TOKYO GHOUL

SUI ISHIDA

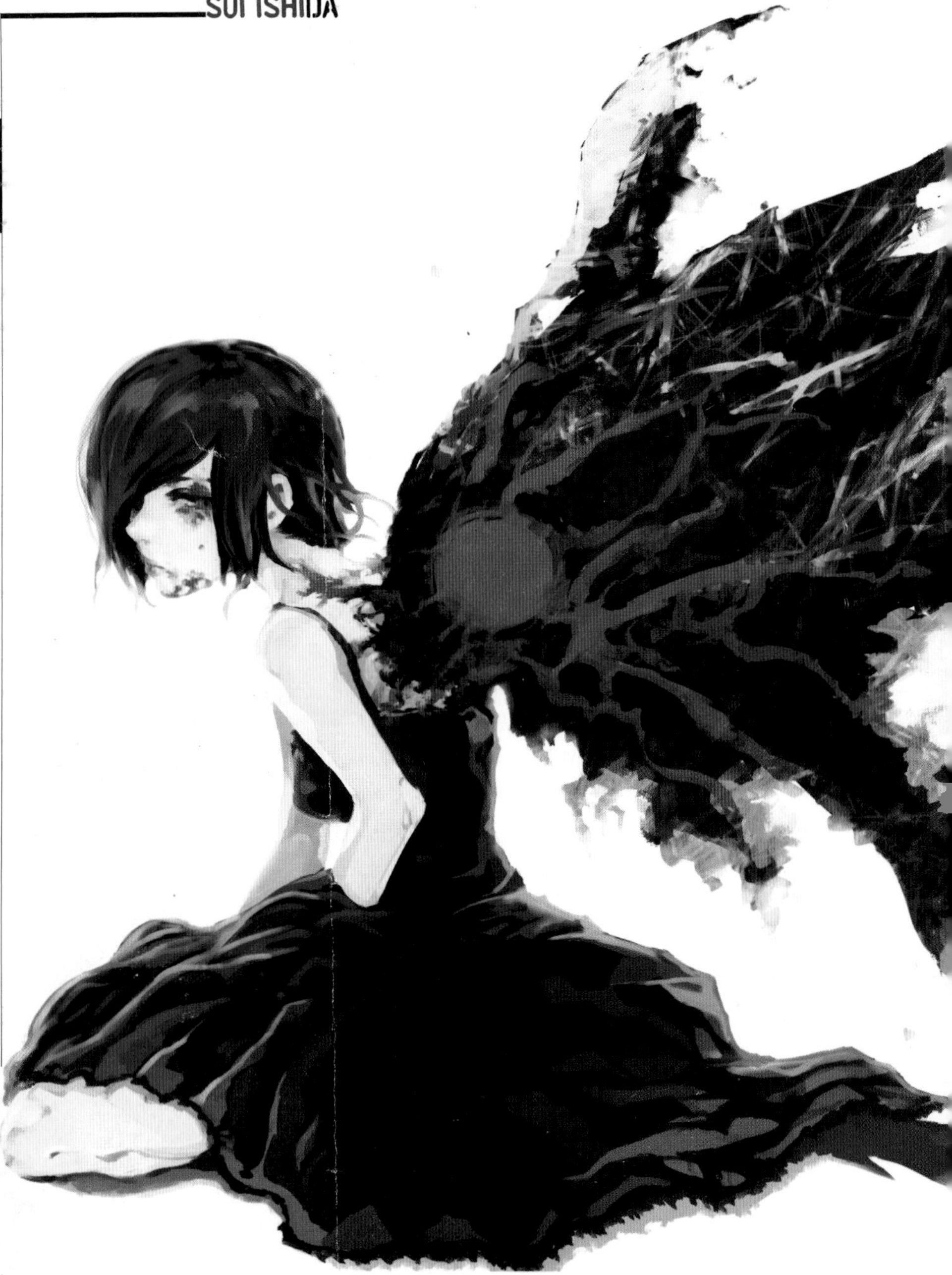

T O K Y O G H O U

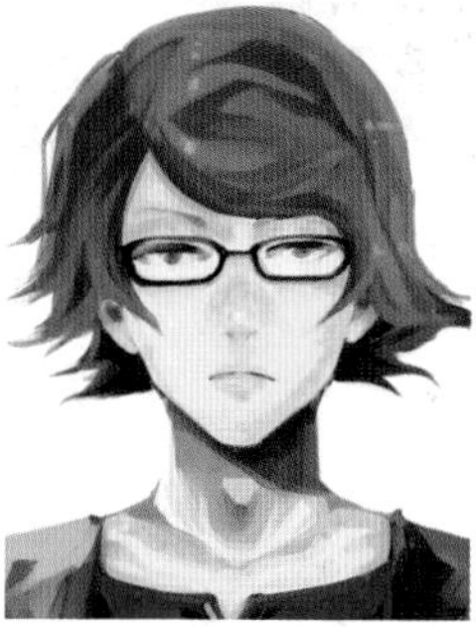

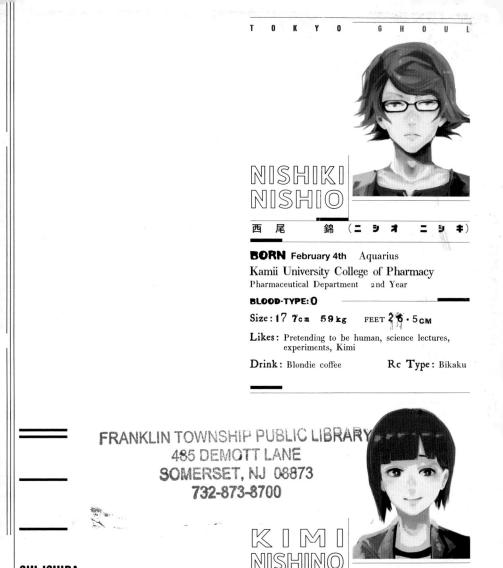

NISHIKI NISHIO

西尾　錦（ニシオ　ニシキ）

BORN February 4th　Aquarius

Kamii University College of Pharmacy

Pharmaceutical Department　2nd Year

BLOOD-TYPE: O

Size: 177cm　59kg　FEET 26.5cm

Likes: Pretending to be human, science lectures, experiments, Kimi

Drink: Blondie coffee　**Rc Type:** Bikaku

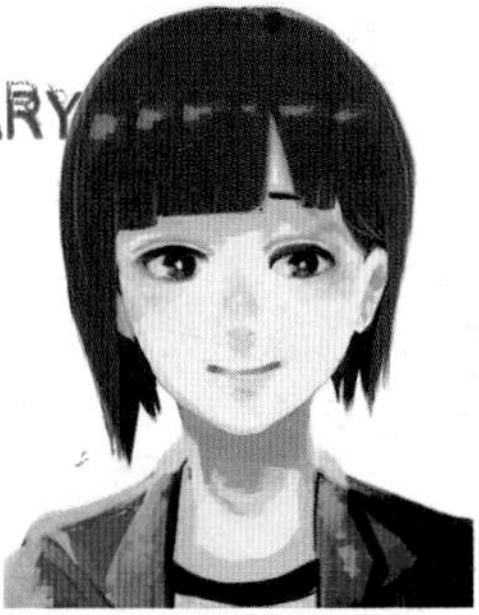

KIMI NISHINO

西野貴未（ニシノ　キミ）

BORN October 1st　Libra

Kamii University College of Medicine

Medical Department　2nd Year

BLOOD-TYPE: O

Size: 163cm　50kg　FEET 23.5cm

Likes: Eating, archery (member of High School Archery Club), Nishiki

Food: Yakisoba, melon pan from the school store

SUI ISHIDA was born in Fukuoka, Japan. He is the author of ***Tokyo Ghoul*** and several ***Tokyo Ghoul*** one-shots, including one that won him second place in the *Weekly Young Jump* 113th Grand Prix award in 2010. ***Tokyo Ghoul*** began serialization in *Weekly Young Jump* in 2011 and was adapted into an anime series in 2014.

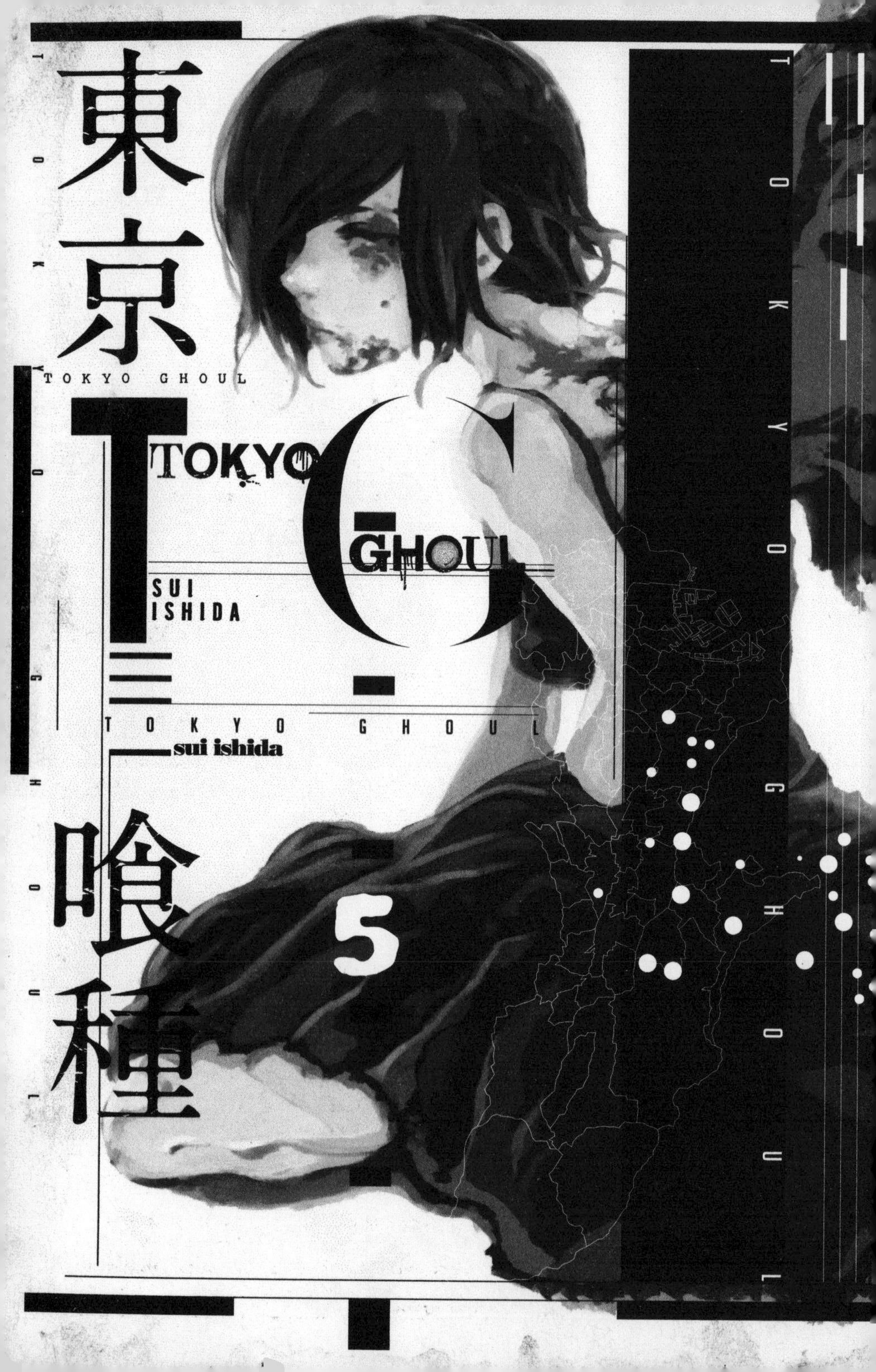
東京喰種
TOKYO GHOUL
TOKYO GHOUL
SUI ISHIDA
T O K Y O G H O U L
sui ishida
5
T O K Y O G H O U L
T O K Y O G H O U L

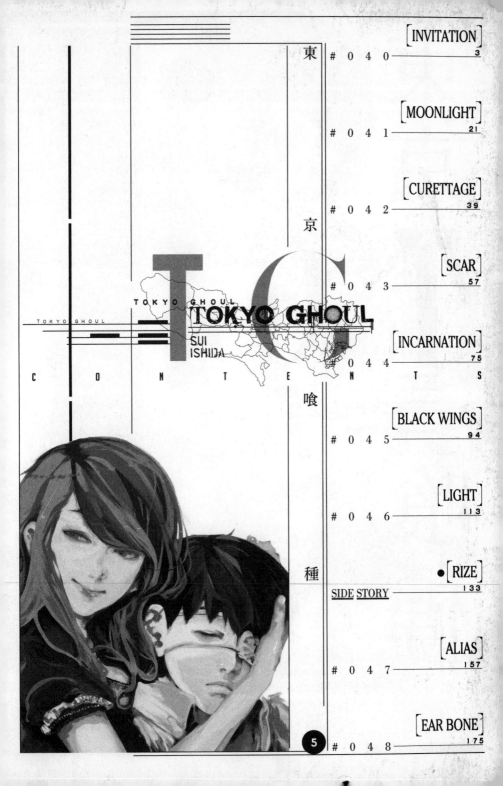

東

京

喰

種

TOKYO GHOUL
SUI ISHIDA

C O N T E N T S

5

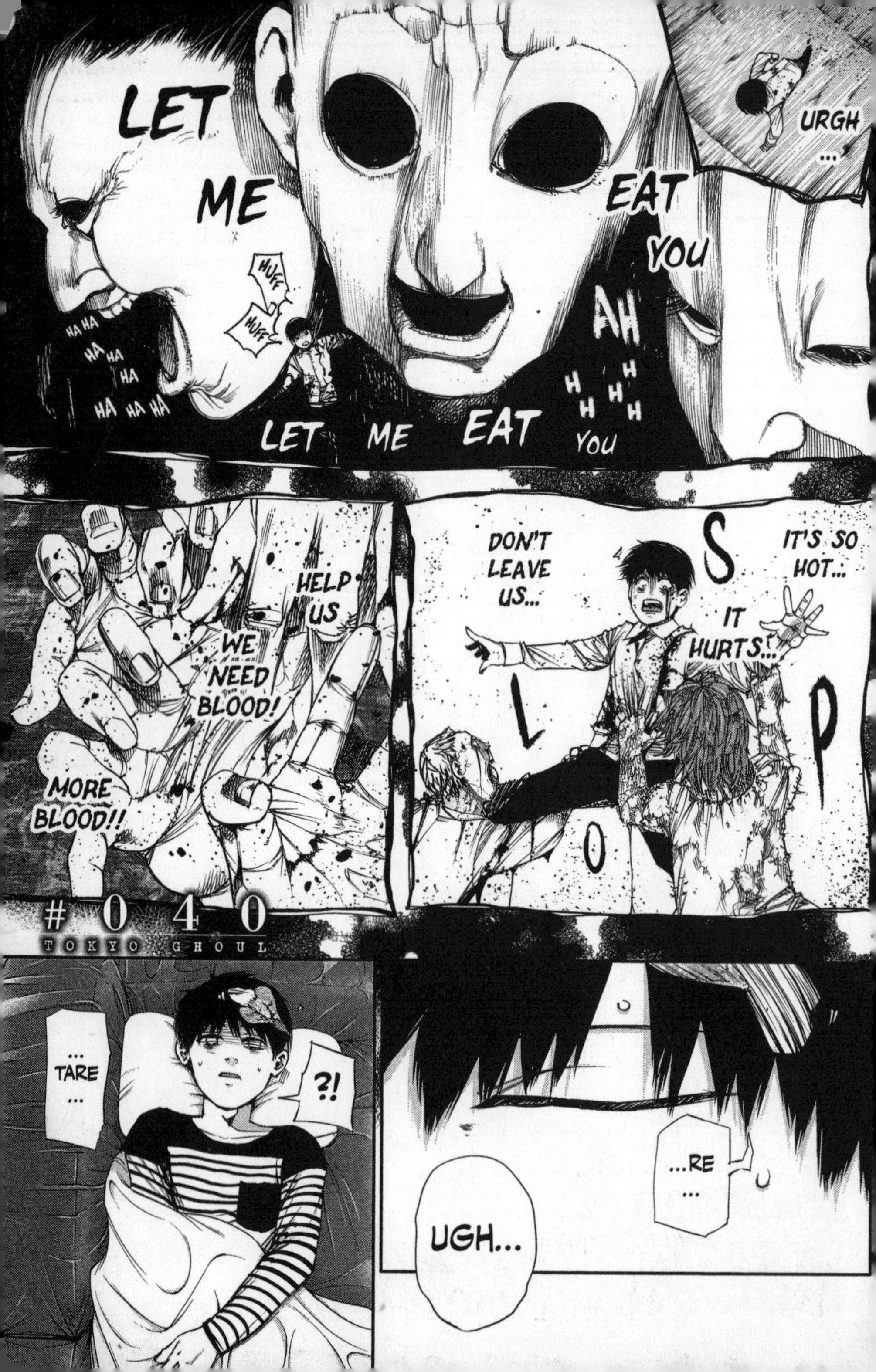
URGH ...
LET ME EAT YOU
HUFF
HUFF
HA HA HA HA HA HA HA HA
AH HHHHHH
LET ME EAT YOU
IT'S SO HOT...
IT HURTS...
DON'T LEAVE US...
SLOP
HELP US
WE NEED BLOOD!
MORE BLOOD!!
#040
TOKYO GHOUL
...RE ...
UGH...
?!
... TARE ...

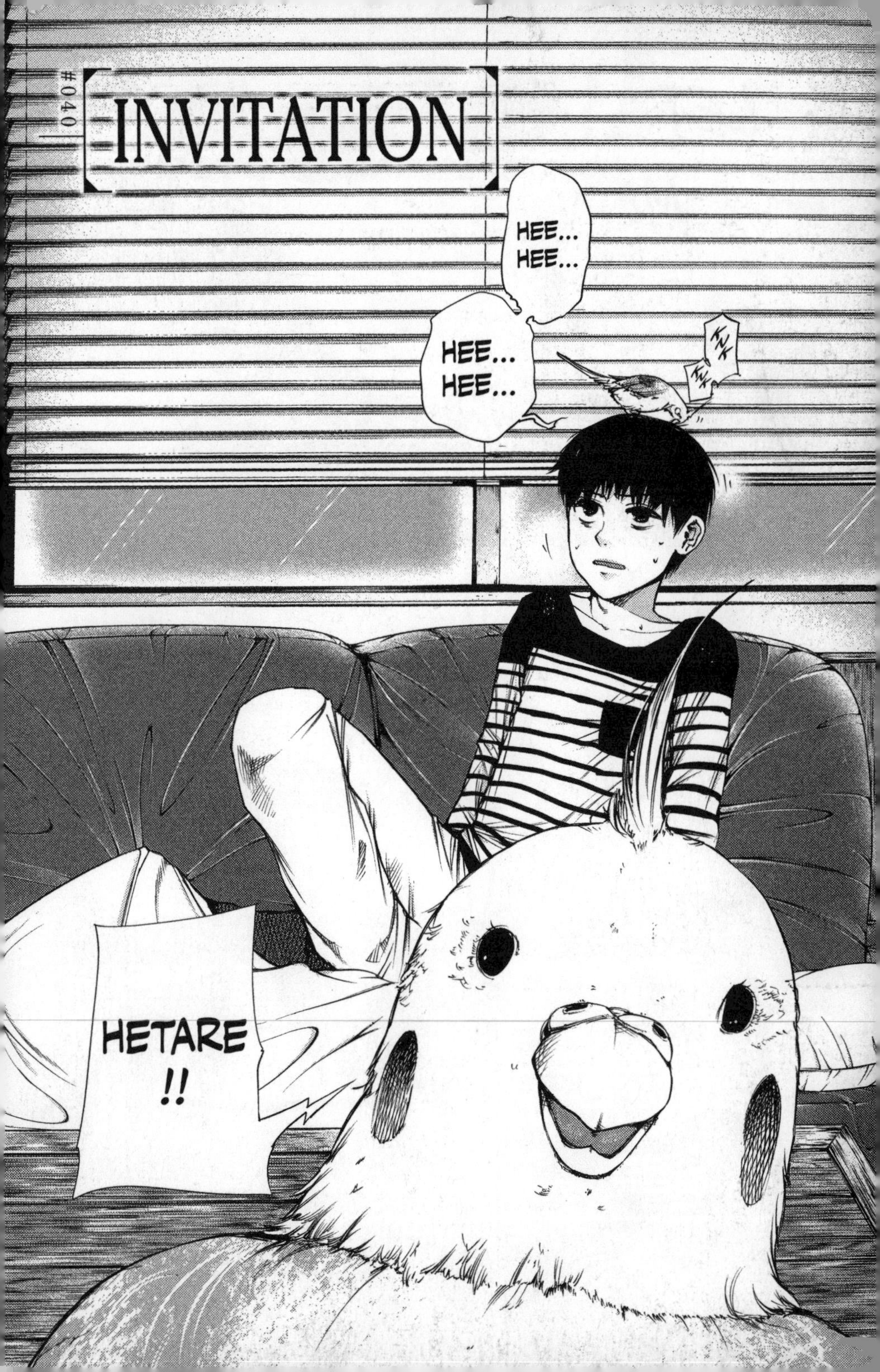
#040
INVITATION
HEE... HEE...
HEE... HEE...
KNK
KNK
HETARE !!

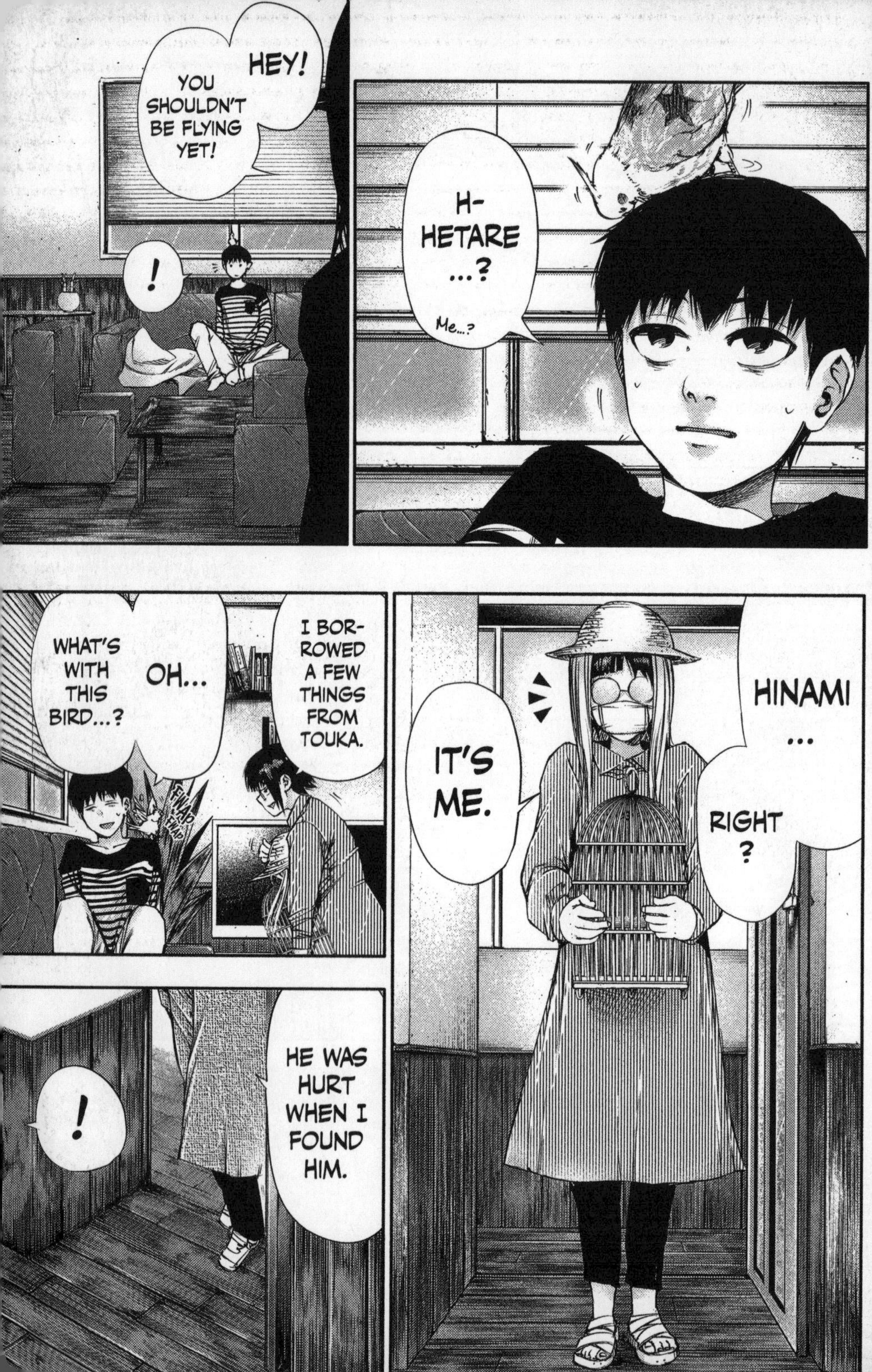
H-HETARE ...?
Me...?
HEY! YOU SHOULDN'T BE FLYING YET!
!
HINAMI ... RIGHT?
IT'S ME.
I BOR-ROWED A FEW THINGS FROM TOUKA.
OH...
WHAT'S WITH THIS BIRD...?
FWAP FWAP
HE WAS HURT WHEN I FOUND HIM.
!

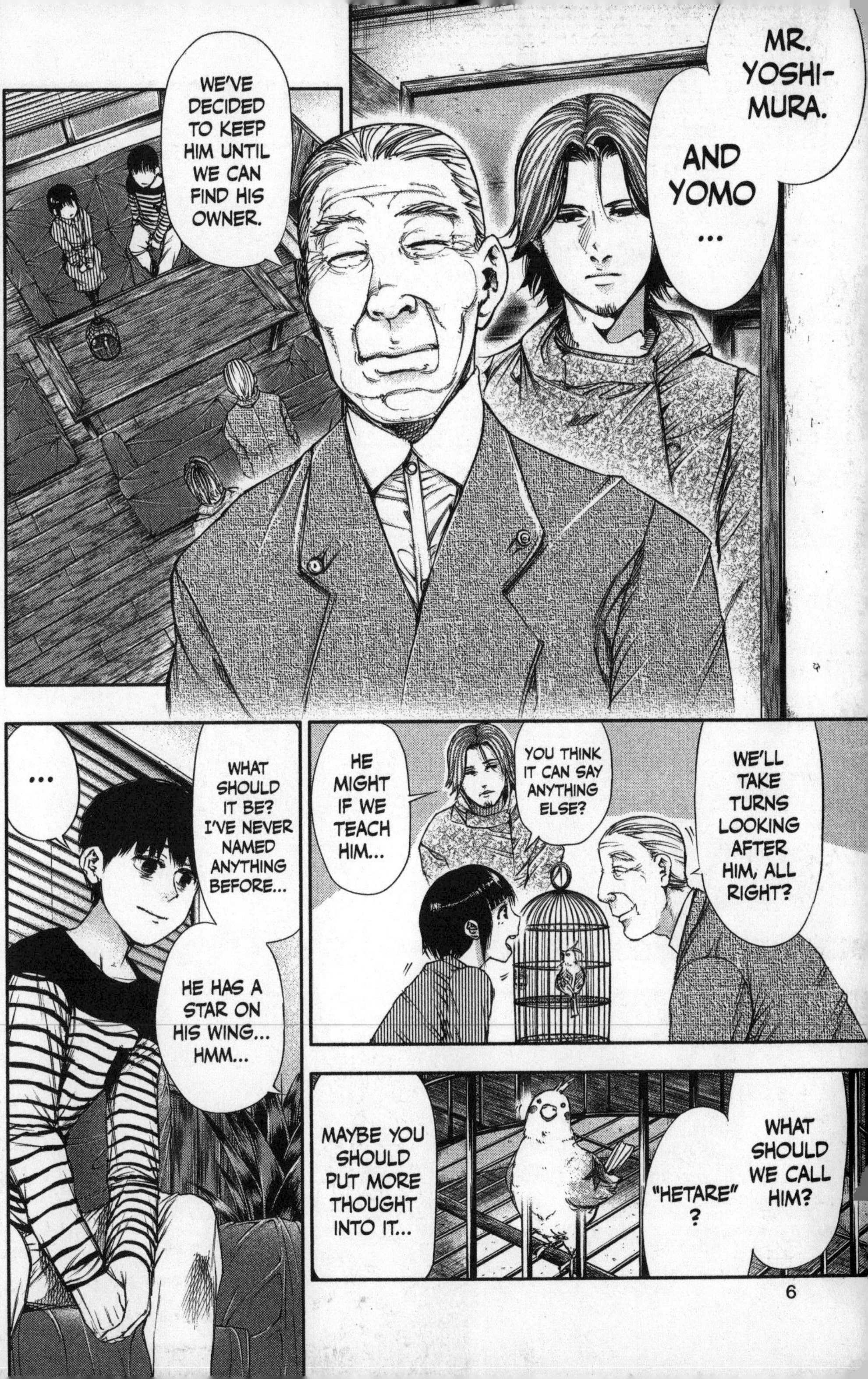
MR. YOSHIMURA.
AND YOMO ...
WE'VE DECIDED TO KEEP HIM UNTIL WE CAN FIND HIS OWNER.
WE'LL TAKE TURNS LOOKING AFTER HIM, ALL RIGHT?
YOU THINK IT CAN SAY ANYTHING ELSE?
HE MIGHT IF WE TEACH HIM...
WHAT SHOULD WE CALL HIM?
"HETARE"?
MAYBE YOU SHOULD PUT MORE THOUGHT INTO IT...
WHAT SHOULD IT BE? I'VE NEVER NAMED ANYTHING BEFORE...
...
HE HAS A STAR ON HIS WING... HMM...

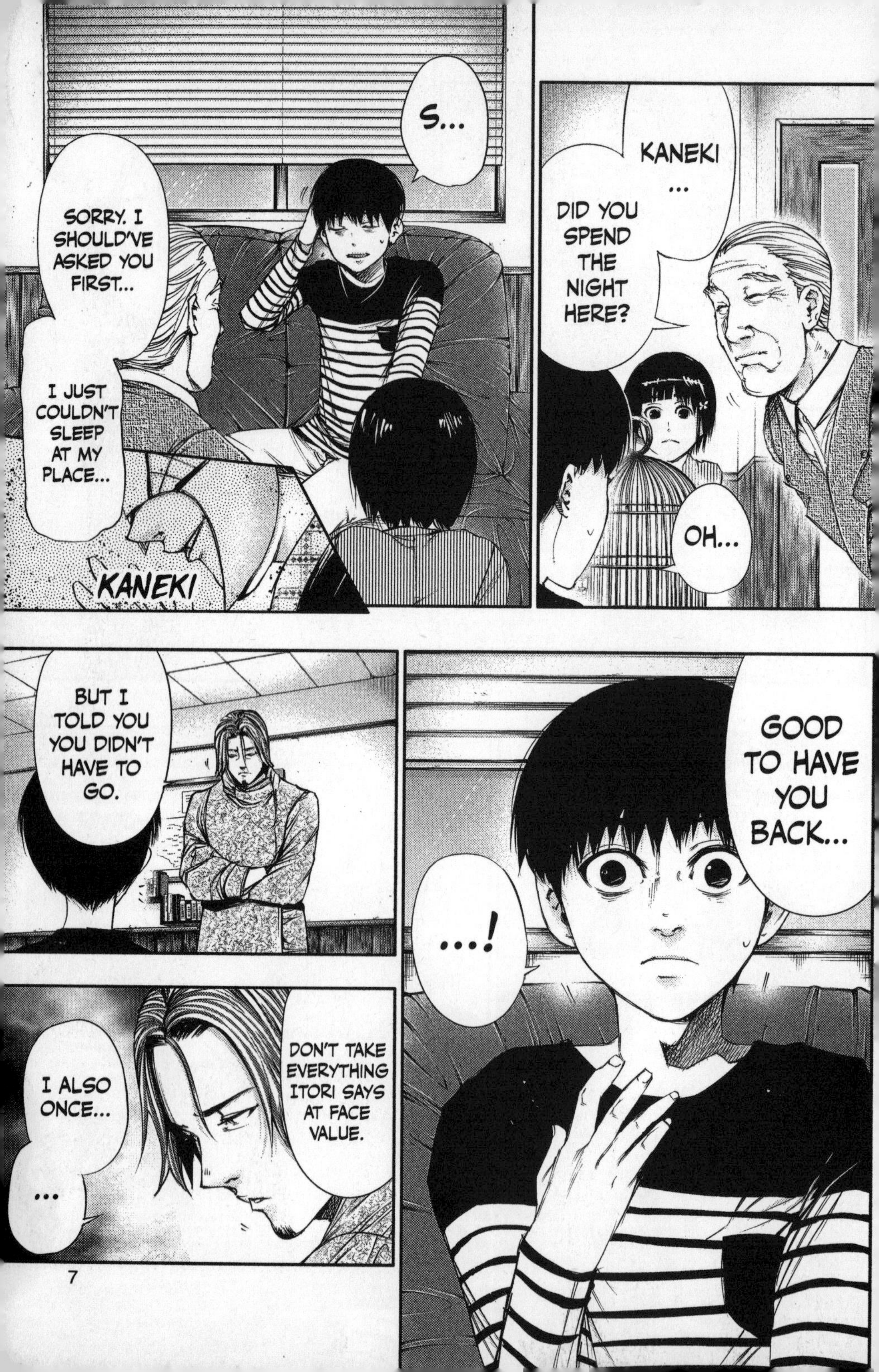
KANEKI ...
DID YOU SPEND THE NIGHT HERE?
OH...
S...
SORRY. I SHOULD'VE ASKED YOU FIRST...
I JUST COULDN'T SLEEP AT MY PLACE...
KANEKI
GOOD TO HAVE YOU BACK...
...!
BUT I TOLD YOU YOU DIDN'T HAVE TO GO.
DON'T TAKE EVERYTHING ITORI SAYS AT FACE VALUE.
I ALSO ONCE...
...

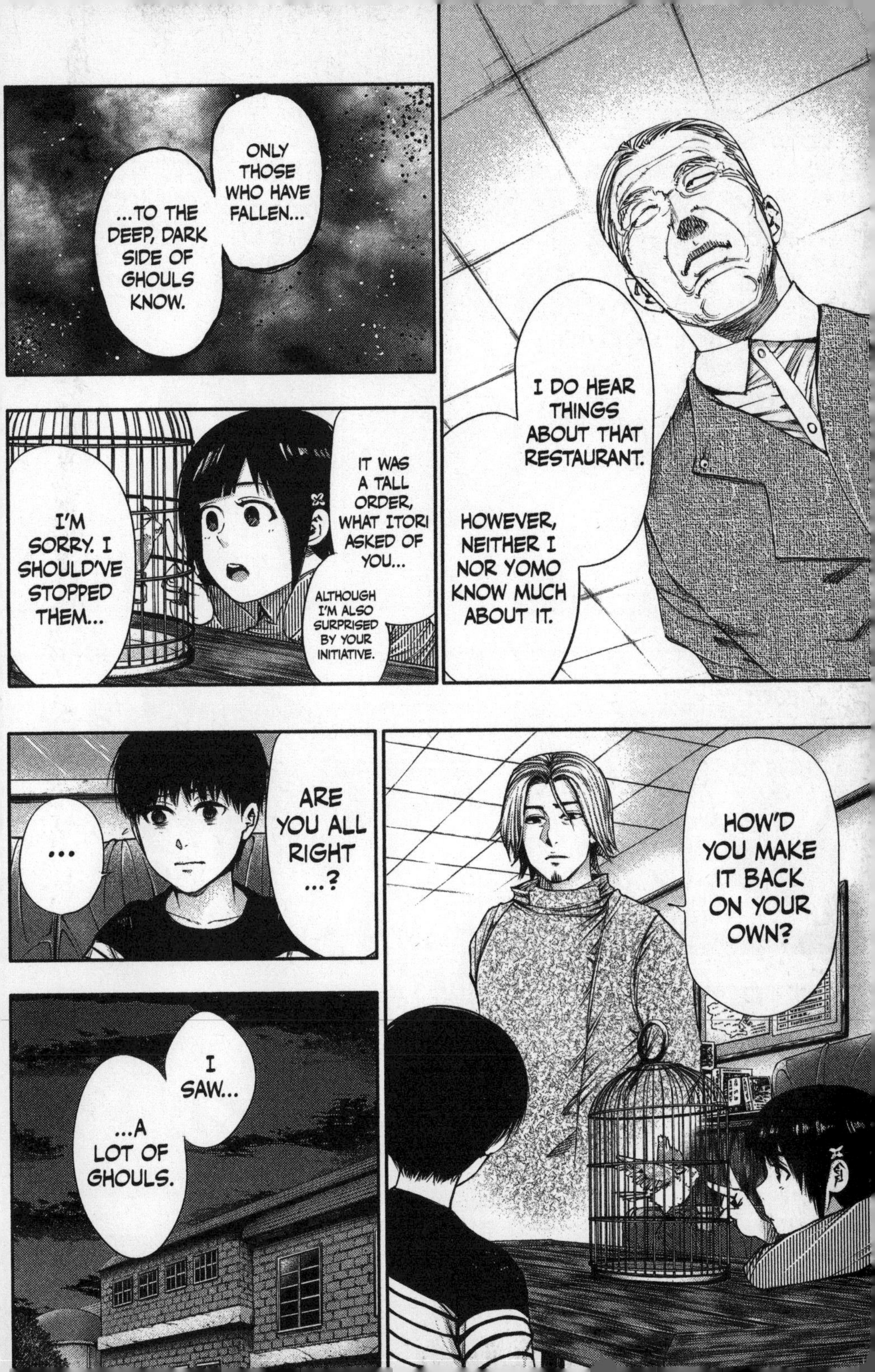
I DO HEAR THINGS ABOUT THAT RESTAURANT.
HOWEVER, NEITHER I NOR YOMO KNOW MUCH ABOUT IT.
ONLY THOSE WHO HAVE FALLEN...
...TO THE DEEP, DARK SIDE OF GHOULS KNOW.
IT WAS A TALL ORDER, WHAT ITORI ASKED OF YOU...
ALTHOUGH I'M ALSO SURPRISED BY YOUR INITIATIVE.
I'M SORRY. I SHOULD'VE STOPPED THEM...
HOW'D YOU MAKE IT BACK ON YOUR OWN?
ARE YOU ALL RIGHT ...?
...
I SAW...
...A LOT OF GHOULS.

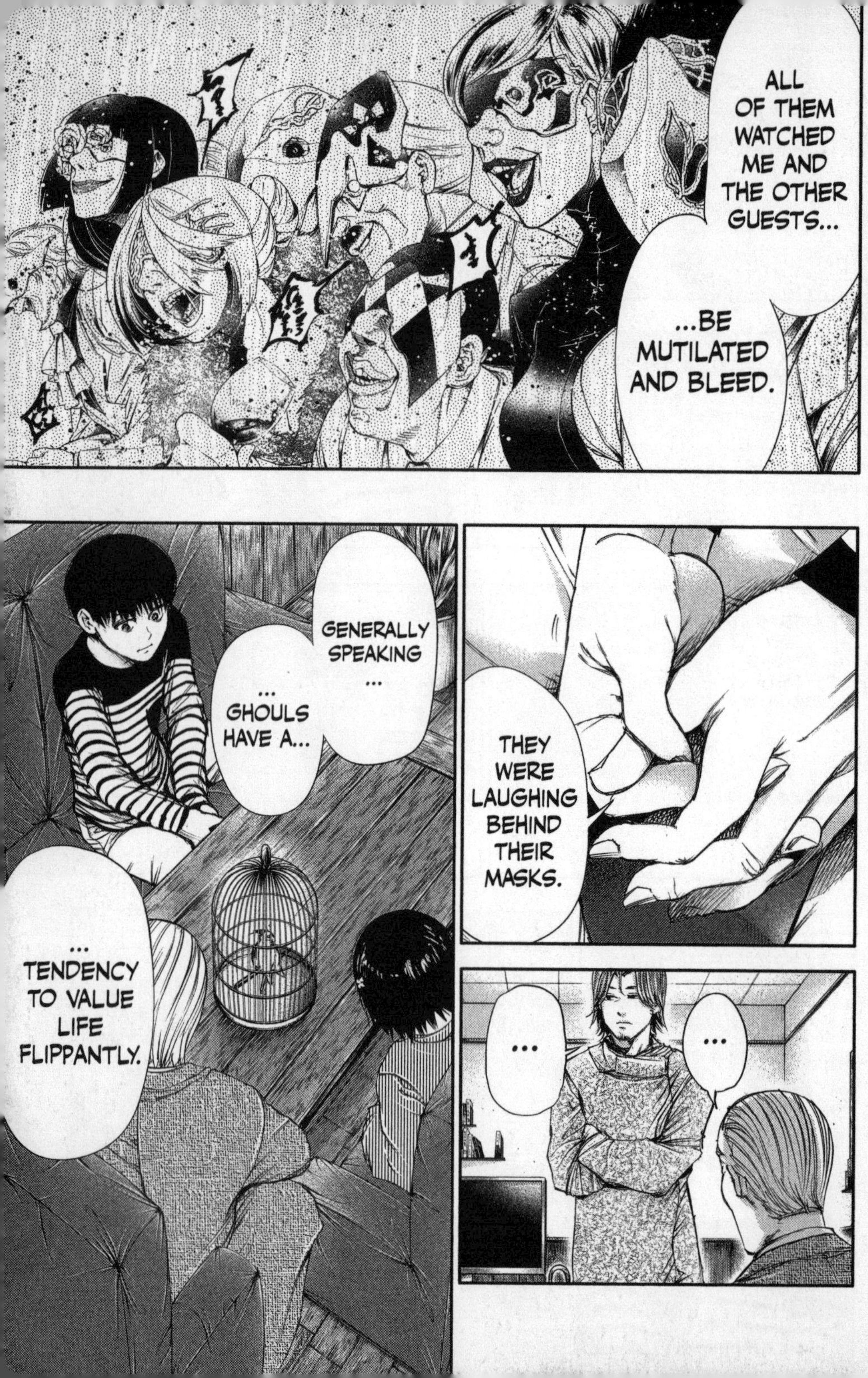
ALL OF THEM WATCHED ME AND THE OTHER GUESTS...
...BE MUTILATED AND BLEED.
THEY WERE LAUGHING BEHIND THEIR MASKS.
...
...
GENERALLY SPEAKING ...
... GHOULS HAVE A...
... TENDENCY TO VALUE LIFE FLIPPANTLY.

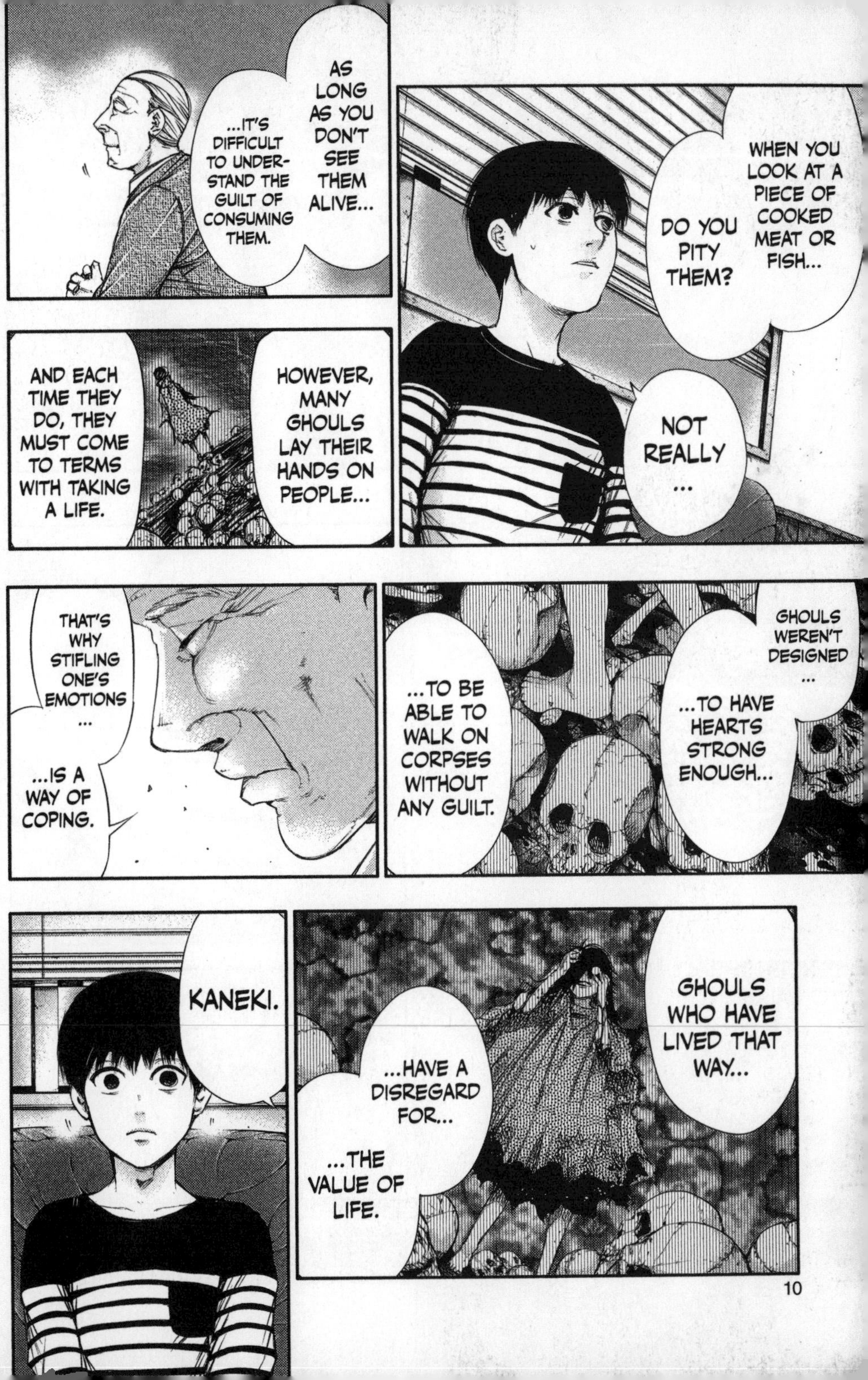
WHEN YOU LOOK AT A PIECE OF COOKED MEAT OR FISH...
DO YOU PITY THEM?
NOT REALLY ...
AS LONG AS YOU DON'T SEE THEM ALIVE...
...IT'S DIFFICULT TO UNDER-STAND THE GUILT OF CONSUMING THEM.
HOWEVER, MANY GHOULS LAY THEIR HANDS ON PEOPLE...
AND EACH TIME THEY DO, THEY MUST COME TO TERMS WITH TAKING A LIFE.
GHOULS WEREN'T DESIGNED ...
...TO HAVE HEARTS STRONG ENOUGH...
...TO BE ABLE TO WALK ON CORPSES WITHOUT ANY GUILT.
THAT'S WHY STIFLING ONE'S EMOTIONS ...
...IS A WAY OF COPING.
GHOULS WHO HAVE LIVED THAT WAY...
...HAVE A DISREGARD FOR...
...THE VALUE OF LIFE.
KANEKI.

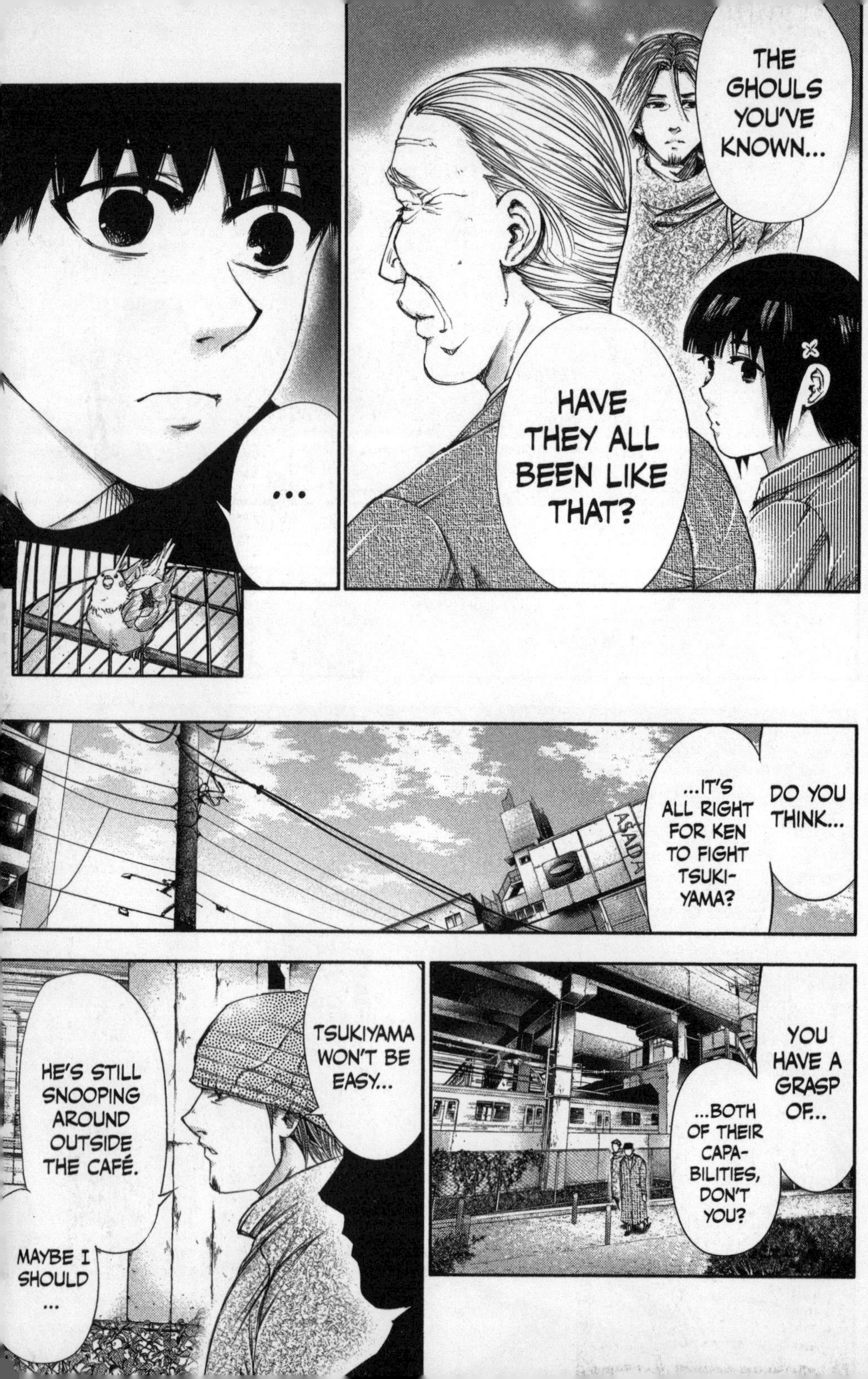
THE GHOULS YOU'VE KNOWN...
HAVE THEY ALL BEEN LIKE THAT?
...
DO YOU THINK...
...IT'S ALL RIGHT FOR KEN TO FIGHT TSUKIYAMA?
ASADA
YOU HAVE A GRASP OF...
...BOTH OF THEIR CAPABILITIES, DON'T YOU?
TSUKIYAMA WON'T BE EASY...
HE'S STILL SNOOPING AROUND OUTSIDE THE CAFÉ.
MAYBE I SHOULD ...

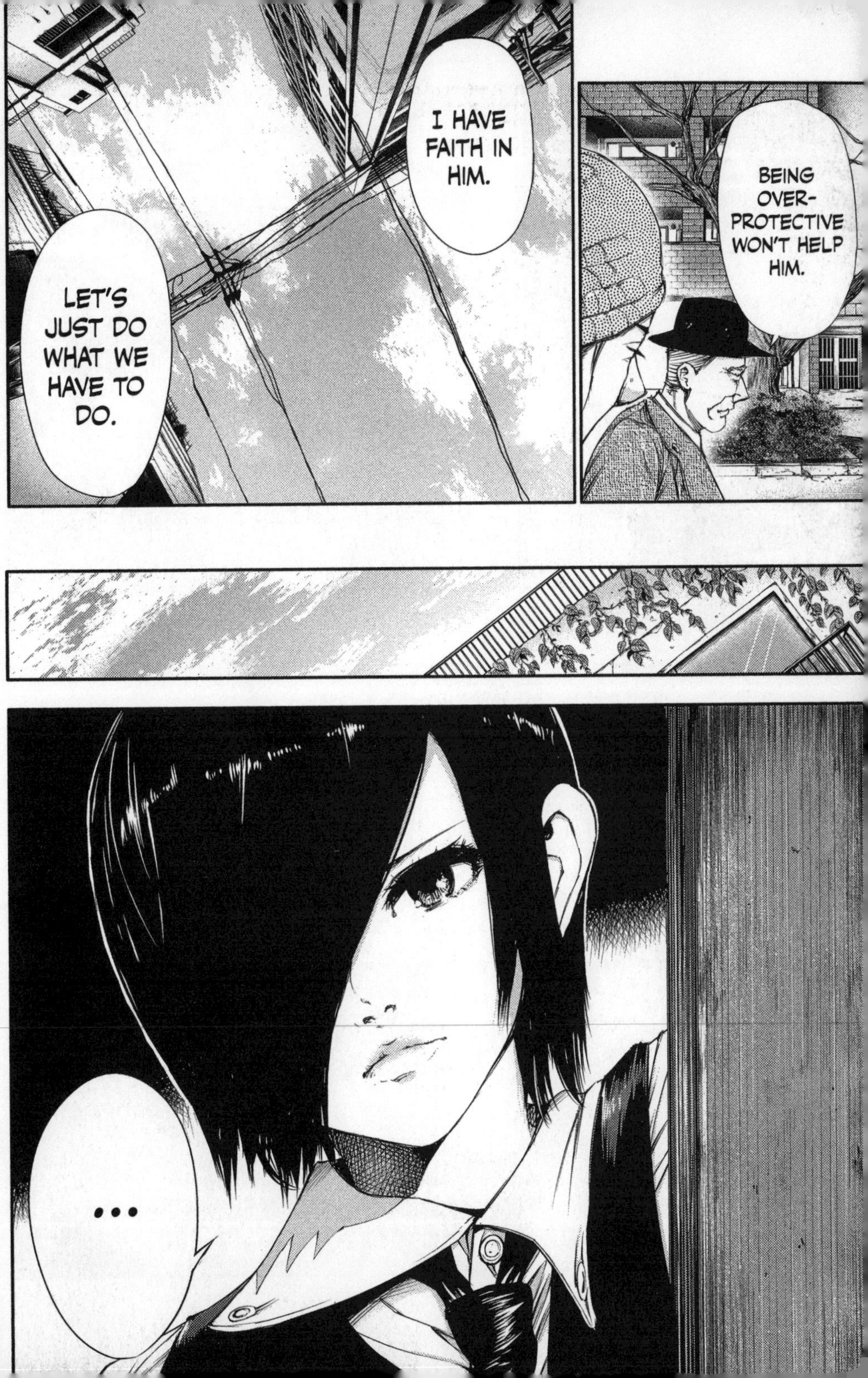
BEING OVER-PROTECTIVE WON'T HELP HIM.
I HAVE FAITH IN HIM.
LET'S JUST DO WHAT WE HAVE TO DO.
...

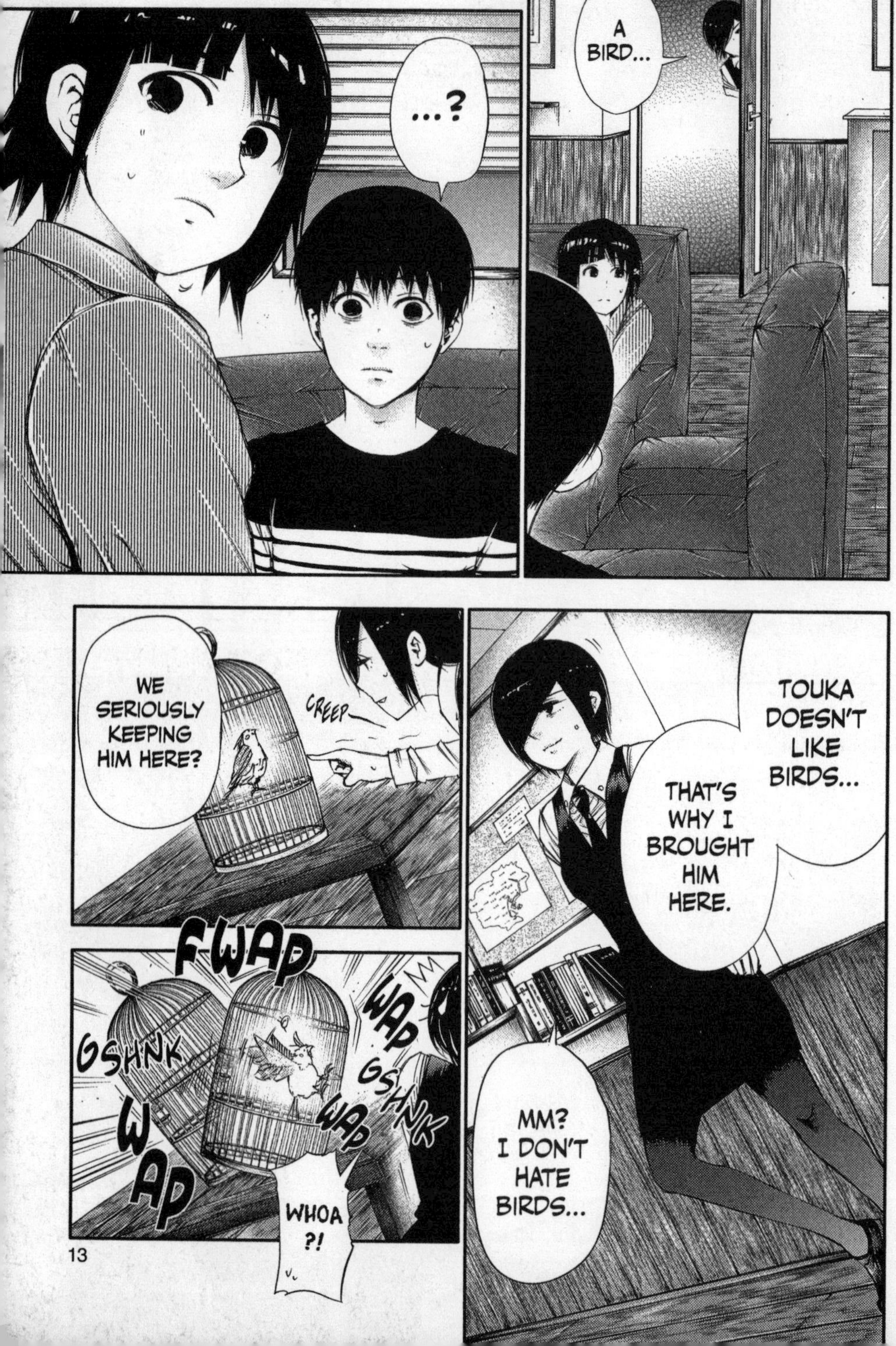
A BIRD...
...?
TOUKA DOESN'T LIKE BIRDS...
THAT'S WHY I BROUGHT HIM HERE.
MM? I DON'T HATE BIRDS...
WE SERIOUSLY KEEPING HIM HERE?
CREEP
FWAP
WAP
GSHNK
WAP
GSHNK
WAP
WAP
WHOA?!

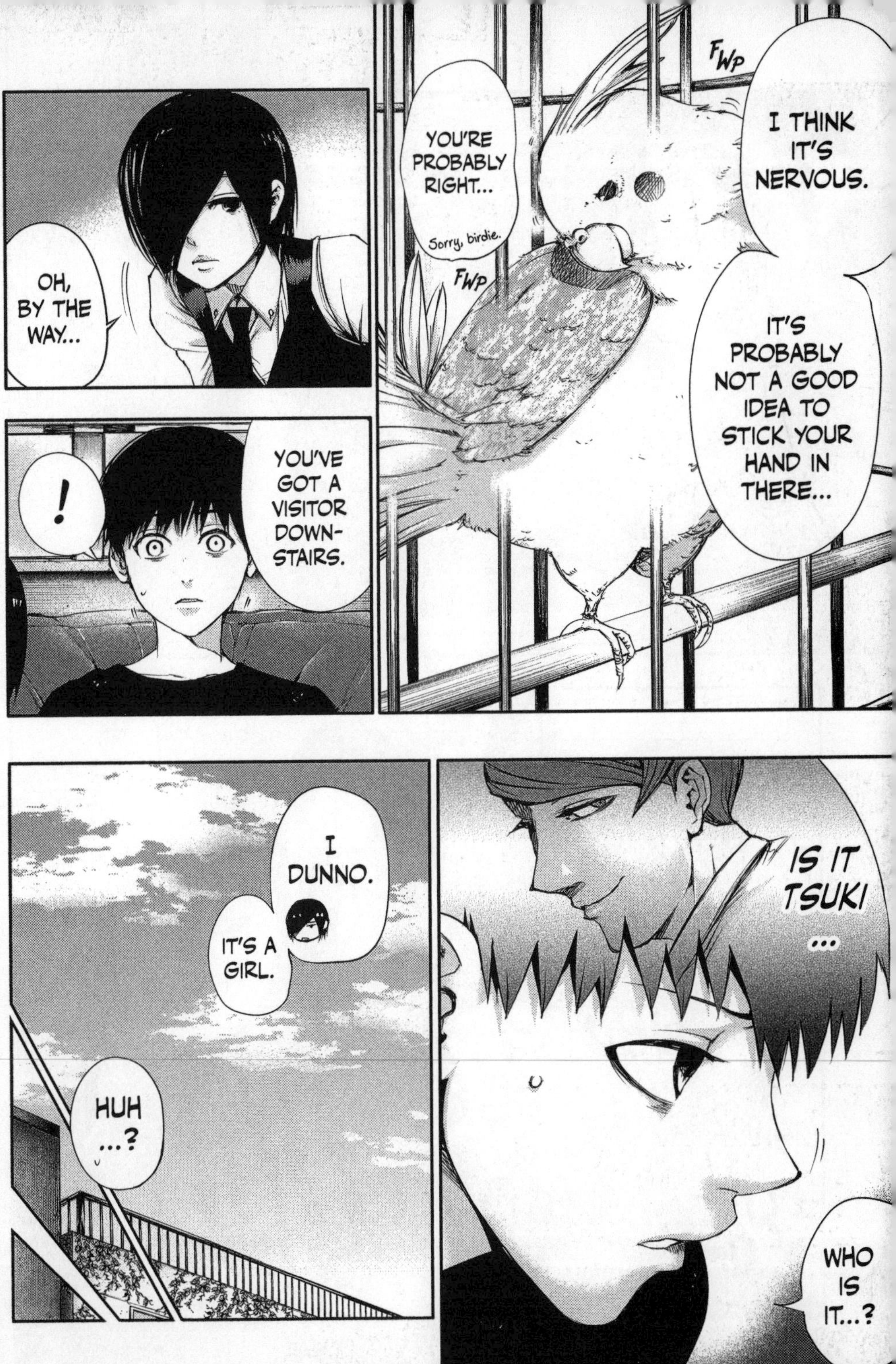
FWP
I THINK IT'S NERVOUS.
IT'S PROBABLY NOT A GOOD IDEA TO STICK YOUR HAND IN THERE...
YOU'RE PROBABLY RIGHT...
Sorry, birdie.
FWP
OH, BY THE WAY...
YOU'VE GOT A VISITOR DOWN-STAIRS.
!
IS IT TSUKI...
WHO IS IT...?
I DUNNO.
IT'S A GIRL.
HUH...?

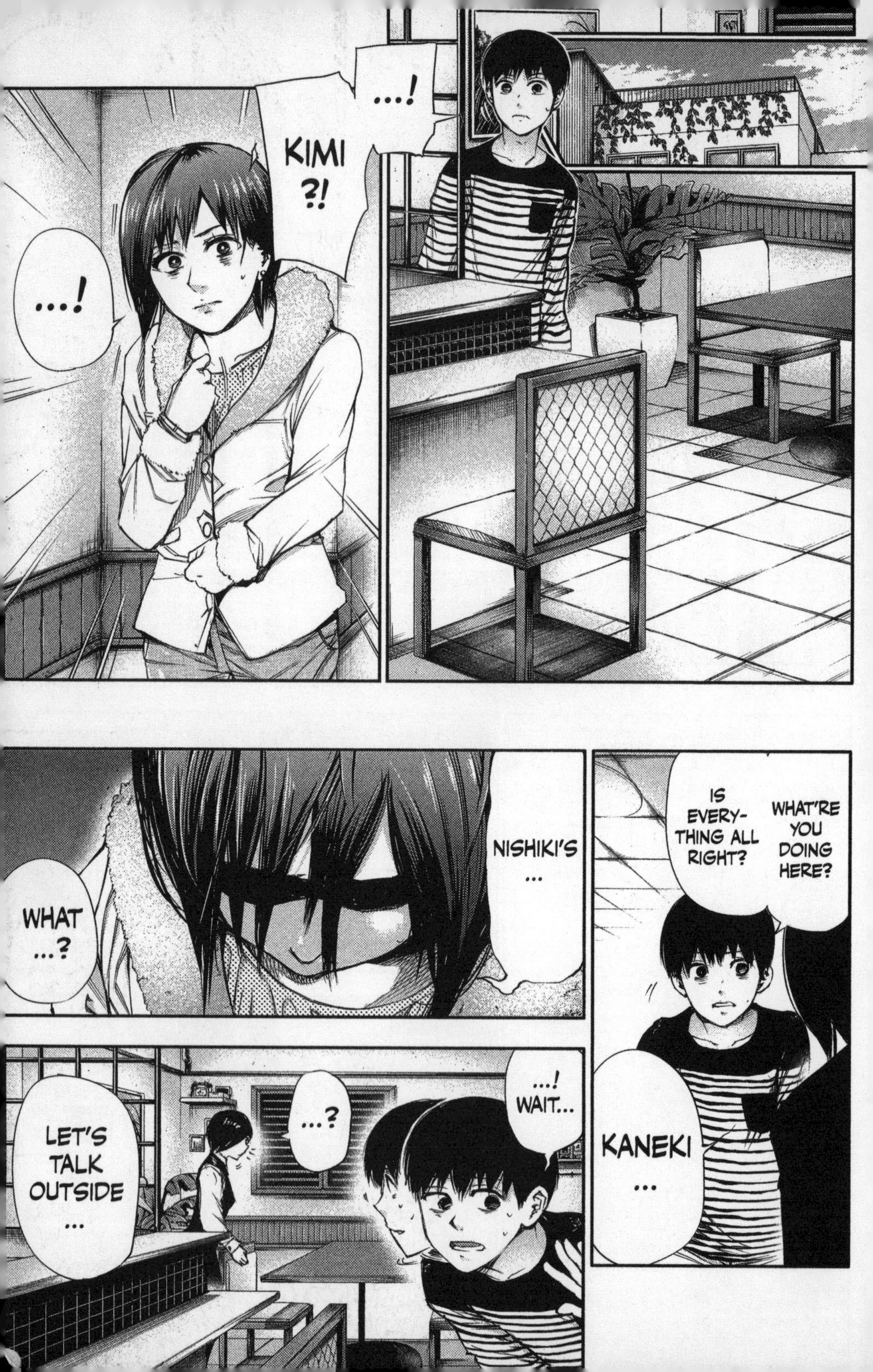
...!
KIMI ?!
...!
WHAT'RE YOU DOING HERE?
IS EVERY-THING ALL RIGHT?
KANEKI ...
NISHIKI'S ...
WHAT ...?
...! WAIT...
...?
LET'S TALK OUTSIDE ...

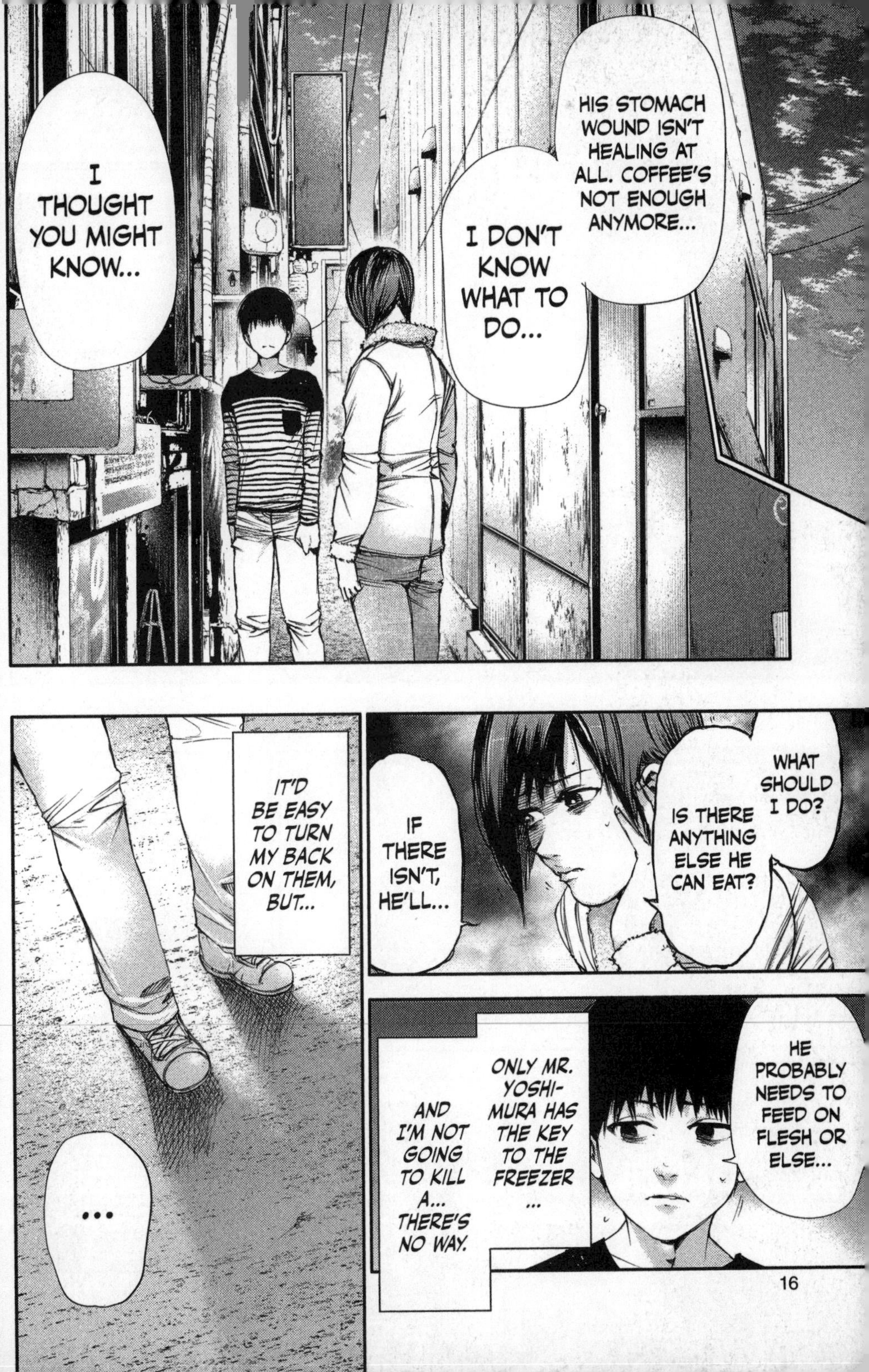
HIS STOMACH WOUND ISN'T HEALING AT ALL. COFFEE'S NOT ENOUGH ANYMORE...
I DON'T KNOW WHAT TO DO...
I THOUGHT YOU MIGHT KNOW...
WHAT SHOULD I DO?
IS THERE ANYTHING ELSE HE CAN EAT?
IF THERE ISN'T, HE'LL...
HE PROBABLY NEEDS TO FEED ON FLESH OR ELSE...
ONLY MR. YOSHIMURA HAS THE KEY TO THE FREEZER...
AND I'M NOT GOING TO KILL A... THERE'S NO WAY.
IT'D BE EASY TO TURN MY BACK ON THEM, BUT...
...

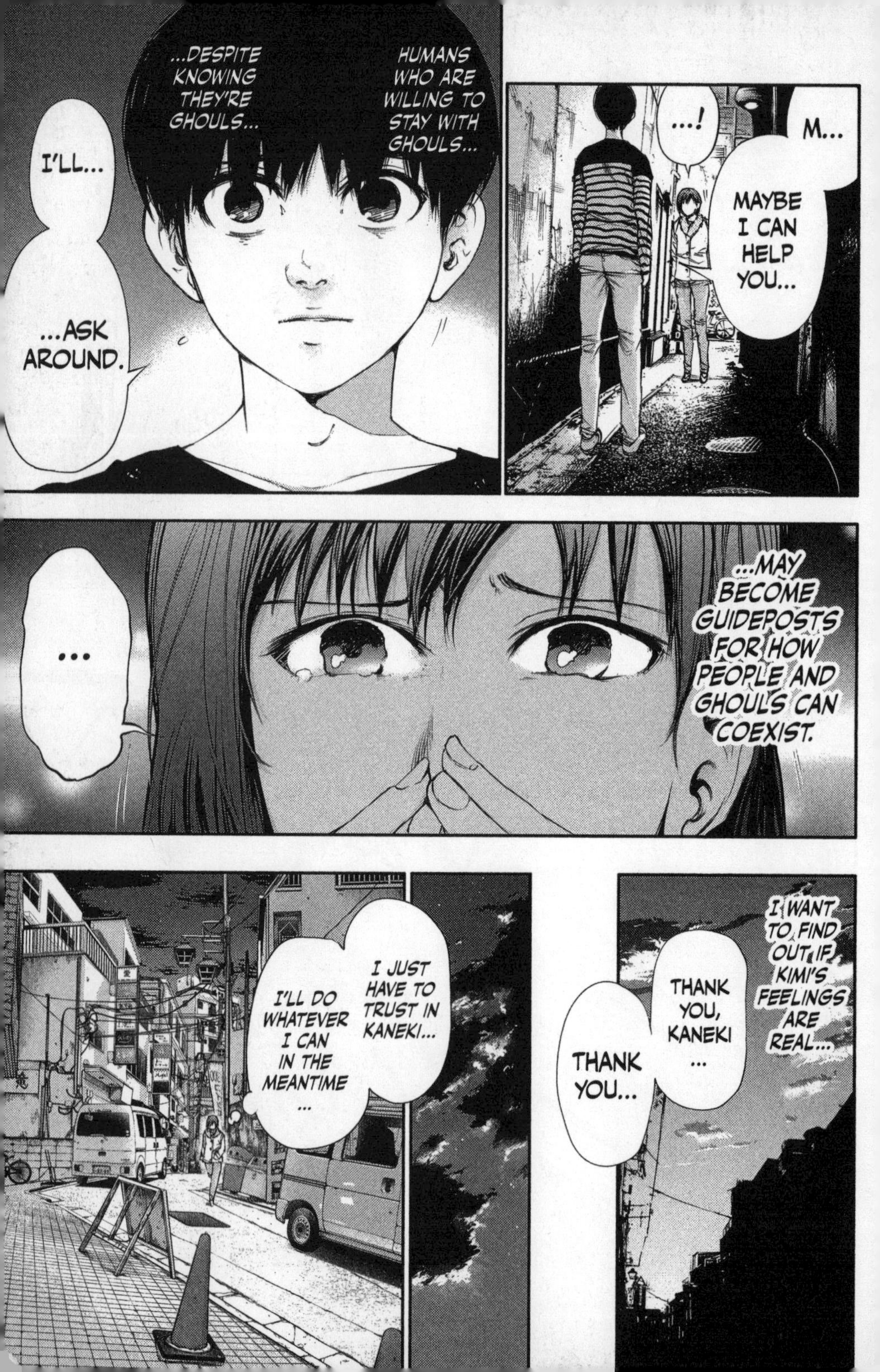
...!
M... MAYBE I CAN HELP YOU...
HUMANS WHO ARE WILLING TO STAY WITH GHOULS...
...DESPITE KNOWING THEY'RE GHOULS...
I'LL... ...ASK AROUND.
...MAY BECOME GUIDEPOSTS FOR HOW PEOPLE AND GHOULS CAN COEXIST.
...
I WANT TO FIND OUT IF KIMI'S FEELINGS ARE REAL...
THANK YOU, KANEKI ...
THANK YOU...
I JUST HAVE TO TRUST IN KANEKI...
I'LL DO WHATEVER I CAN IN THE MEANTIME ...

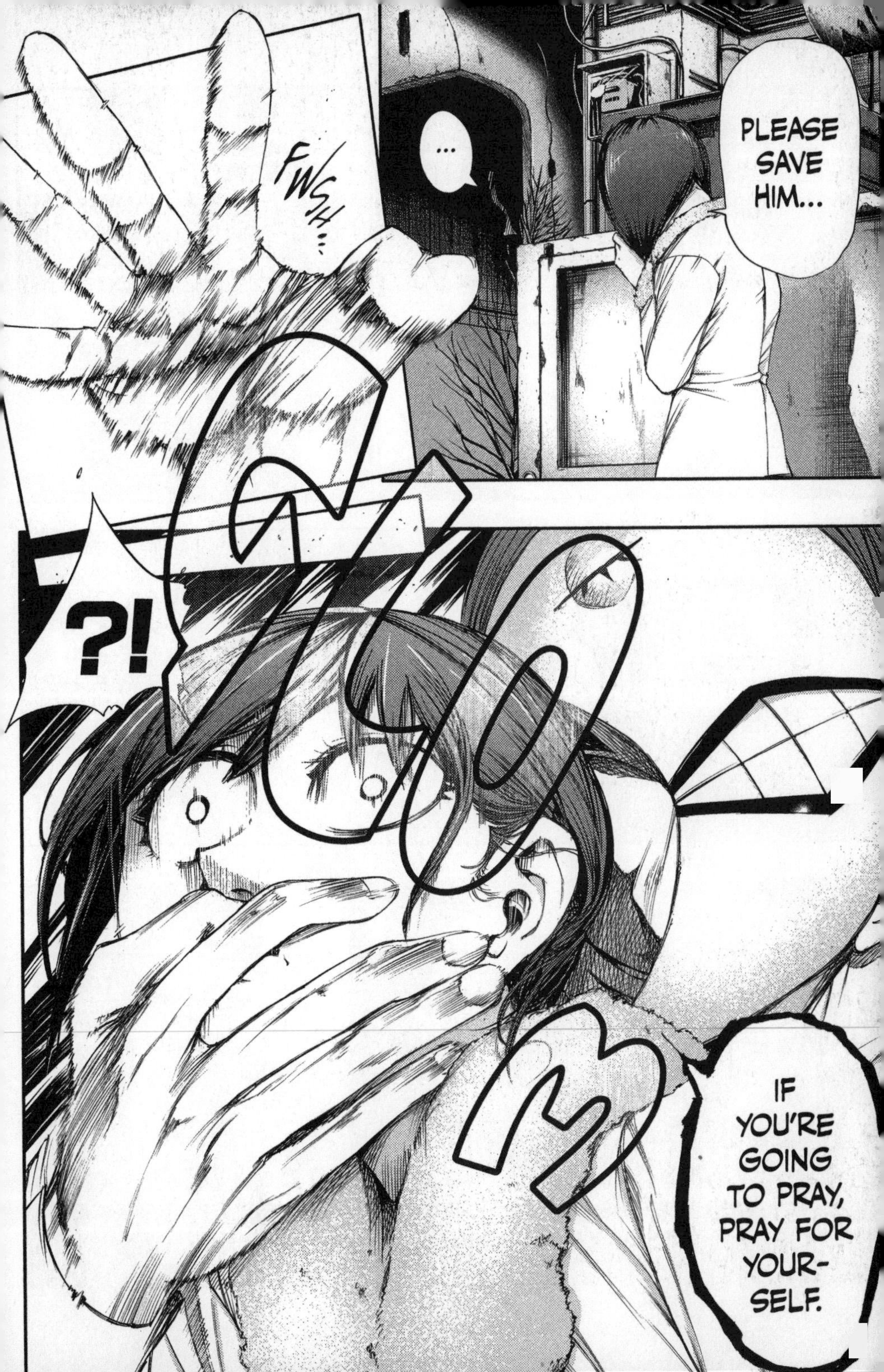
PLEASE SAVE HIM...
...
FWSH...
?!
IF YOU'RE GOING TO PRAY, PRAY FOR YOUR-SELF.

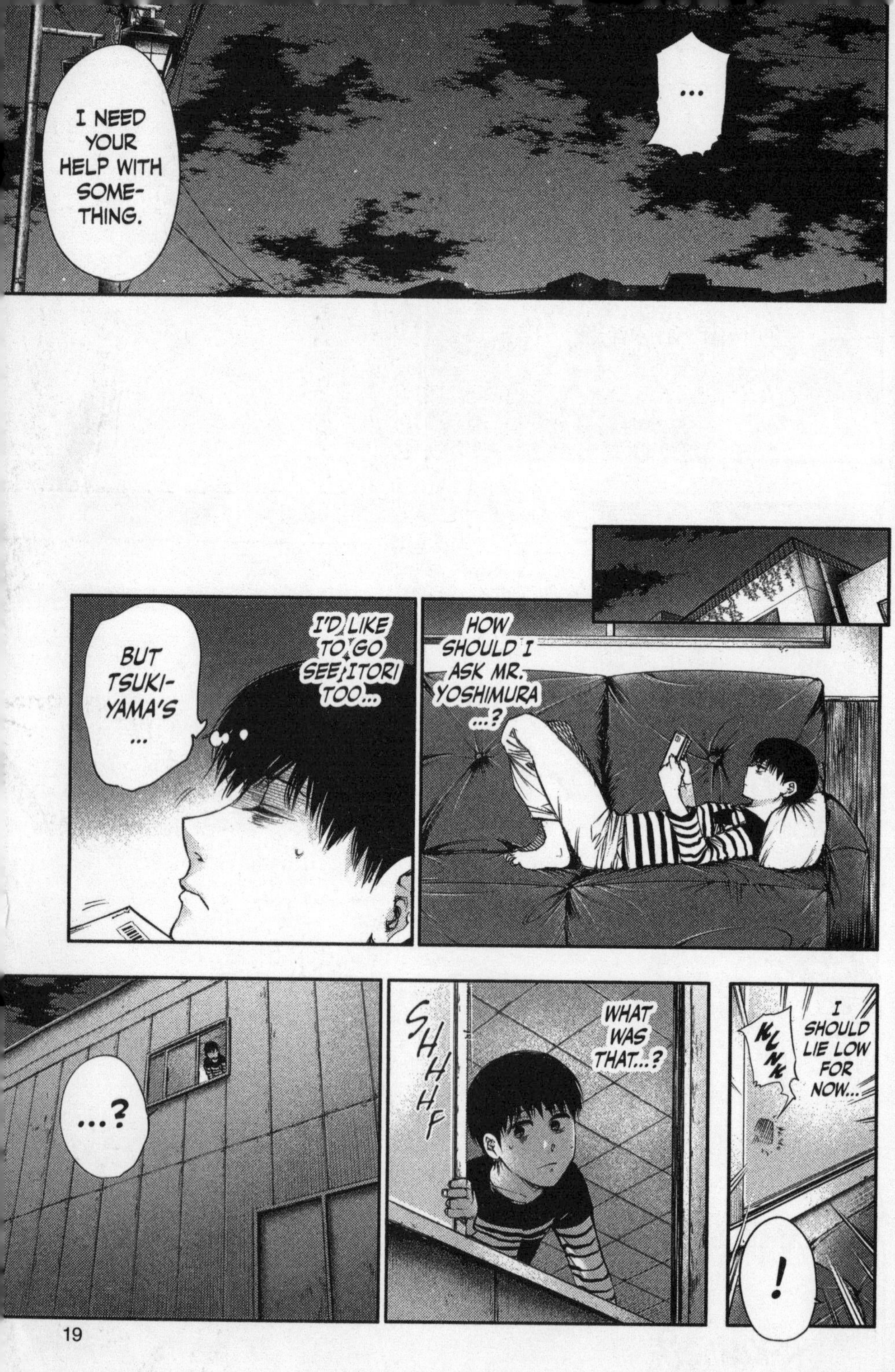
...
I NEED YOUR HELP WITH SOME-THING.
HOW SHOULD I ASK MR. YOSHIMURA ...?
I'D LIKE TO GO SEE ITORI TOO...
BUT TSUKI-YAMA'S ...
KLINK
I SHOULD LIE LOW FOR NOW...
!
SHHHF
WHAT WAS THAT...?
...?

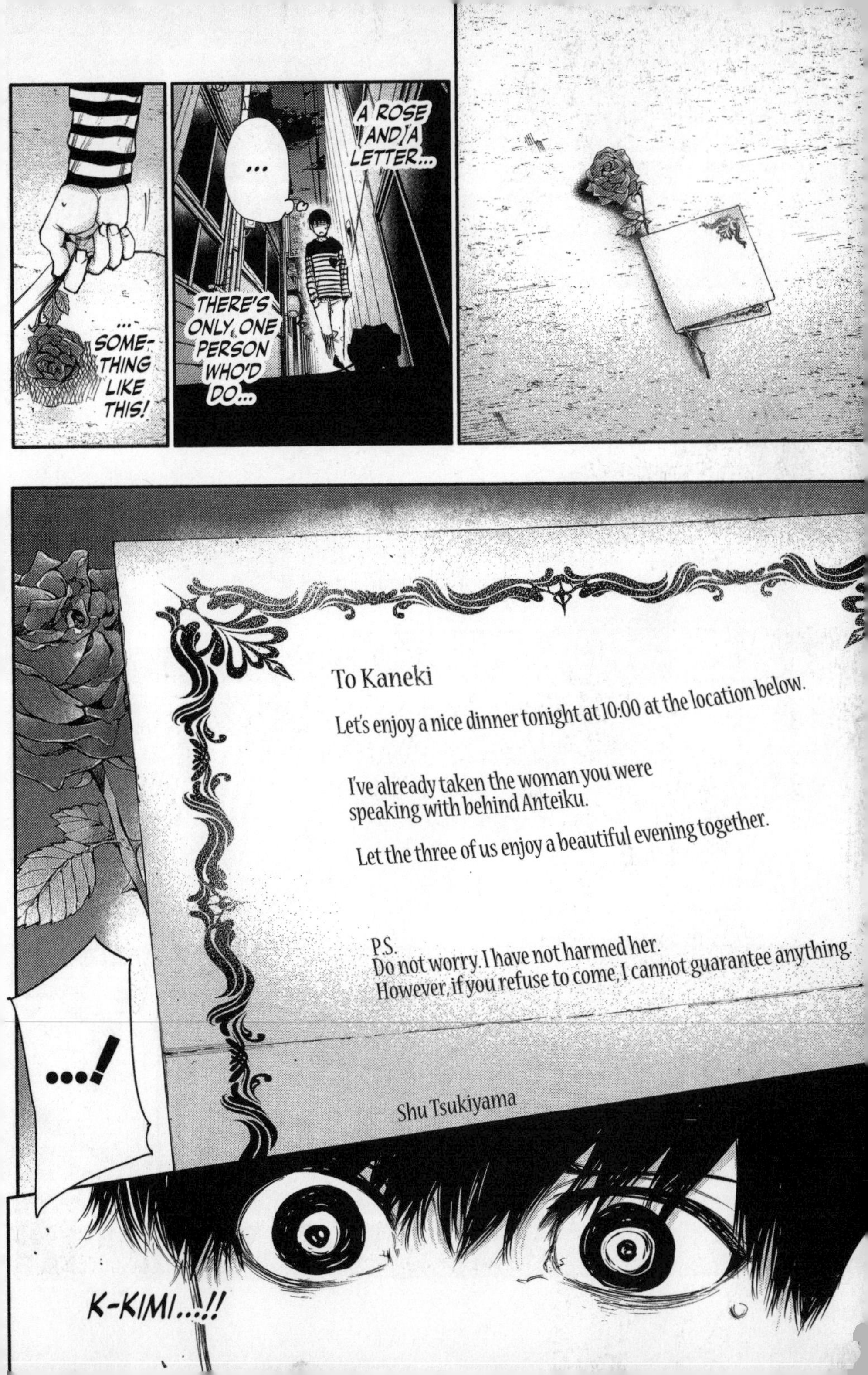
A ROSE AND A LETTER...
...
THERE'S ONLY ONE PERSON WHO'D DO...
...SOMETHING LIKE THIS!
To Kaneki
Let's enjoy a nice dinner tonight at 10:00 at the location below.
I've already taken the woman you were speaking with behind Anteiku.
Let the three of us enjoy a beautiful evening together.
P.S.
Do not worry. I have not harmed her.
However, if you refuse to come, I cannot guarantee anything.
Shu Tsukiyama
...!
K-KIMI...!!

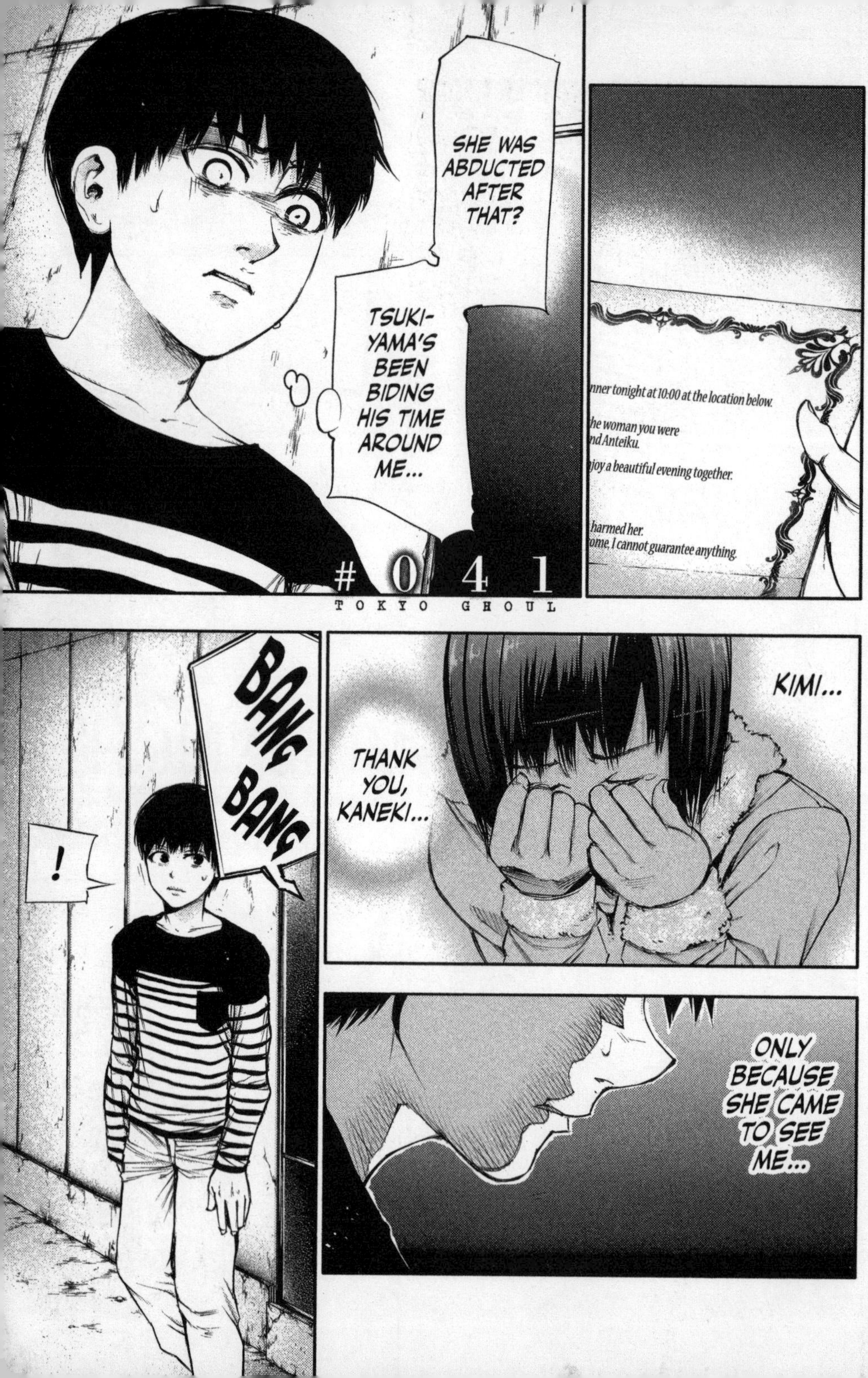
nner tonight at 10:00 at the location below.
he woman you were
nd Anteiku.
njoy a beautiful evening together.
harmed her.
ome, I cannot guarantee anything.
SHE WAS ABDUCTED AFTER THAT?
TSUKI-YAMA'S BEEN BIDING HIS TIME AROUND ME...
#041
TOKYO GHOUL
KIMI...
THANK YOU, KANEKI...
ONLY BECAUSE SHE CAME TO SEE ME...
BANG BANG
!

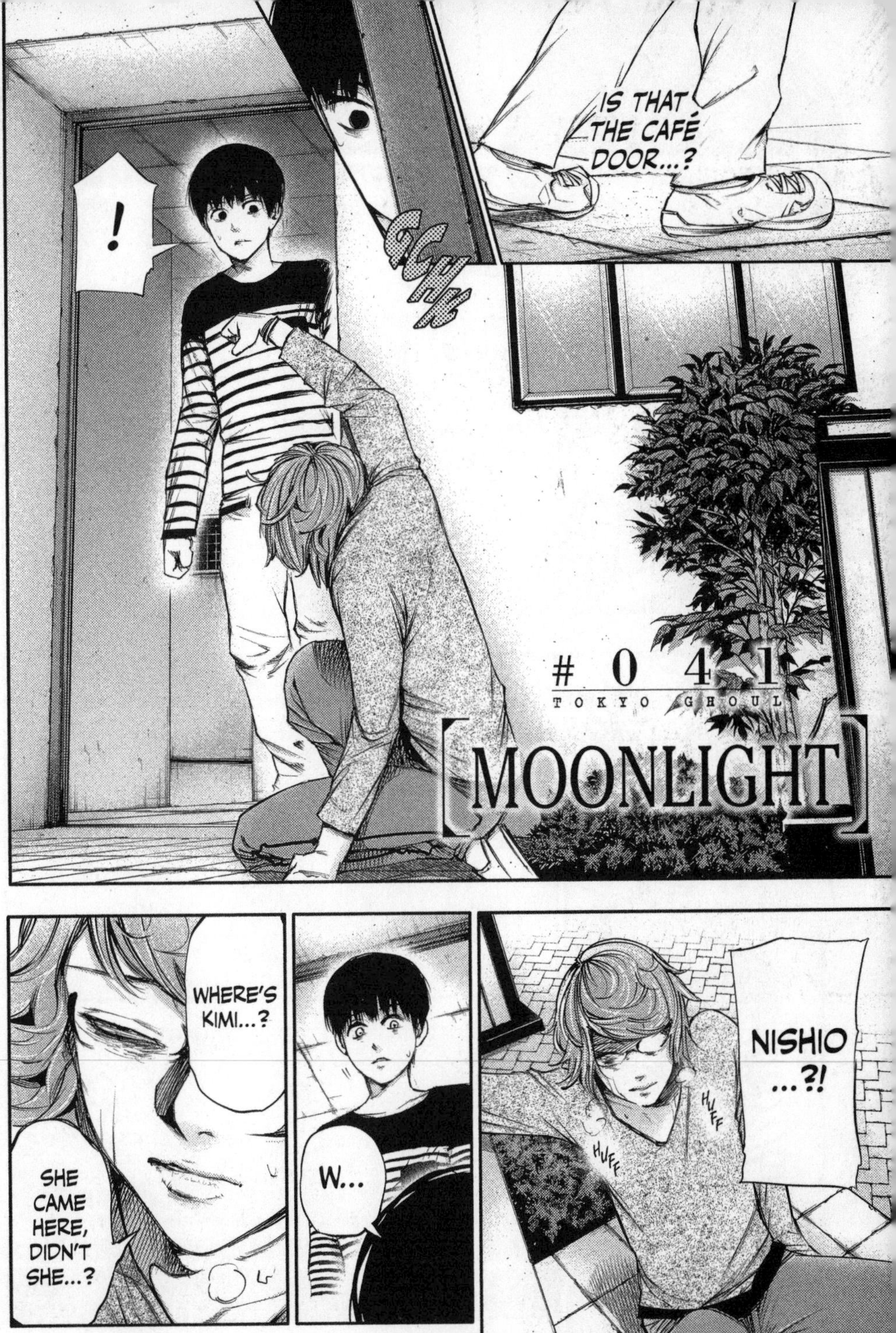
IS THAT THE CAFÉ DOOR...?
GCHHH
!
0 4 1
TOKYO GHOUL
MOONLIGHT
NISHIO ...?!
HUFF
HUFF
W...
WHERE'S KIMI...?
SHE CAME HERE, DIDN'T SHE...?

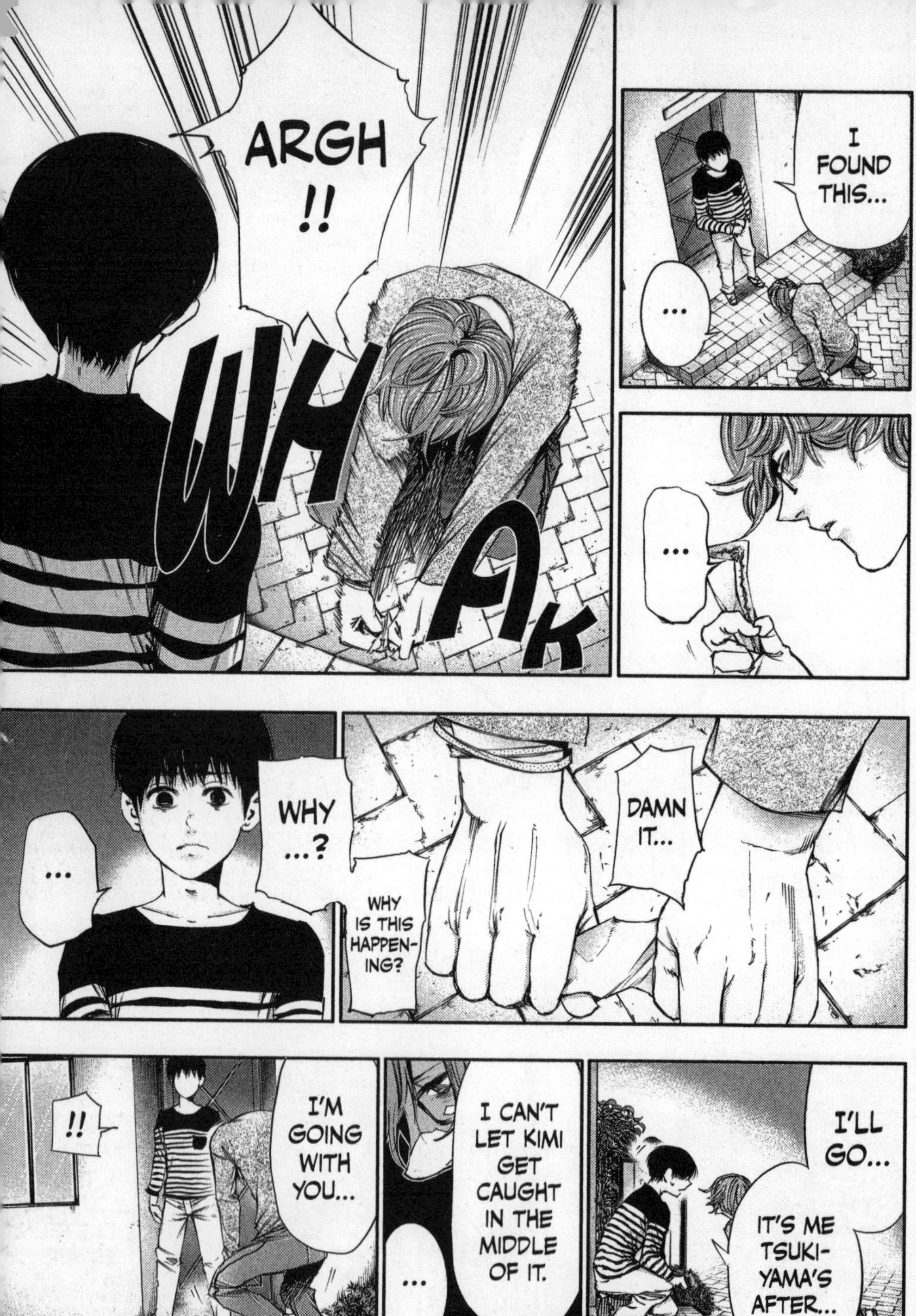
I FOUND THIS...
...
...
ARGH !!
WHAK
DAMN IT...
WHY ...?
WHY IS THIS HAPPENING?
...
I'LL GO...
IT'S ME TSUKIYAMA'S AFTER...
I CAN'T LET KIMI GET CAUGHT IN THE MIDDLE OF IT.
...
I'M GOING WITH YOU...
!!

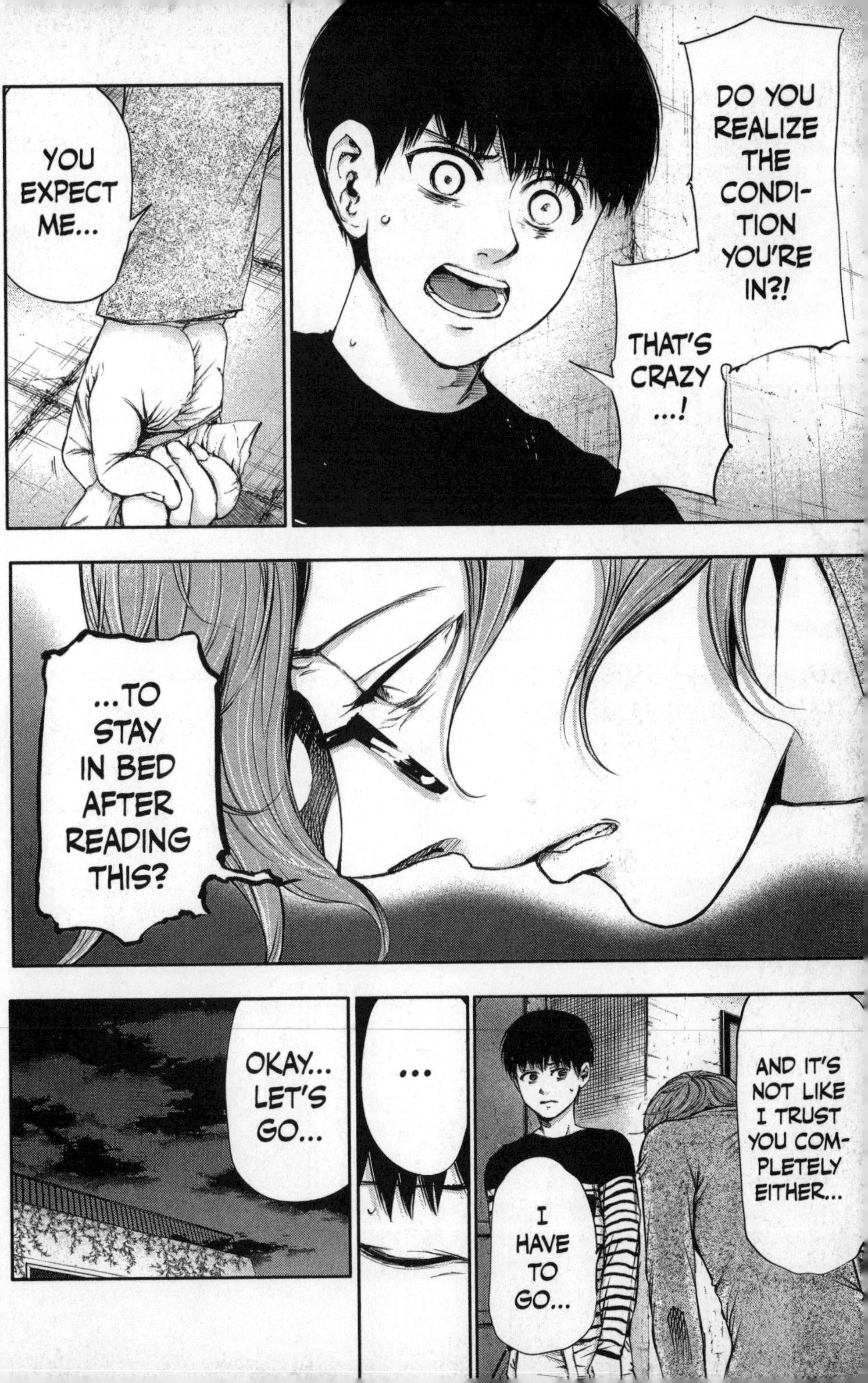
DO YOU REALIZE THE CONDITION YOU'RE IN?!
THAT'S CRAZY ...!
YOU EXPECT ME...
...TO STAY IN BED AFTER READING THIS?
AND IT'S NOT LIKE I TRUST YOU COMPLETELY EITHER...
I HAVE TO GO...
...
OKAY... LET'S GO...

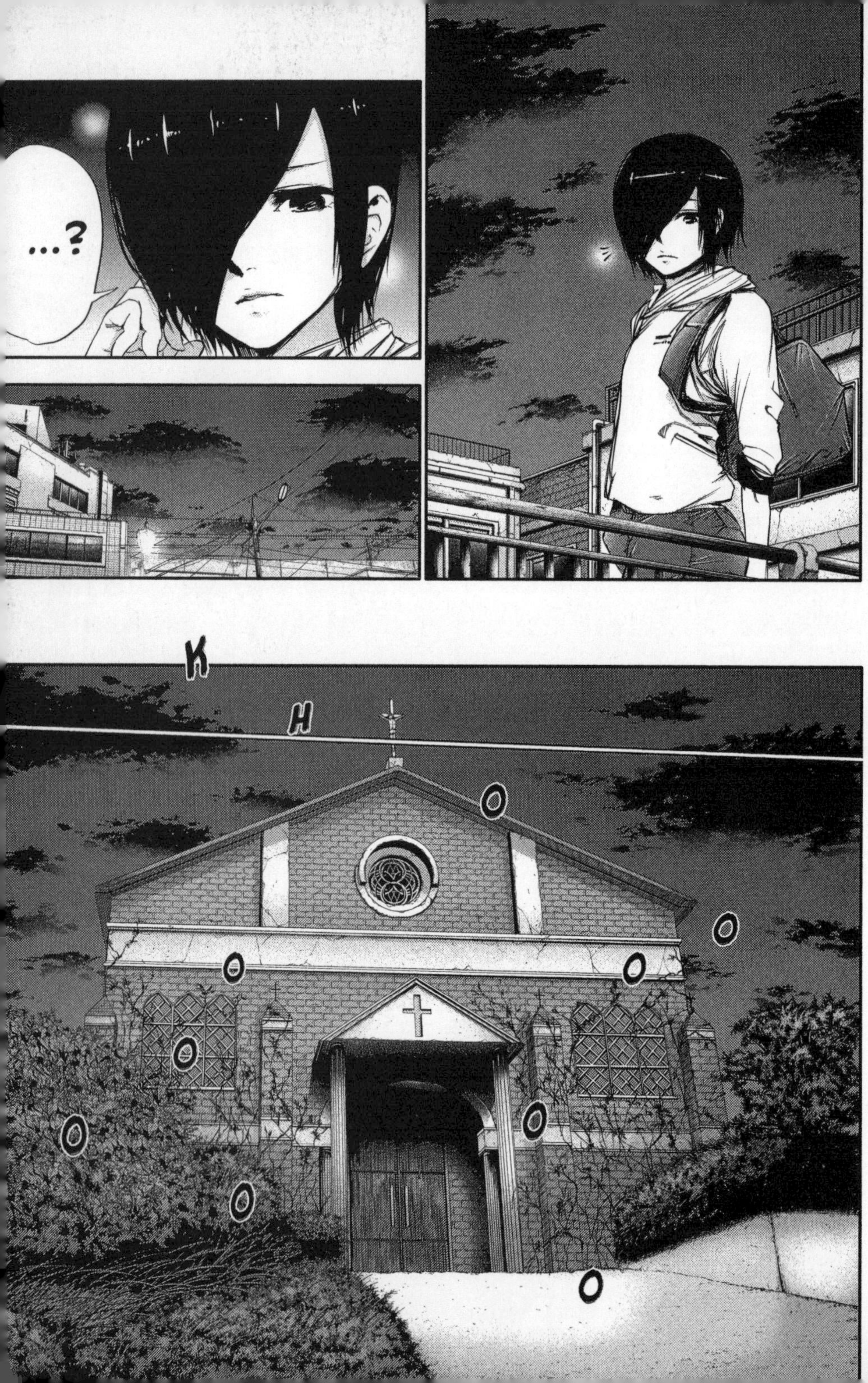
...?
KHOOOOOOOOO

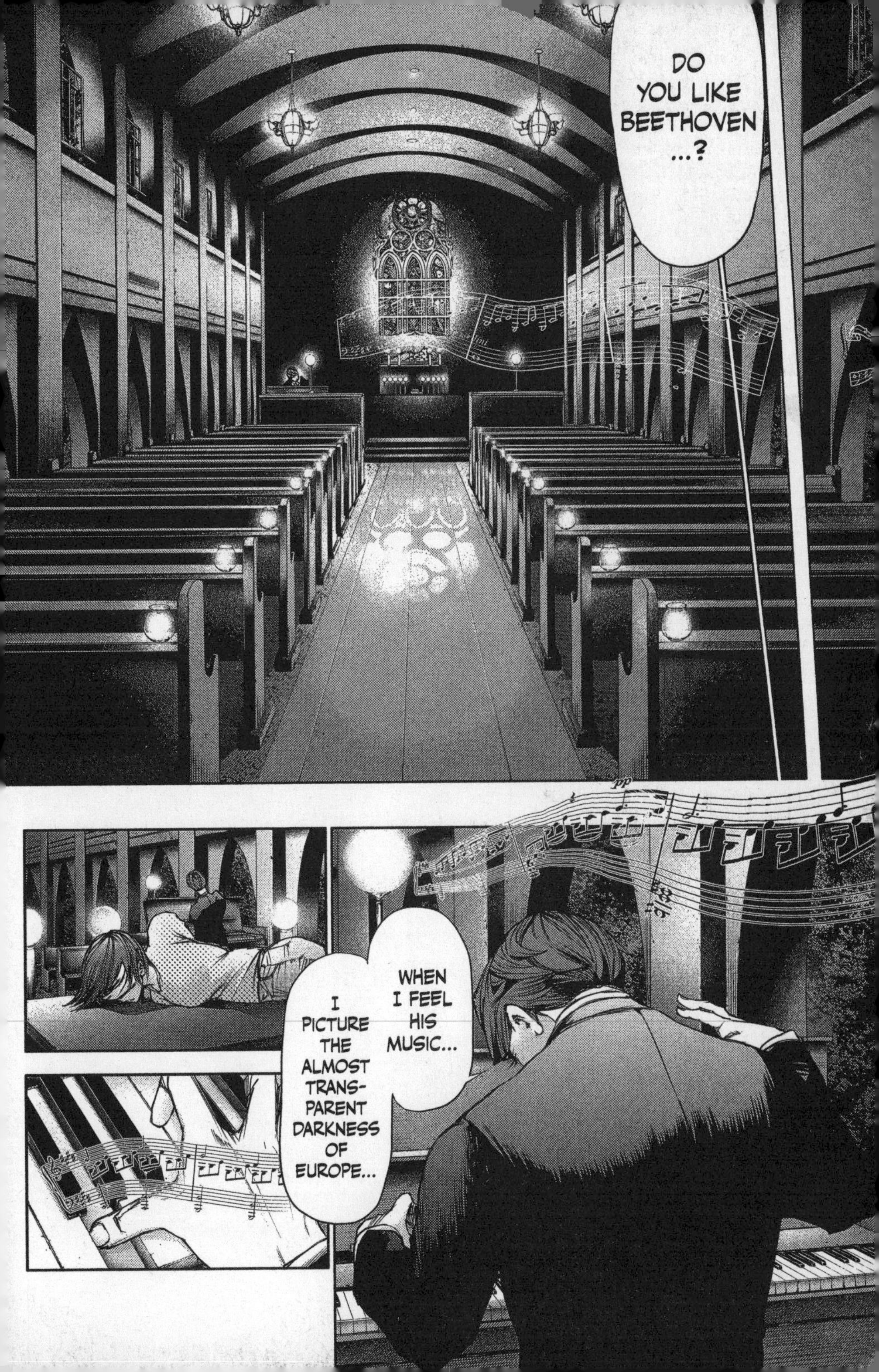
DO YOU LIKE BEETHOVEN ...?
WHEN I FEEL HIS MUSIC...
I PICTURE THE ALMOST TRANS-PARENT DARKNESS OF EUROPE...

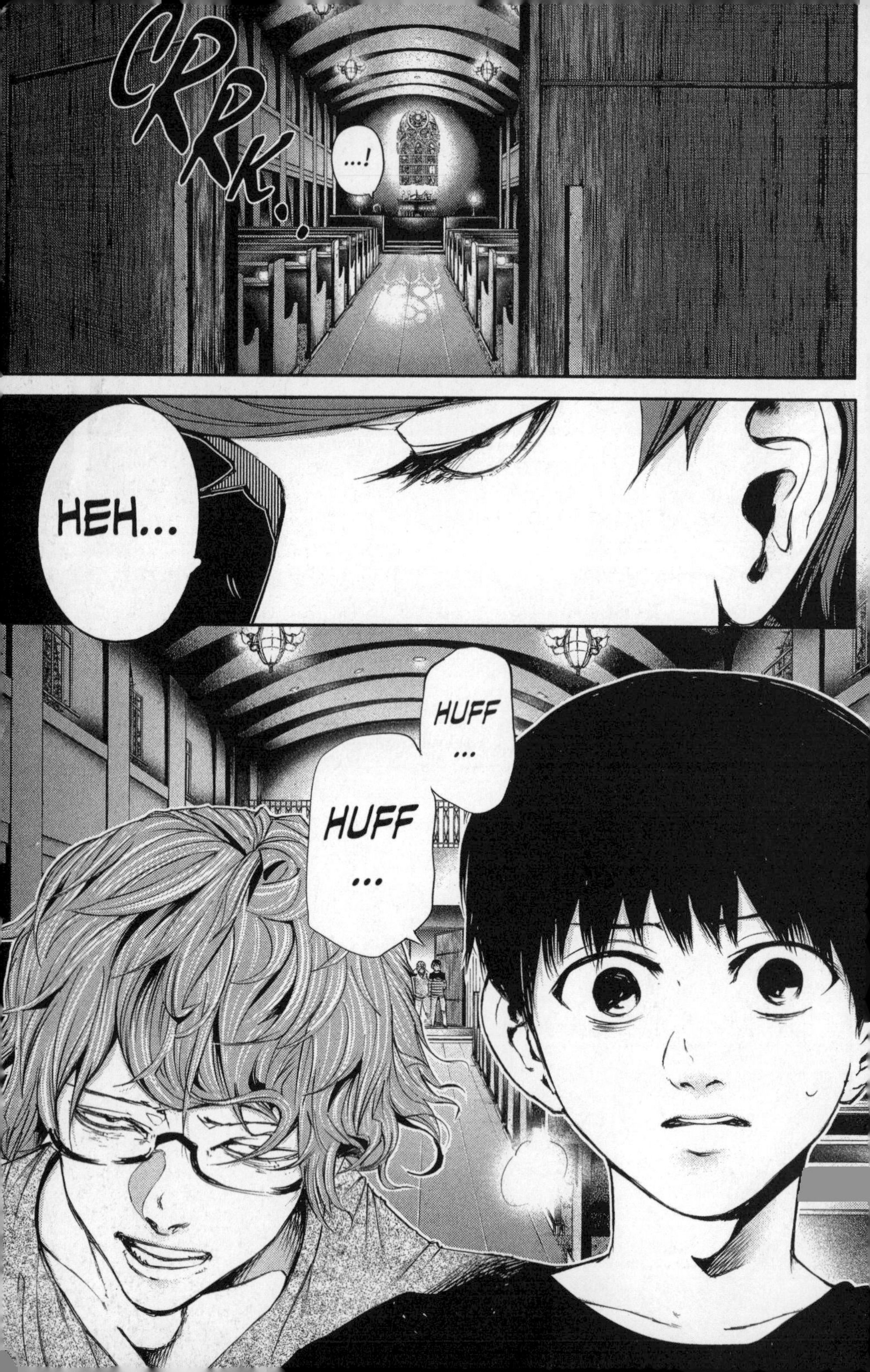
CRRK...
...!
HEH...
HUFF...
HUFF...

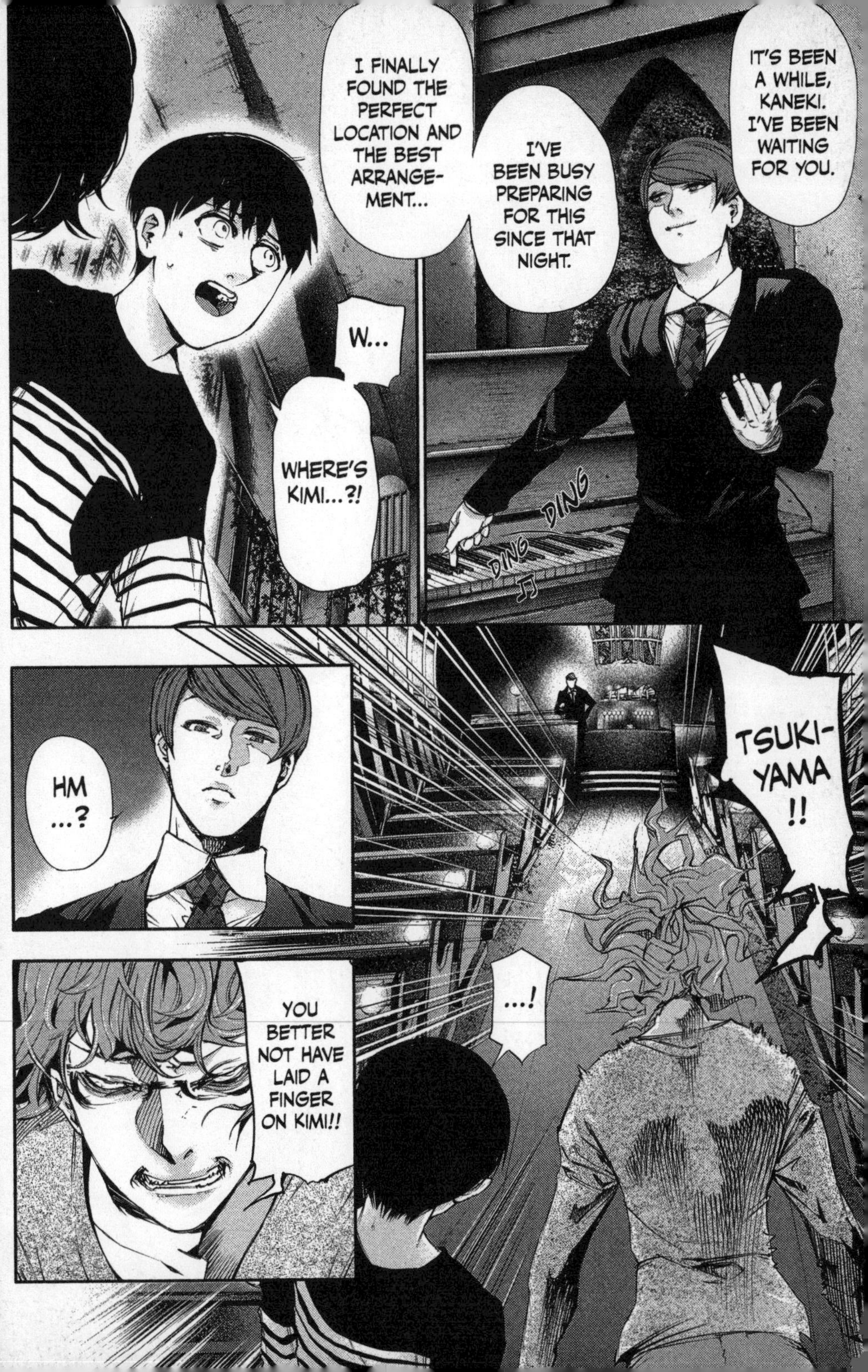

IT'S BEEN A WHILE, KANEKI. I'VE BEEN WAITING FOR YOU.
I'VE BEEN BUSY PREPARING FOR THIS SINCE THAT NIGHT.
I FINALLY FOUND THE PERFECT LOCATION AND THE BEST ARRANGEMENT...
DING
DING
W...
WHERE'S KIMI...?!
TSUKI-YAMA!!
...!
HM ...?
YOU BETTER NOT HAVE LAID A FINGER ON KIMI!!

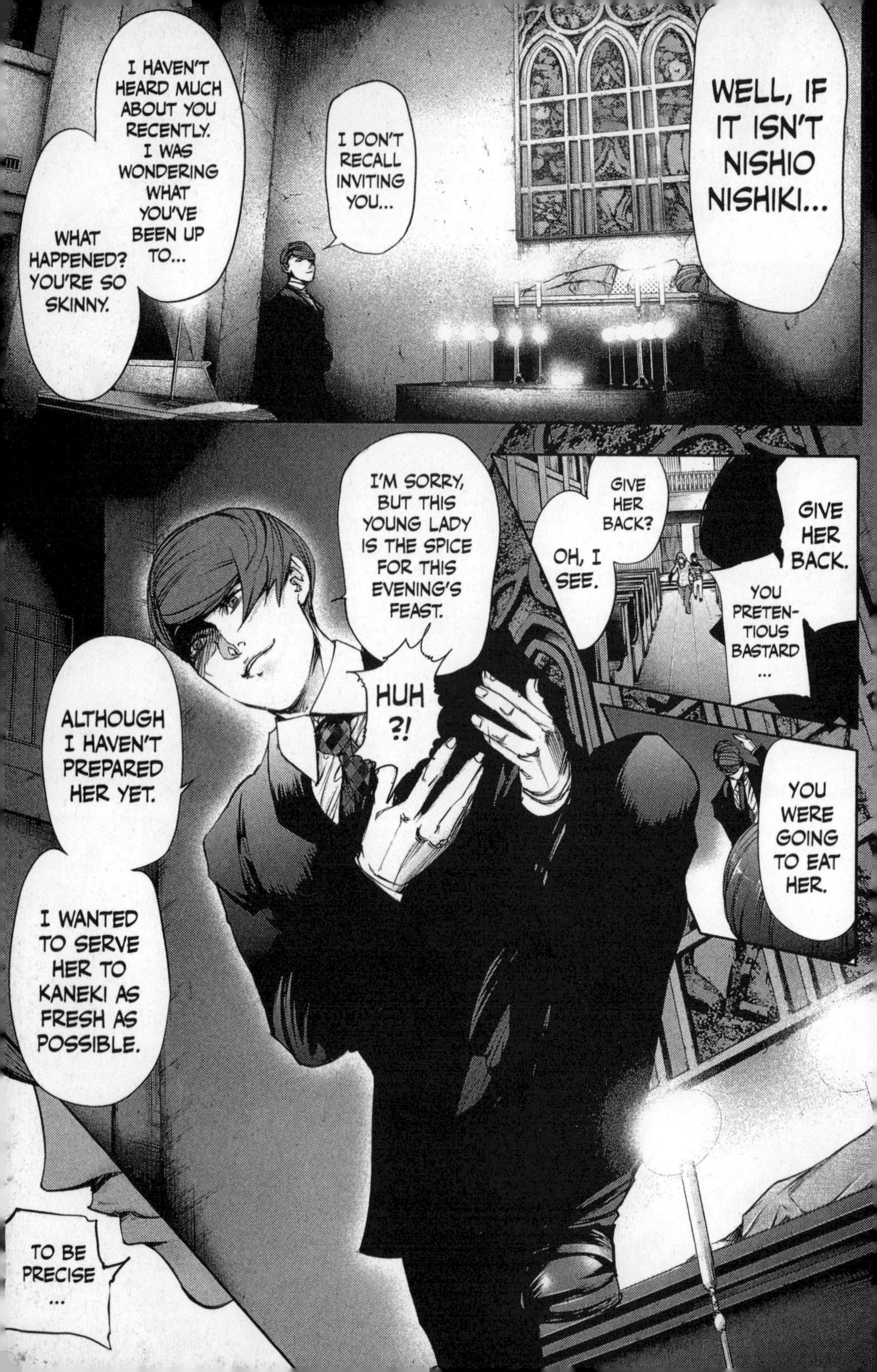
WELL, IF IT ISN'T NISHIO NISHIKI...
I DON'T RECALL INVITING YOU...
I HAVEN'T HEARD MUCH ABOUT YOU RECENTLY. I WAS WONDERING WHAT YOU'VE BEEN UP TO...
WHAT HAPPENED? YOU'RE SO SKINNY.
GIVE HER BACK.
YOU PRETEN-TIOUS BASTARD ...
GIVE HER BACK?
OH, I SEE.
YOU WERE GOING TO EAT HER.
I'M SORRY, BUT THIS YOUNG LADY IS THE SPICE FOR THIS EVENING'S FEAST.
HUH ?!
ALTHOUGH I HAVEN'T PREPARED HER YET.
I WANTED TO SERVE HER TO KANEKI AS FRESH AS POSSIBLE.
TO BE PRECISE ...

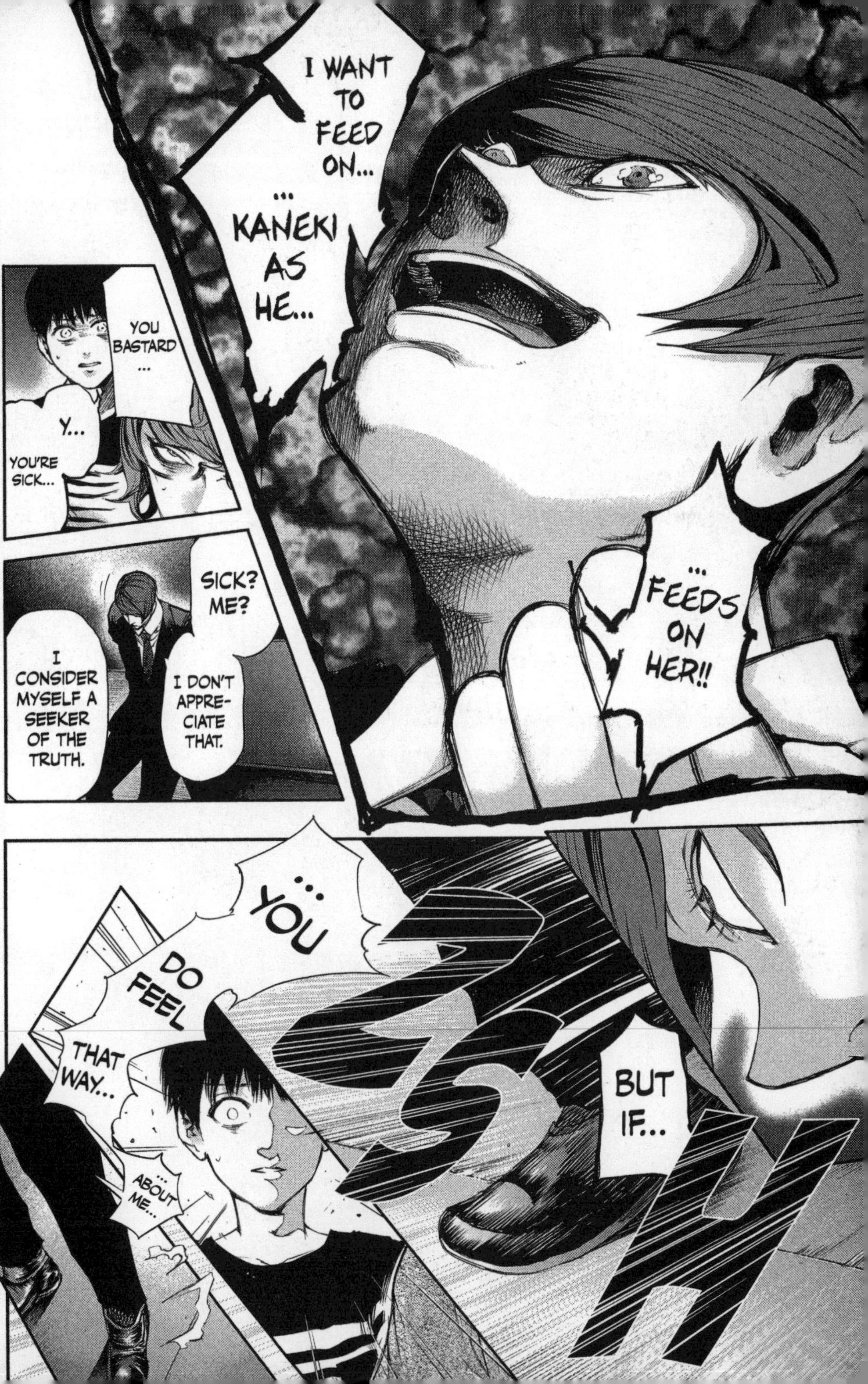
I WANT TO FEED ON...
...KANEKI AS HE...
...FEEDS ON HER!!
YOU BASTARD...
Y...
YOU'RE SICK...
SICK? ME?
I DON'T APPRECIATE THAT.
I CONSIDER MYSELF A SEEKER OF THE TRUTH.
BUT IF...
...YOU DO FEEL THAT WAY...
...ABOUT ME...

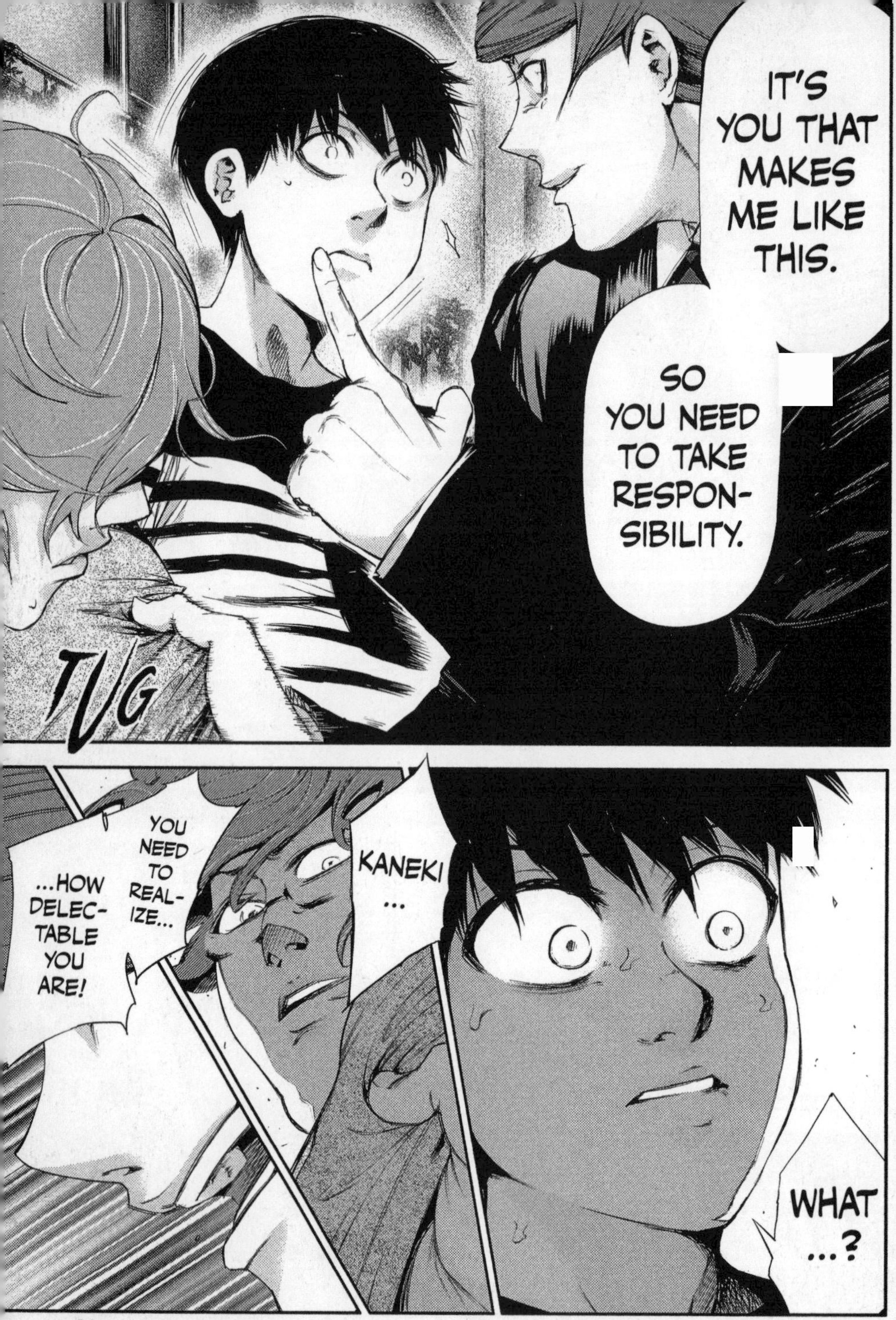
IT'S YOU THAT MAKES ME LIKE THIS.
SO YOU NEED TO TAKE RESPON-SIBILITY.
TUG
WHAT ...?
KANEKI ...
YOU NEED TO REAL-IZE...
...HOW DELEC-TABLE YOU ARE!

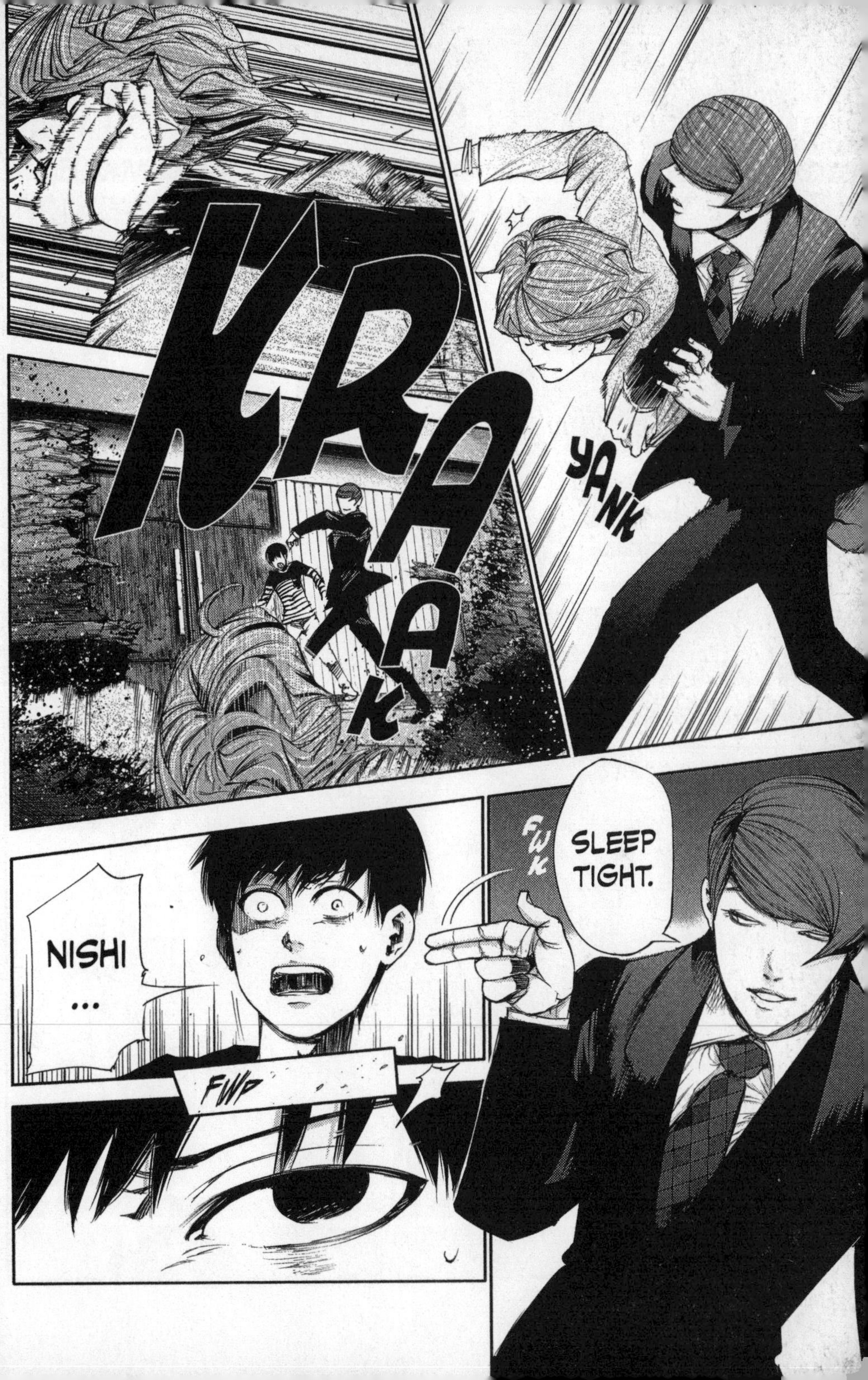
YANK
KRAAAK
FWK
SLEEP TIGHT.
NISHI
...
FWP

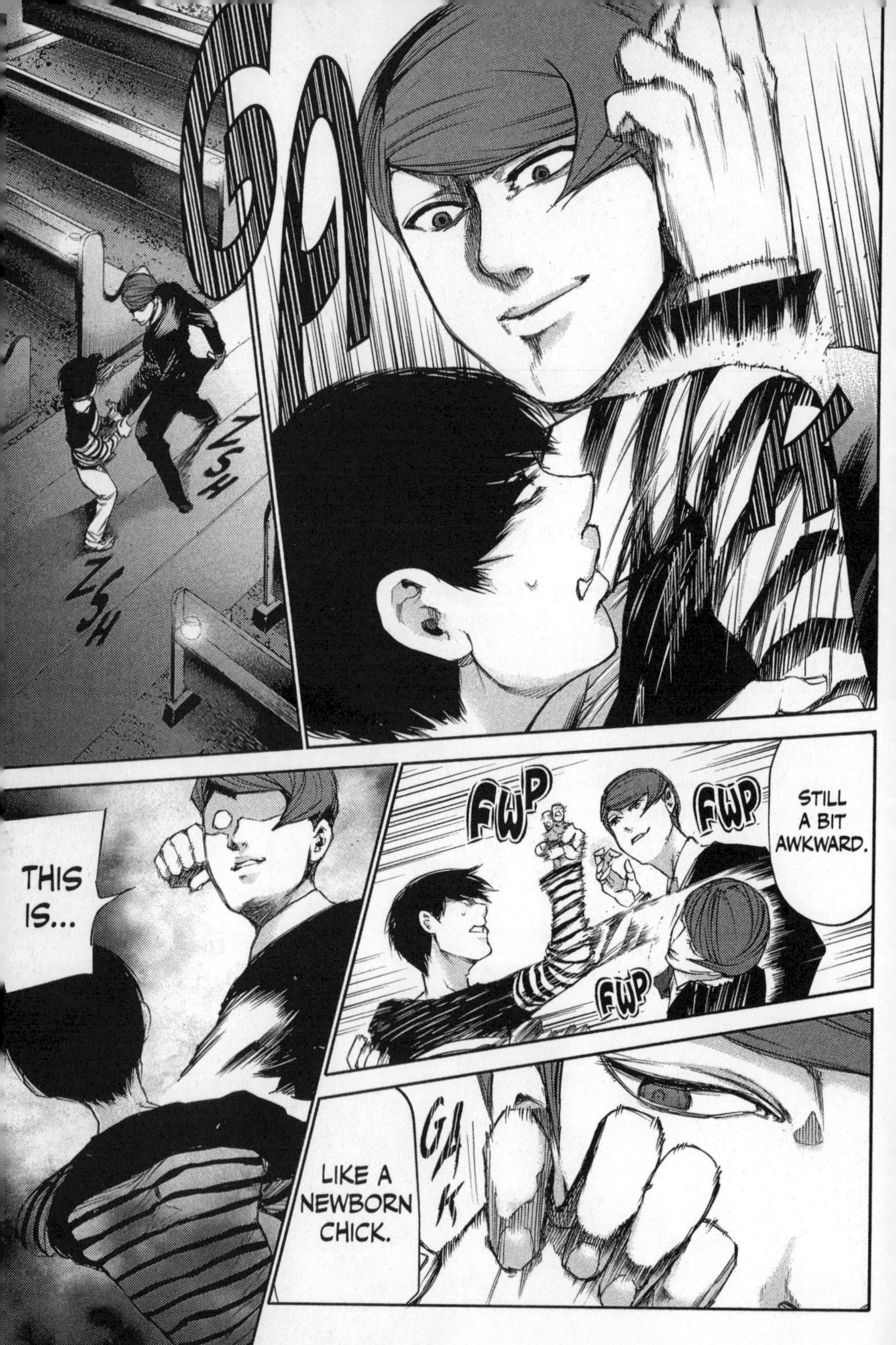
ZSH
ZSH
FWP
FWP
FWP
STILL A BIT AWKWARD.
GAK
LIKE A NEWBORN CHICK.
THIS IS...

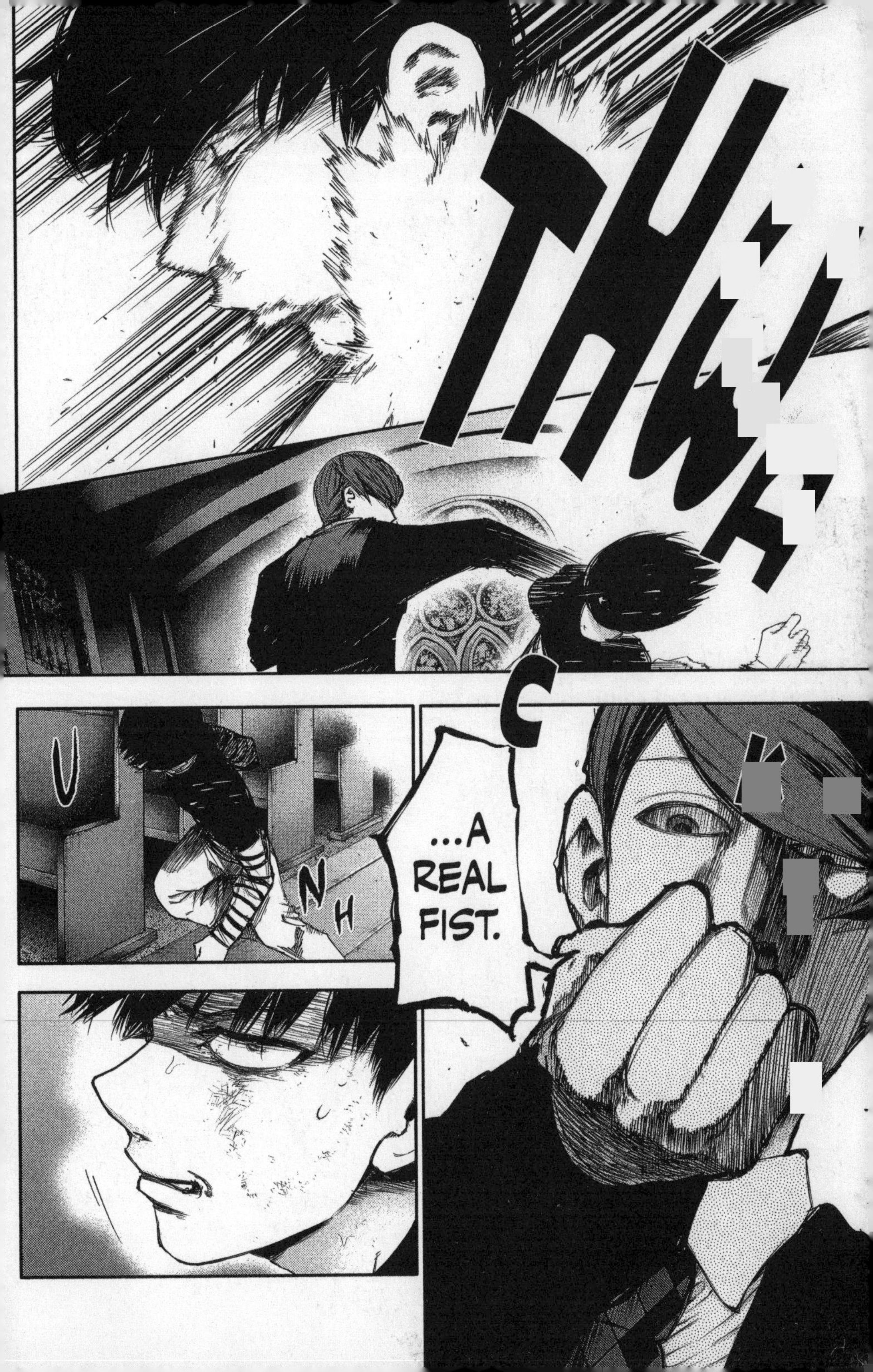
THWAK
C
...A REAL FIST.
U
NH

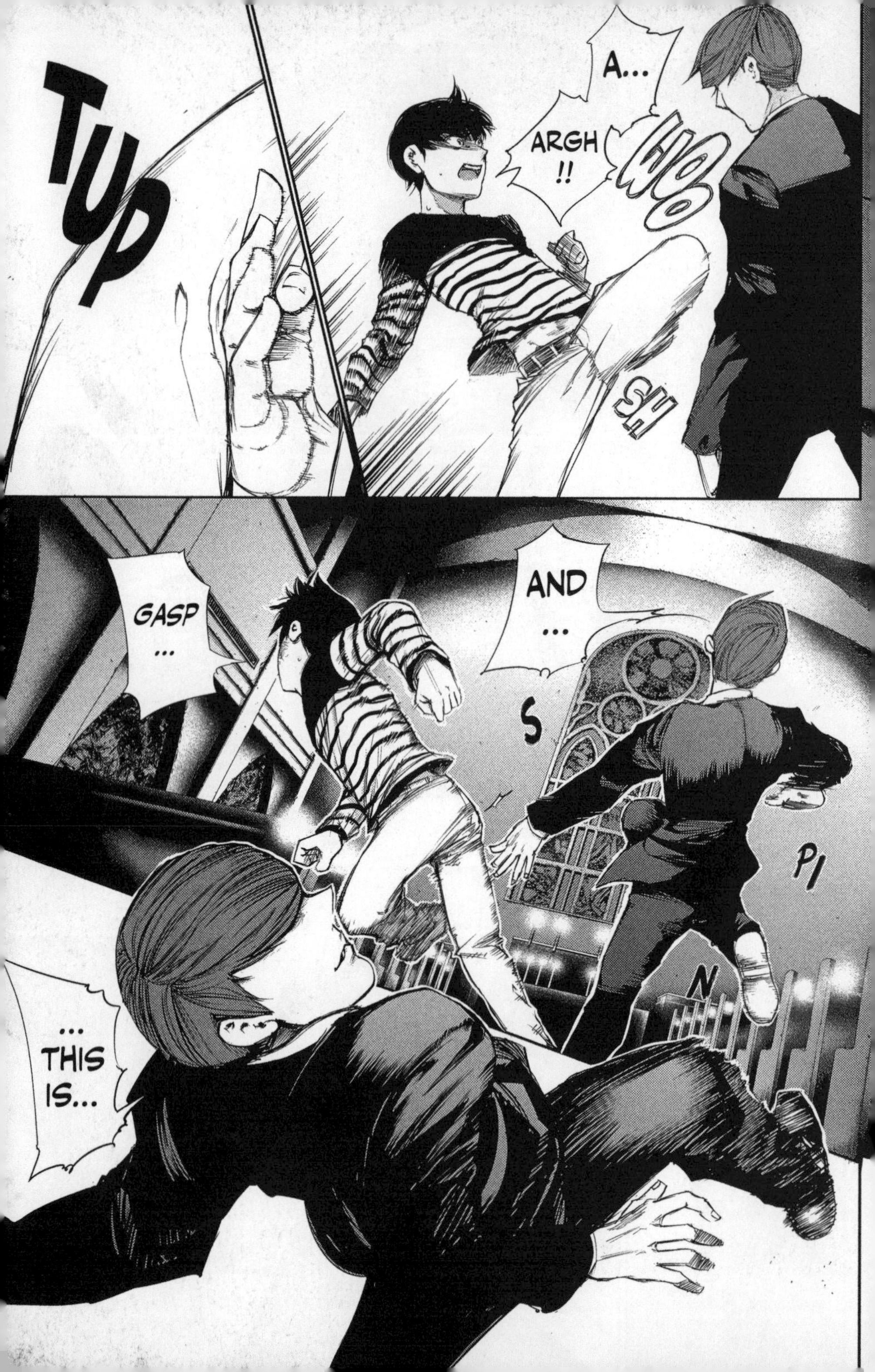
A...
ARGH!!
WHOO
SH
TUP
AND...
S
PI
N
GASP...
...THIS IS...

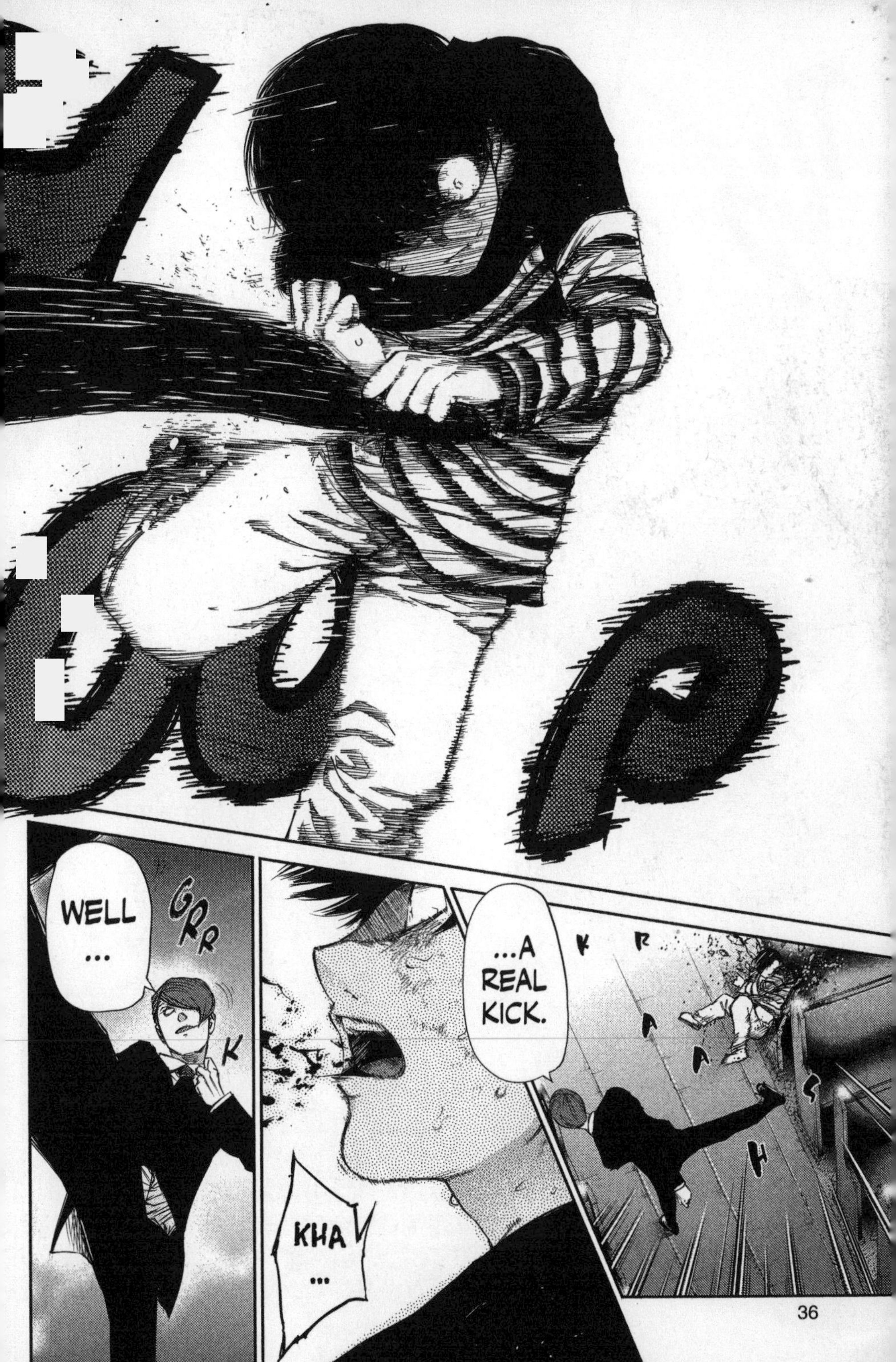
KRAASH
...A REAL KICK.
KHA ...
WELL ...
GRR
K

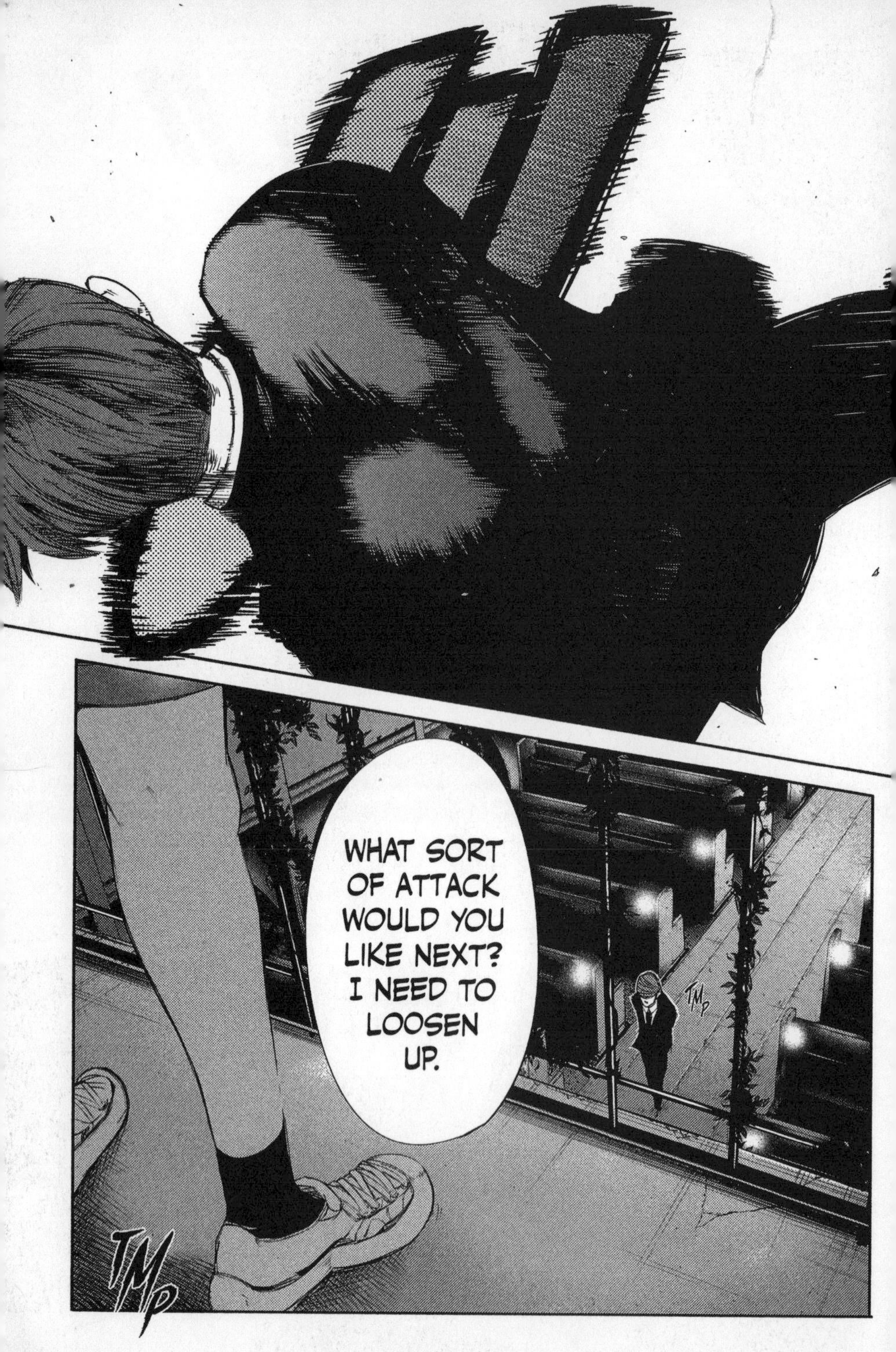
WHAT SORT OF ATTACK WOULD YOU LIKE NEXT? I NEED TO LOOSEN UP.
TMP
TMP

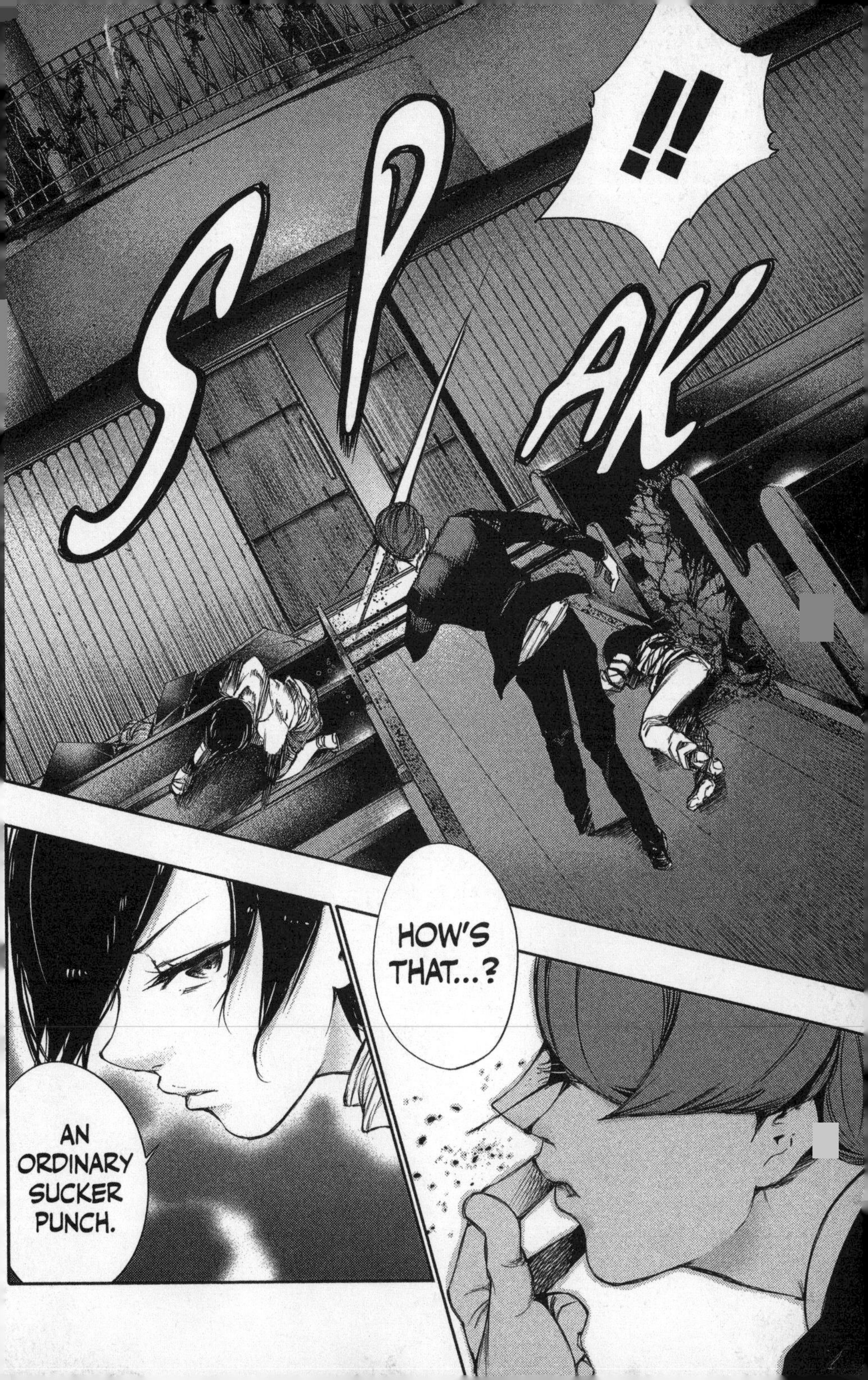
!!
SPAK
HOW'S THAT...?
AN ORDINARY SUCKER PUNCH.

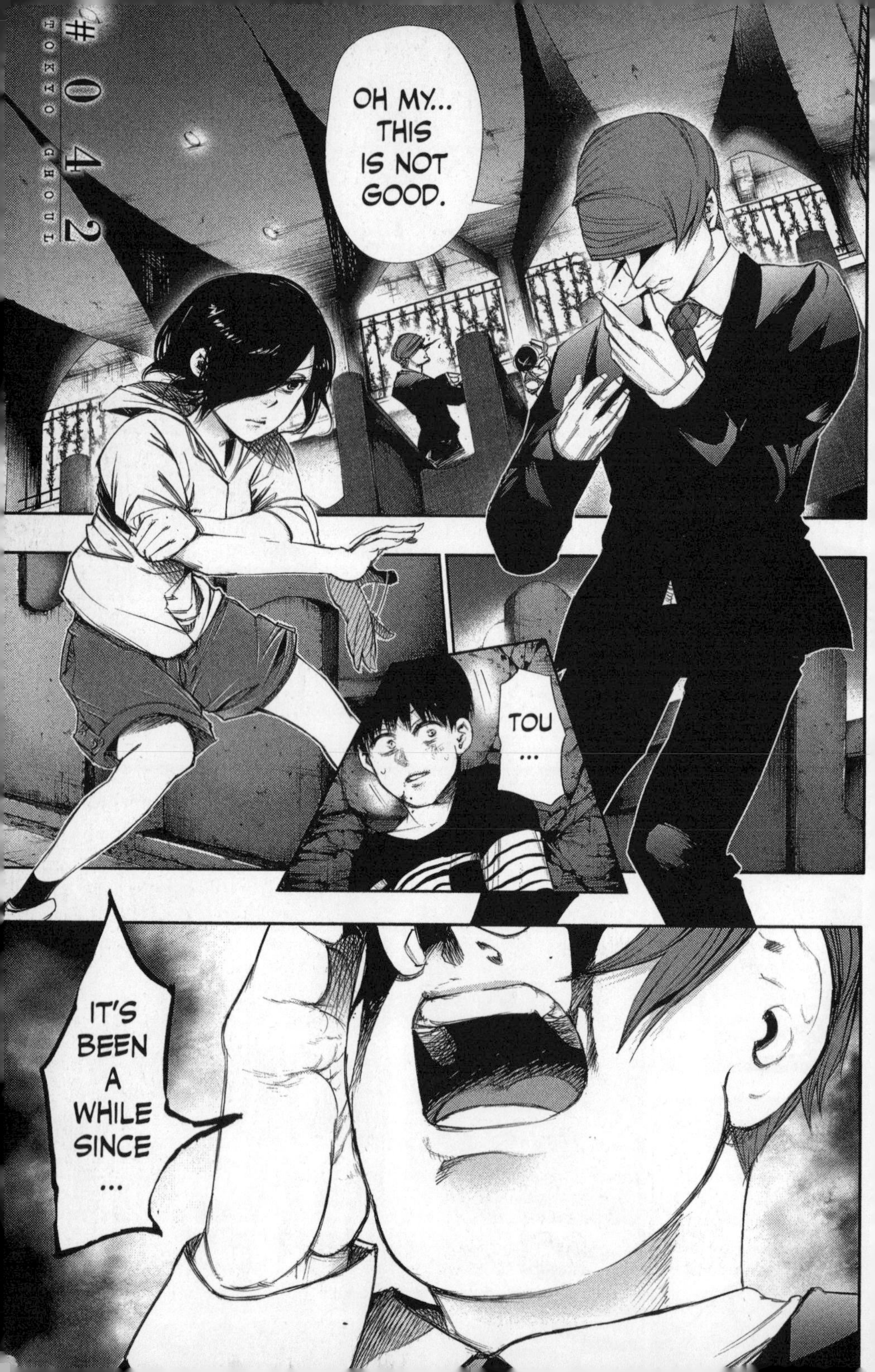
OH MY... THIS IS NOT GOOD.
#042 TOKYO GHOUL
TOU ...
IT'S BEEN A WHILE SINCE ...

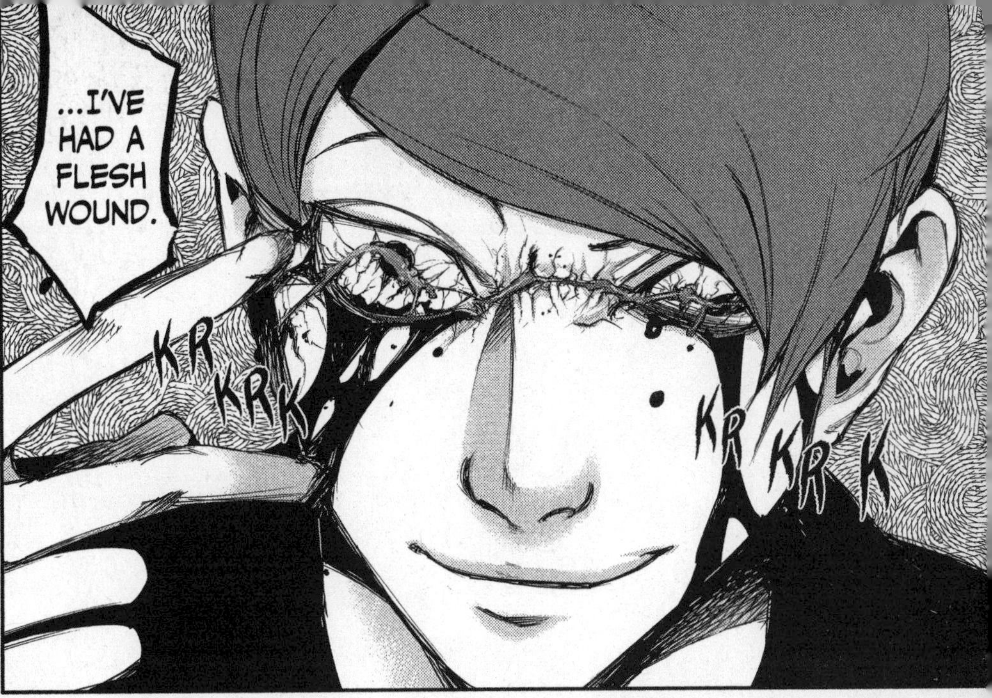
...I'VE HAD A FLESH WOUND.
KR KRK
KR KR KR K

#042 [CURETTAGE]

TOKYO GHOUL

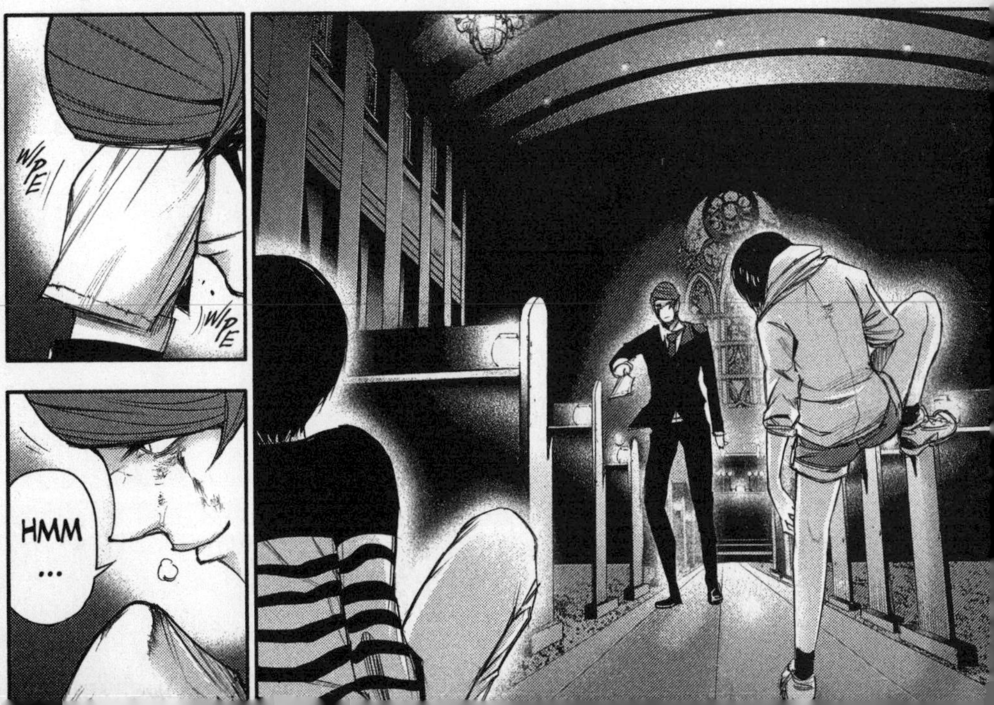
WIPE
WIPE
HMM ...

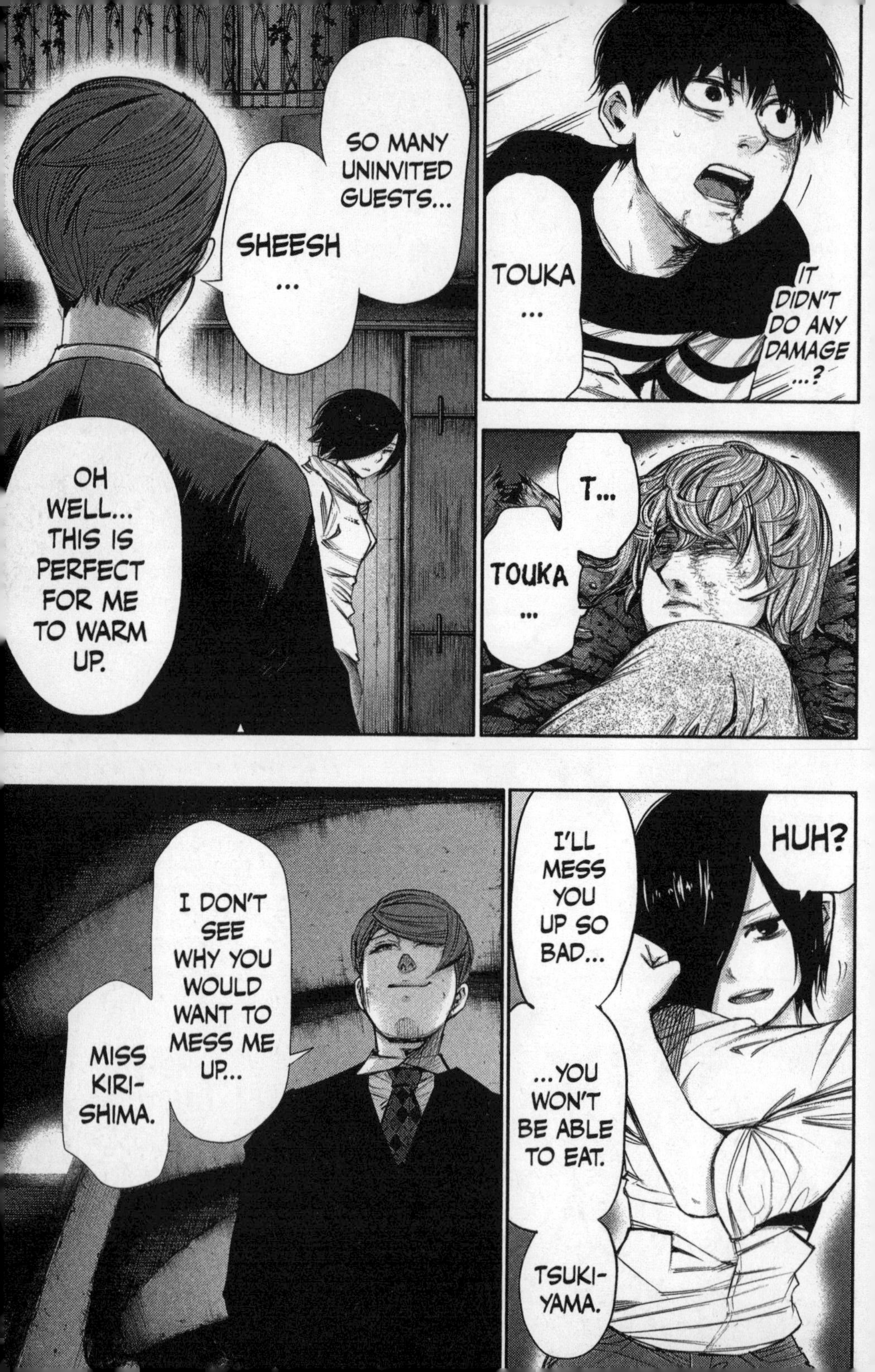
IT DIDN'T DO ANY DAMAGE ...?
TOUKA ...
T...
TOUKA ...
SO MANY UNINVITED GUESTS...
SHEESH ...
OH WELL... THIS IS PERFECT FOR ME TO WARM UP.
HUH?
I'LL MESS YOU UP SO BAD...
...YOU WON'T BE ABLE TO EAT.
TSUKI-YAMA.
I DON'T SEE WHY YOU WOULD WANT TO MESS ME UP...
MISS KIRI-SHIMA.

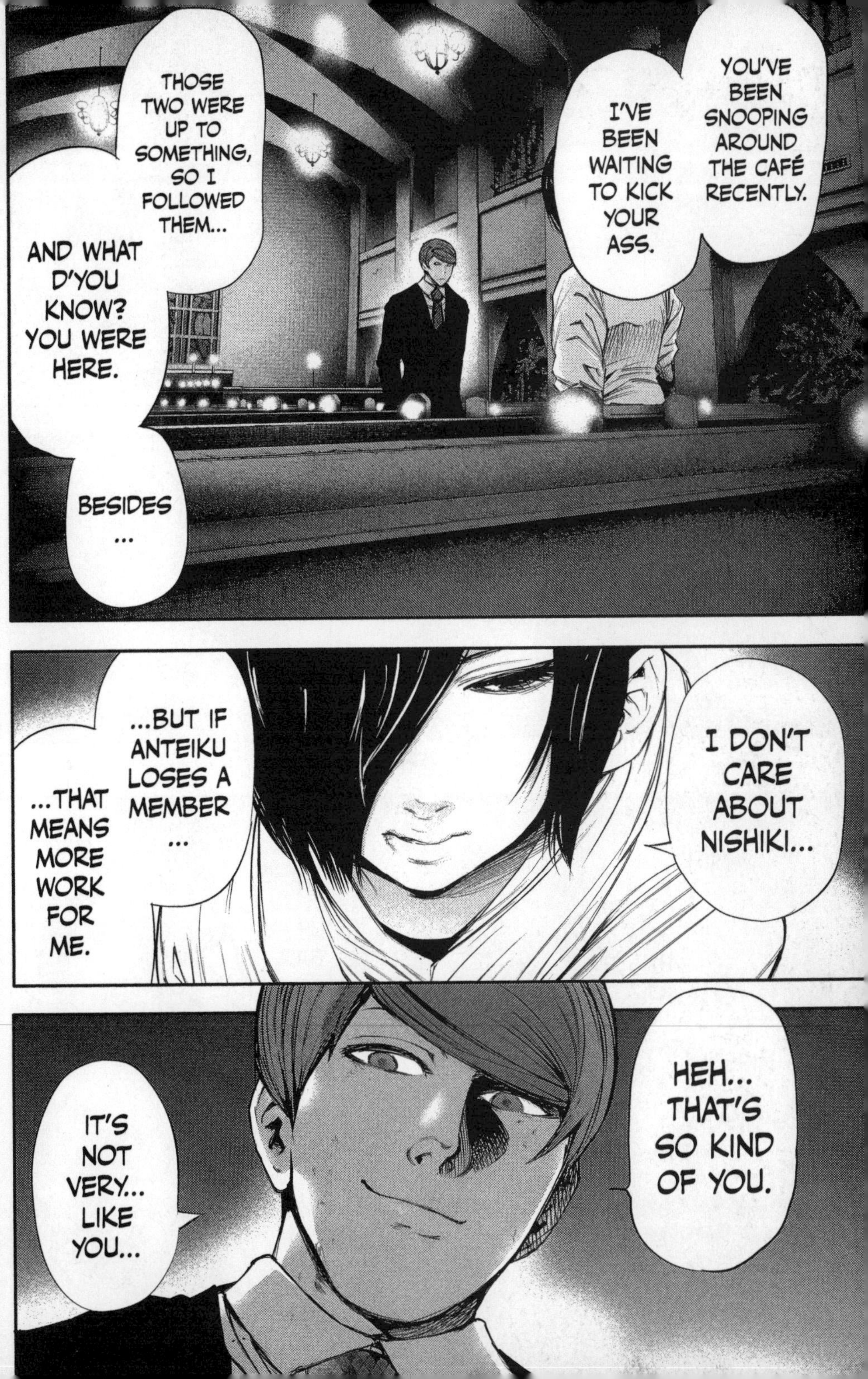
YOU'VE BEEN SNOOPING AROUND THE CAFÉ RECENTLY.
I'VE BEEN WAITING TO KICK YOUR ASS.
THOSE TWO WERE UP TO SOMETHING, SO I FOLLOWED THEM...
AND WHAT D'YOU KNOW? YOU WERE HERE.
BESIDES ...
I DON'T CARE ABOUT NISHIKI...
...BUT IF ANTEIKU LOSES A MEMBER ...
...THAT MEANS MORE WORK FOR ME.
HEH... THAT'S SO KIND OF YOU.
IT'S NOT VERY... LIKE YOU...

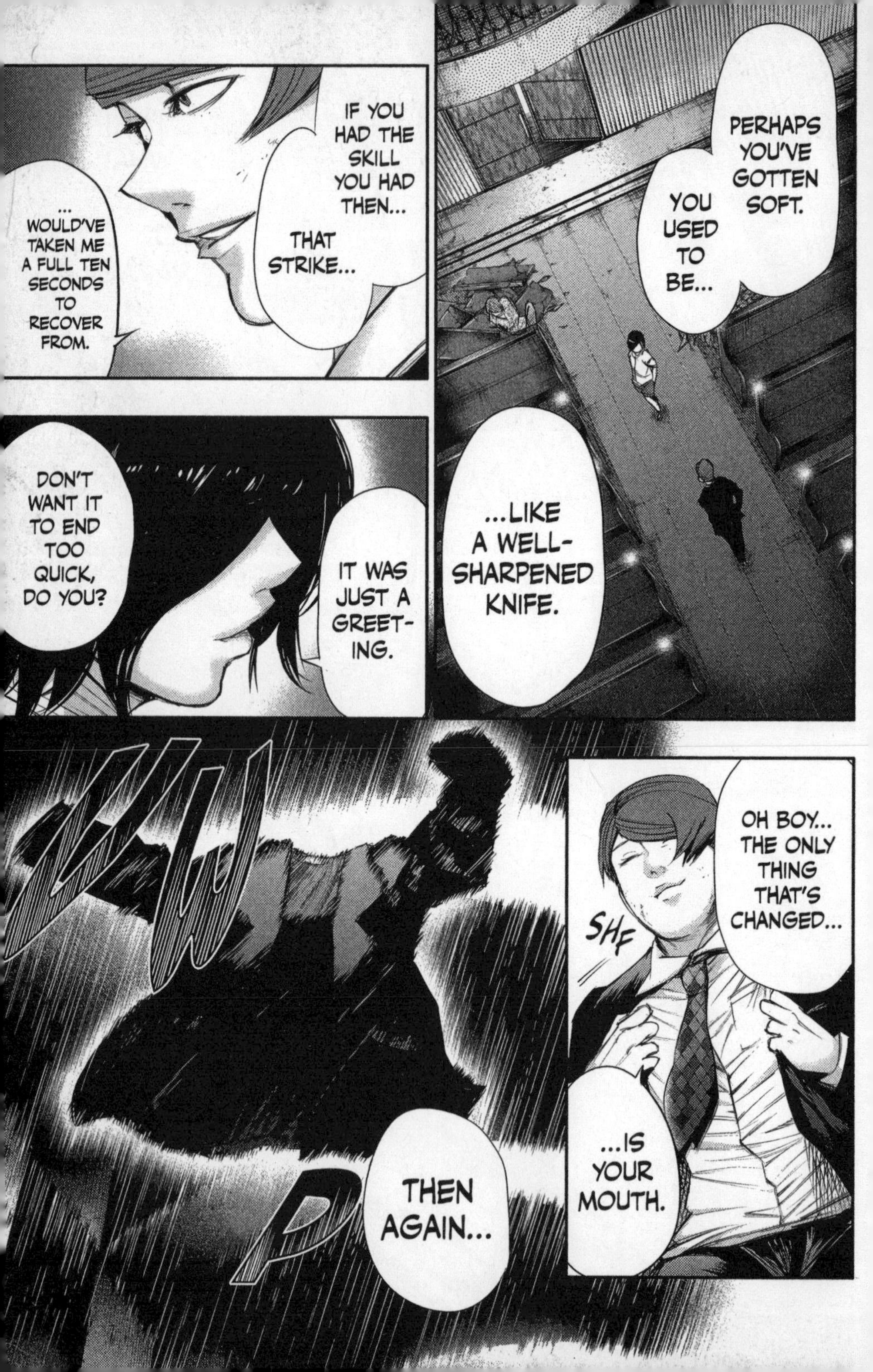
PERHAPS YOU'VE GOTTEN SOFT.
YOU USED TO BE...
...LIKE A WELL-SHARPENED KNIFE.
IF YOU HAD THE SKILL YOU HAD THEN...
THAT STRIKE...
...WOULD'VE TAKEN ME A FULL TEN SECONDS TO RECOVER FROM.
IT WAS JUST A GREET-ING.
DON'T WANT IT TO END TOO QUICK, DO YOU?
OH BOY... THE ONLY THING THAT'S CHANGED...
SHF
...IS YOUR MOUTH.
THEN AGAIN...

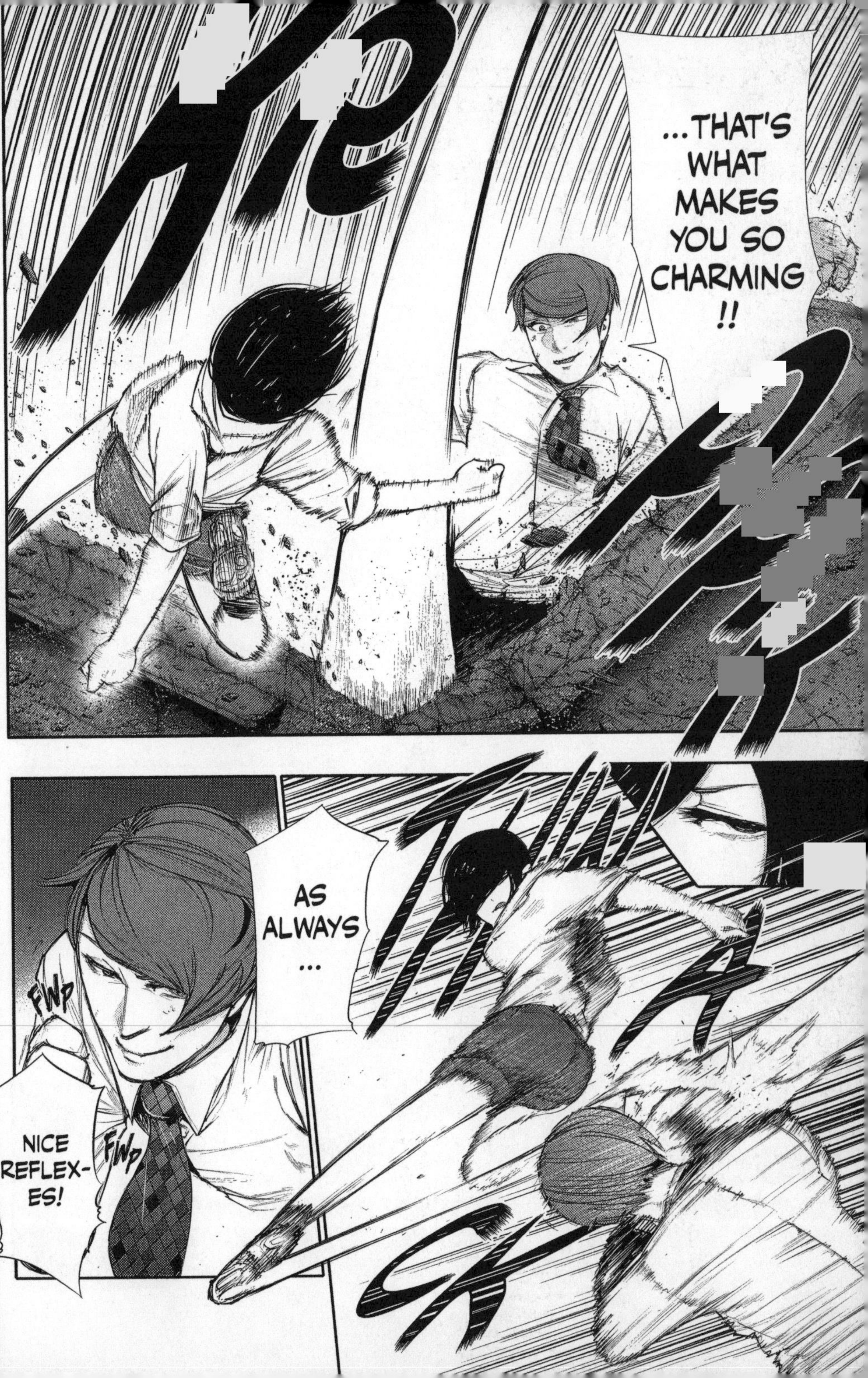
...THAT'S WHAT MAKES YOU SO CHARMING!!
AS ALWAYS...
FWP
NICE REFLEX-ES!
FWP

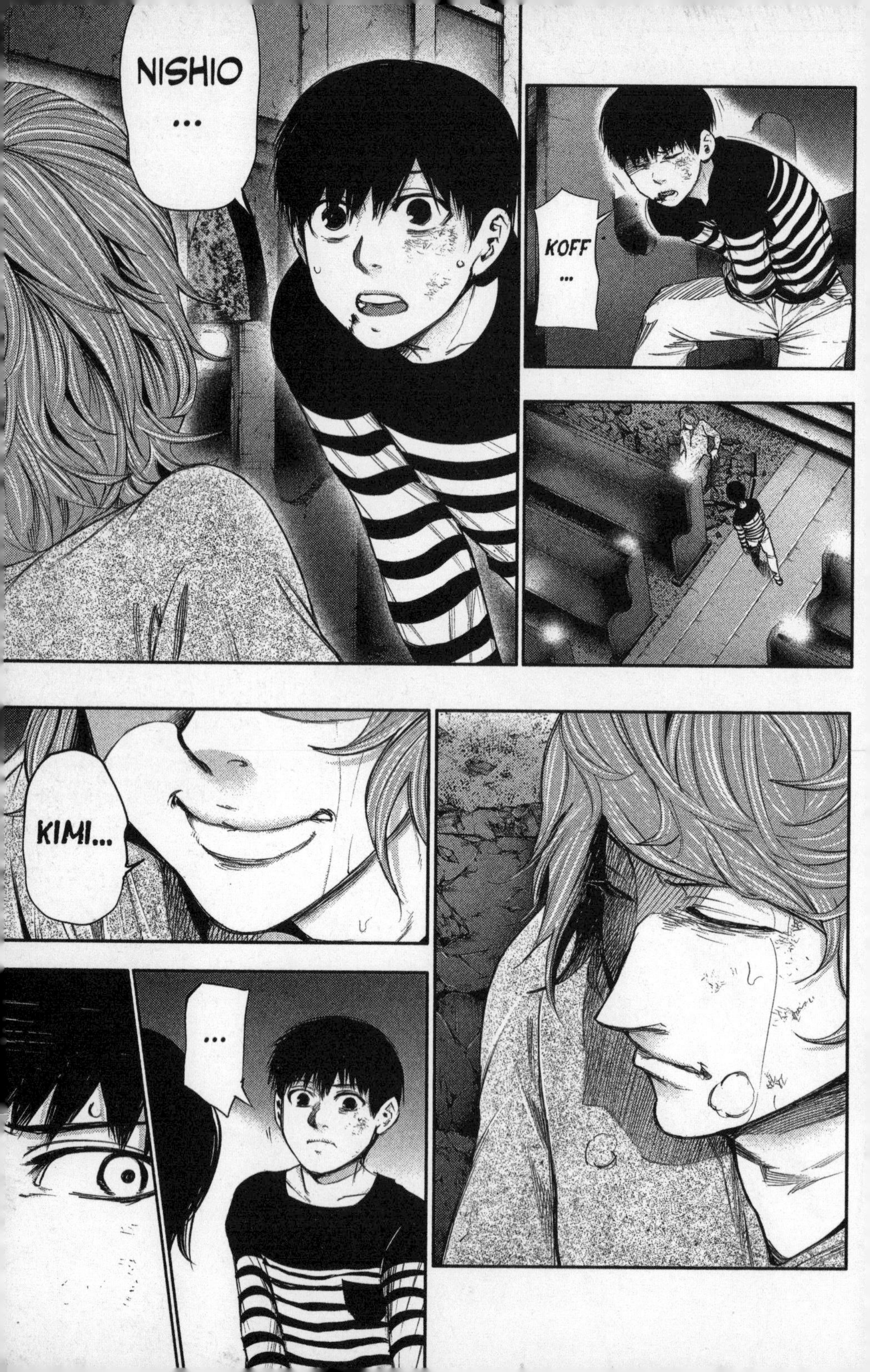
KOFF ...
NISHIO ...
KIMI...
...

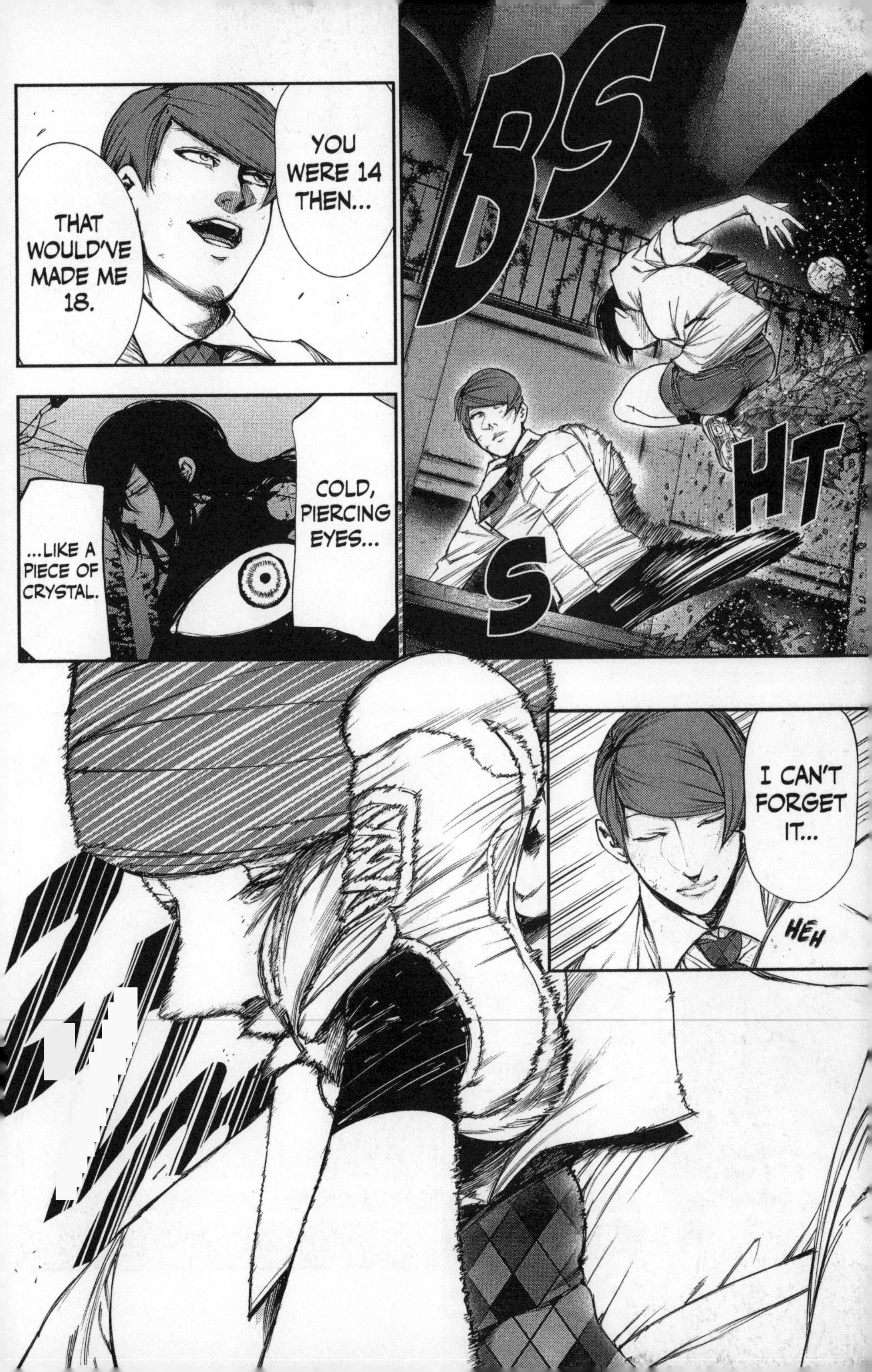
BS
HT
S
YOU WERE 14 THEN...
THAT WOULD'VE MADE ME 18.
COLD, PIERCING EYES...
...LIKE A PIECE OF CRYSTAL.
I CAN'T FORGET IT...
HEH

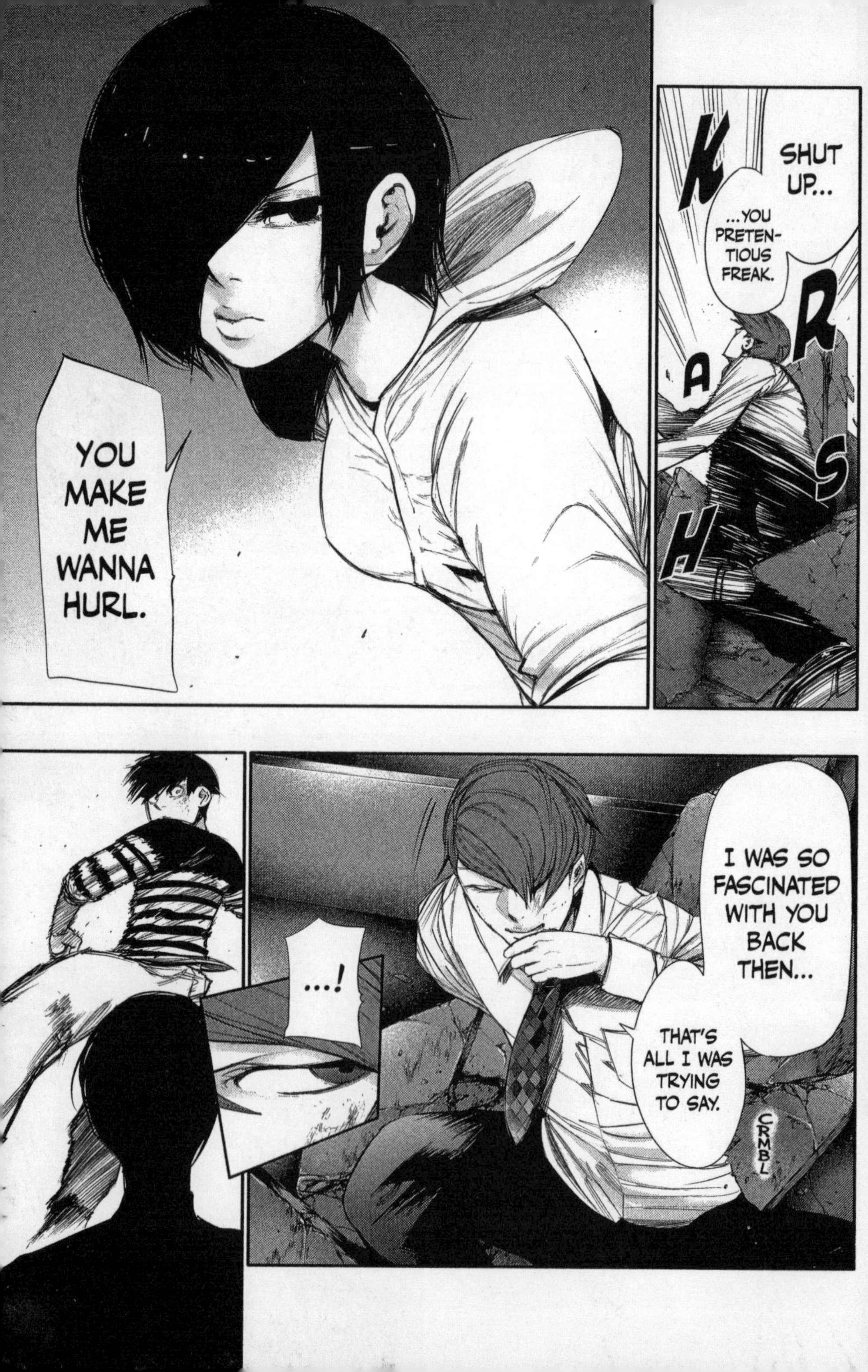
KRASH
SHUT UP...
...YOU PRETEN-TIOUS FREAK.
YOU MAKE ME WANNA HURL.
I WAS SO FASCINATED WITH YOU BACK THEN...
THAT'S ALL I WAS TRYING TO SAY.
CRMBL
...!

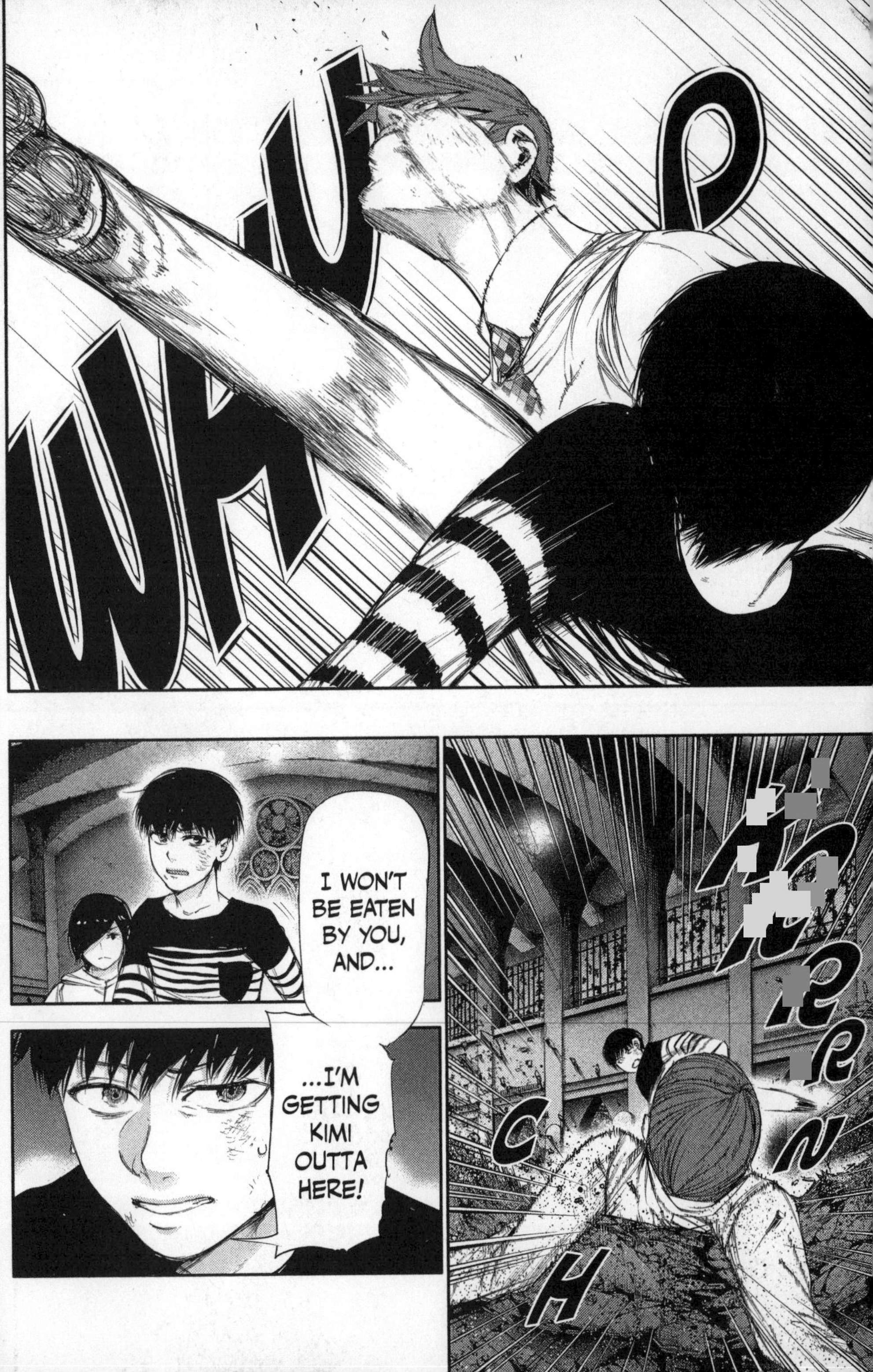
I WON'T BE EATEN BY YOU, AND...
...I'M GETTING KIMI OUTTA HERE!

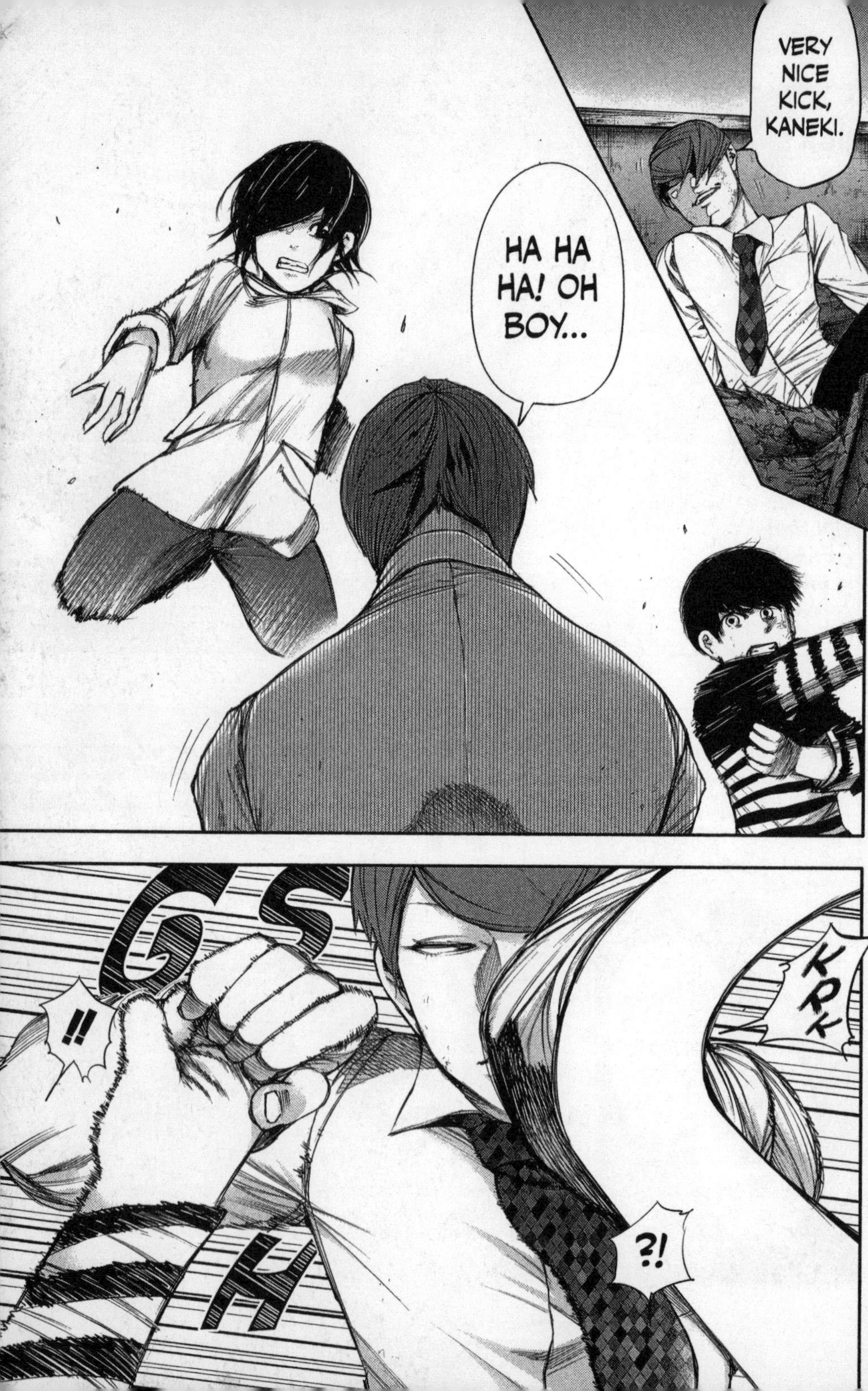
VERY NICE KICK, KANEKI.
HA HA HA! OH BOY...
KRK
GS
!!
?!
H

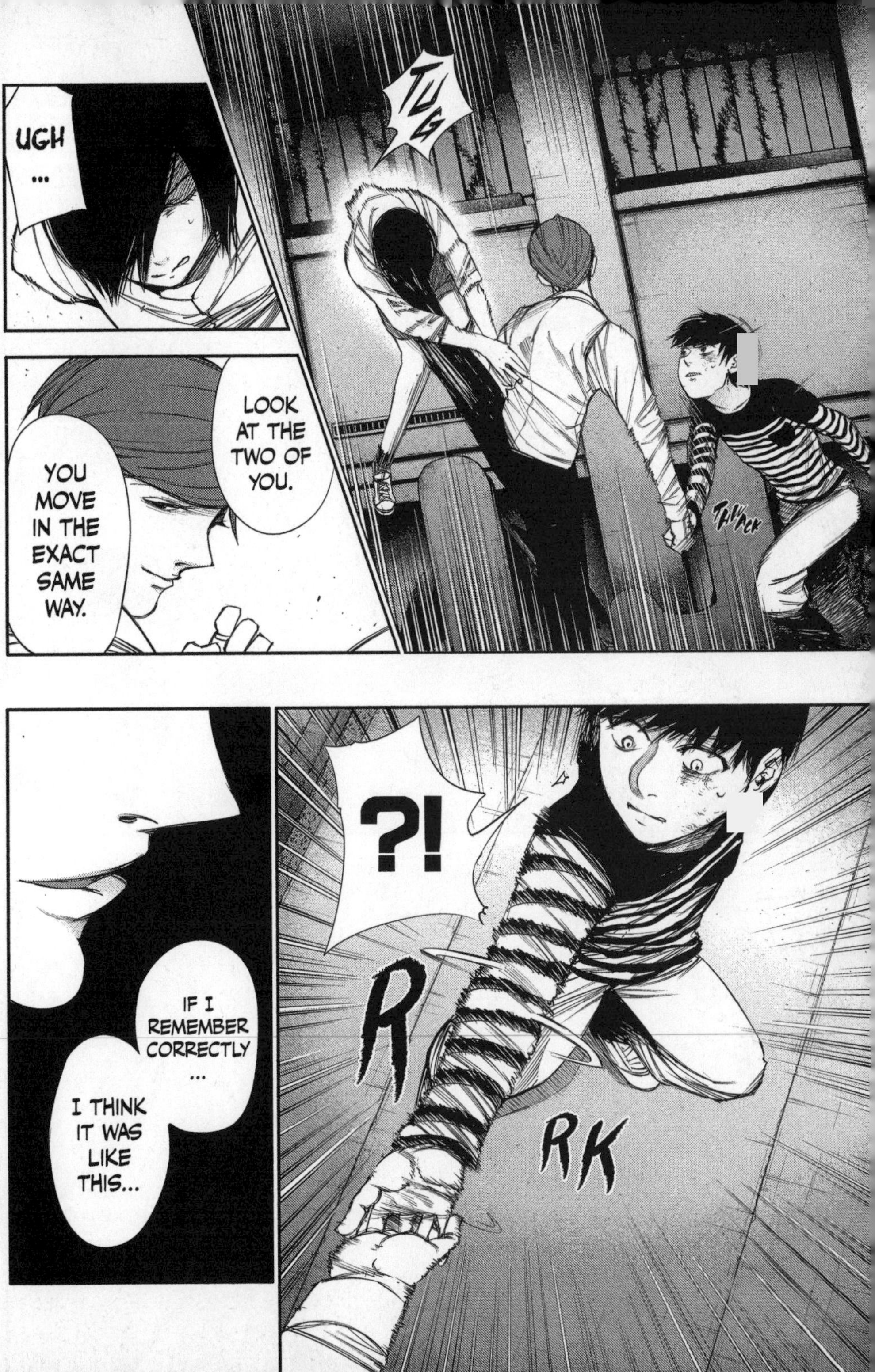
TUG
THWACK
UGH
...
LOOK AT THE TWO OF YOU.
YOU MOVE IN THE EXACT SAME WAY.
?!
RRK
IF I REMEMBER CORRECTLY...
I THINK IT WAS LIKE THIS...

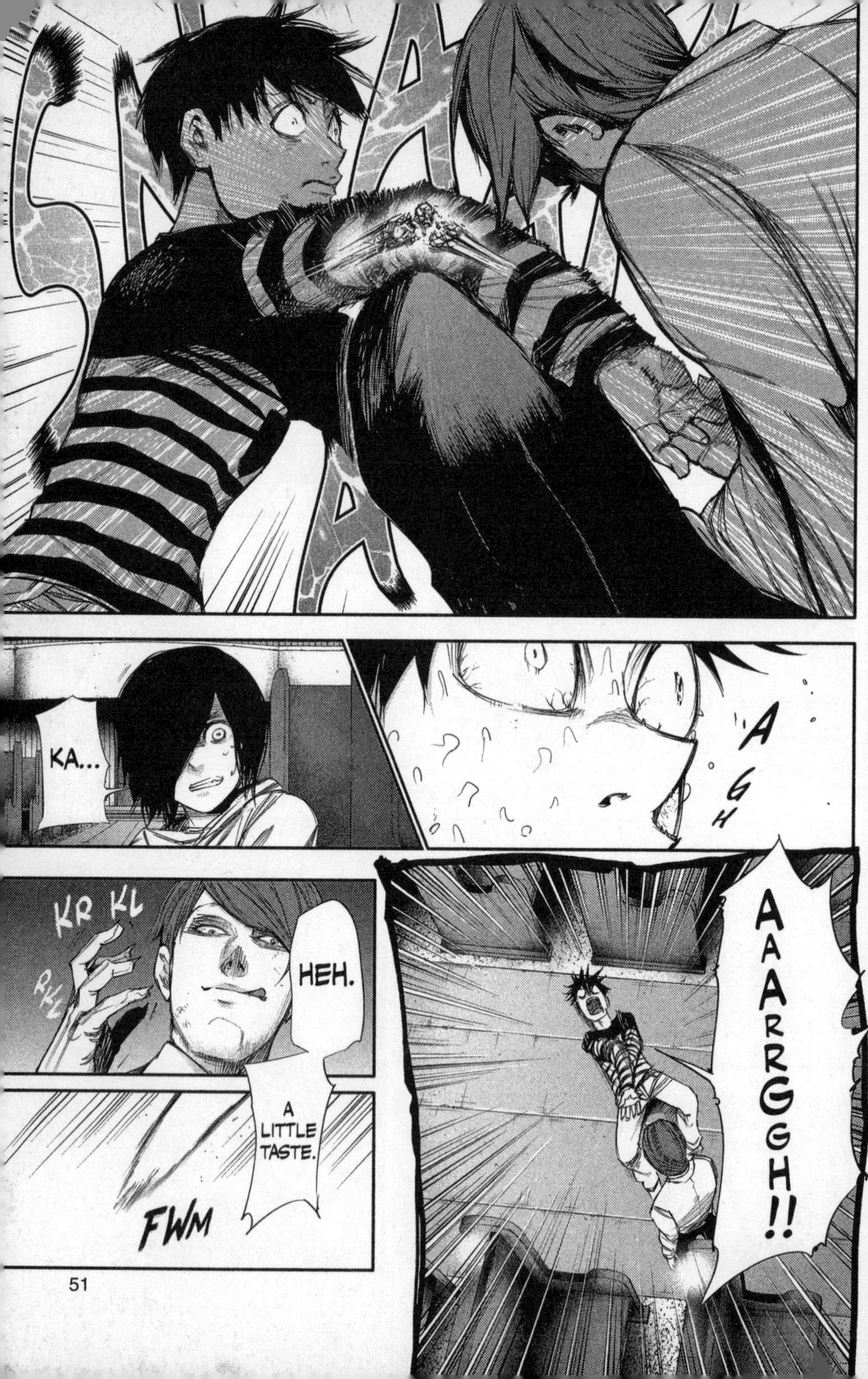
AGH
KA...
AAARRGGH!!
KR KL
RKL
HEH.
A LITTLE TASTE.
FWM

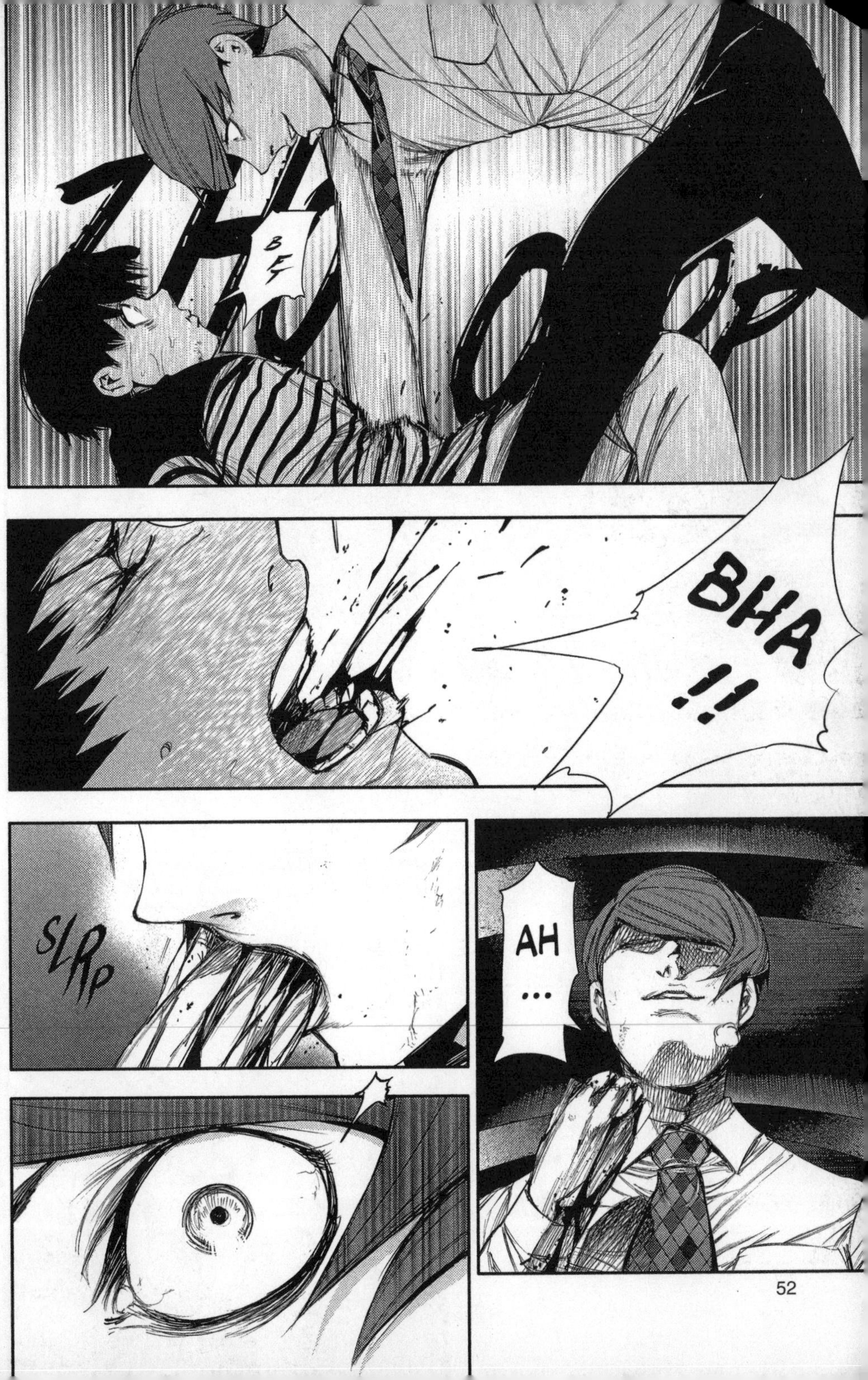
BHA !!
AH ...
SLRP

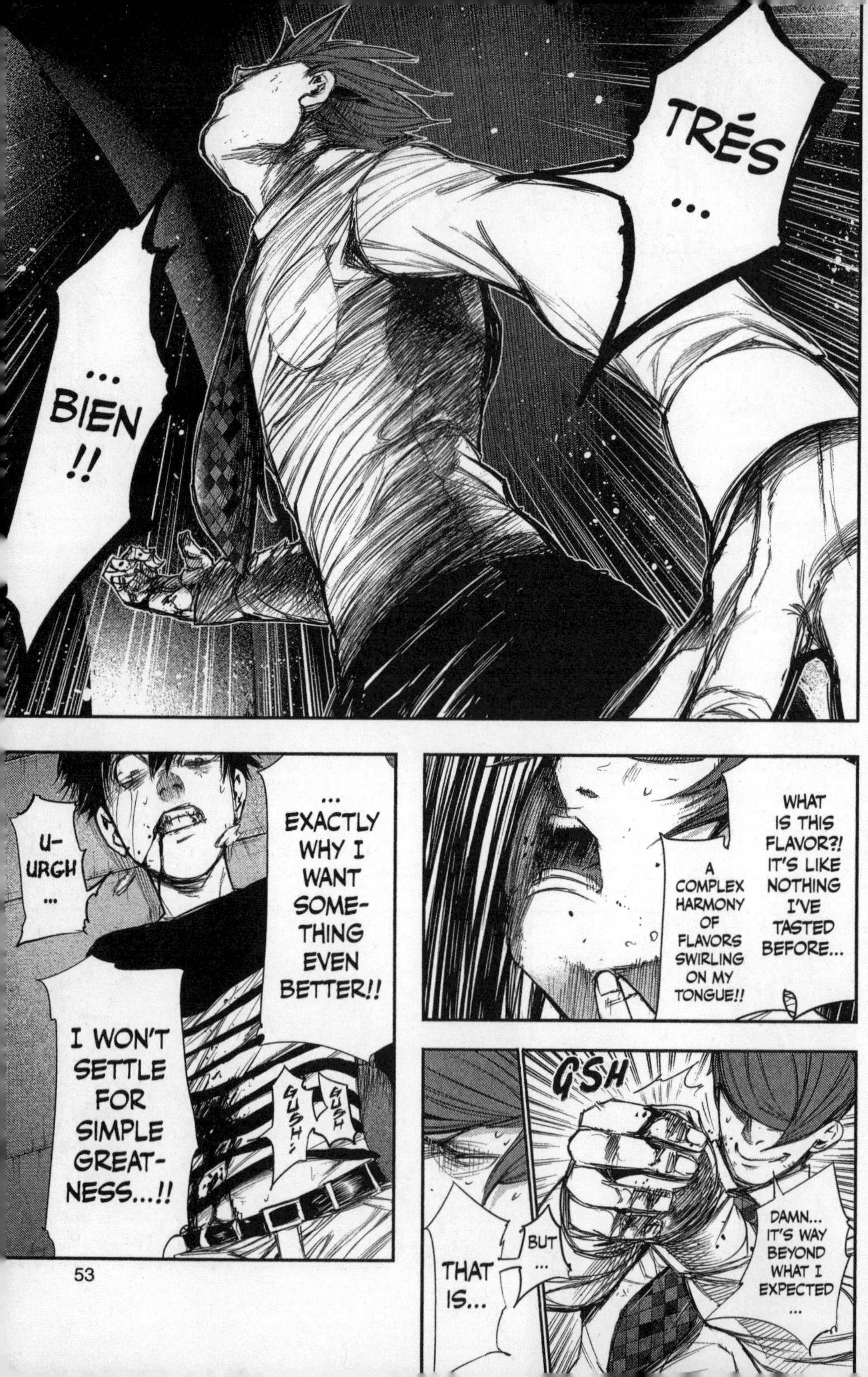
TRÉS ...
... BIEN !!
WHAT IS THIS FLAVOR?! IT'S LIKE NOTHING I'VE TASTED BEFORE...
A COMPLEX HARMONY OF FLAVORS SWIRLING ON MY TONGUE!!
GSH
DAMN... IT'S WAY BEYOND WHAT I EXPECTED ...
BUT ...
THAT IS...
... EXACTLY WHY I WANT SOME-THING EVEN BETTER!!
U-URGH ...
GUSH
GUSH
I WON'T SETTLE FOR SIMPLE GREAT-NESS...!!

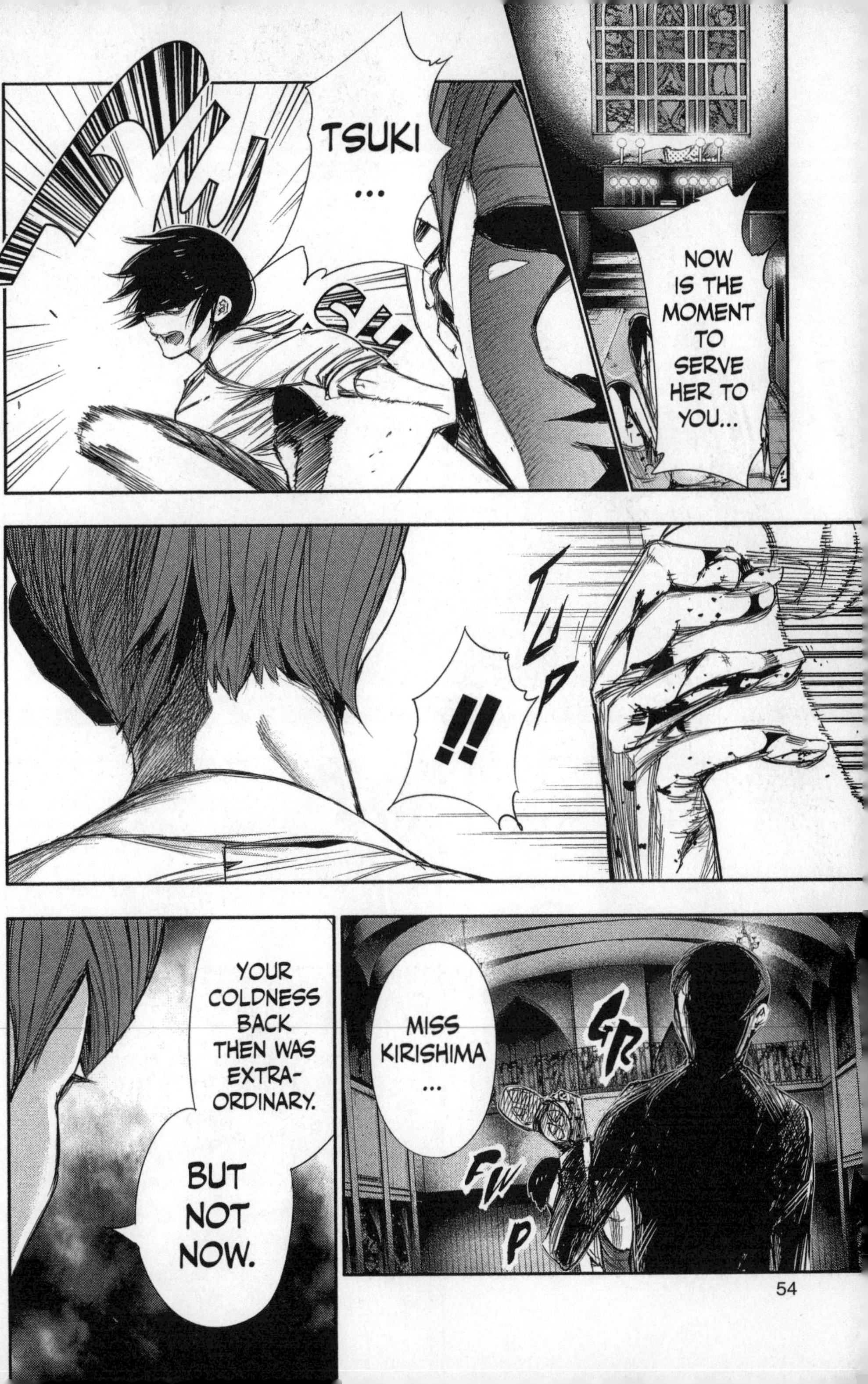
NOW IS THE MOMENT TO SERVE HER TO YOU...
TSUKI ...
TUP
!!
MISS KIRISHIMA ...
GR
FWP
YOUR COLDNESS BACK THEN WAS EXTRA-ORDINARY.
BUT NOT NOW.

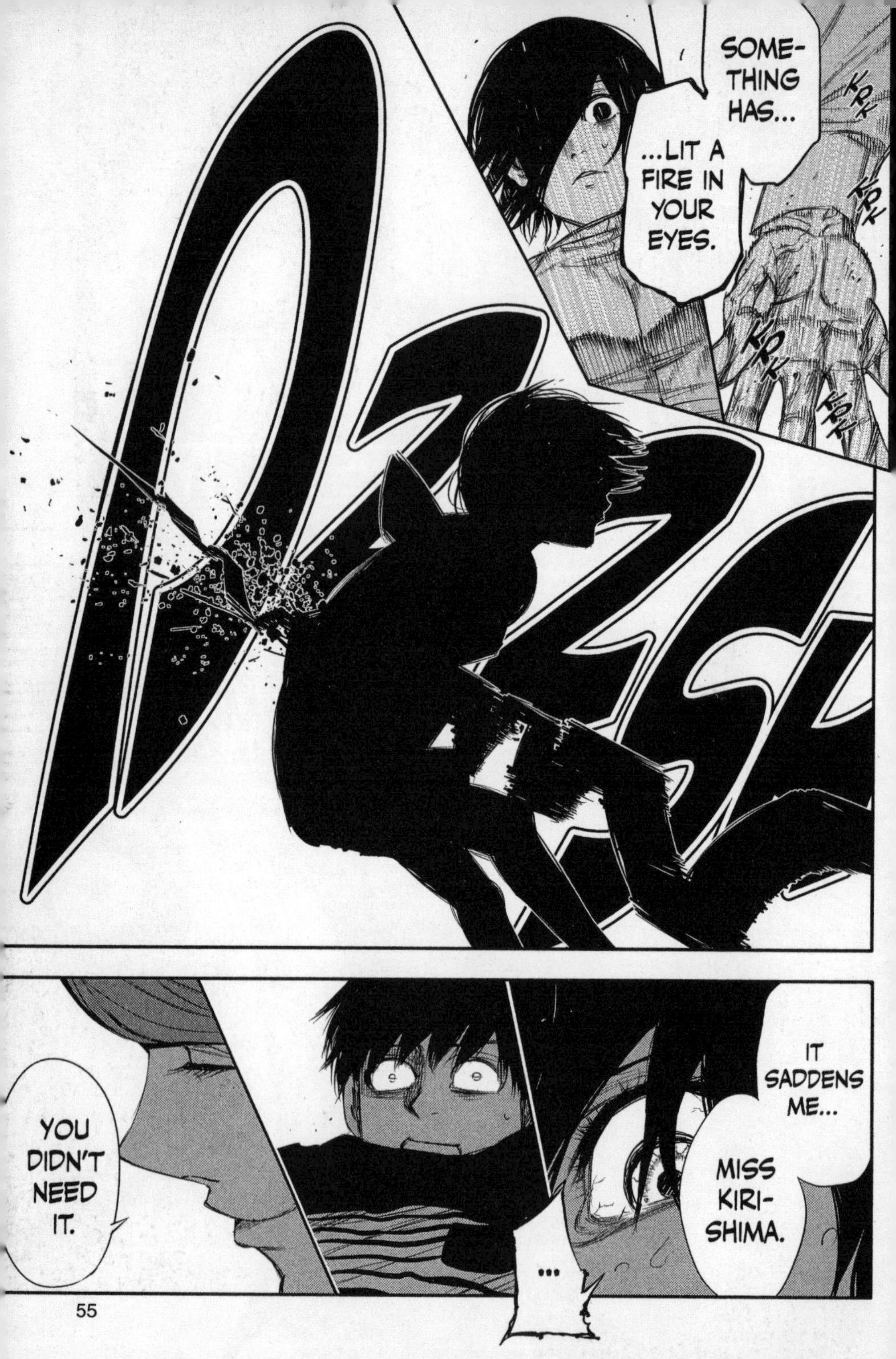
SOME-THING HAS...
...LIT A FIRE IN YOUR EYES.
KRK
KRK
KRK
KRK
KRK
IT SADDENS ME...
MISS KIRI-SHIMA.
...
YOU DIDN'T NEED IT.

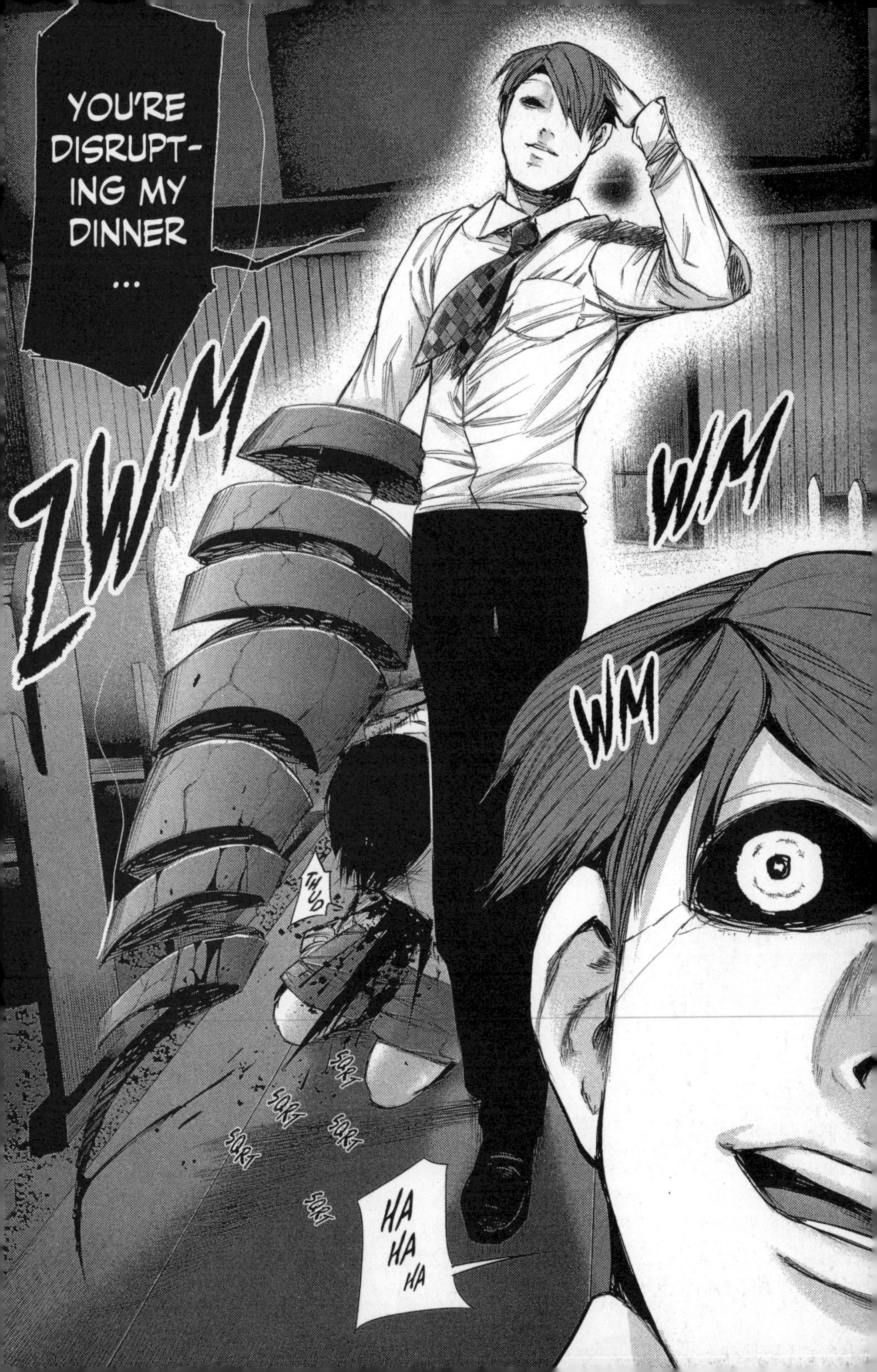
YOU'RE DISRUPT-ING MY DINNER ...
WM
ZWM
WM
THUD
SQRT
SQRT
SQRT
SQRT
SQRT
HA HA HA

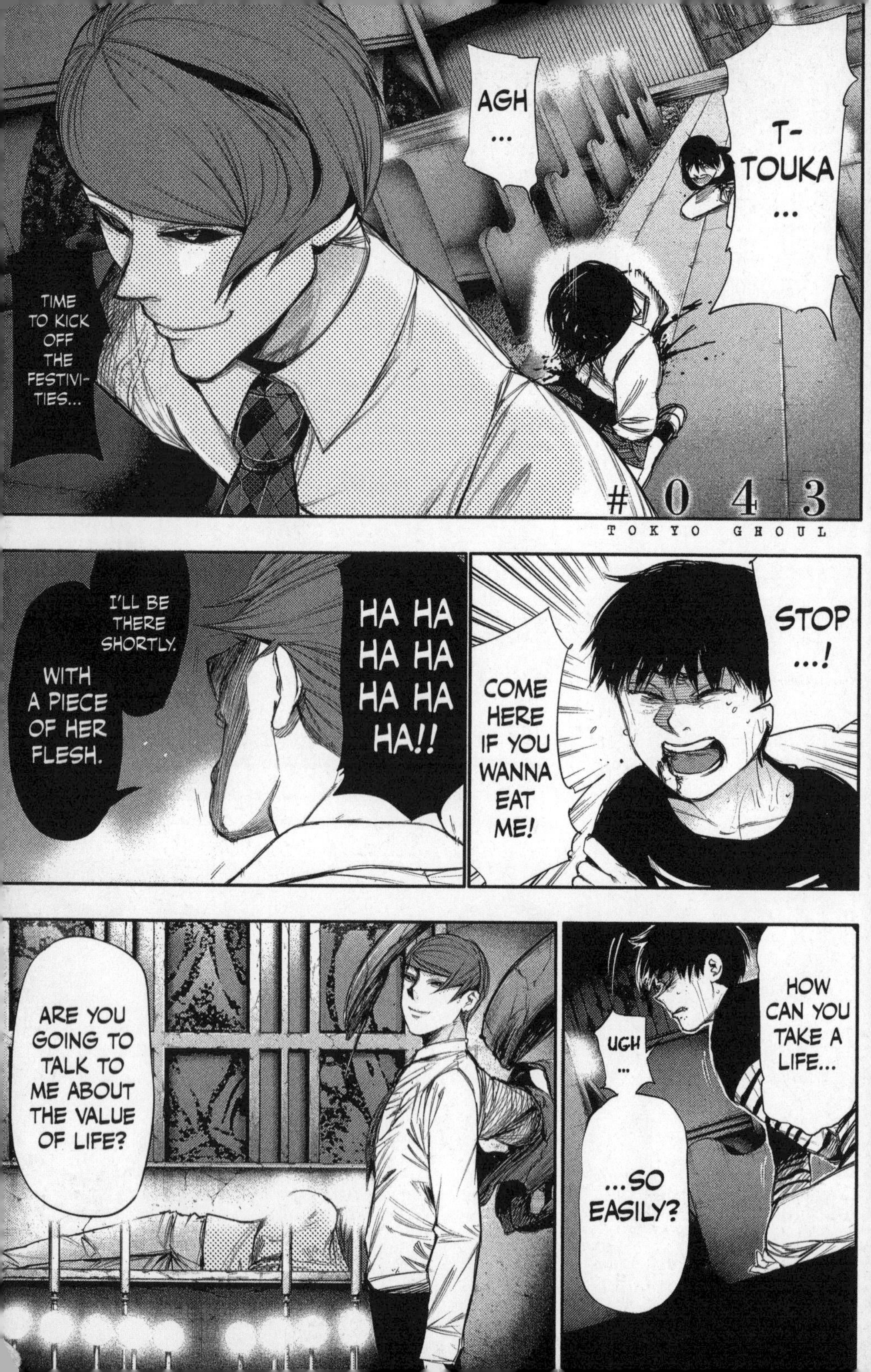
T-TOUKA...
AGH...
TIME TO KICK OFF THE FESTIVITIES...
#043
TOKYO GHOUL
STOP...!
COME HERE IF YOU WANNA EAT ME!
HA HA HA HA HA HA HA!!
I'LL BE THERE SHORTLY.
WITH A PIECE OF HER FLESH.
HOW CAN YOU TAKE A LIFE...
UGH...
...SO EASILY?
ARE YOU GOING TO TALK TO ME ABOUT THE VALUE OF LIFE?

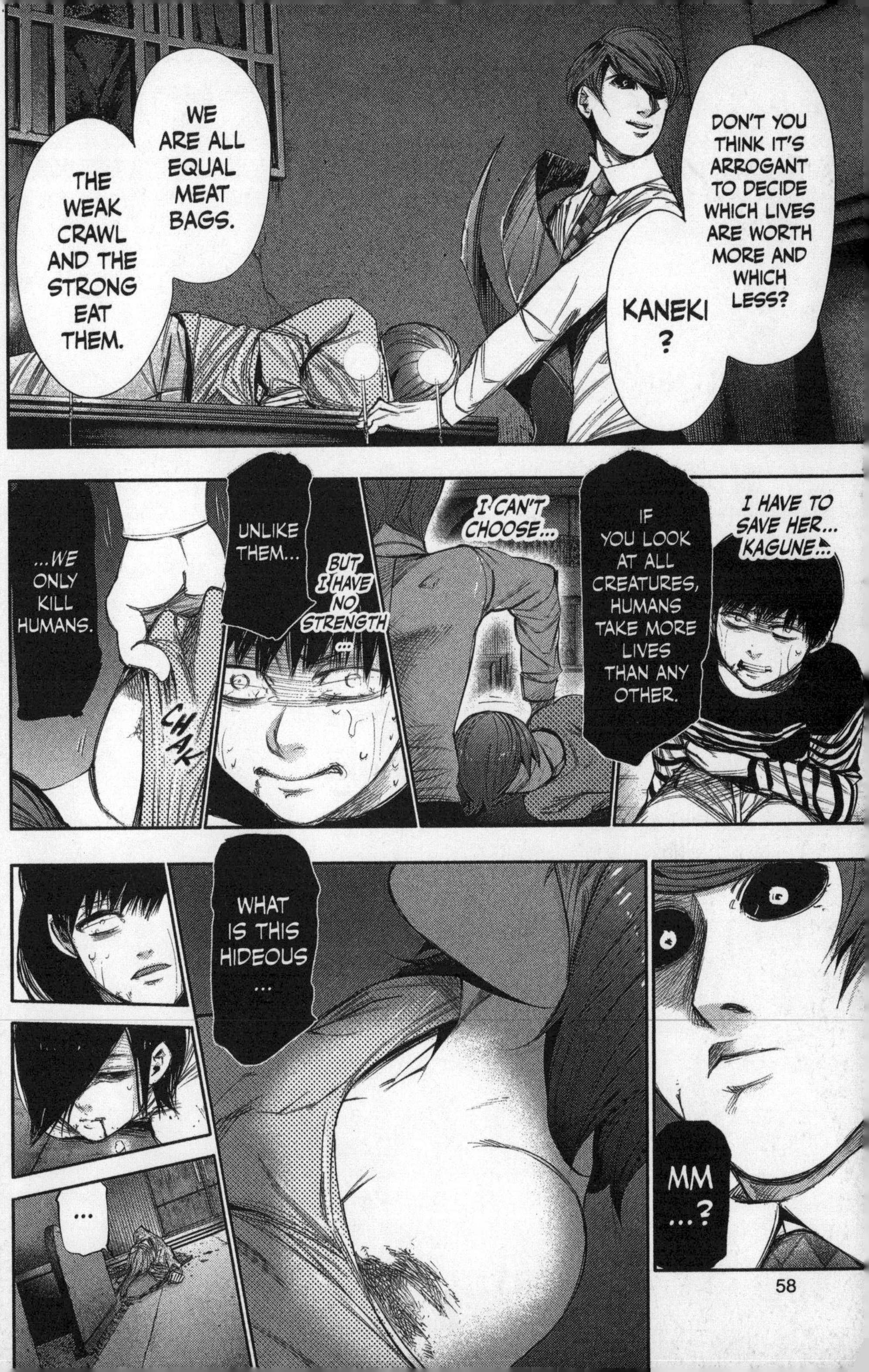
DON'T YOU THINK IT'S ARROGANT TO DECIDE WHICH LIVES ARE WORTH MORE AND WHICH LESS?
KANEKI ?
WE ARE ALL EQUAL MEAT BAGS.
THE WEAK CRAWL AND THE STRONG EAT THEM.
I HAVE TO SAVE HER... KAGUNE...
IF YOU LOOK AT ALL CREATURES, HUMANS TAKE MORE LIVES THAN ANY OTHER.
I CAN'T CHOOSE...
BUT I HAVE NO STRENGTH ...
UNLIKE THEM...
...WE ONLY KILL HUMANS.
CHAK
MM ...?
WHAT IS THIS HIDEOUS ...
...

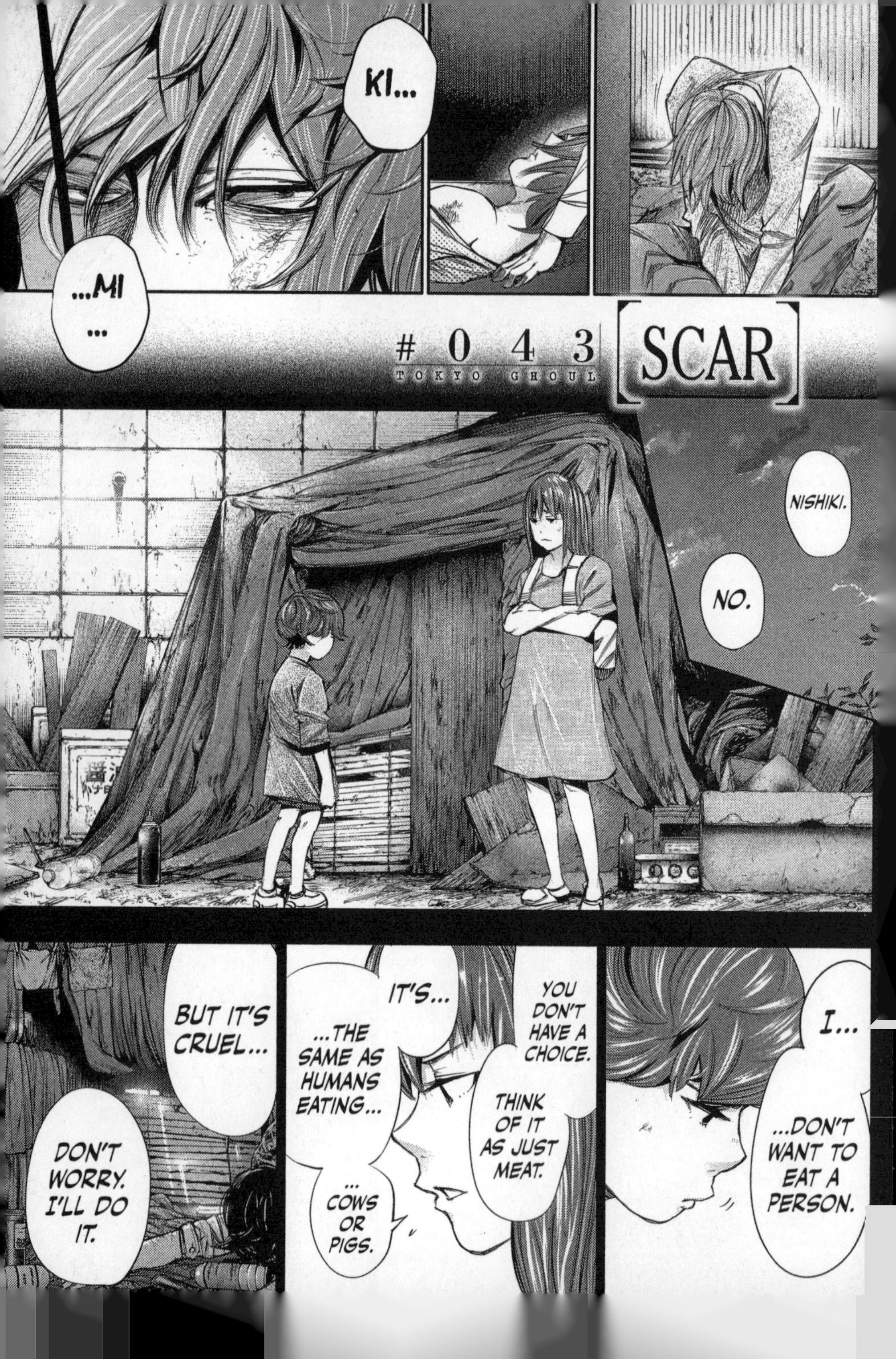
KI...
...MI ...
#043 SCAR
TOKYO GHOUL
NISHIKI.
NO.
I...
...DON'T WANT TO EAT A PERSON.
YOU DON'T HAVE A CHOICE.
IT'S...
THINK OF IT AS JUST MEAT.
...THE SAME AS HUMANS EATING...
... COWS OR PIGS.
BUT IT'S CRUEL...
DON'T WORRY. I'LL DO IT.

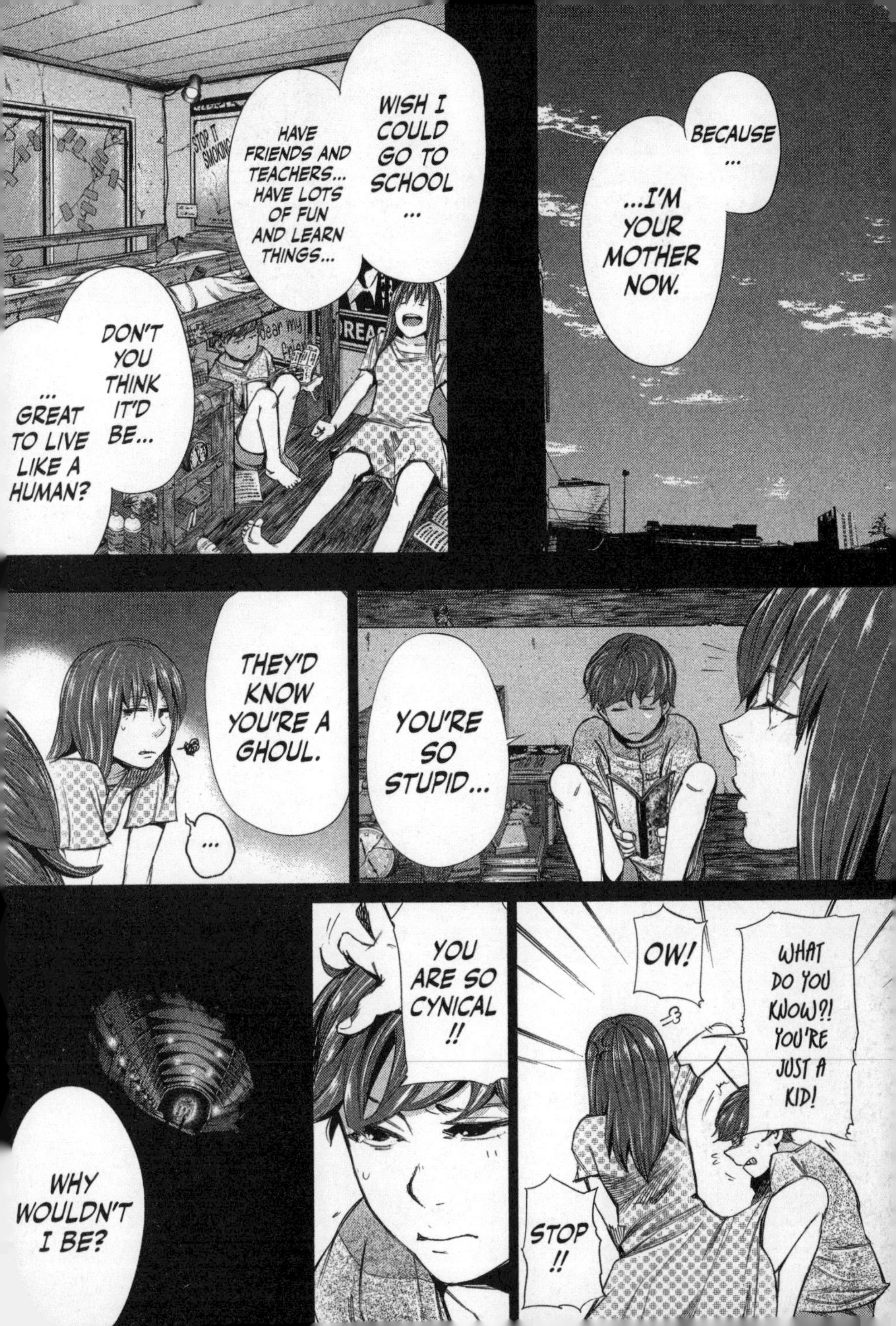
BECAUSE...
...I'M YOUR MOTHER NOW.
WISH I COULD GO TO SCHOOL...
HAVE FRIENDS AND TEACHERS... HAVE LOTS OF FUN AND LEARN THINGS...
DON'T YOU THINK IT'D BE...
...GREAT TO LIVE LIKE A HUMAN?
YOU'RE SO STUPID...
THEY'D KNOW YOU'RE A GHOUL.
...
OW!
WHAT DO YOU KNOW?! YOU'RE JUST A KID!
STOP!!
YOU ARE SO CYNICAL!!
WHY WOULDN'T I BE?

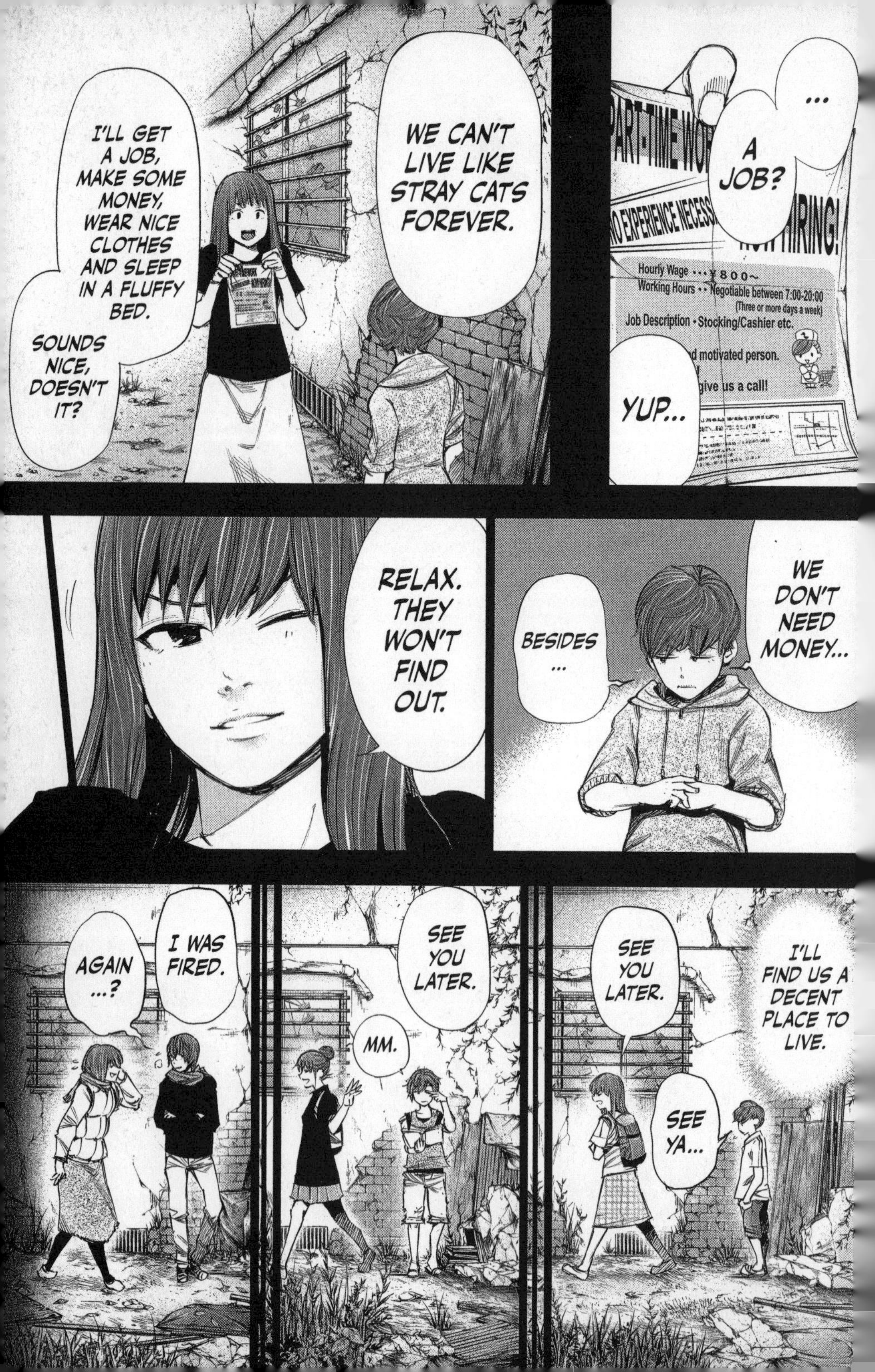
...
A JOB?
Hourly Wage ・・・¥800～
Working Hours ・・ Negotiable between 7:00-20:00
(Three or more days a week)
Job Description ・Stocking/Cashier etc.
give us a call!
YUP...
WE CAN'T LIVE LIKE STRAY CATS FOREVER.
I'LL GET A JOB, MAKE SOME MONEY, WEAR NICE CLOTHES AND SLEEP IN A FLUFFY BED.
SOUNDS NICE, DOESN'T IT?
WE DON'T NEED MONEY...
BESIDES ...
RELAX. THEY WON'T FIND OUT.
I'LL FIND US A DECENT PLACE TO LIVE.
SEE YOU LATER.
SEE YA...
SEE YOU LATER.
MM.
I WAS FIRED.
AGAIN ...?

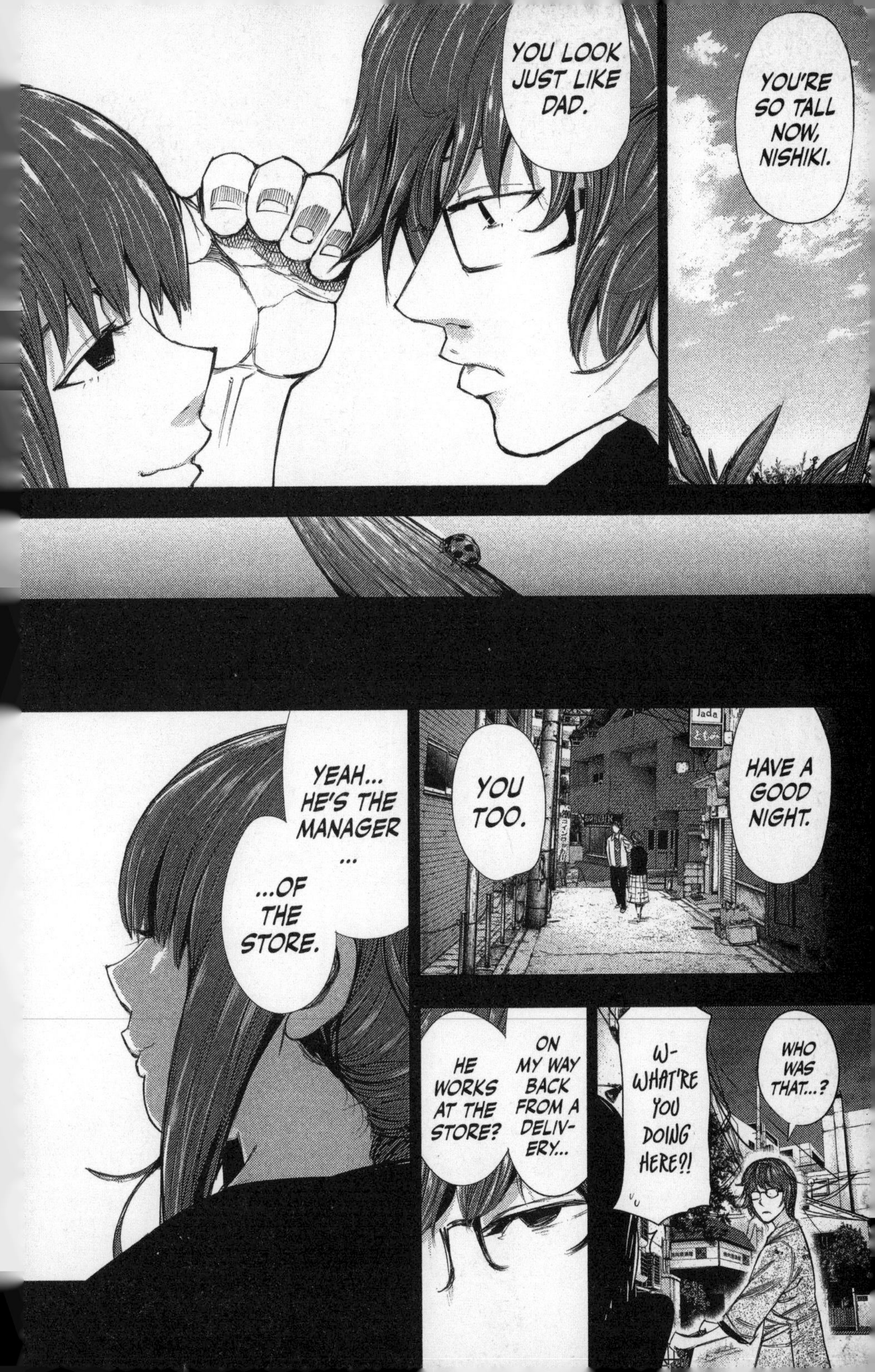
YOU'RE SO TALL NOW, NISHIKI.
YOU LOOK JUST LIKE DAD.
Jada
HAVE A GOOD NIGHT.
YOU TOO.
WHO WAS THAT...?
W-WHAT'RE YOU DOING HERE?!
ON MY WAY BACK FROM A DELIVERY...
HE WORKS AT THE STORE?
YEAH... HE'S THE MANAGER ...
...OF THE STORE.

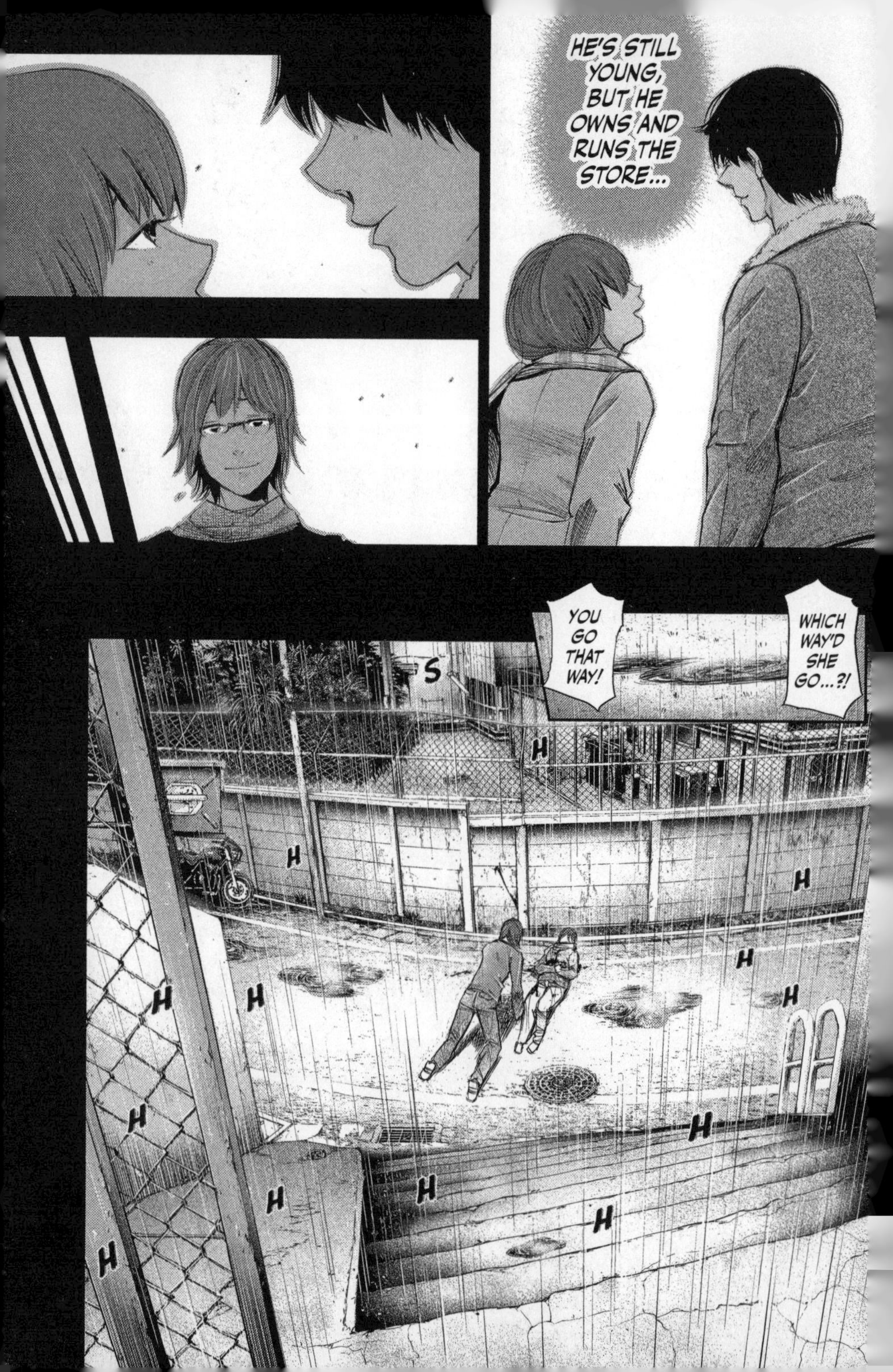
HE'S STILL YOUNG, BUT HE OWNS AND RUNS THE STORE...
WHICH WAY'D SHE GO...?!
YOU GO THAT WAY!
S
H H H H H H H H H H H H H H

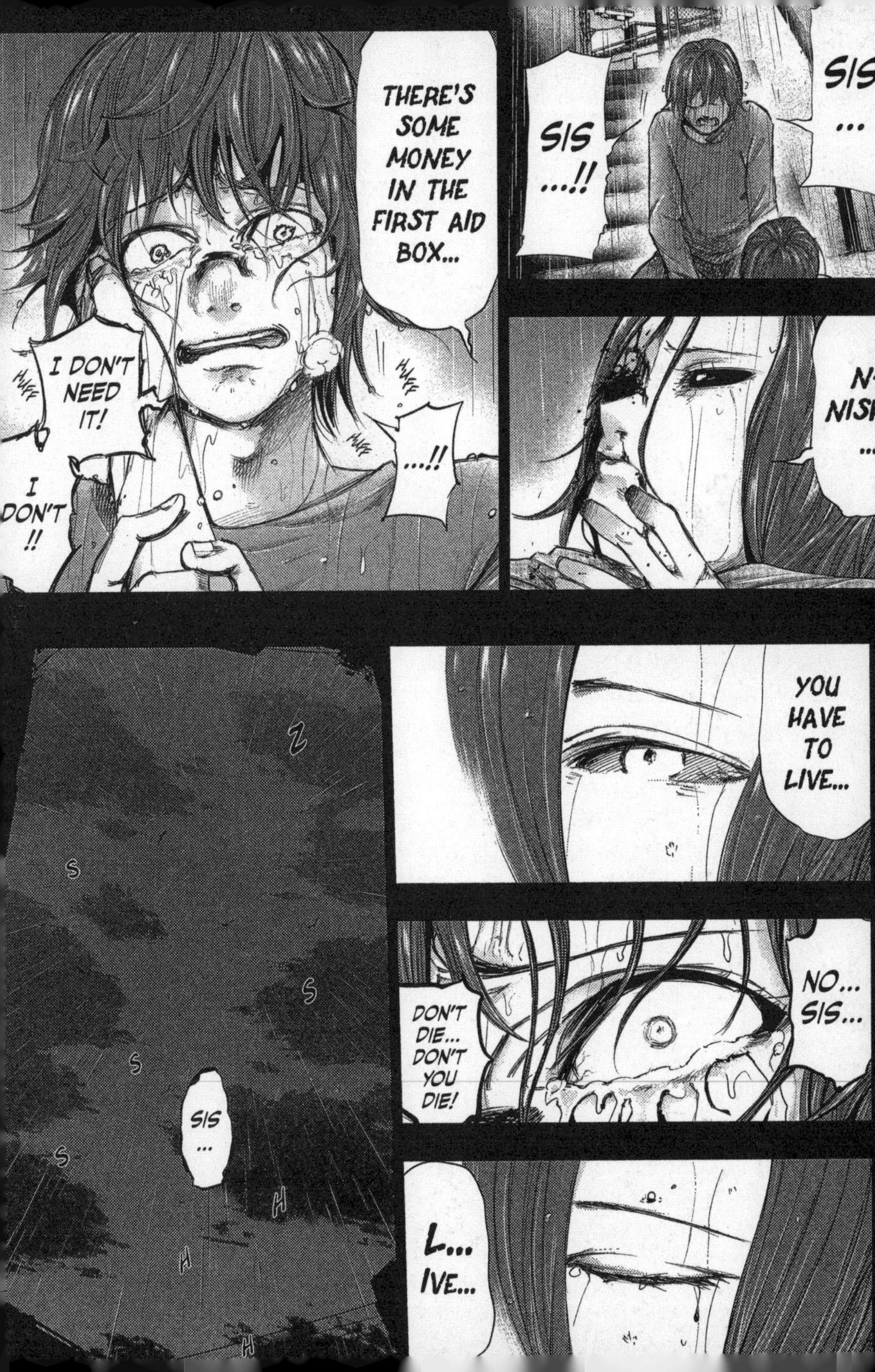
SIS ...
SIS ...!!
N-NISHIKI ...
THERE'S SOME MONEY IN THE FIRST AID BOX...
HUFF
...!!
HUFF
I DON'T NEED IT!
HUFF
I DON'T !!
YOU HAVE TO LIVE...
NO... SIS...
DON'T DIE... DON'T YOU DIE!
L... IVE...
SIS ...

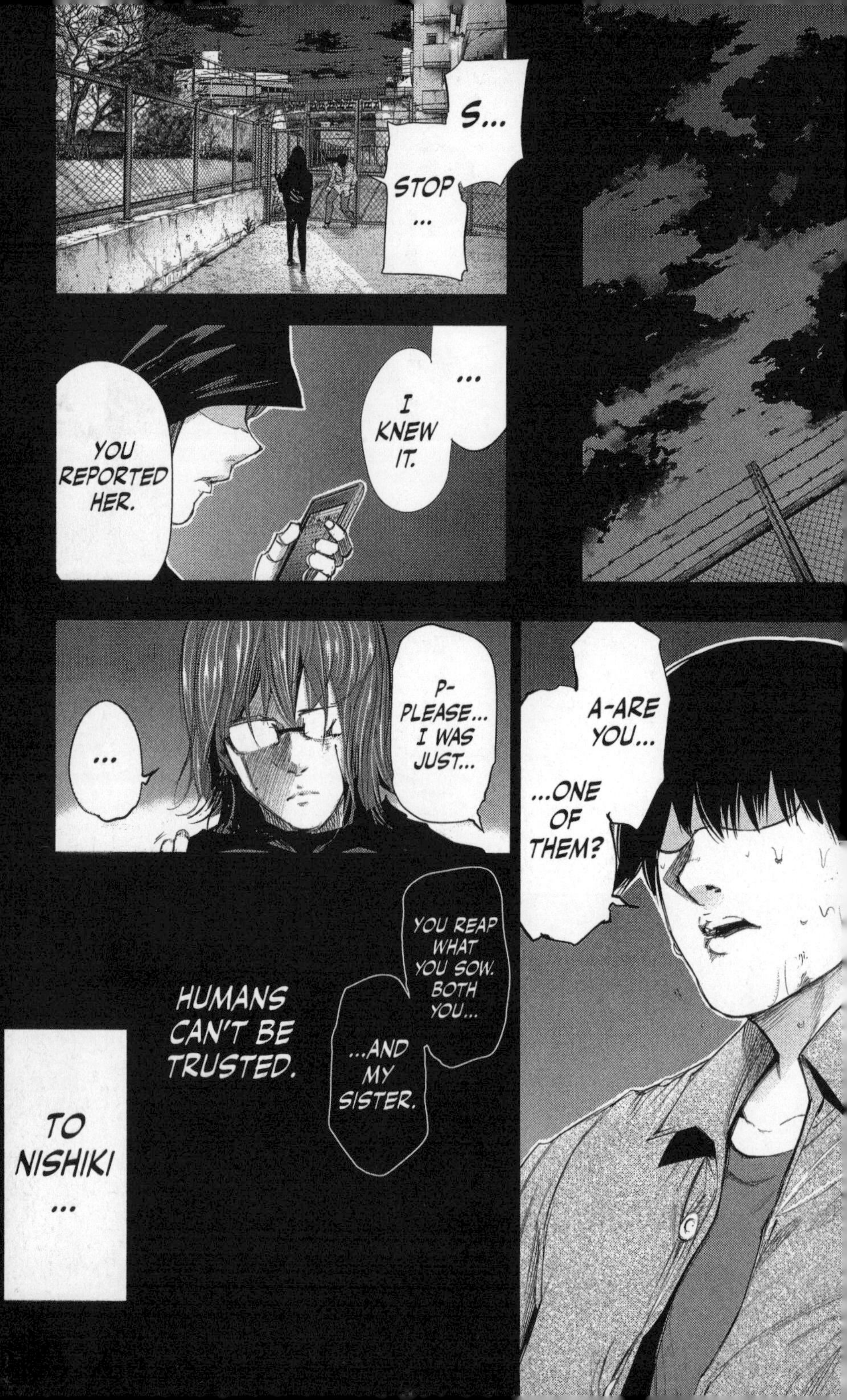
S...
STOP...
... I KNEW IT.
YOU REPORTED HER.
A-ARE YOU...
...ONE OF THEM?
P-PLEASE... I WAS JUST...
...
YOU REAP WHAT YOU SOW. BOTH YOU...
...AND MY SISTER.
HUMANS CAN'T BE TRUSTED.
TO NISHIKI...

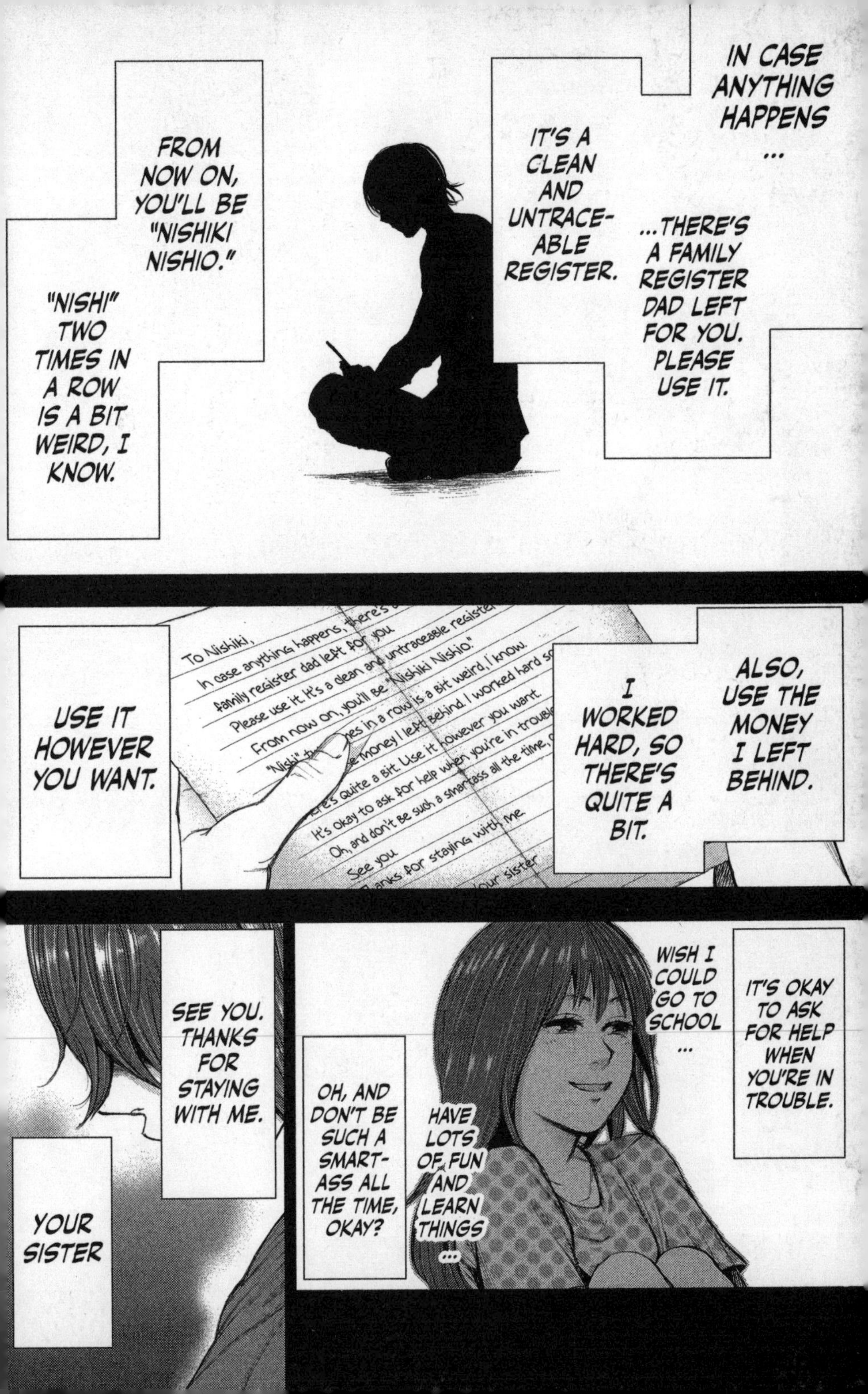
IN CASE ANYTHING HAPPENS...
...THERE'S A FAMILY REGISTER DAD LEFT FOR YOU. PLEASE USE IT.
IT'S A CLEAN AND UNTRACEABLE REGISTER.
FROM NOW ON, YOU'LL BE "NISHIKI NISHIO."
"NISHI" TWO TIMES IN A ROW IS A BIT WEIRD, I KNOW.
ALSO, USE THE MONEY I LEFT BEHIND.
I WORKED HARD, SO THERE'S QUITE A BIT.
To Nishiki,
family register dad left for you.
From now on, you'll be "Nishiki Nishio."
Oh, and don't be such a smartass all the time,
See you
USE IT HOWEVER YOU WANT.
IT'S OKAY TO ASK FOR HELP WHEN YOU'RE IN TROUBLE.
WISH I COULD GO TO SCHOOL...
HAVE LOTS OF FUN AND LEARN THINGS...
OH, AND DON'T BE SUCH A SMART-ASS ALL THE TIME, OKAY?
SEE YOU. THANKS FOR STAYING WITH ME.
YOUR SISTER

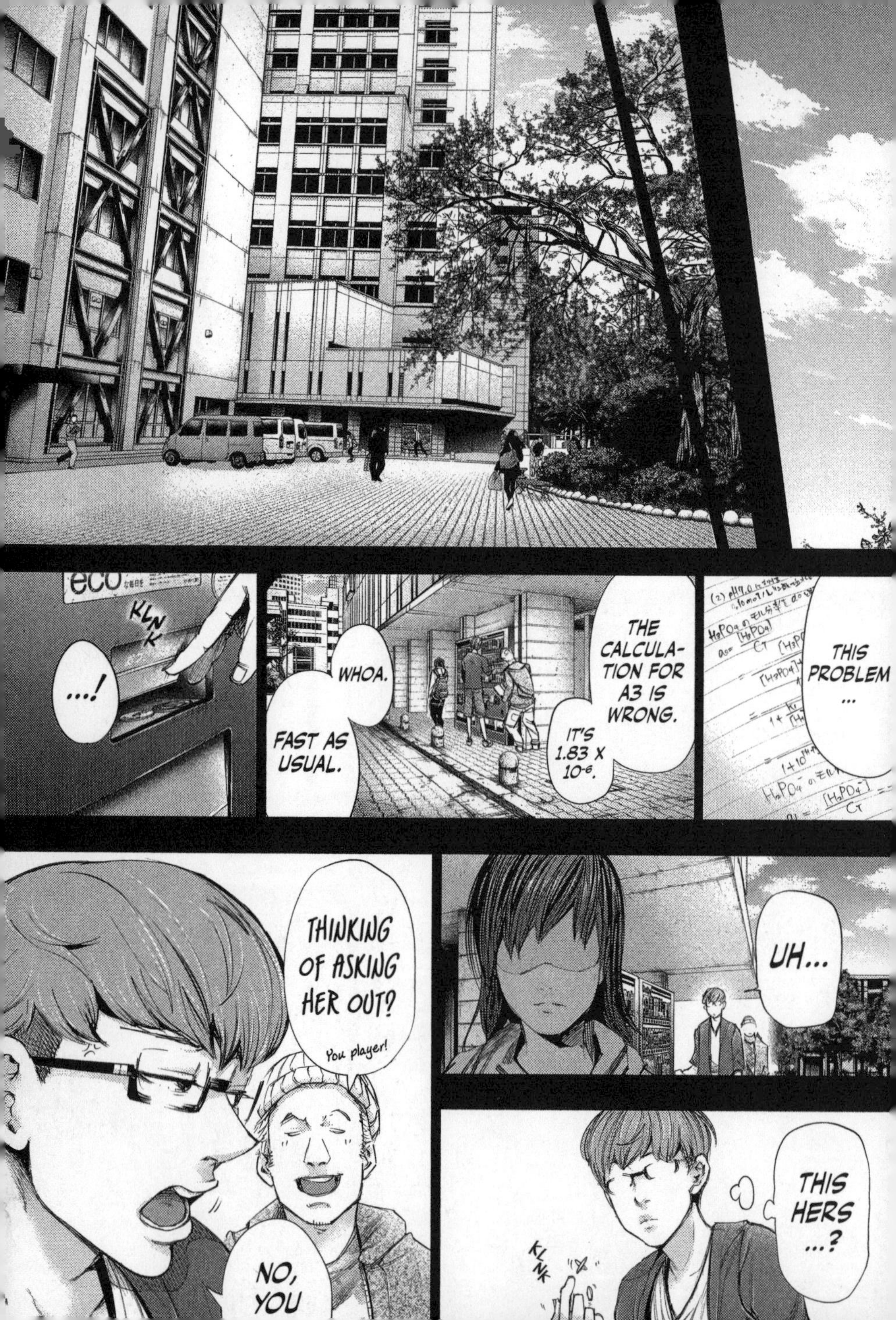
THIS PROBLEM ...
THE CALCULATION FOR A3 IS WRONG.
IT'S 1.83 X 10-6.
WHOA.
FAST AS USUAL.
KLNK
...!
UH...
THIS HERS ...?
KLNK
THINKING OF ASKING HER OUT?
You player!
NO, YOU

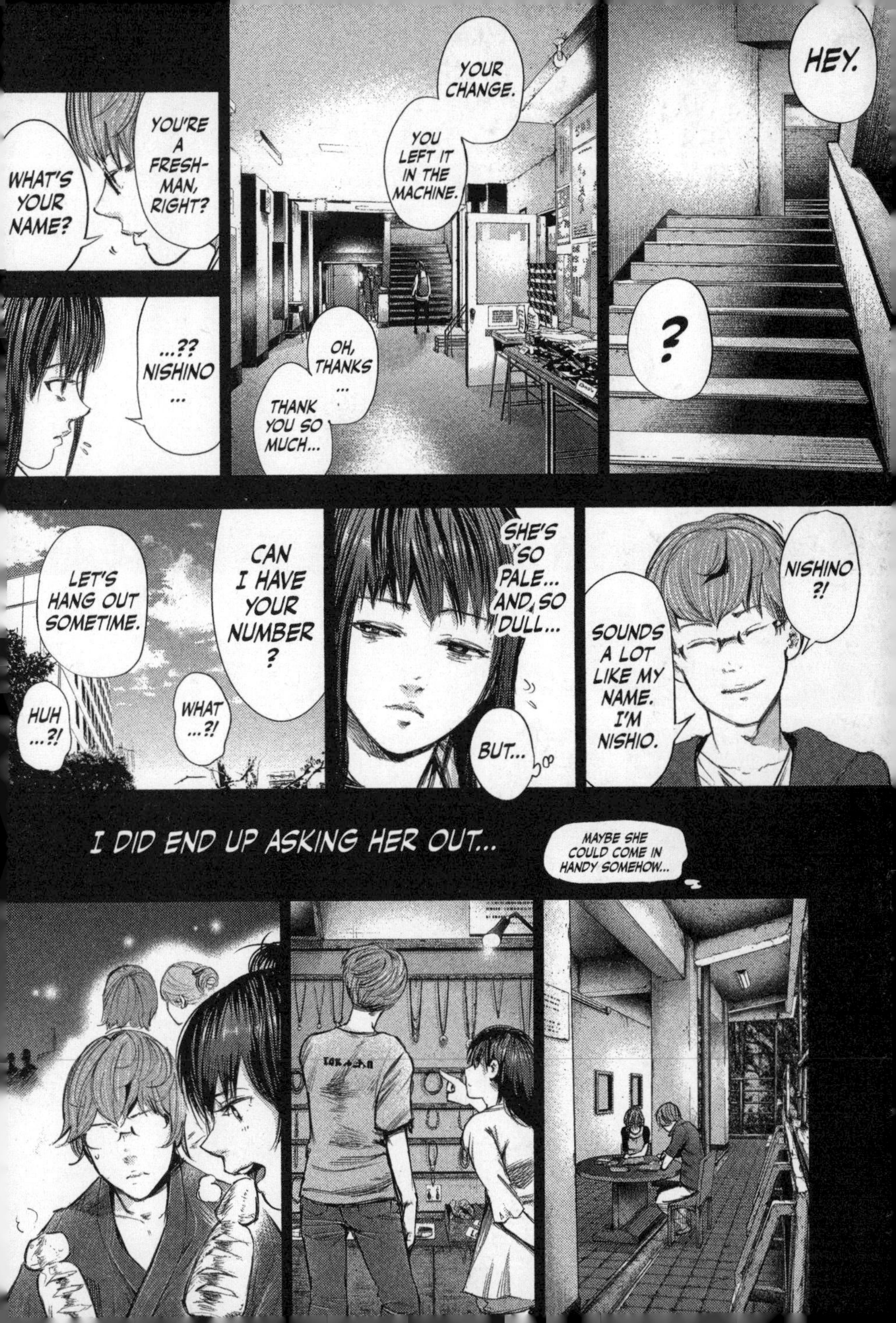
HEY.
?
YOUR CHANGE.
YOU LEFT IT IN THE MACHINE.
OH, THANKS...
THANK YOU SO MUCH...
YOU'RE A FRESH-MAN, RIGHT?
WHAT'S YOUR NAME?
...?? NISHINO...
NISHINO?!
SOUNDS A LOT LIKE MY NAME. I'M NISHIO.
SHE'S SO PALE... AND SO DULL...
BUT...
CAN I HAVE YOUR NUMBER?
LET'S HANG OUT SOMETIME.
WHAT...?!
HUH...?!
MAYBE SHE COULD COME IN HANDY SOMEHOW...
I DID END UP ASKING HER OUT...

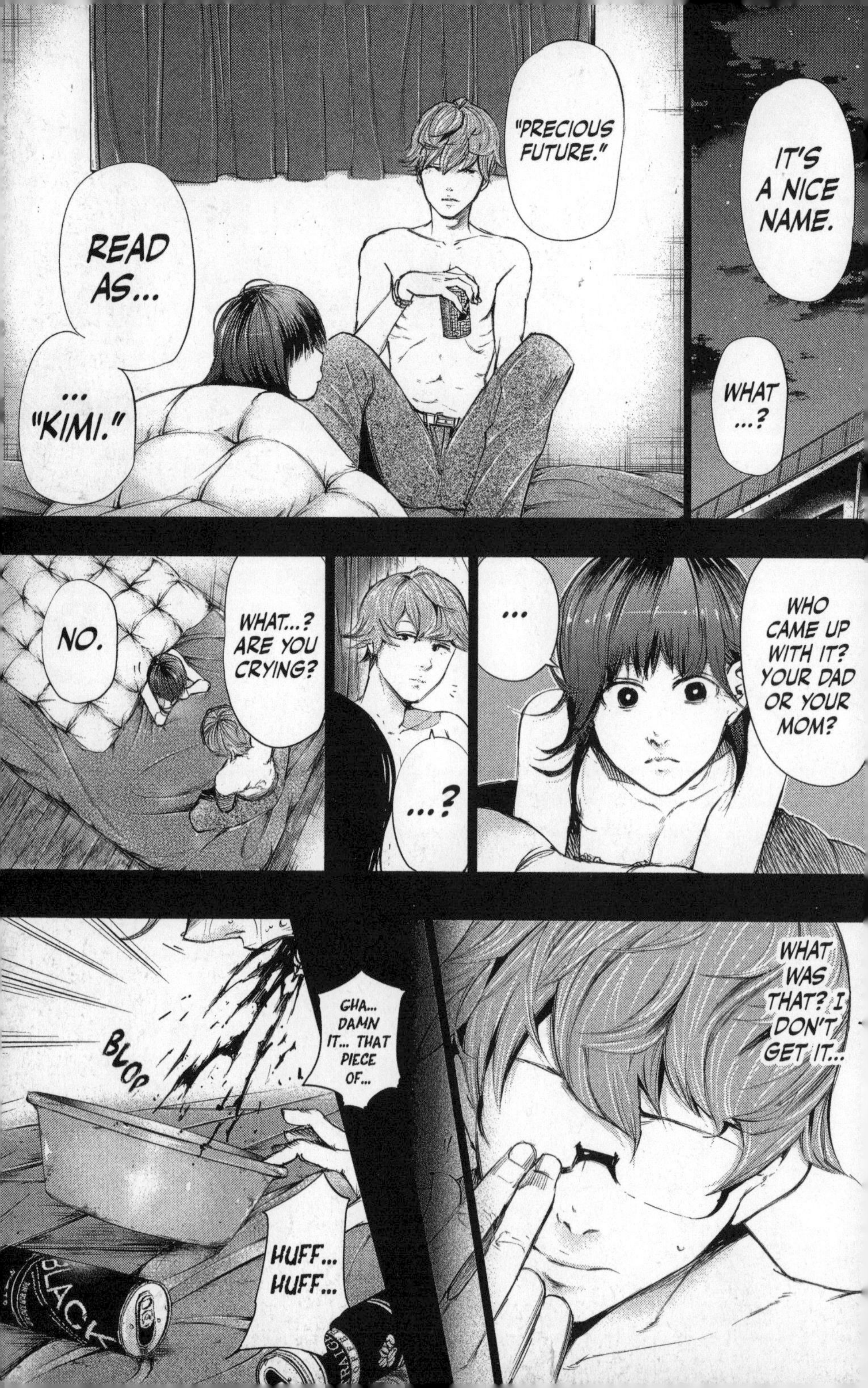
IT'S A NICE NAME.
WHAT ...?
"PRECIOUS FUTURE."
READ AS...
... "KIMI."
WHO CAME UP WITH IT? YOUR DAD OR YOUR MOM?
...
...?
WHAT...? ARE YOU CRYING?
NO.
WHAT WAS THAT? I DON'T GET IT...
GHA... DAMN IT... THAT PIECE OF...
BLOP
HUFF... HUFF...
BLACK

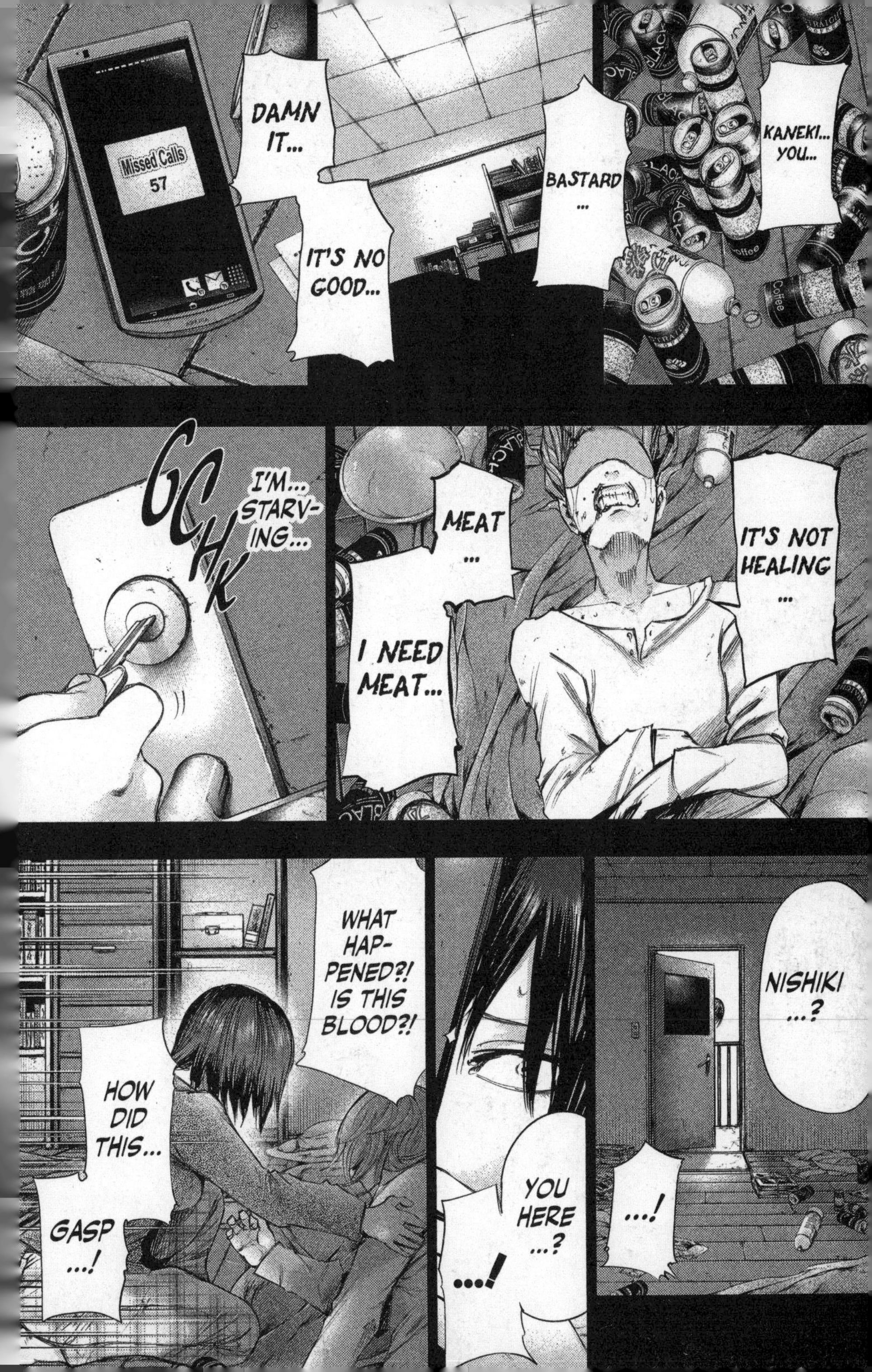
KANEKI... YOU...
BASTARD ...
DAMN IT...
IT'S NO GOOD...
Missed Calls 57
IT'S NOT HEALING ...
MEAT ...
I NEED MEAT...
GCHK
I'M... STARV-ING...
NISHIKI ...?
...!
YOU HERE ...?
...!
WHAT HAP-PENED?! IS THIS BLOOD?!
HOW DID THIS...
GASP ...!

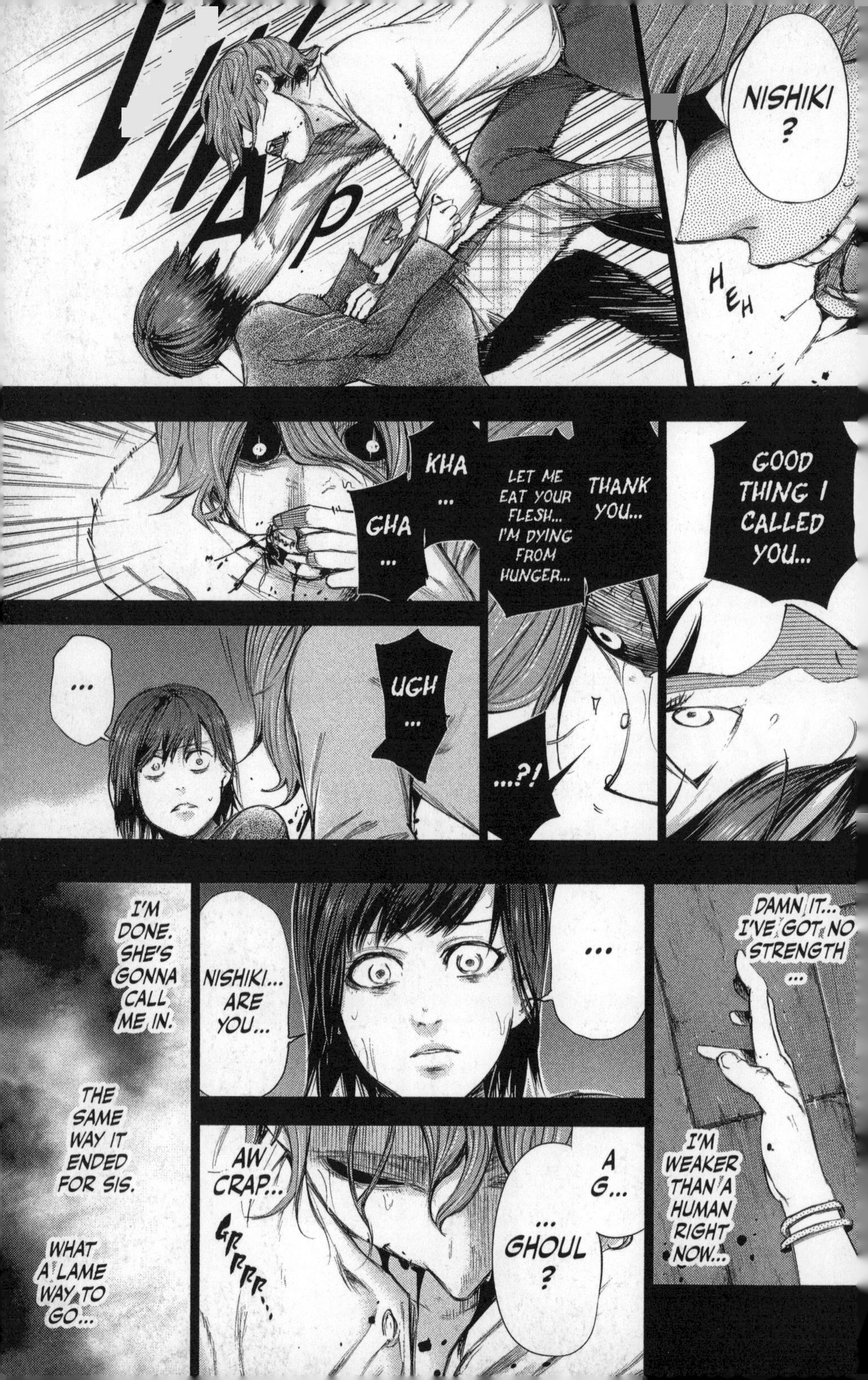
NISHIKI ?
HEH
WAP
GOOD THING I CALLED YOU...
THANK YOU...
LET ME EAT YOUR FLESH... I'M DYING FROM HUNGER...
KHA ...
GHA ...
...?!
UGH ...
...
DAMN IT... I'VE GOT NO STRENGTH ...
I'M WEAKER THAN A HUMAN RIGHT NOW...
...
NISHIKI... ARE YOU...
A G... ... GHOUL ?
AW CRAP...
GRRRR...
I'M DONE. SHE'S GONNA CALL ME IN.
THE SAME WAY IT ENDED FOR SIS.
WHAT A LAME WAY TO GO...

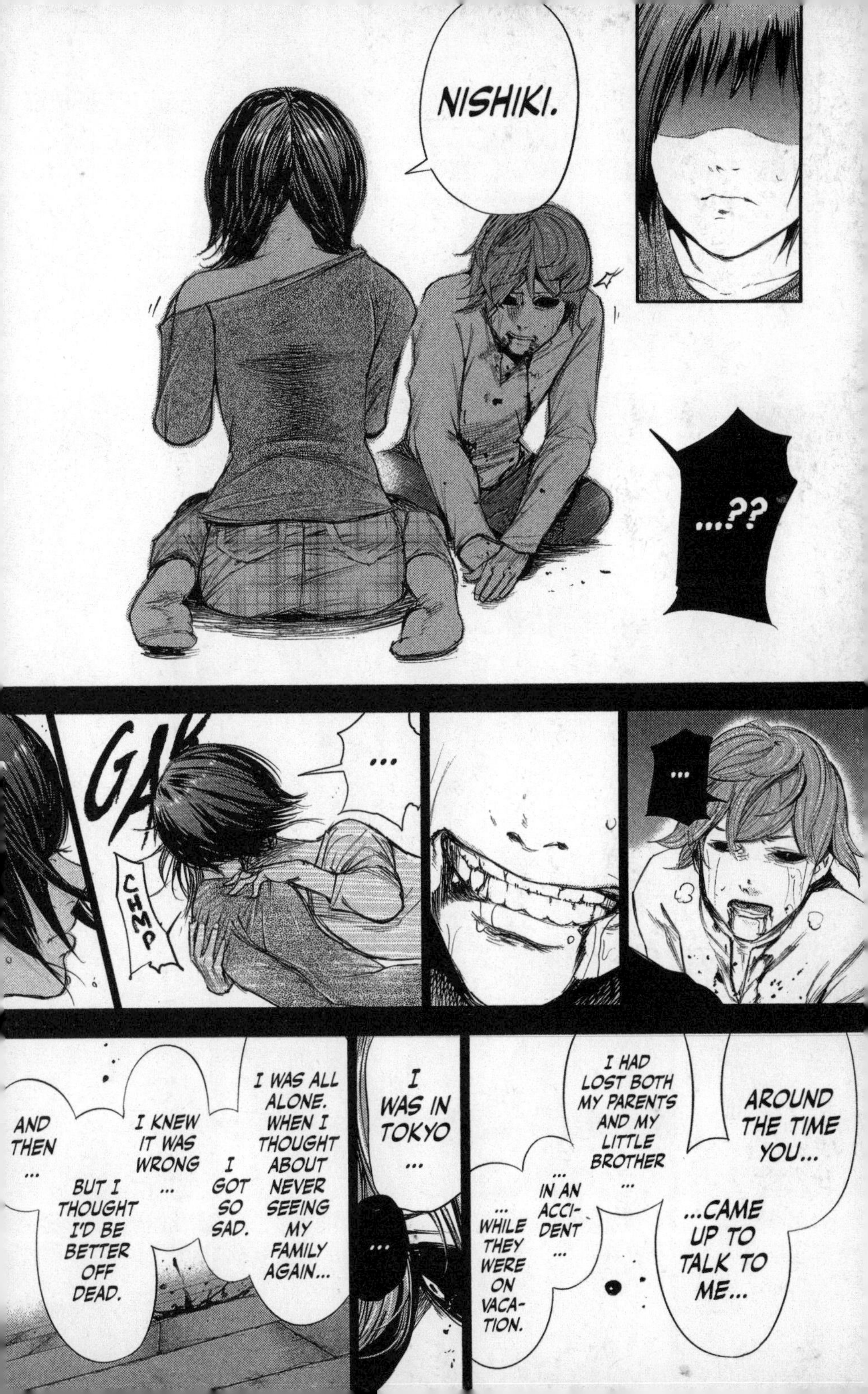
...??
NISHIKI.
...
...
CHMP
AROUND THE TIME YOU...
...CAME UP TO TALK TO ME...
I HAD LOST BOTH MY PARENTS AND MY LITTLE BROTHER ...
... IN AN ACCI-DENT ...
... WHILE THEY WERE ON VACA-TION.
I WAS IN TOKYO ...
...
I WAS ALL ALONE. WHEN I THOUGHT ABOUT NEVER SEEING MY FAMILY AGAIN...
I GOT SO SAD.
I KNEW IT WAS WRONG ...
BUT I THOUGHT I'D BE BETTER OFF DEAD.
AND THEN ...

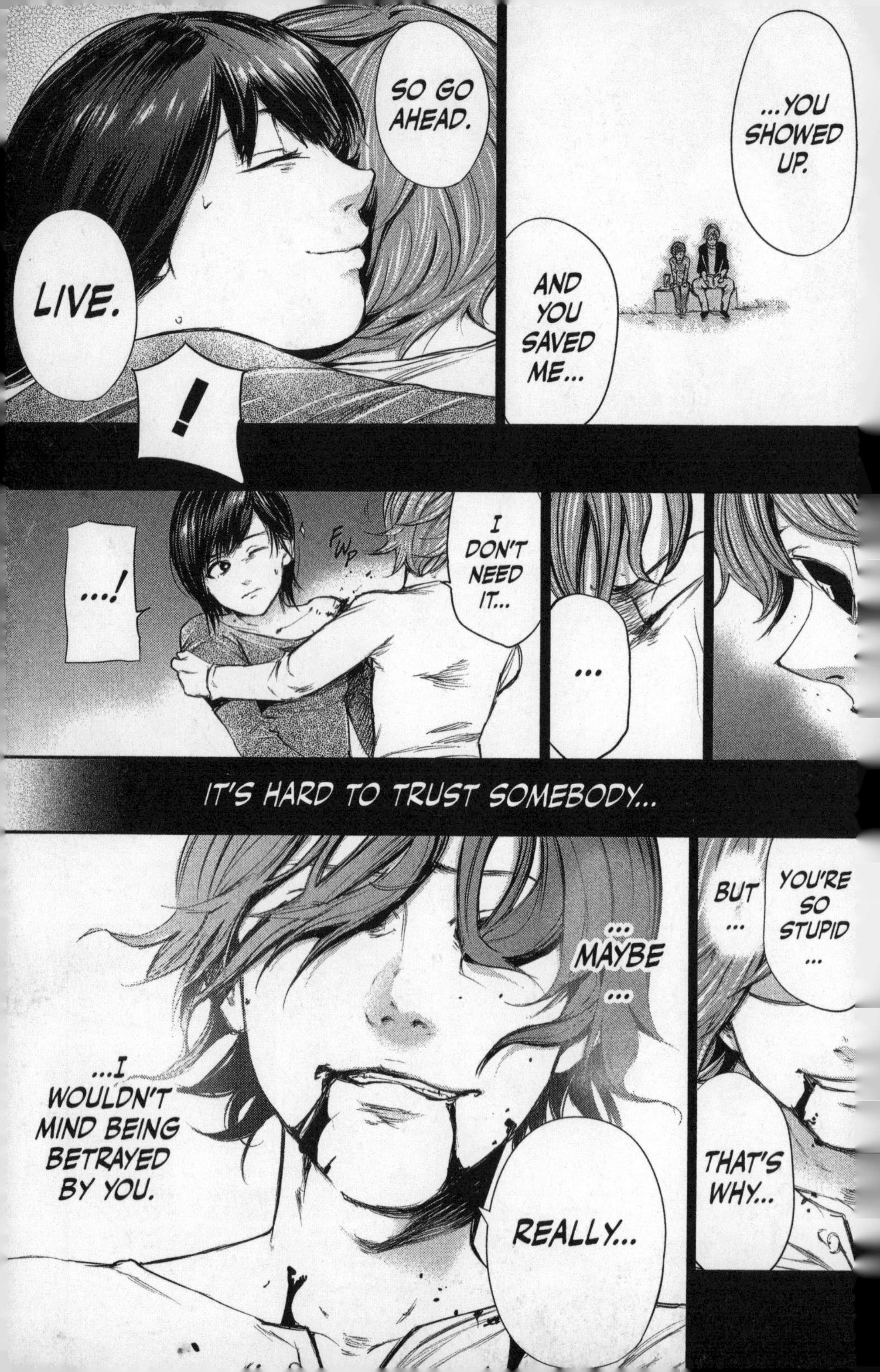
...YOU SHOWED UP.
AND YOU SAVED ME...
SO GO AHEAD.
LIVE.
!
...
I DON'T NEED IT...
FWP
...!
IT'S HARD TO TRUST SOMEBODY...
YOU'RE SO STUPID...
BUT...
THAT'S WHY...
...MAYBE...
...I WOULDN'T MIND BEING BETRAYED BY YOU.
REALLY...

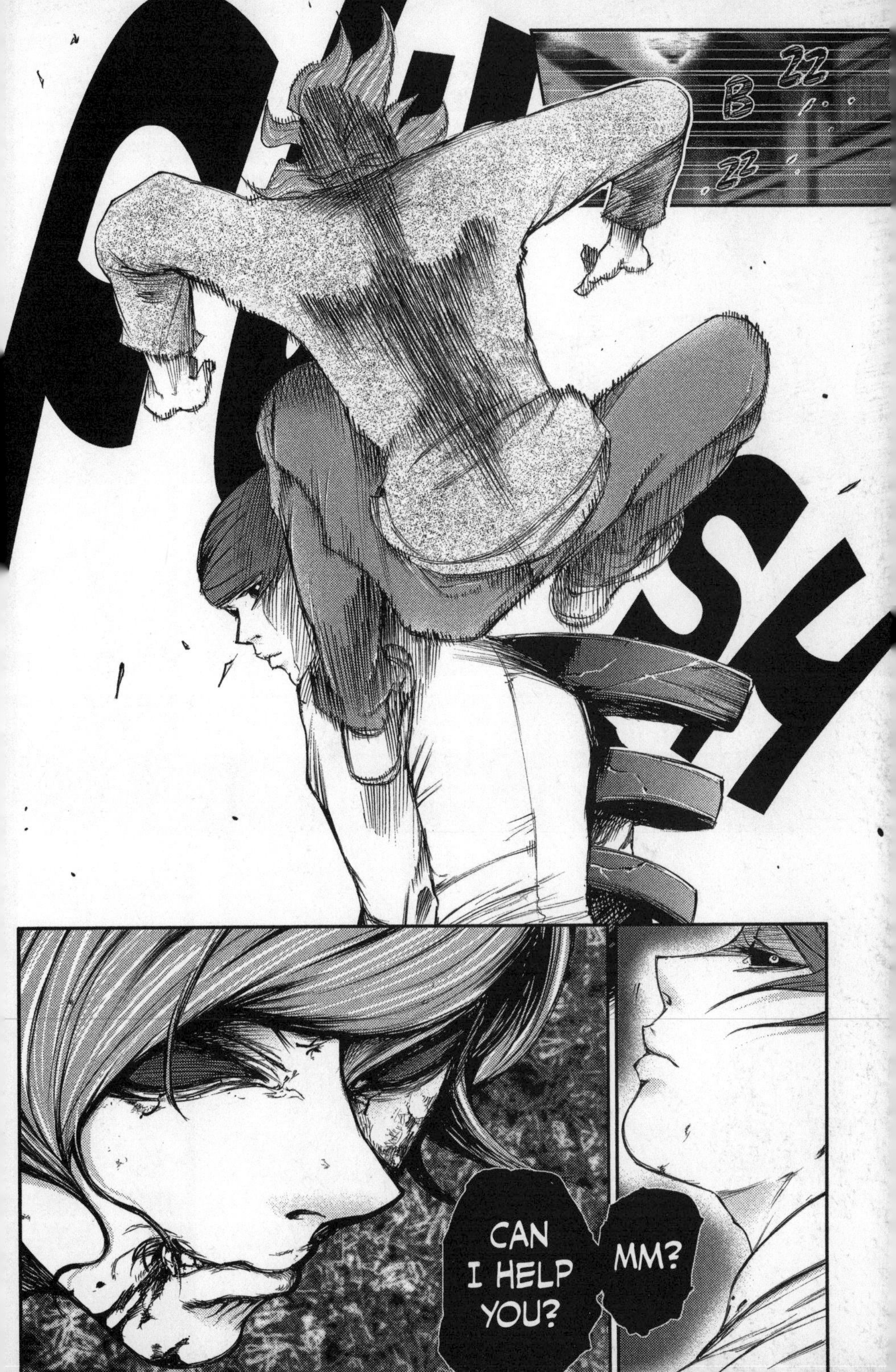
BZZ
ZZ
MM?
CAN I HELP YOU?

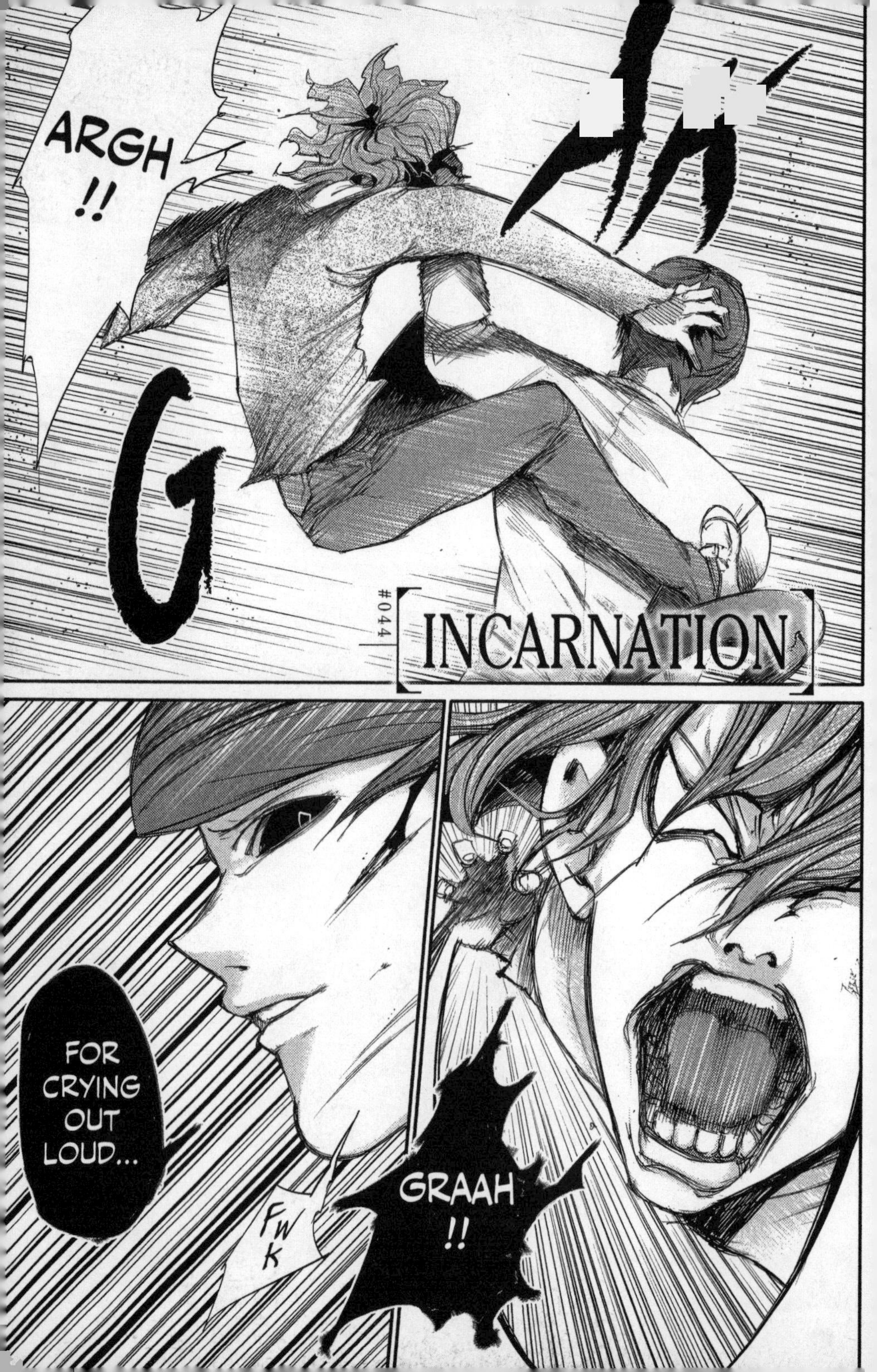
ARGH !!
G
#044 INCARNATION
GRAAH !!
FOR CRYING OUT LOUD...
FWK

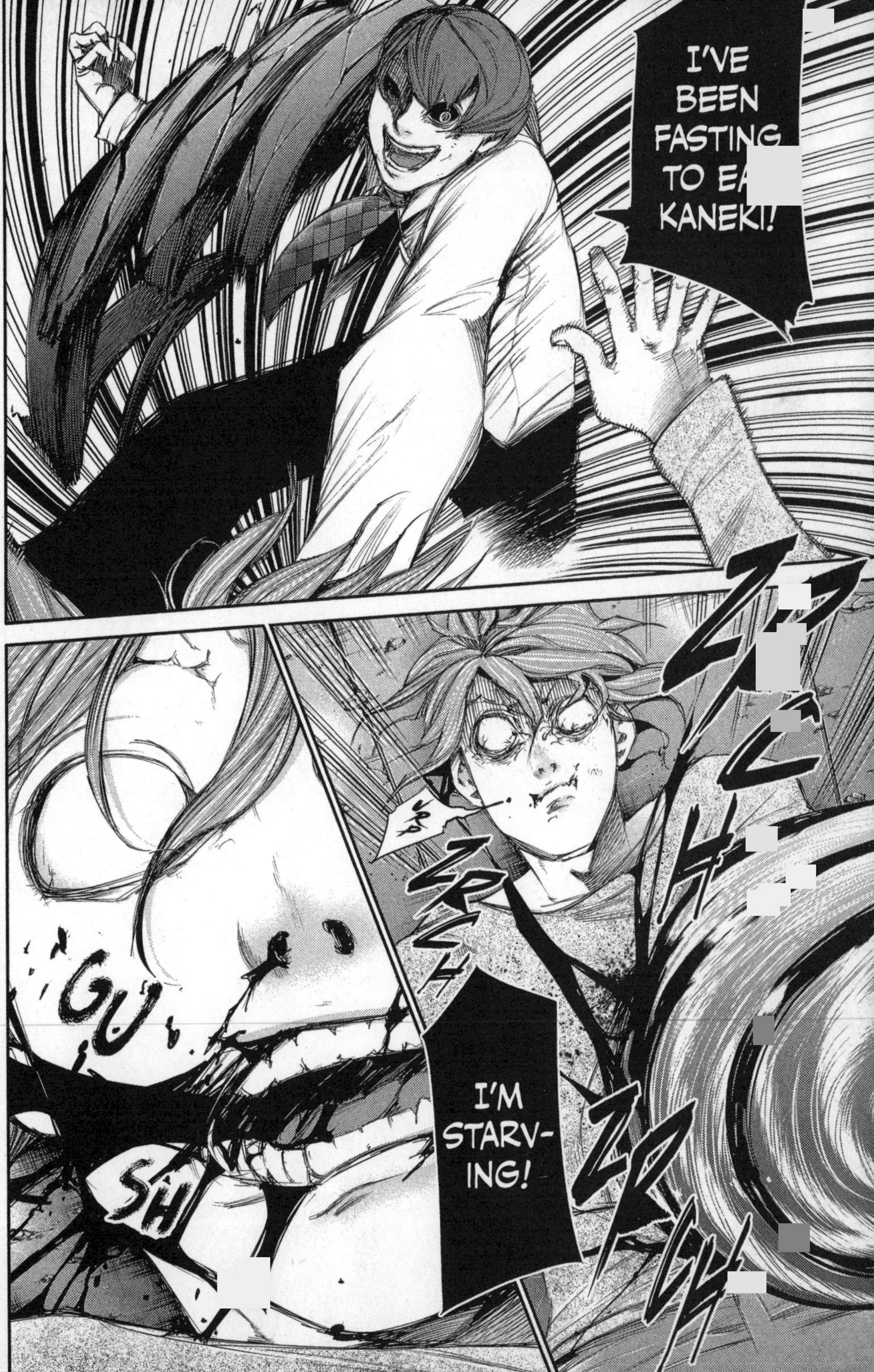
I'VE BEEN FASTING TO EAT KANEKI!
I'M STARV-ING!
GU
SH

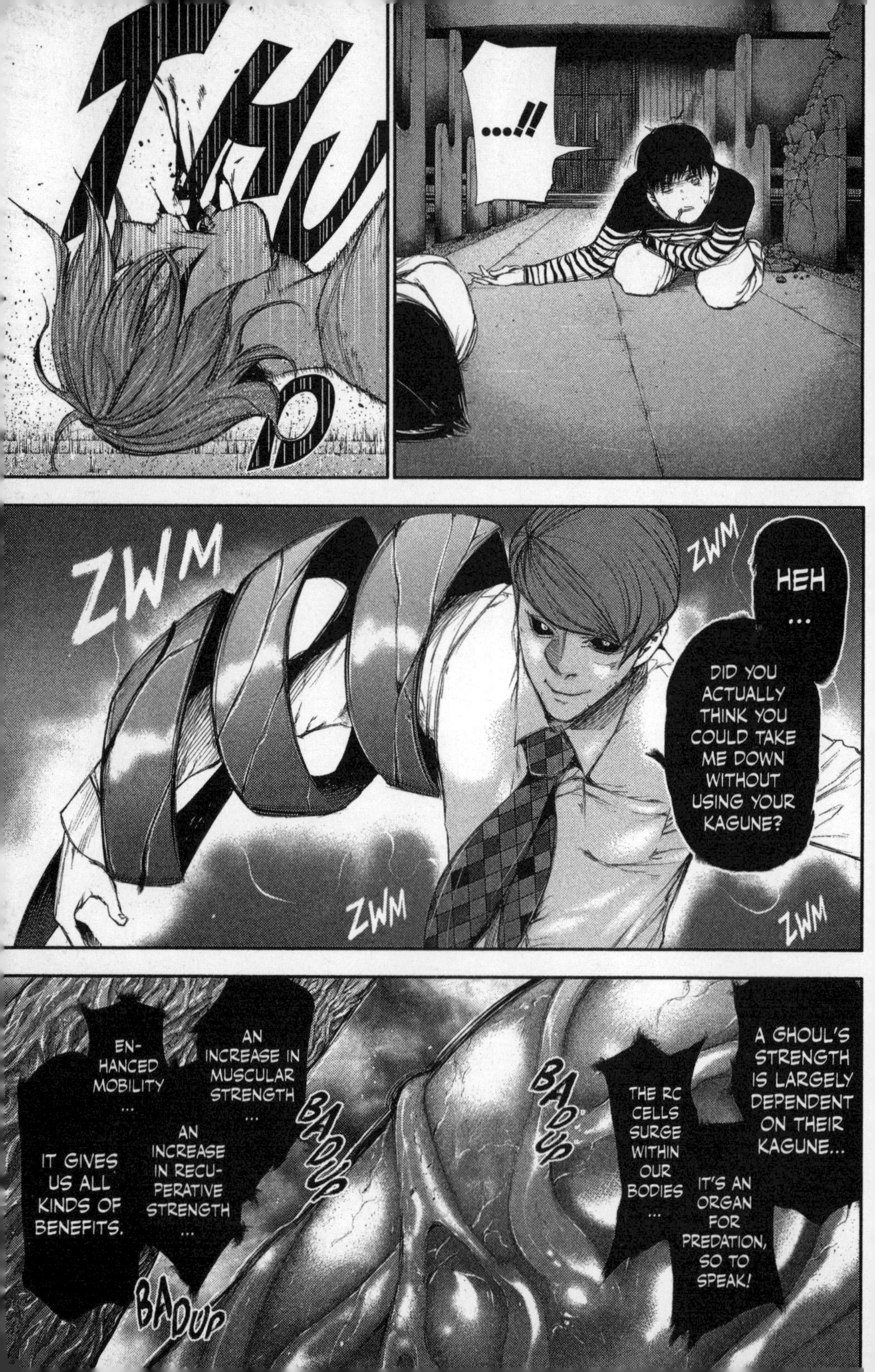
...!!
ZWM
ZWM
HEH...
DID YOU ACTUALLY THINK YOU COULD TAKE ME DOWN WITHOUT USING YOUR KAGUNE?
ZWM
ZWM
A GHOUL'S STRENGTH IS LARGELY DEPENDENT ON THEIR KAGUNE...
IT'S AN ORGAN FOR PREDATION, SO TO SPEAK!
BADUP
THE RC CELLS SURGE WITHIN OUR BODIES...
BADUP
AN INCREASE IN MUSCULAR STRENGTH...
EN-HANCED MOBILITY...
AN INCREASE IN RECU-PERATIVE STRENGTH...
IT GIVES US ALL KINDS OF BENEFITS.
BADUP

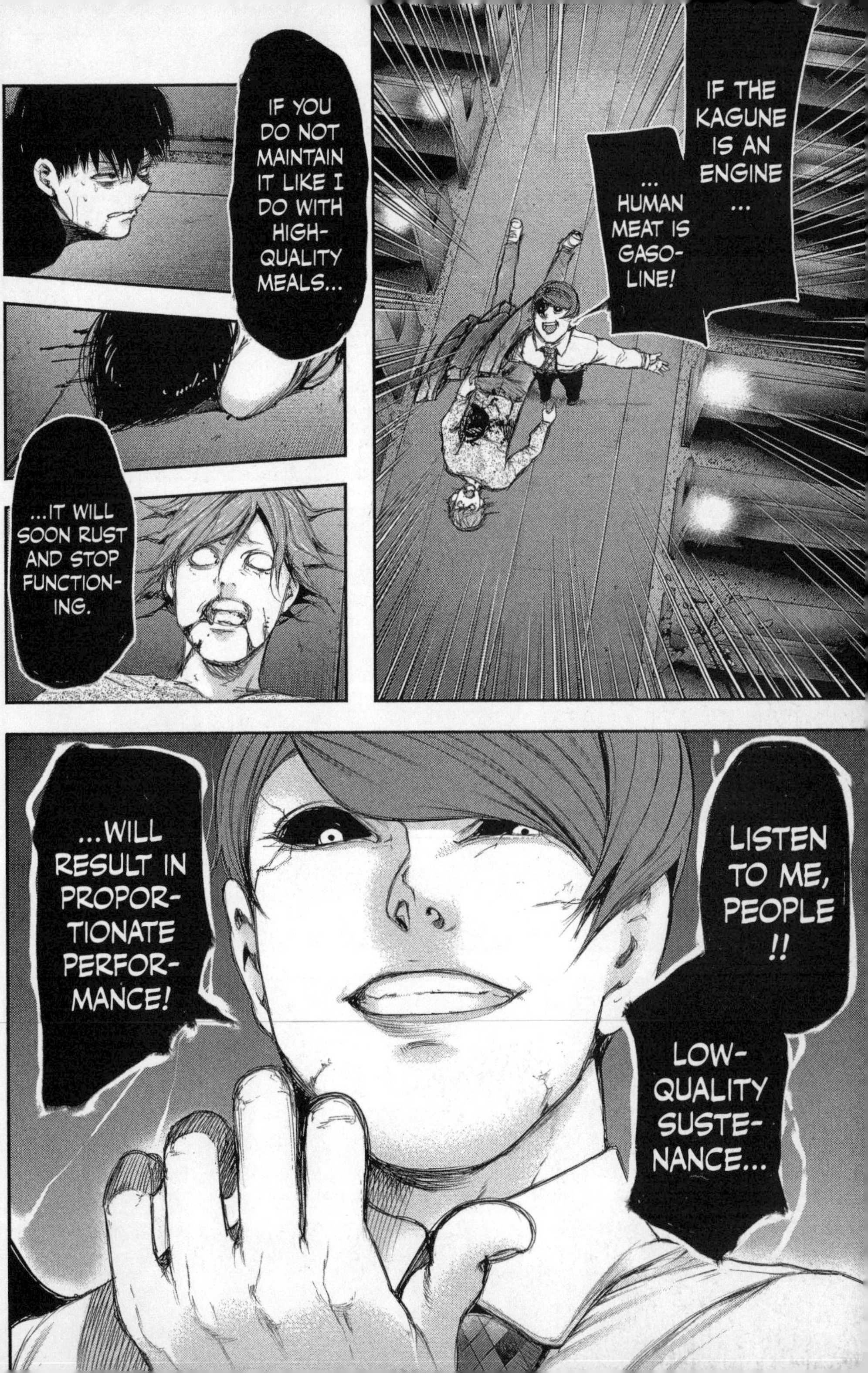
IF THE KAGUNE IS AN ENGINE ...
... HUMAN MEAT IS GASO-LINE!
IF YOU DO NOT MAINTAIN IT LIKE I DO WITH HIGH-QUALITY MEALS...
...IT WILL SOON RUST AND STOP FUNCTION-ING.
LISTEN TO ME, PEOPLE !!
LOW-QUALITY SUSTE-NANCE...
...WILL RESULT IN PROPOR-TIONATE PERFOR-MANCE!

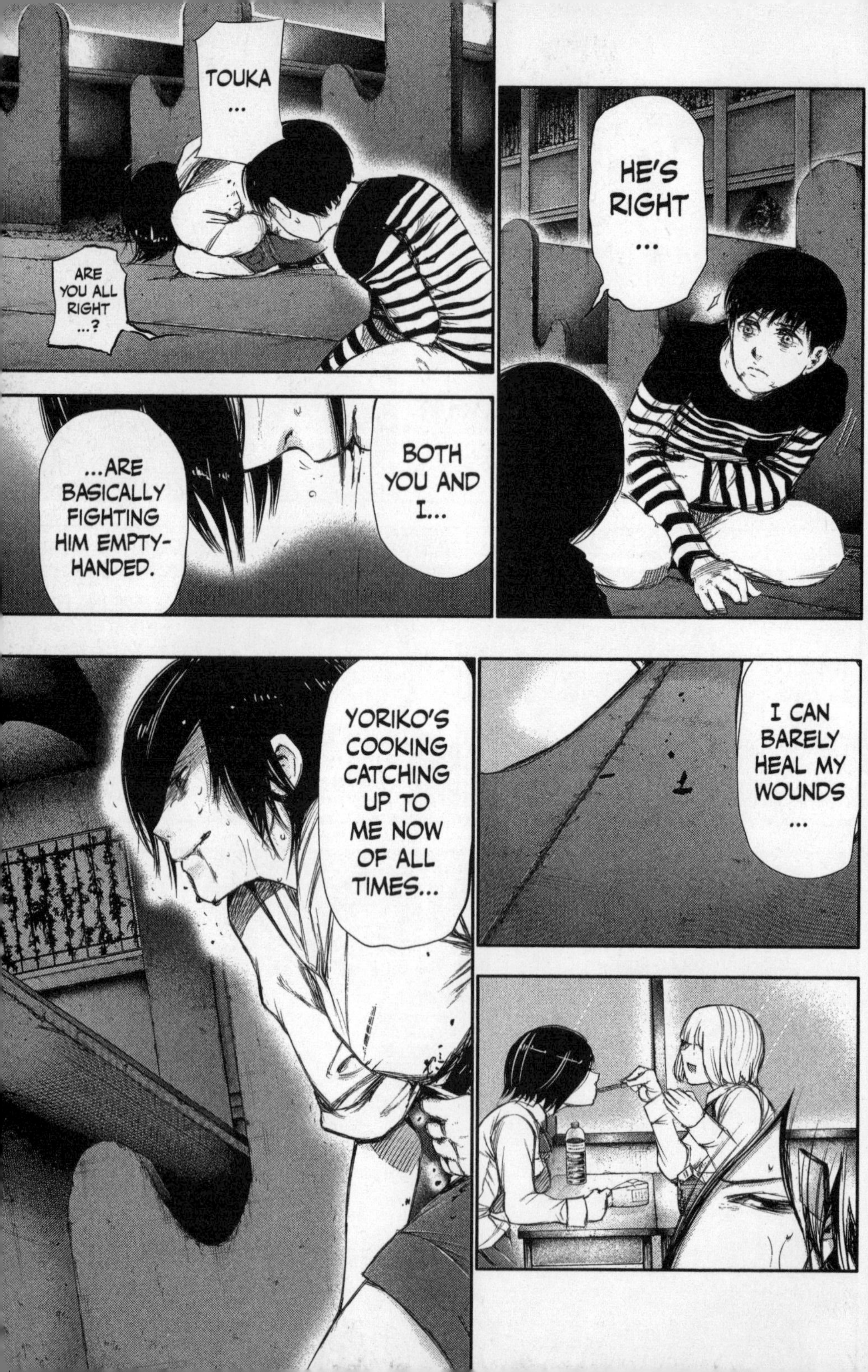
TOUKA ...
ARE YOU ALL RIGHT ...?
HE'S RIGHT ...
BOTH YOU AND I...
...ARE BASICALLY FIGHTING HIM EMPTY-HANDED.
I CAN BARELY HEAL MY WOUNDS ...
YORIKO'S COOKING CATCHING UP TO ME NOW OF ALL TIMES...

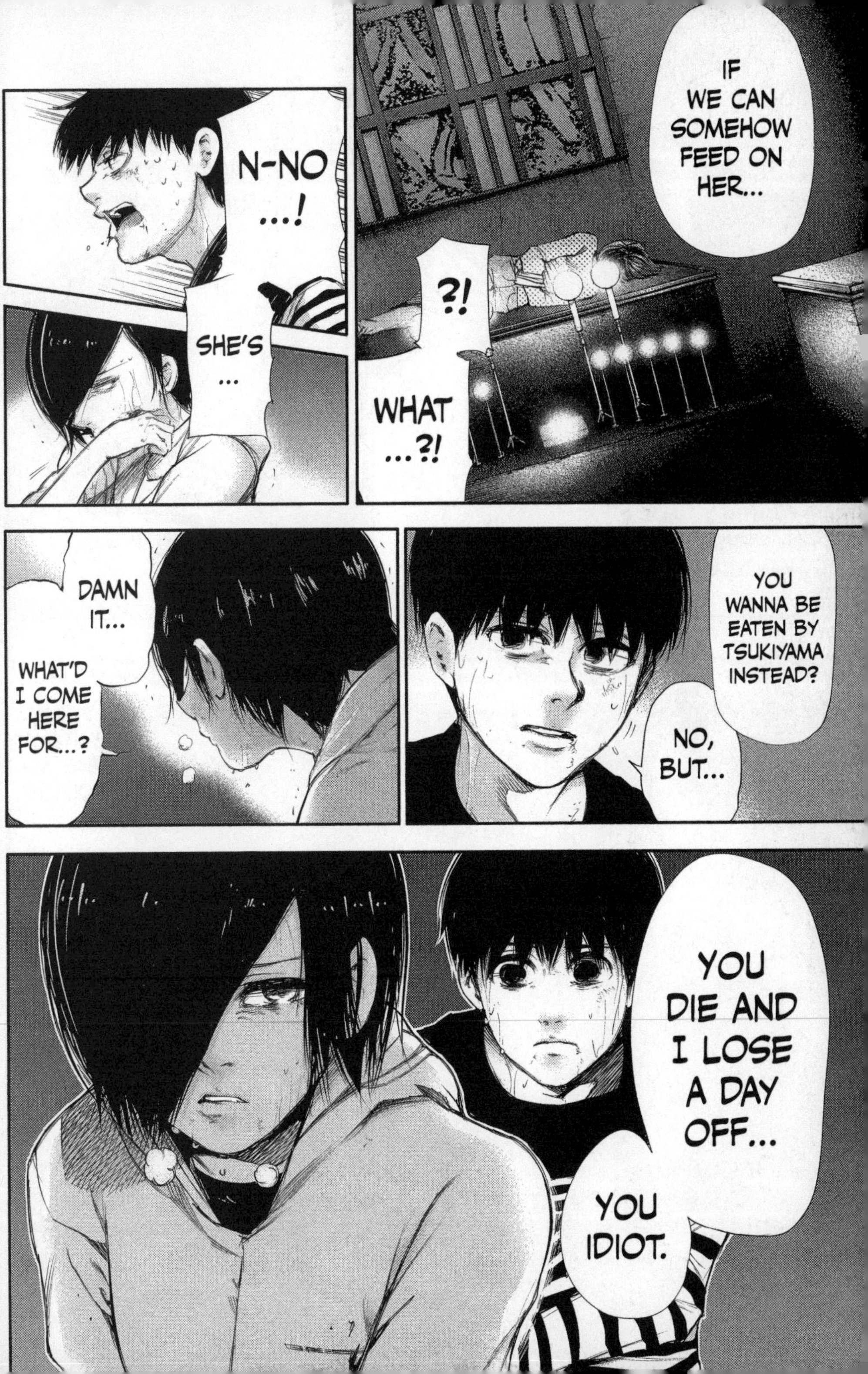
IF WE CAN SOMEHOW FEED ON HER...
?!
WHAT ...?!
N-NO ...!
SHE'S ...
YOU WANNA BE EATEN BY TSUKIYAMA INSTEAD?
NO, BUT...
DAMN IT...
WHAT'D I COME HERE FOR...?
YOU DIE AND I LOSE A DAY OFF...
YOU IDIOT.

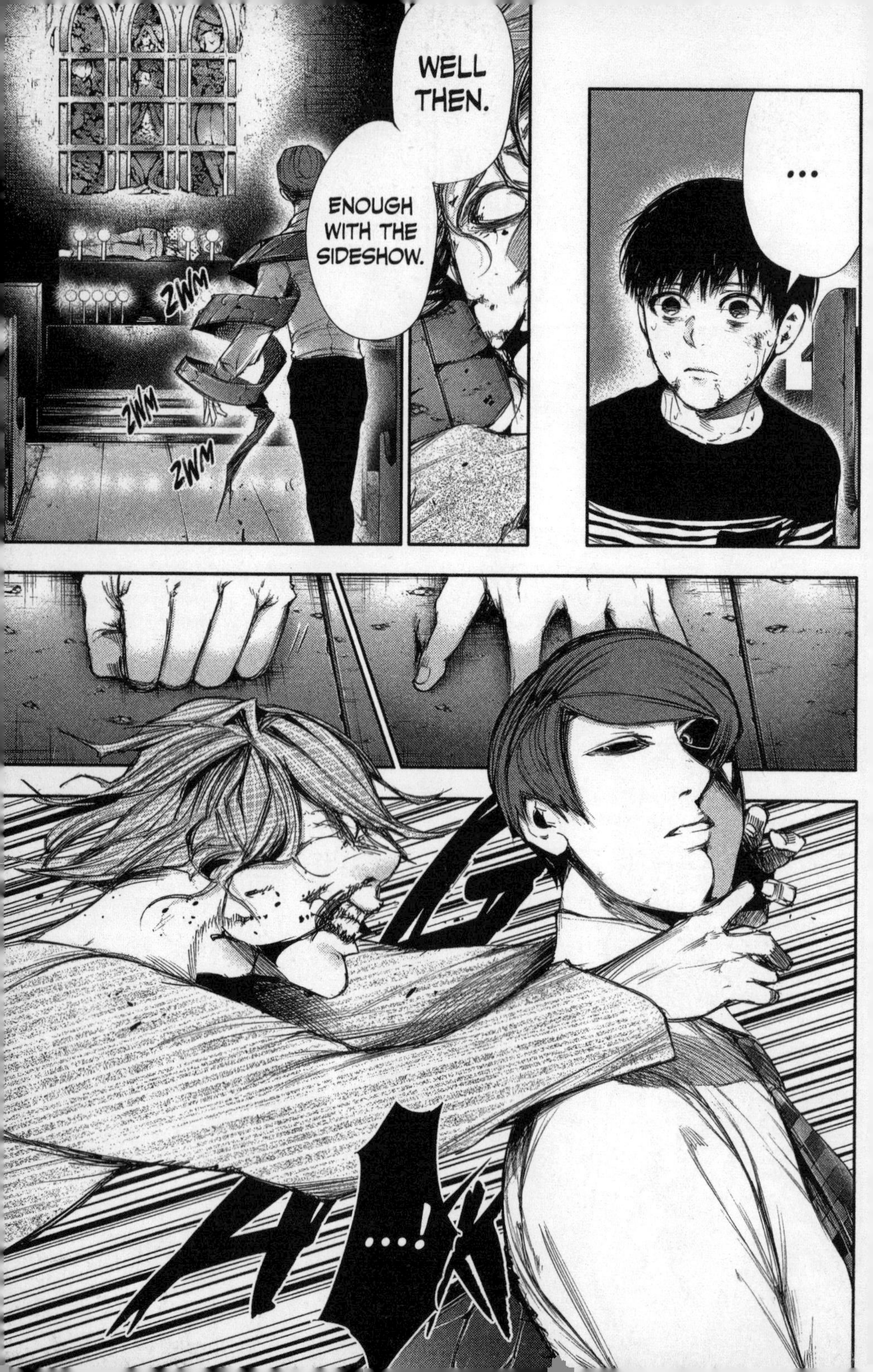
...
WELL THEN.
ENOUGH WITH THE SIDESHOW.
ZWM
ZWM
ZWM
....!

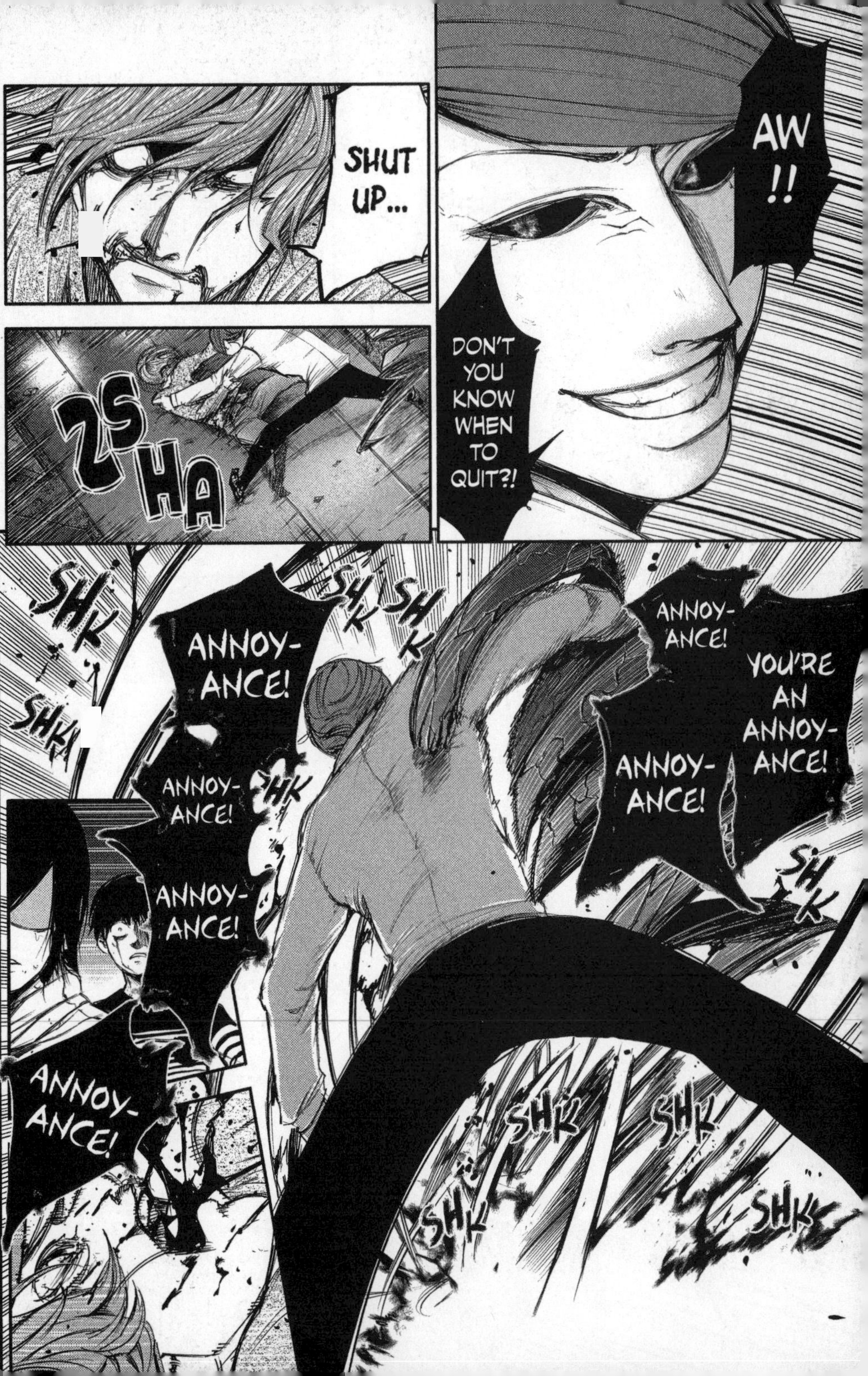
AW!!
DON'T YOU KNOW WHEN TO QUIT?!
SHUT UP...
ZSHA
ANNOY-ANCE!
YOU'RE AN ANNOY-ANCE!
ANNOY-ANCE!
SHK
SHK
SHK
SHK
ANNOY-ANCE!
SHK
SHK
ANNOY-ANCE!
SHK
ANNOY-ANCE!
ANNOY-ANCE!
SHK
SHK
SHK
SHK

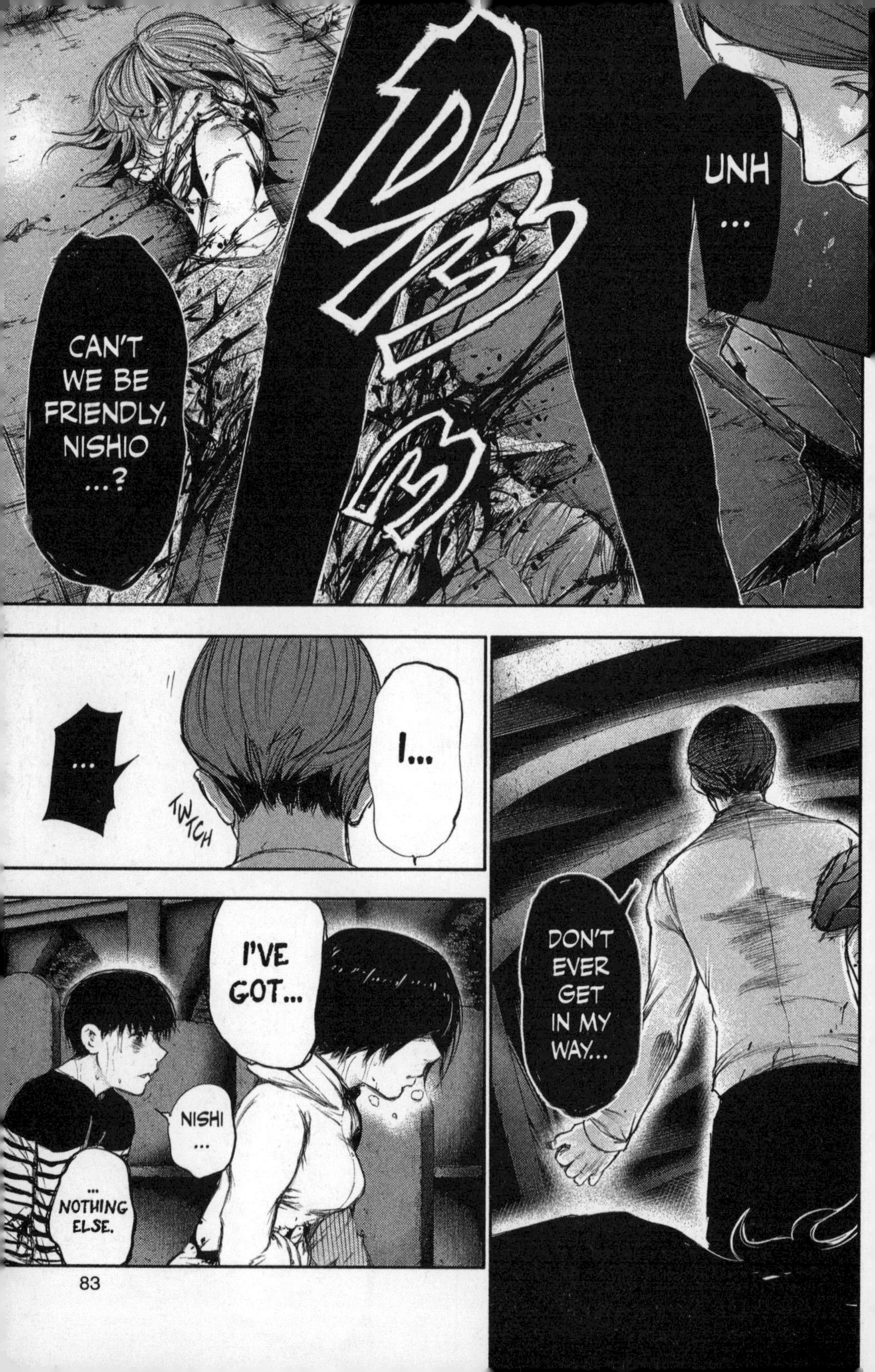
UNH ...
CAN'T WE BE FRIENDLY, NISHIO ...?
DON'T EVER GET IN MY WAY...
I...
...
TWITCH
I'VE GOT...
NISHI ...
... NOTHING ELSE.

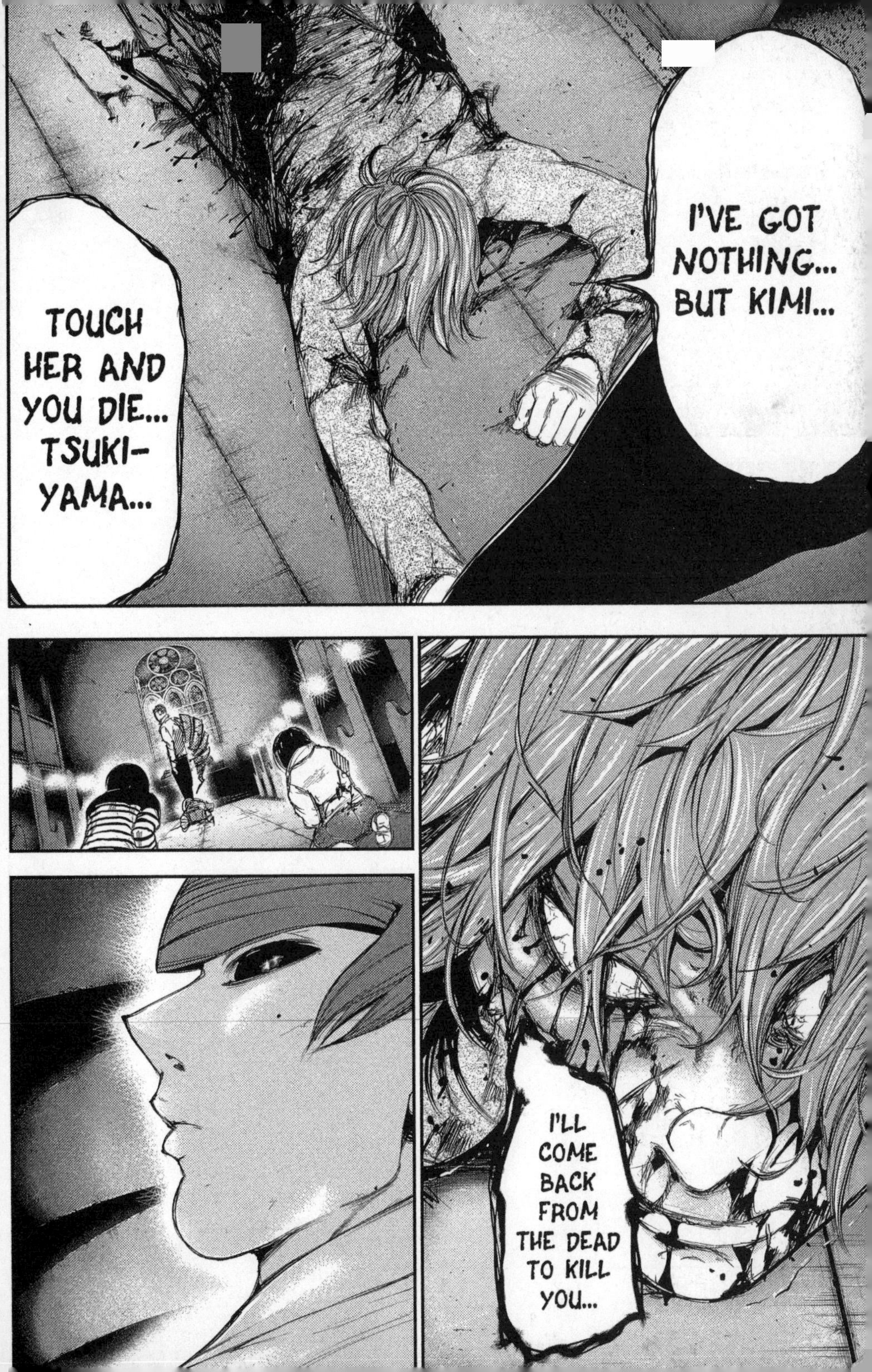
I'VE GOT NOTHING... BUT KIMI...
TOUCH HER AND YOU DIE... TSUKI-YAMA...
I'LL COME BACK FROM THE DEAD TO KILL YOU...

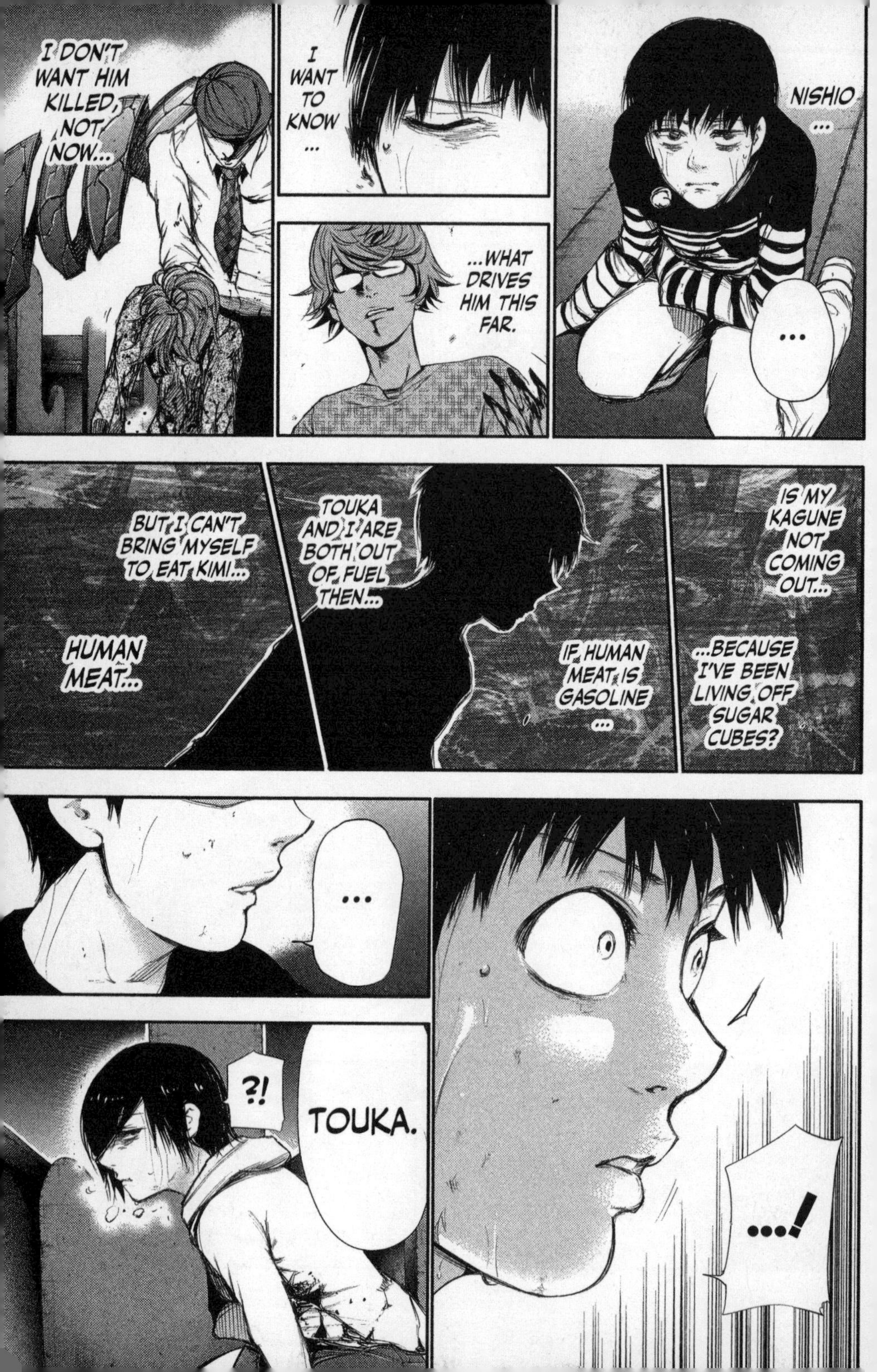
NISHIO
...
...
I WANT TO KNOW
...
...WHAT DRIVES HIM THIS FAR.
I DON'T WANT HIM KILLED, NOT NOW...
IS MY KAGUNE NOT COMING OUT...
...BECAUSE I'VE BEEN LIVING OFF SUGAR CUBES?
IF HUMAN MEAT IS GASOLINE
...
TOUKA AND I ARE BOTH OUT OF FUEL THEN...
BUT I CAN'T BRING MYSELF TO EAT KIMI...
HUMAN MEAT...
...!
...
TOUKA.
?!

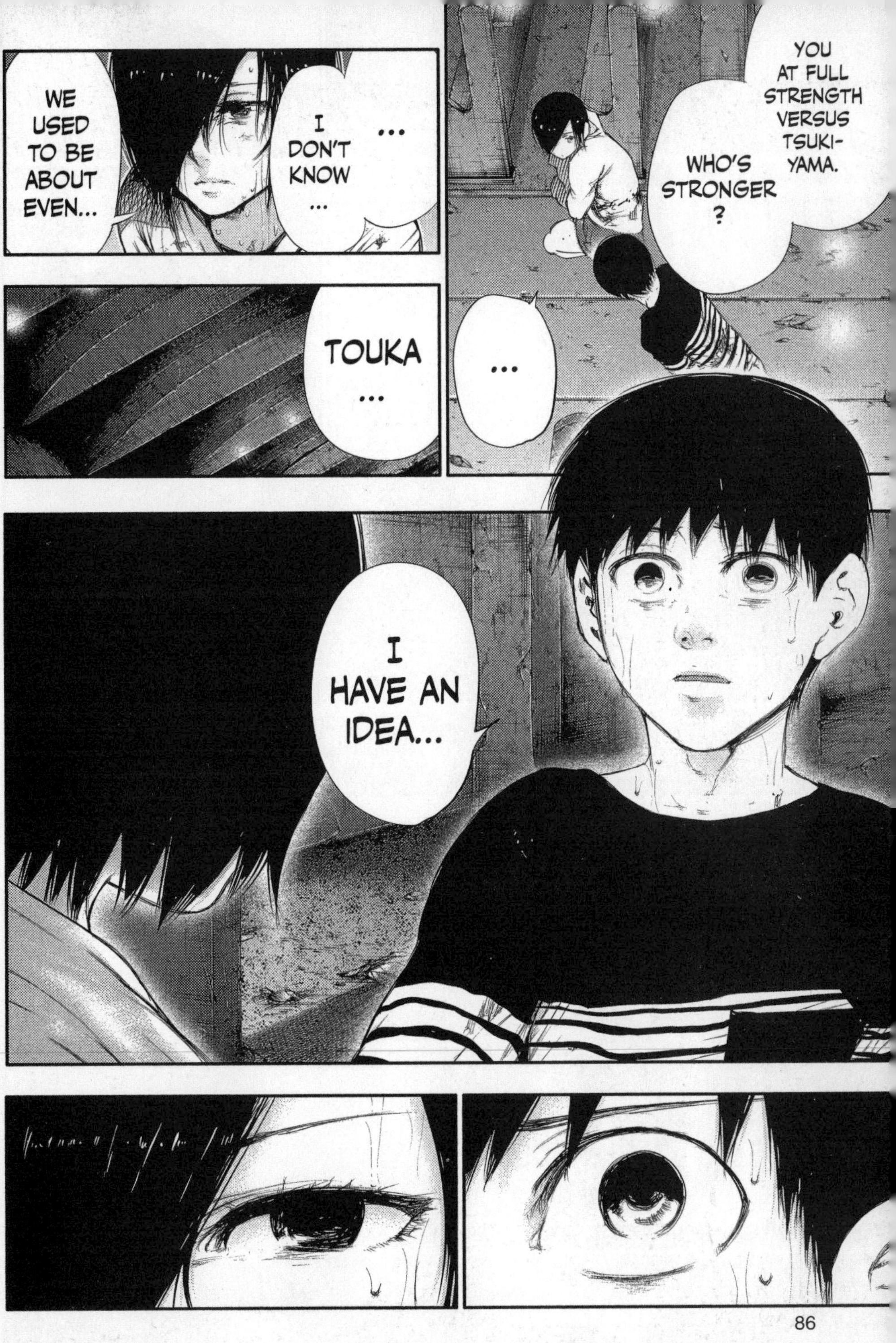
YOU AT FULL STRENGTH VERSUS TSUKI-YAMA.
WHO'S STRONGER?
...
... I DON'T KNOW ...
WE USED TO BE ABOUT EVEN...
TOUKA ...
I HAVE AN IDEA...

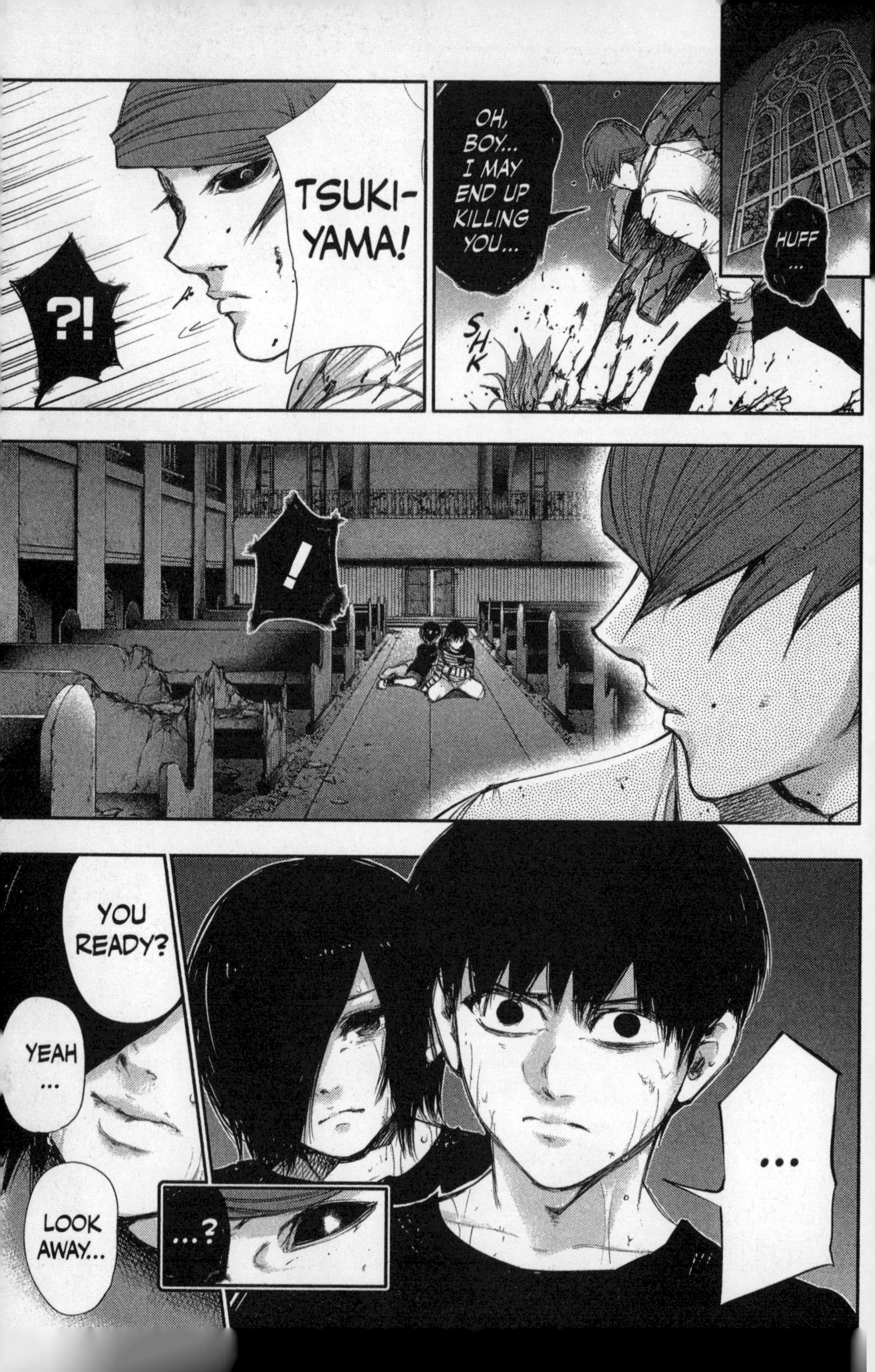
HUFF...
OH, BOY... I MAY END UP KILLING YOU...
SHK
TSUKI-YAMA!
?!
!
...
...?
YOU READY?
YEAH...
LOOK AWAY...

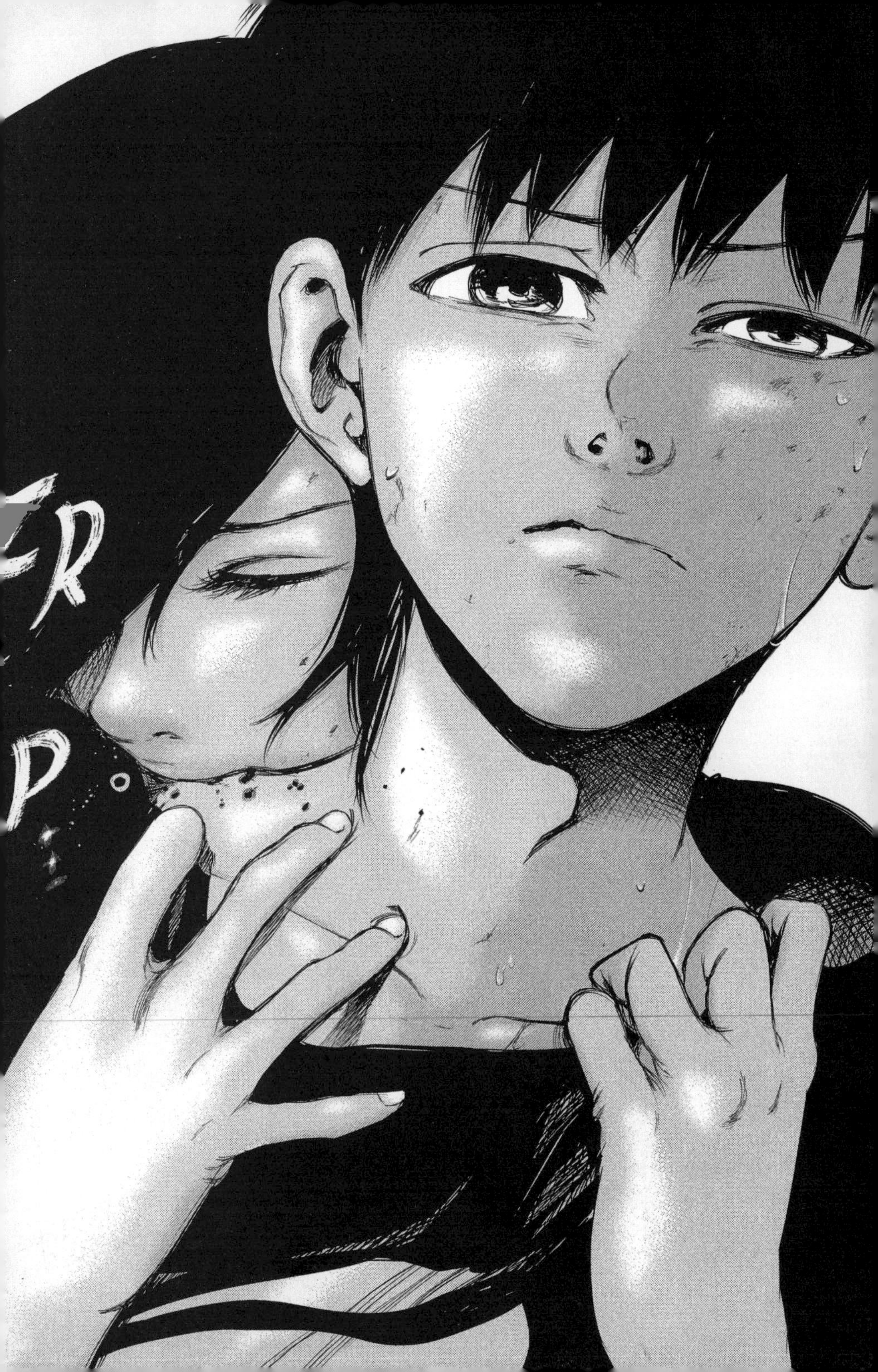

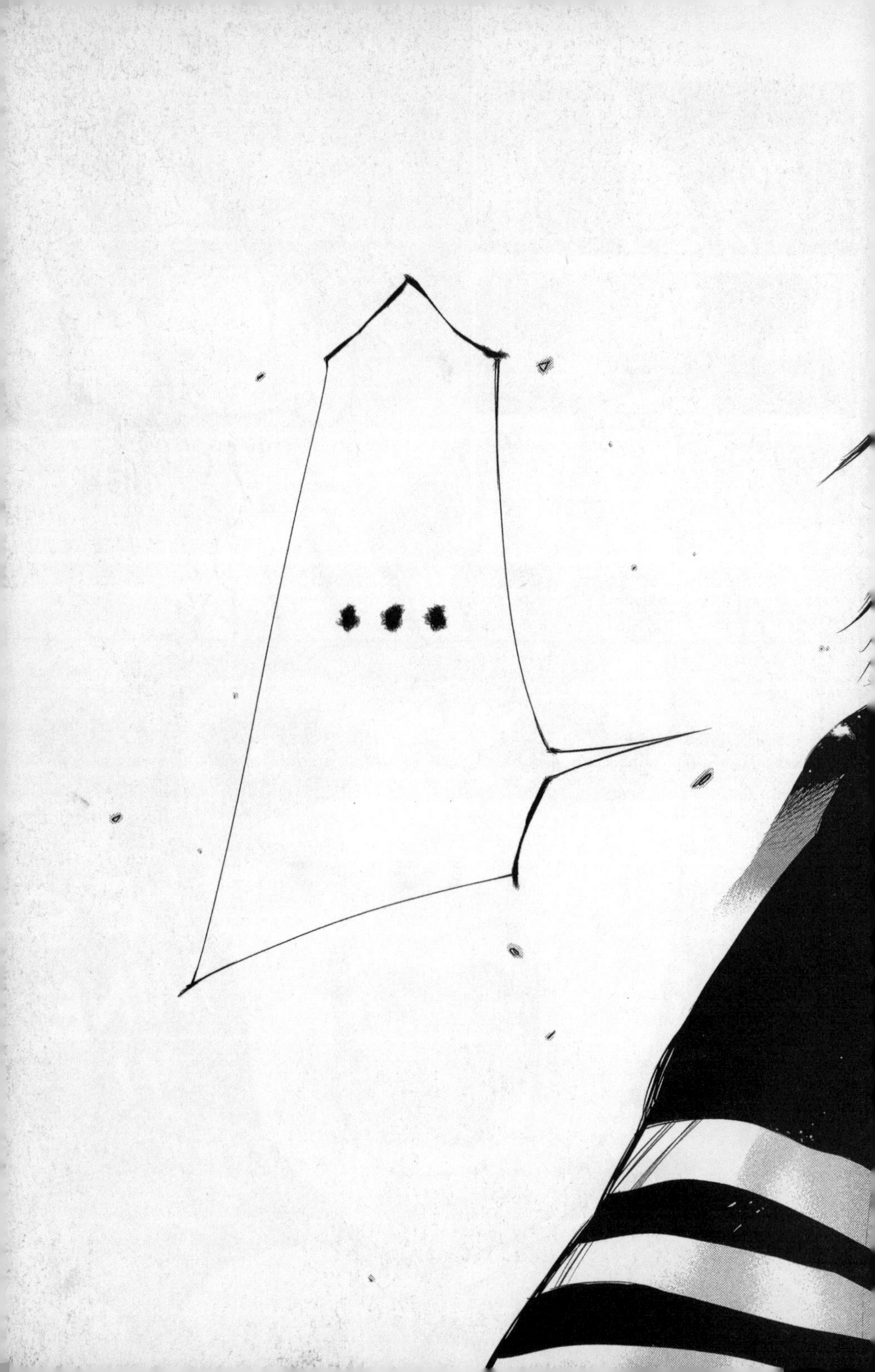
...

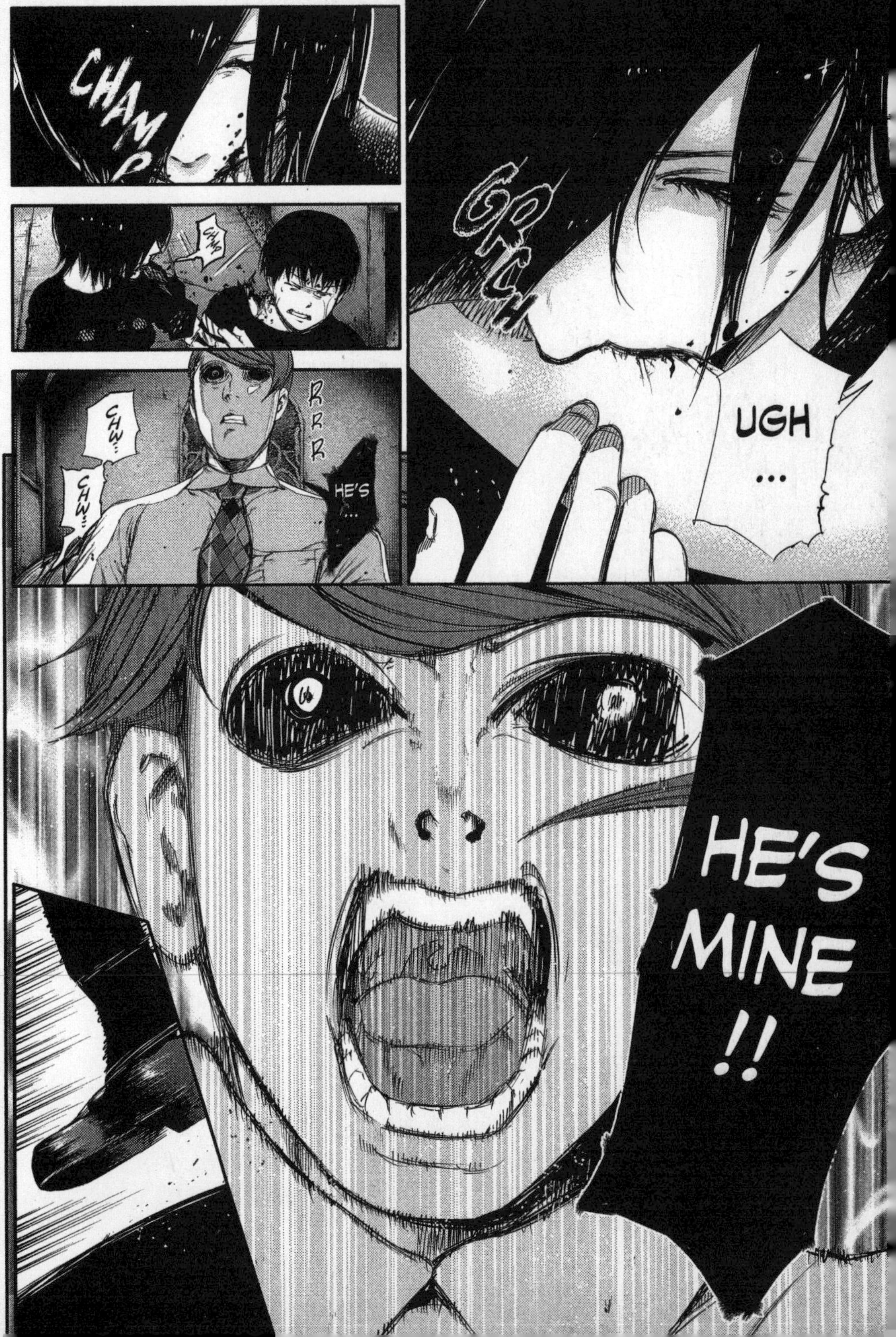
GRCH
UGH ...
CHAMP
CHMP
CHW...
CHW...
RRR
HE'S ...
HE'S MINE !!

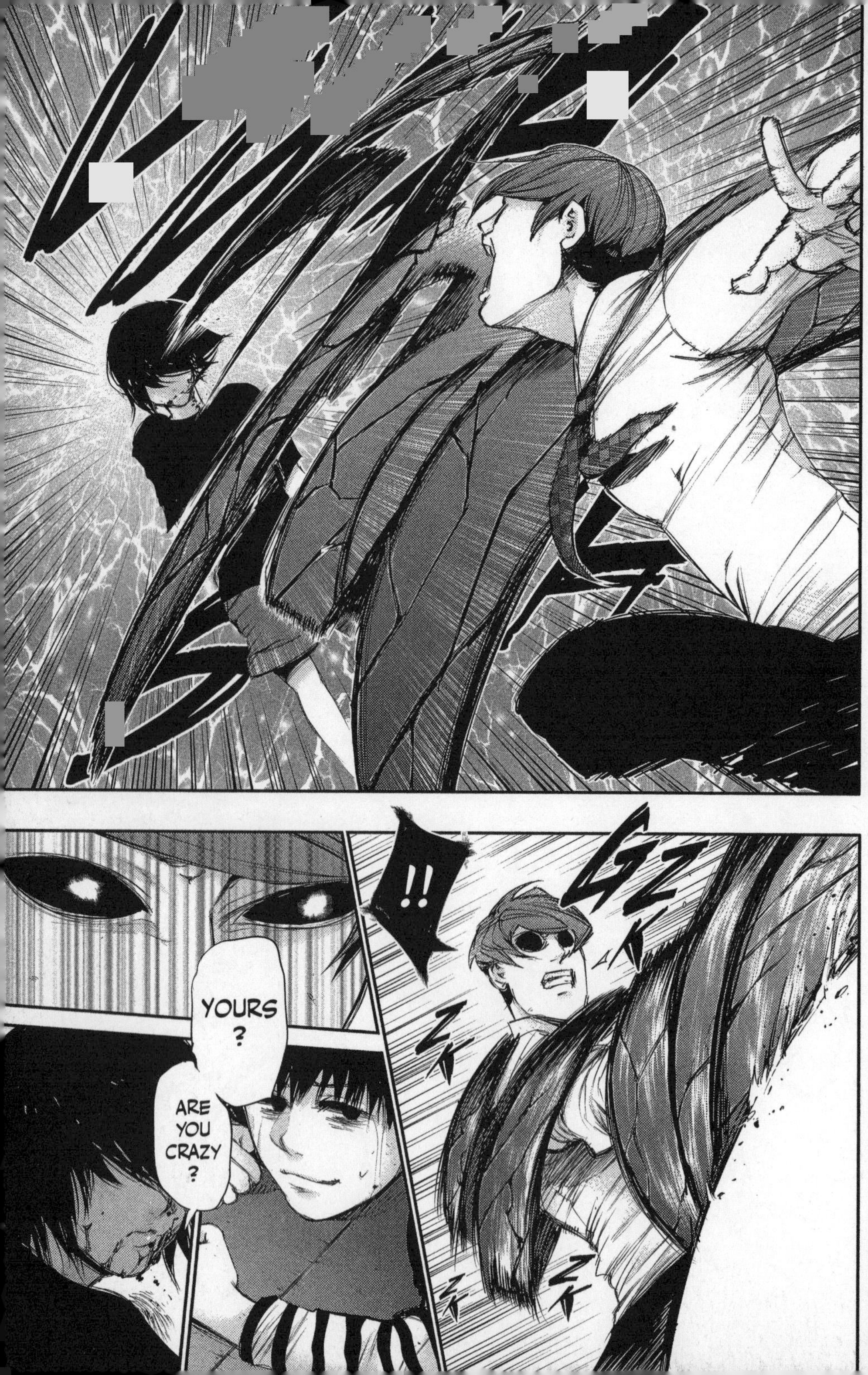
!!
YOURS ?
ARE YOU CRAZY ?

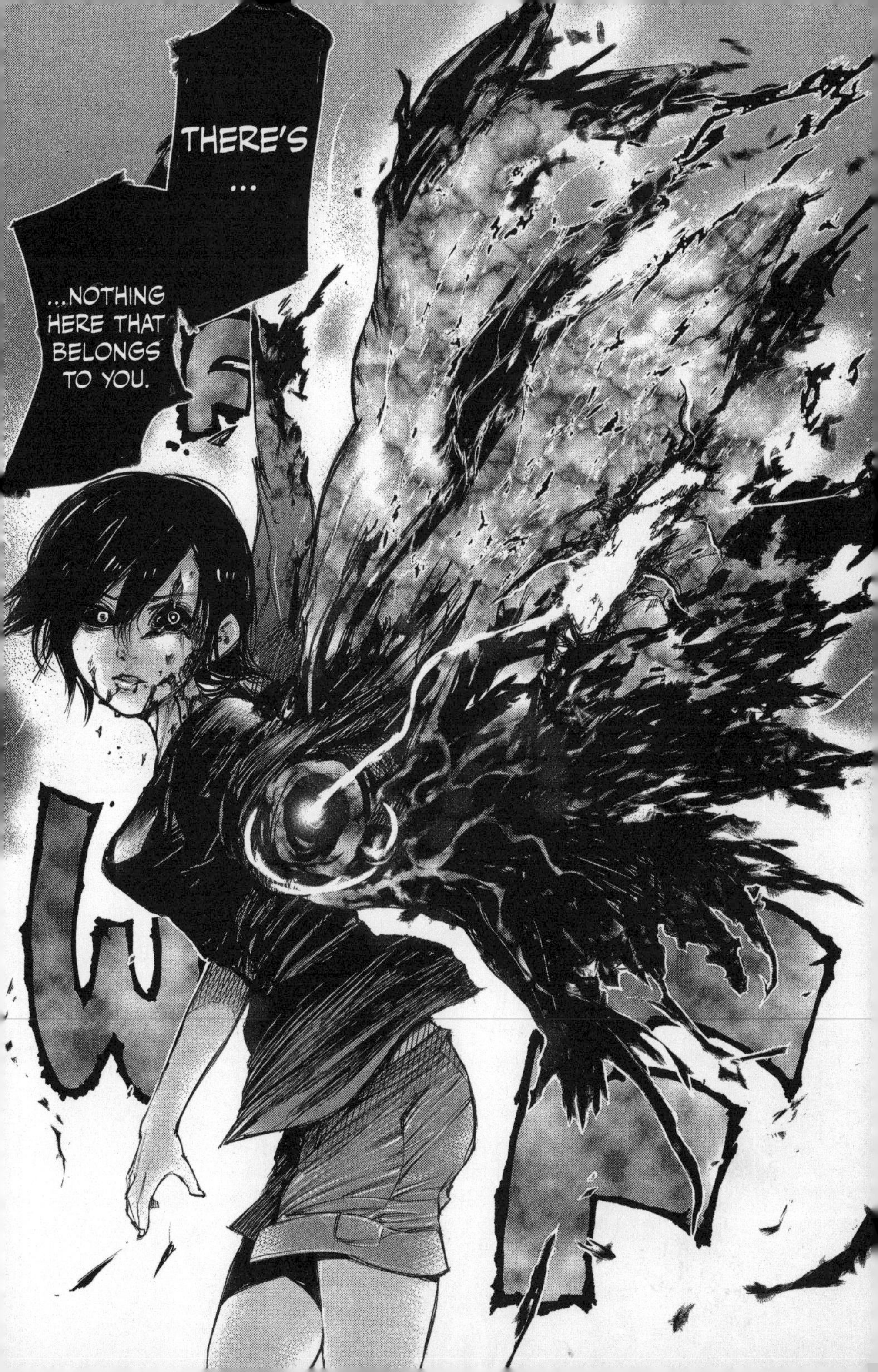
THERE'S ...
...NOTHING HERE THAT BELONGS TO YOU.

東京喰種
トーキョーグール
Tokyo Ghoul

#0 4 5 TOKYO GHOUL

[BLACK WINGS]

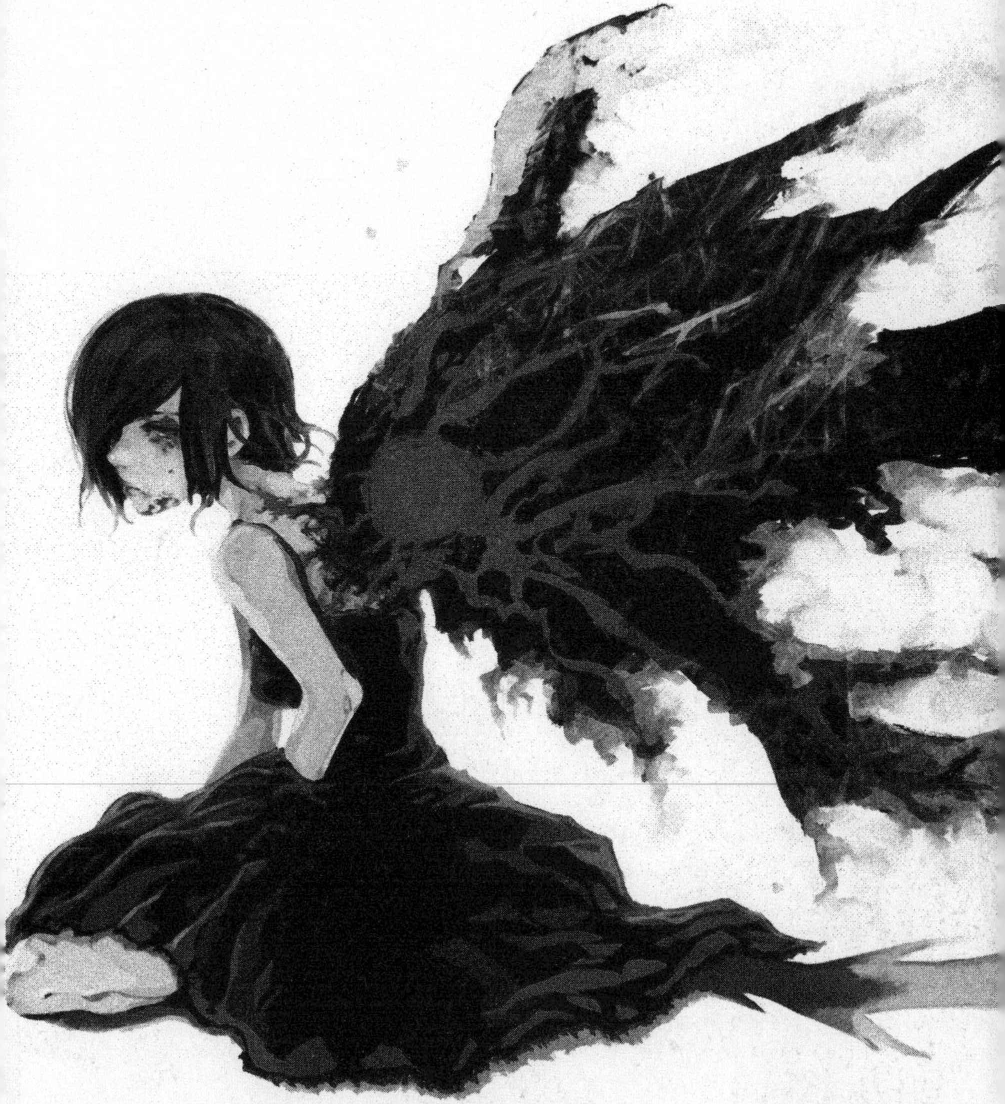

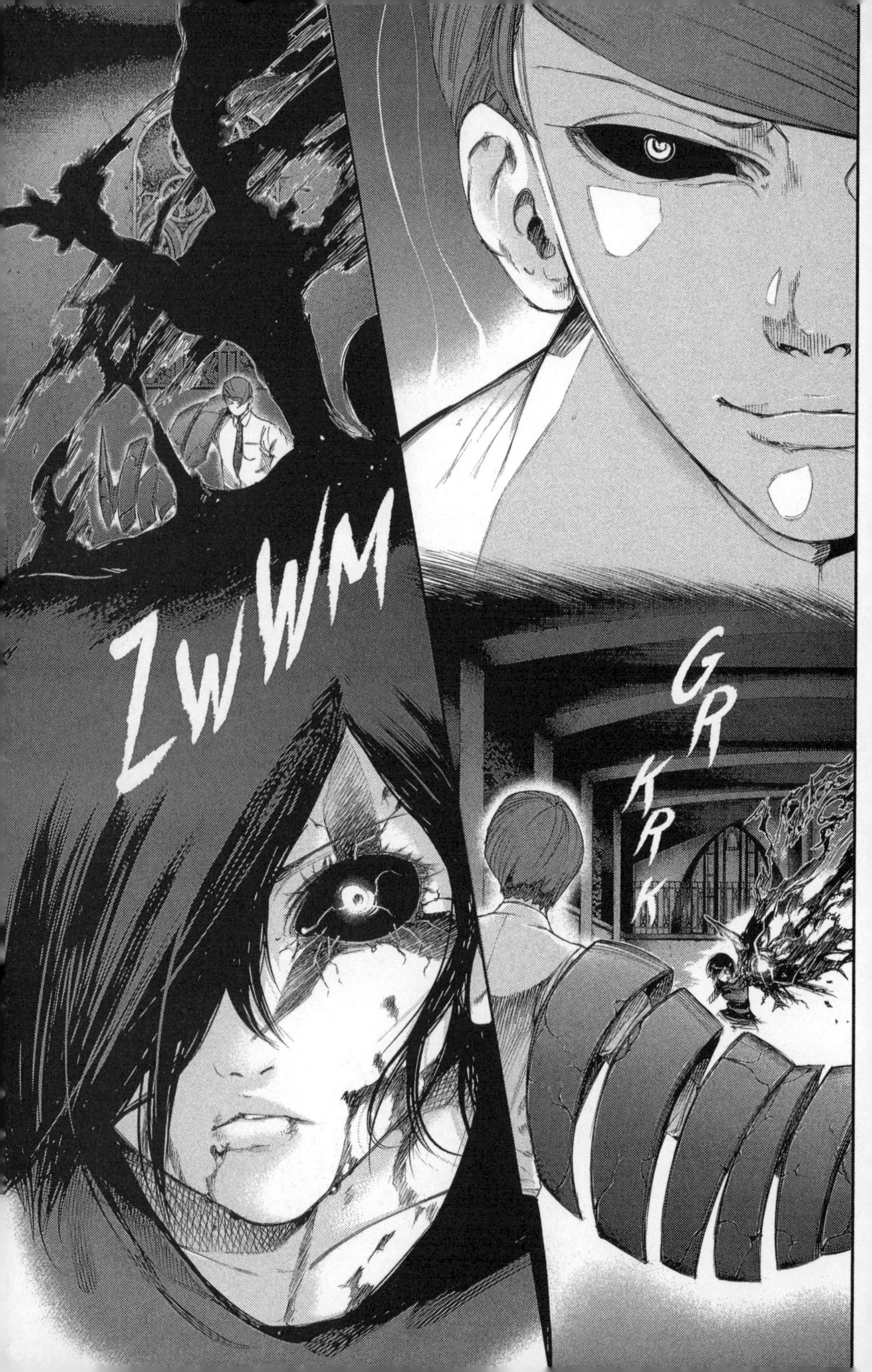
ZWWM
GRKRK

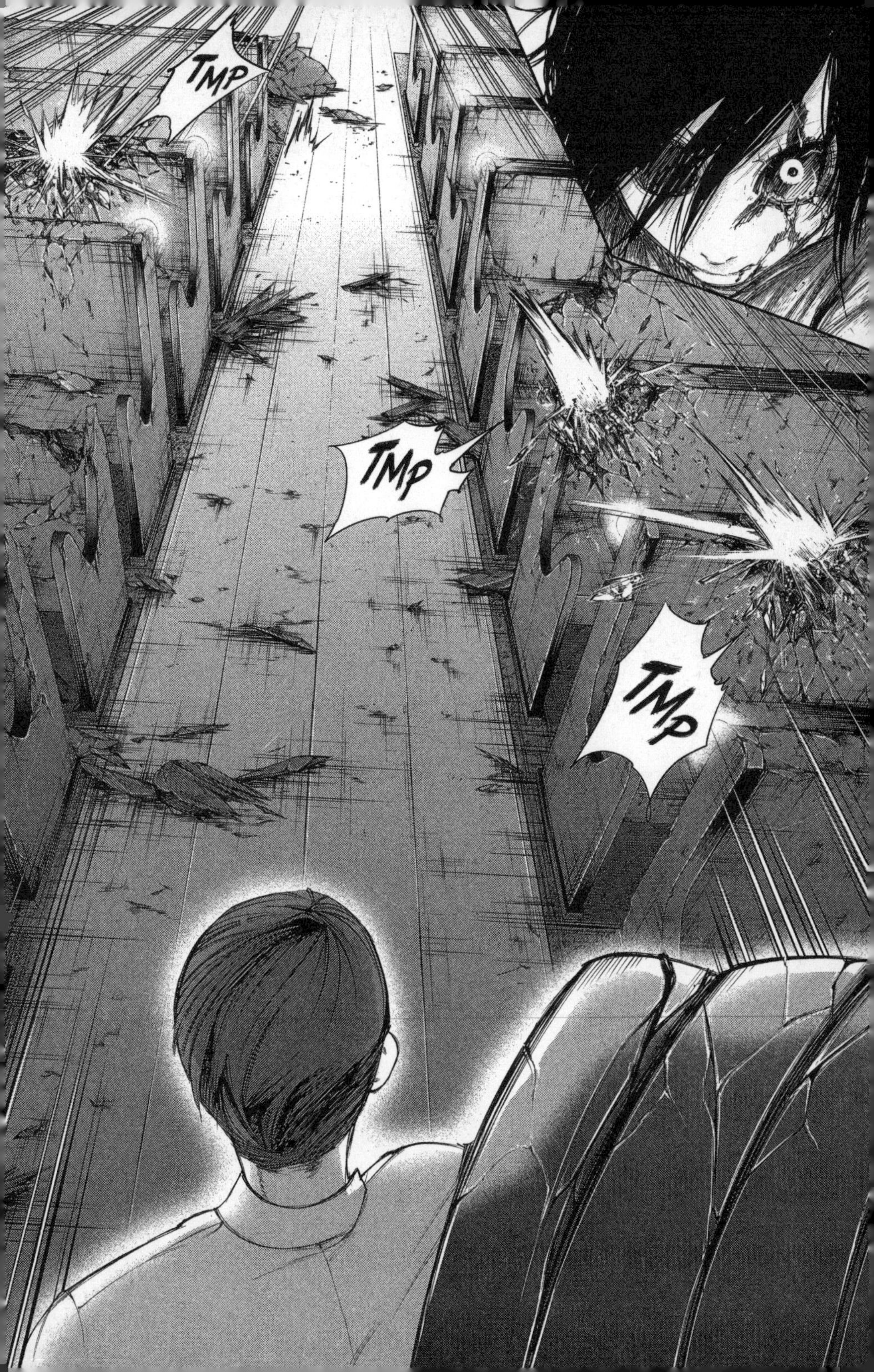
TMP
TMP
TMP

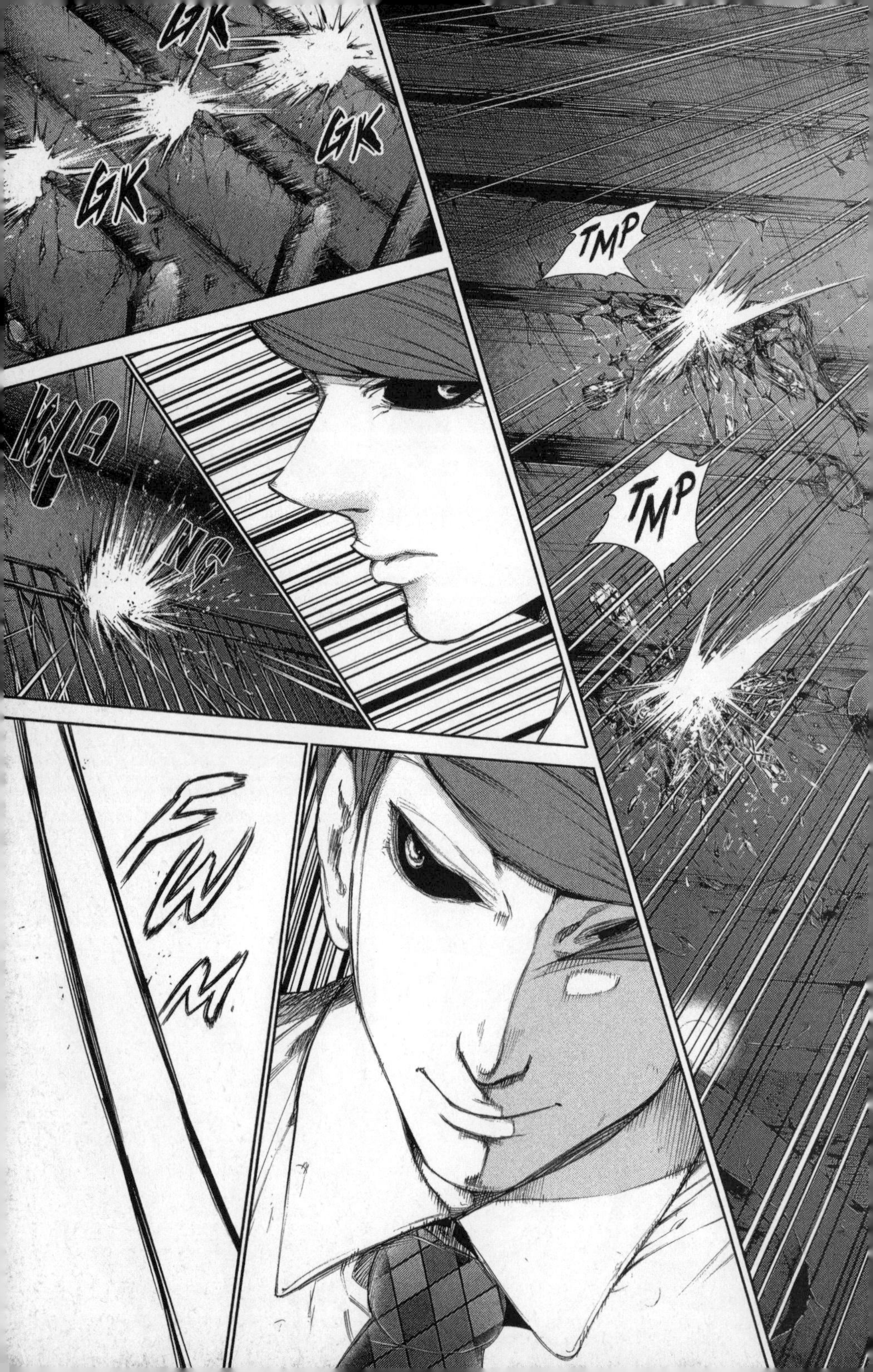
TMP
TMP
GK
GK
GK
KLANG
FWM

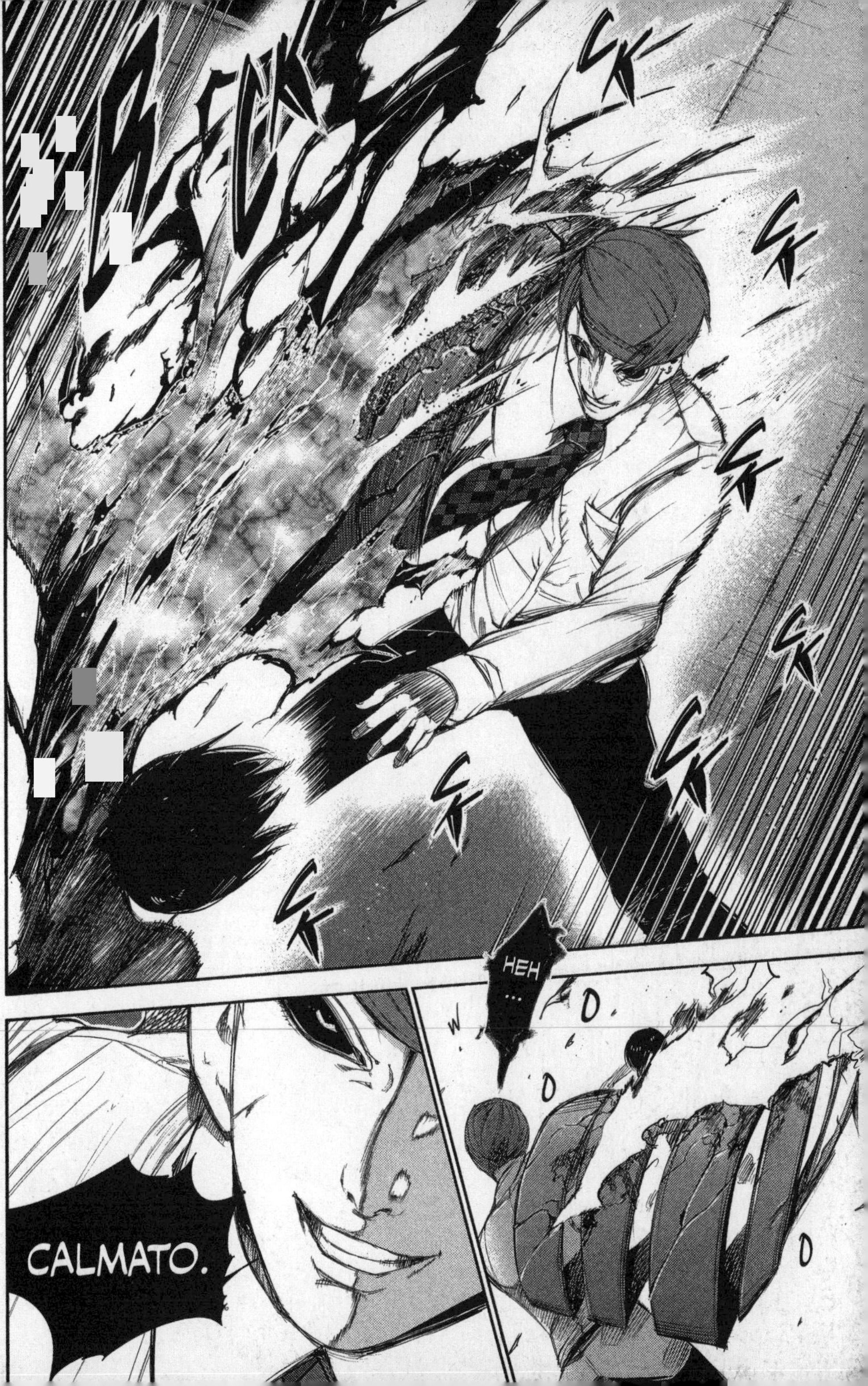
CK
CK
CK
CK
CK
CK
CK
HEH ...
CALMATO.

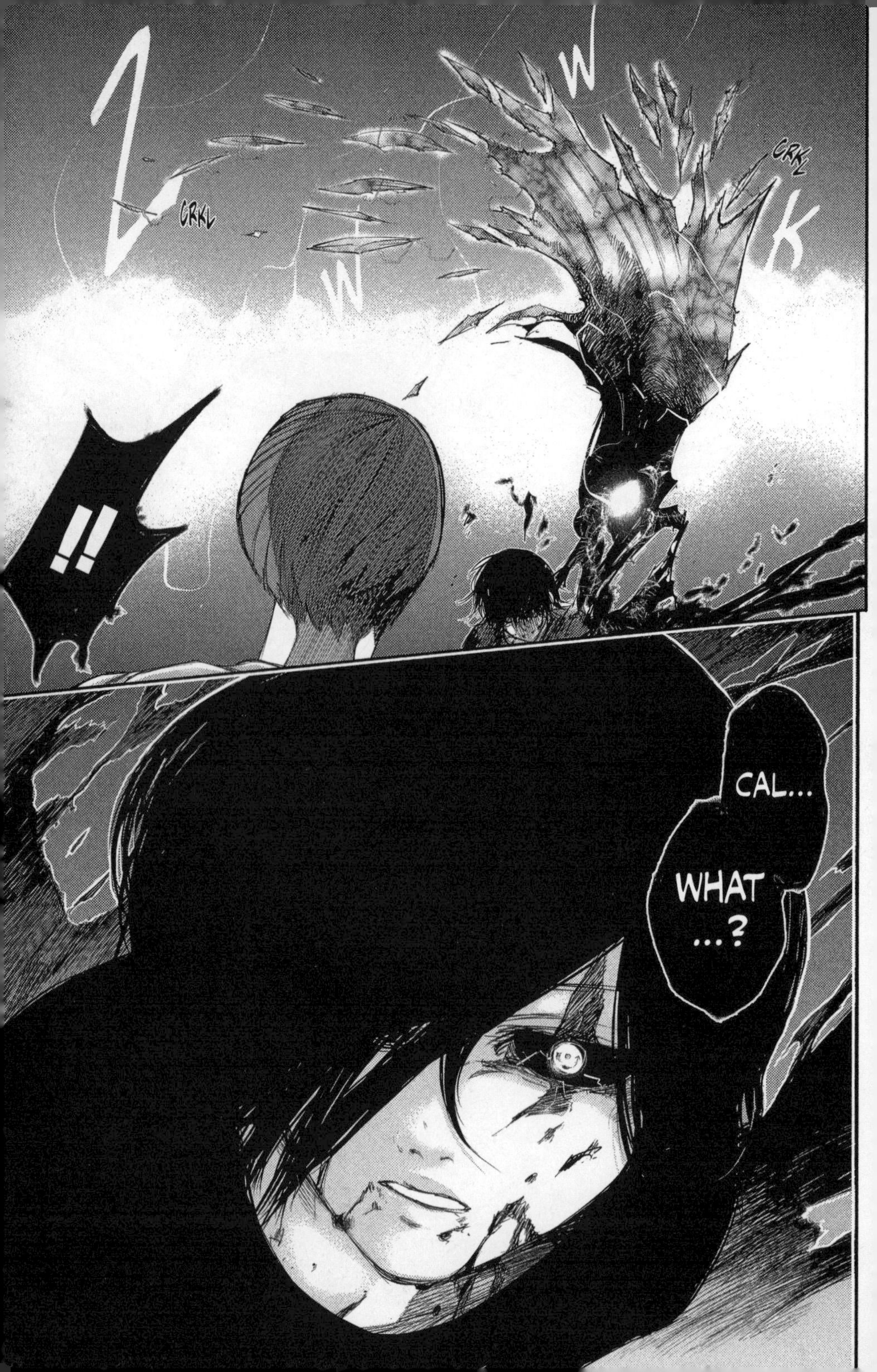
CRKL
CRKL
!!
CAL...
WHAT ...?

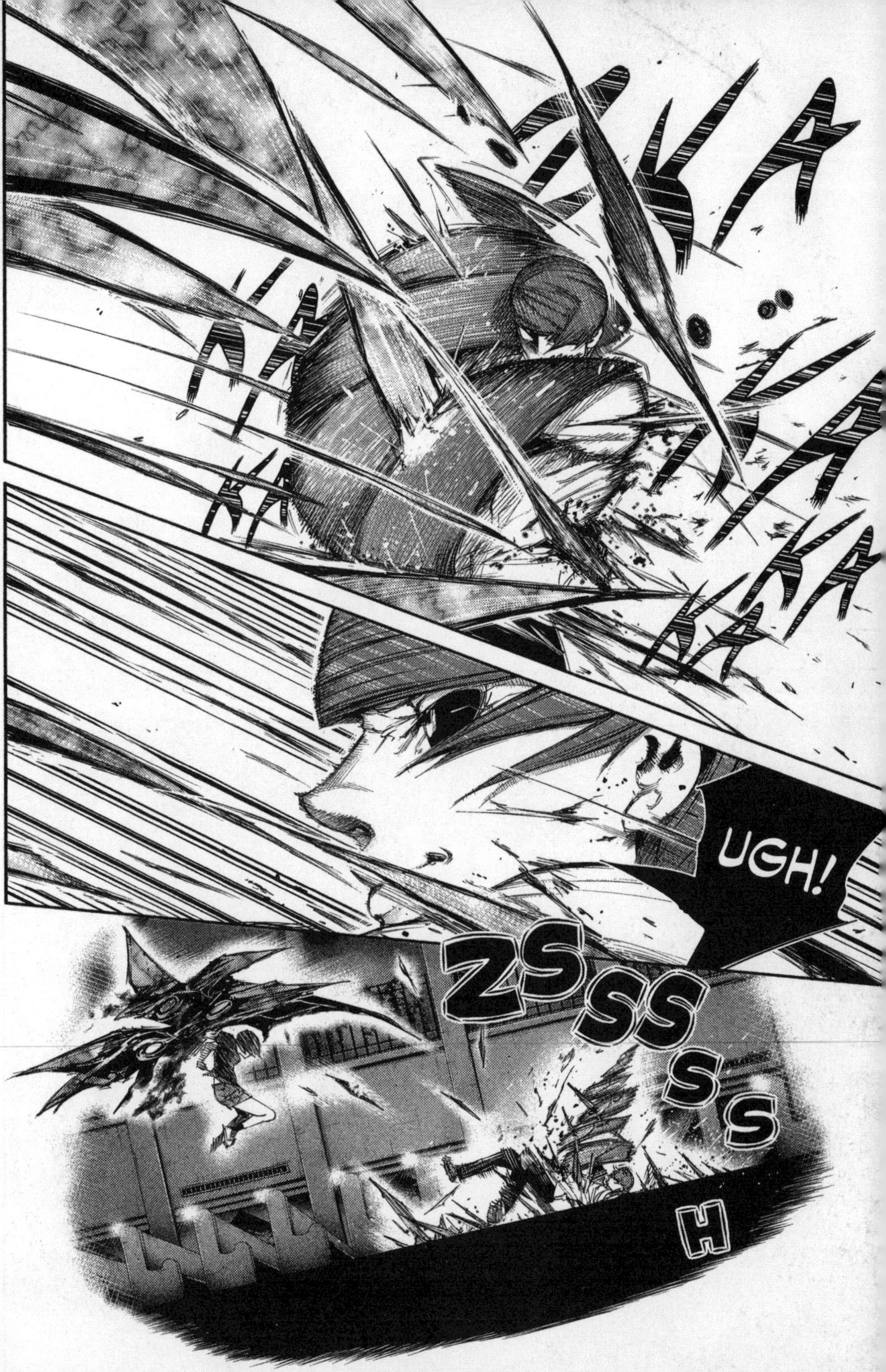
UGH!
ZSSSSSH

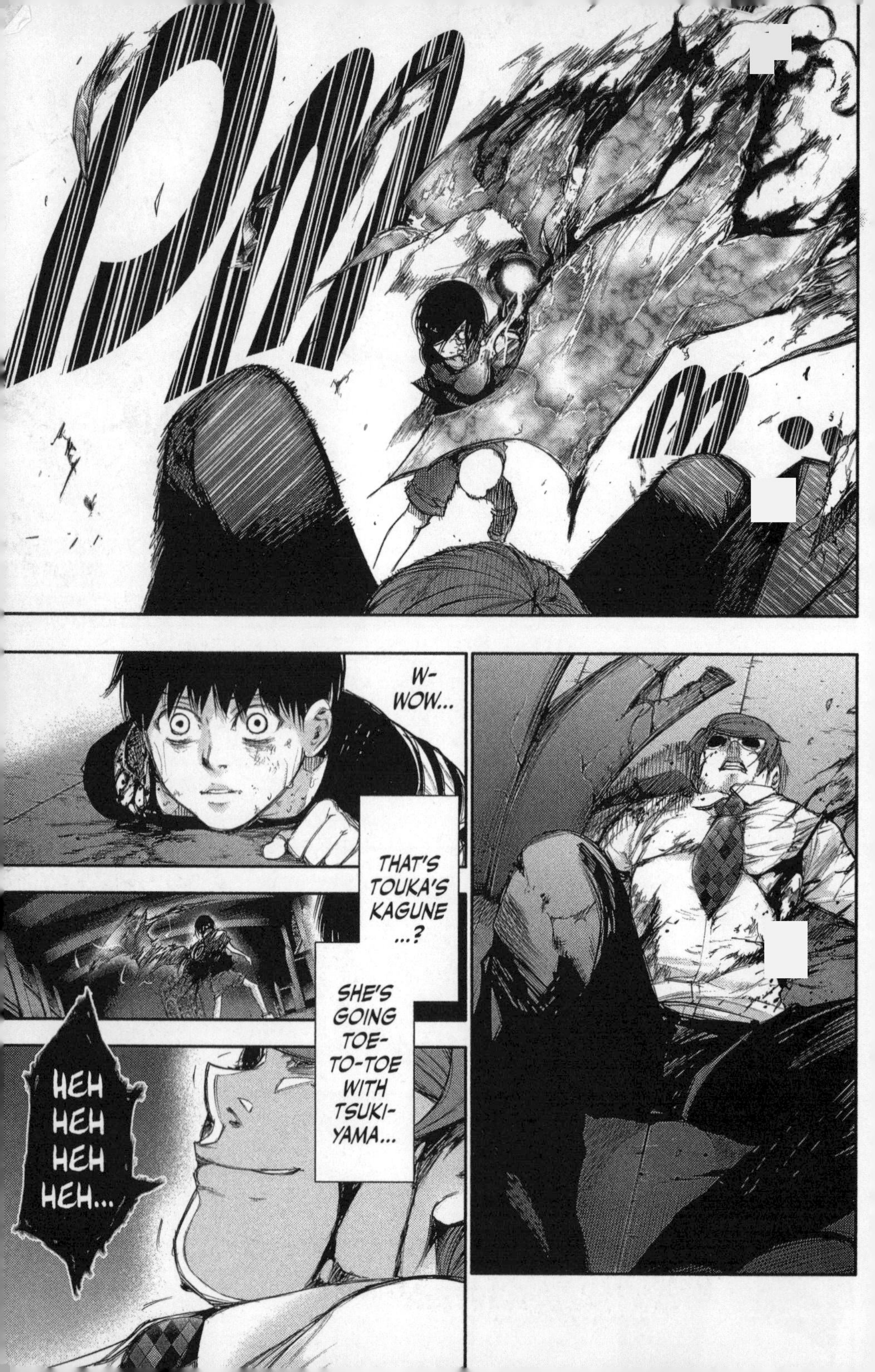
W-WOW...
THAT'S TOUKA'S KAGUNE ...?
SHE'S GOING TOE-TO-TOE WITH TSUKI-YAMA...
HEH HEH HEH HEH...

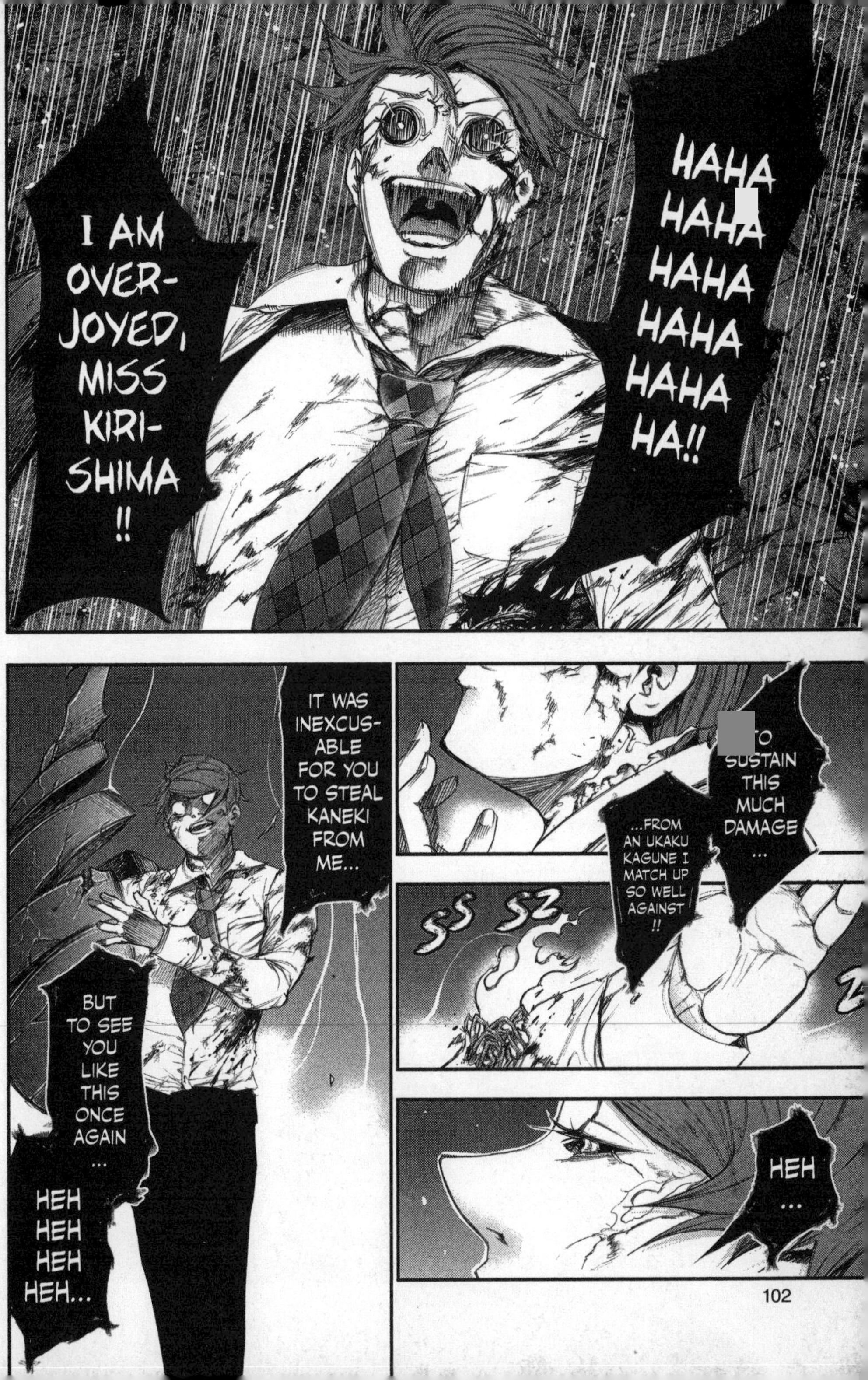
HAHA HAHA HAHA HAHA HAHA HA!!
I AM OVER-JOYED, MISS KIRI-SHIMA!!
TO SUSTAIN THIS MUCH DAMAGE...
...FROM AN UKAKU KAGUNE I MATCH UP SO WELL AGAINST!!
SS SZ
HEH...
IT WAS INEXCUS-ABLE FOR YOU TO STEAL KANEKI FROM ME...
BUT TO SEE YOU LIKE THIS ONCE AGAIN...
HEH HEH HEH HEH...

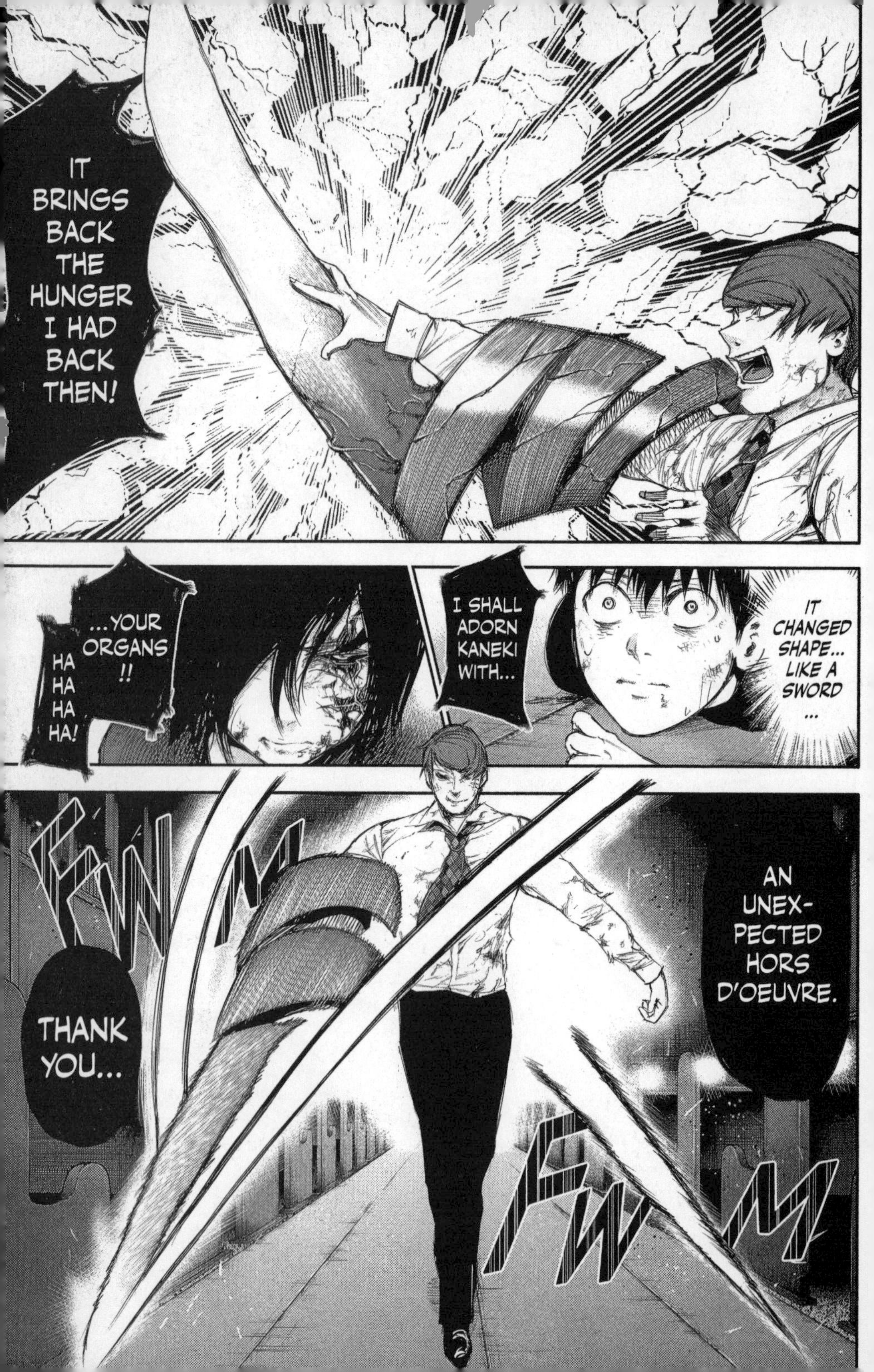
IT BRINGS BACK THE HUNGER I HAD BACK THEN!
IT CHANGED SHAPE... LIKE A SWORD ...
I SHALL ADORN KANEKI WITH...
...YOUR ORGANS!!
HA HA HA HA!
AN UNEX-PECTED HORS D'OEUVRE.
FWM
THANK YOU...
FWM

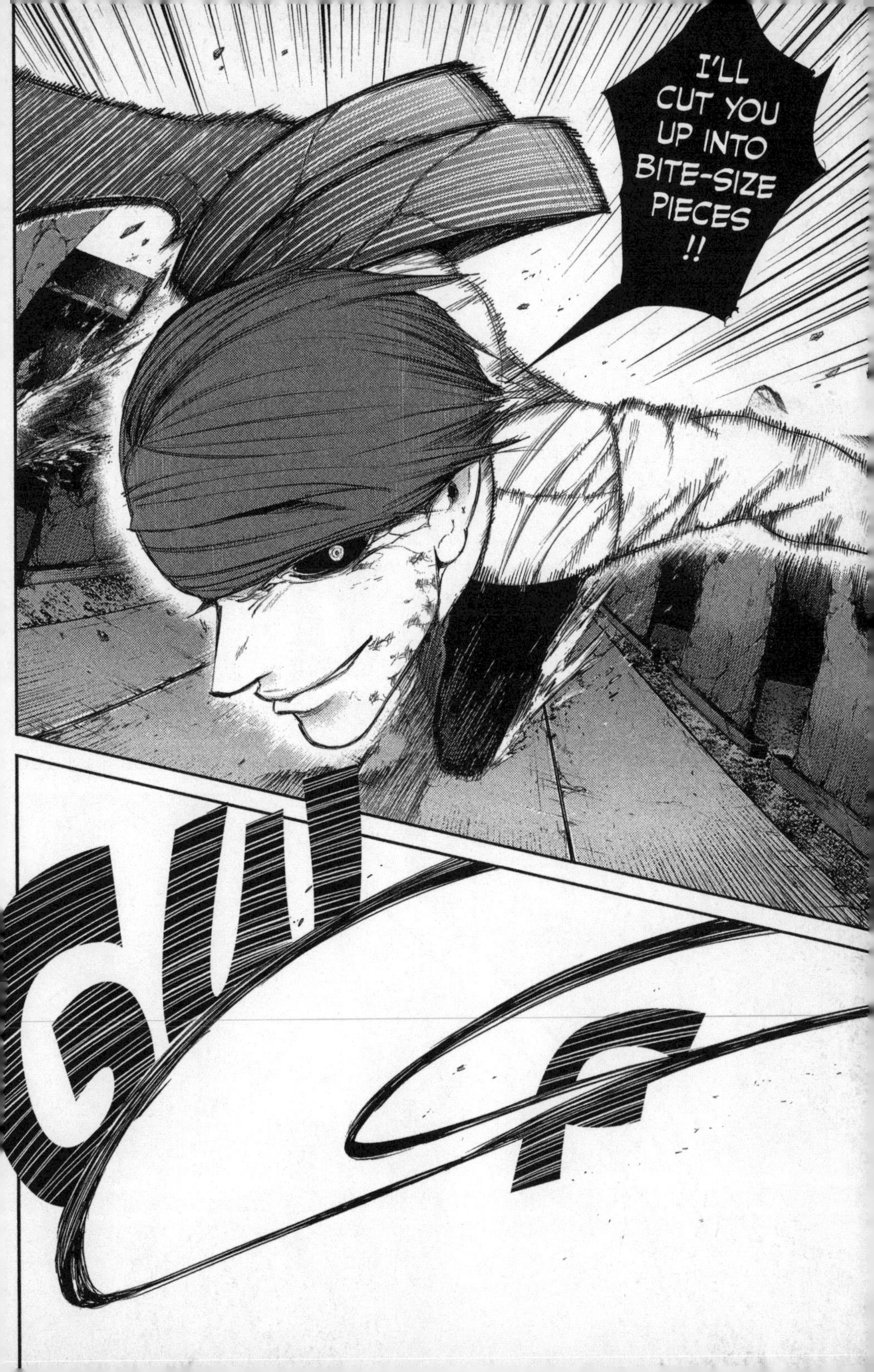
I'LL CUT YOU UP INTO BITE-SIZE PIECES !!

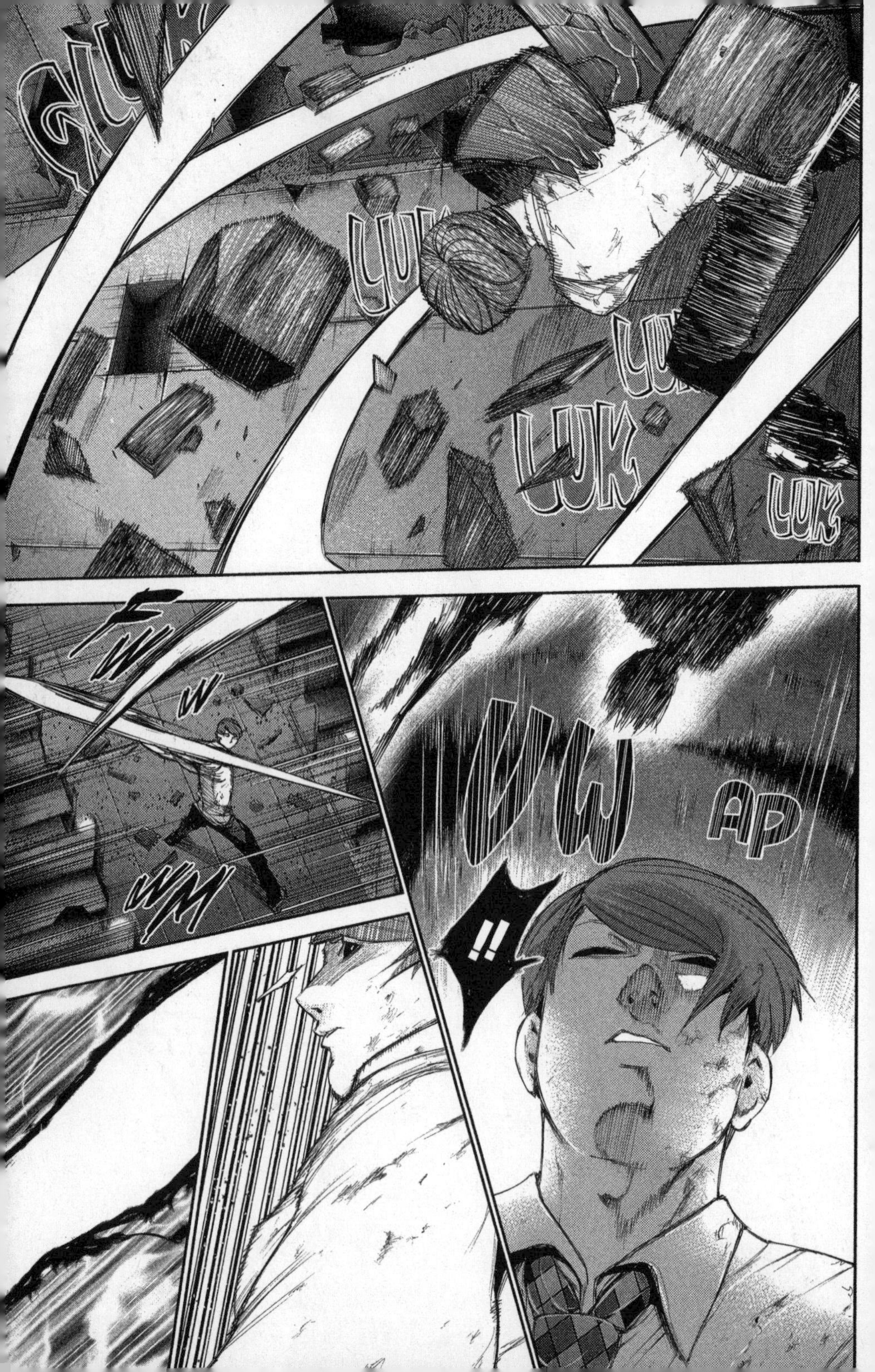
LUK
LUK
LUK
LUK
GLUK
UUW
AP
!!
FWW
WM

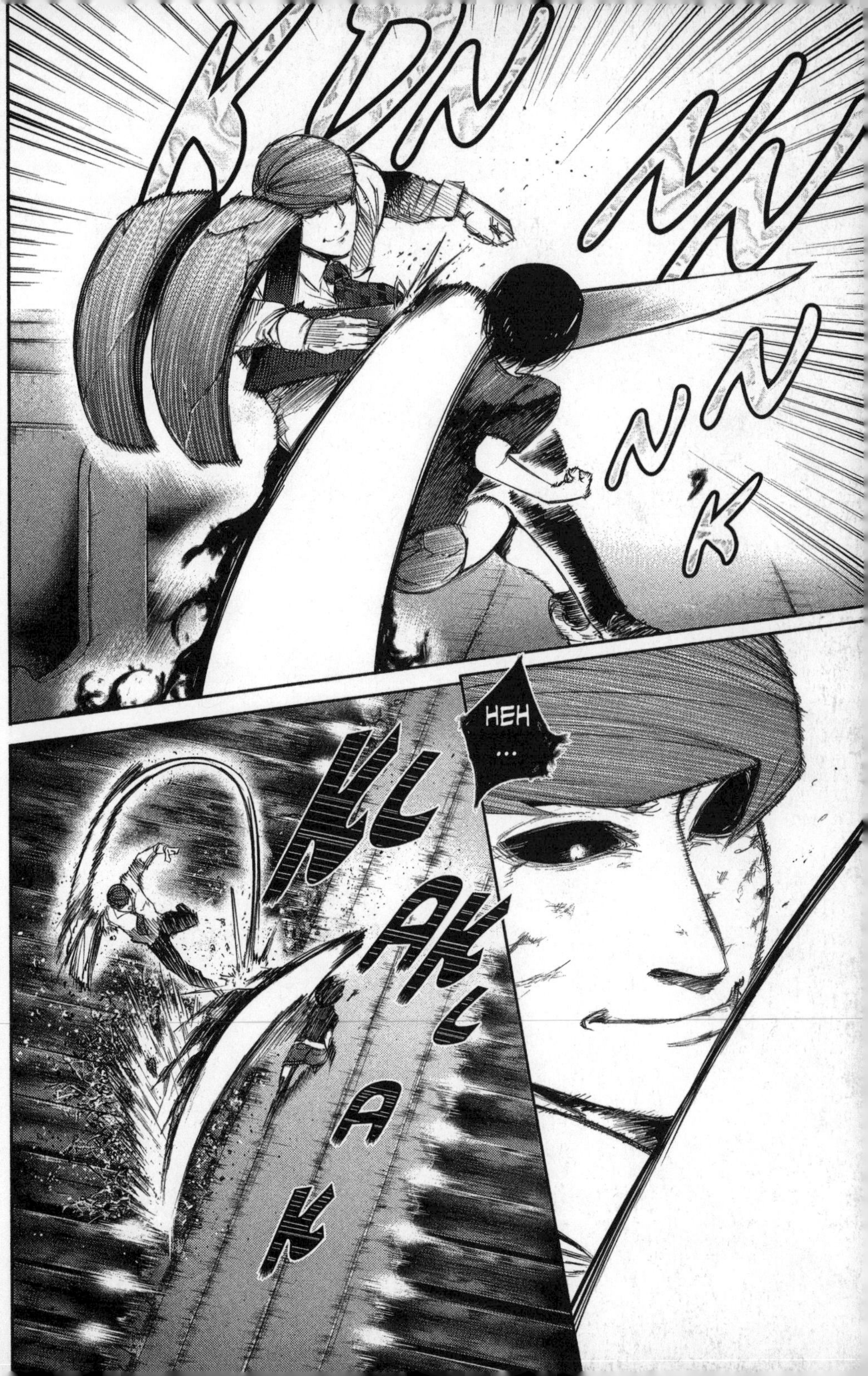
KDNNNNNNK
HEH...
KLAKLAK

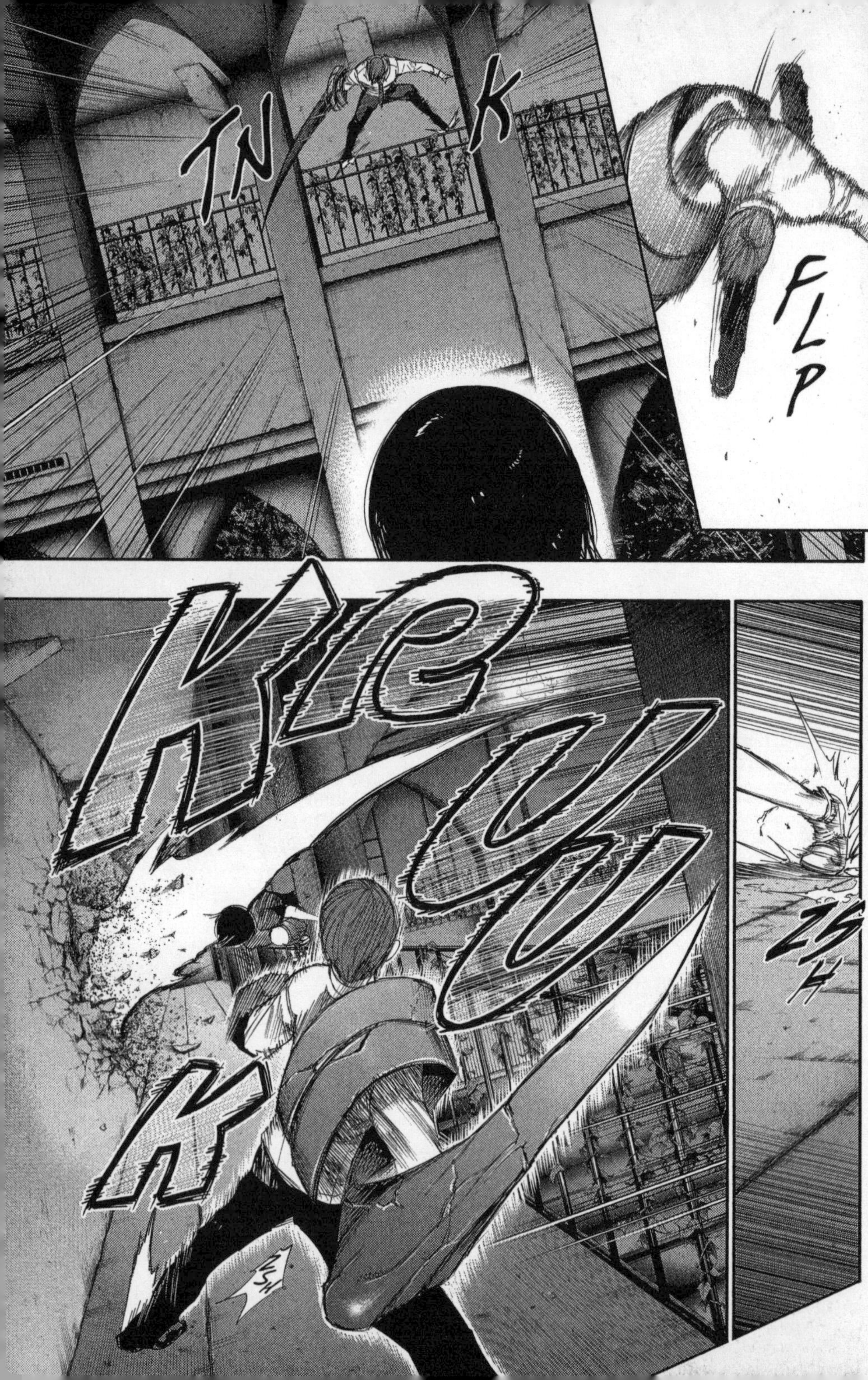
FLP
TNK
ZSH
KRCHUNK
WSH

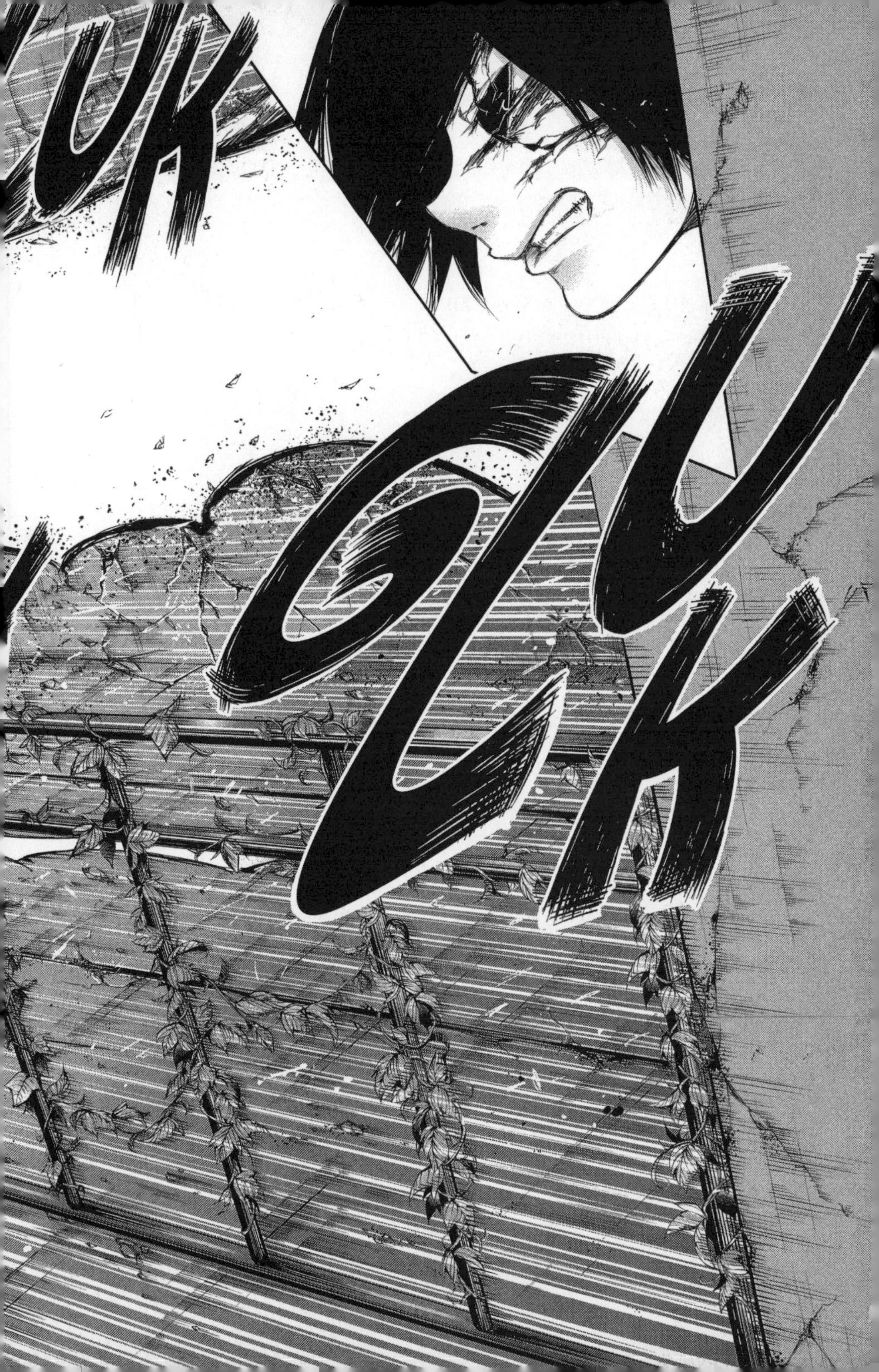
UK

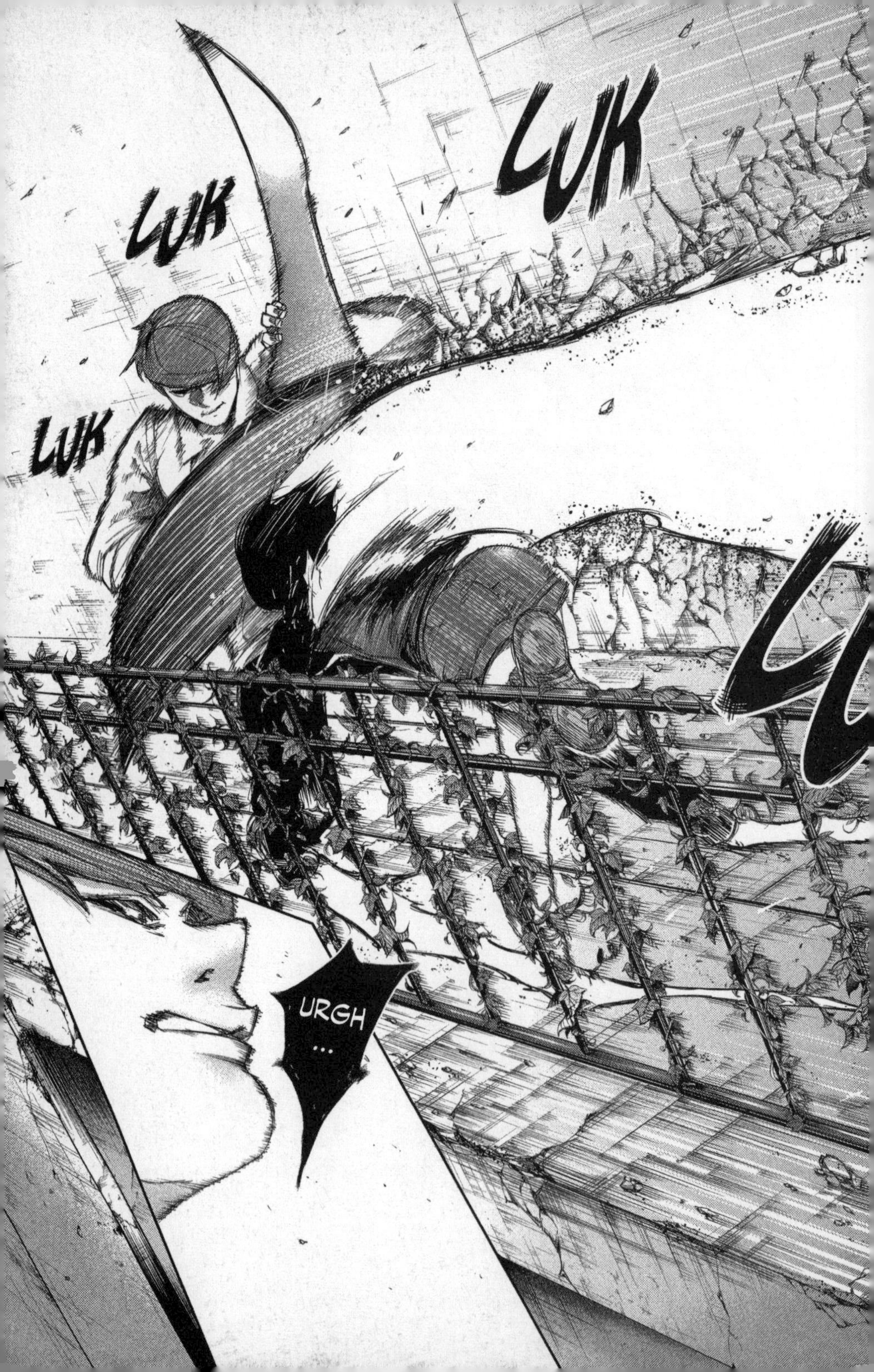
LUK
LUK
LUK
LU
URGH
...

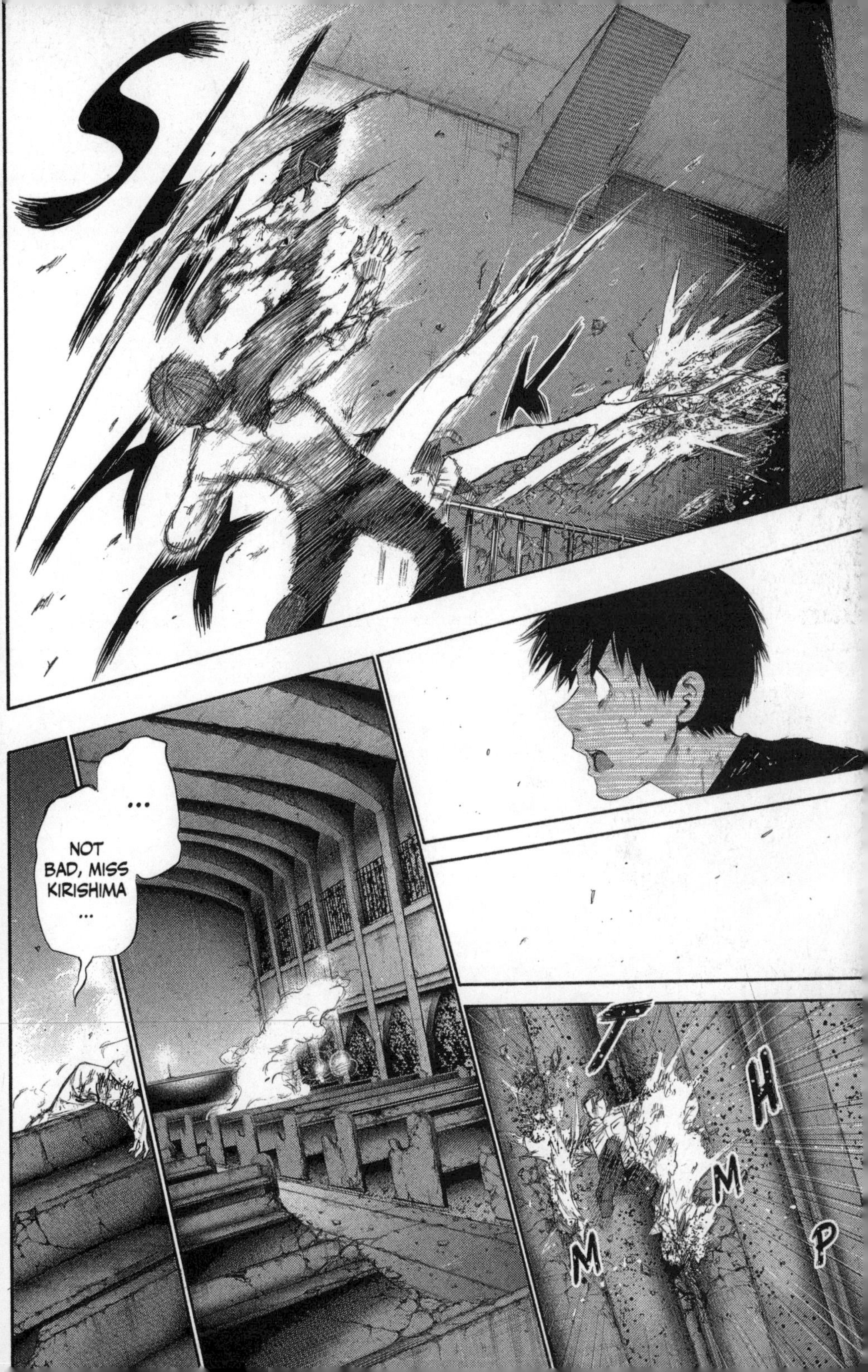

SHAKK
THMMP
...
NOT BAD, MISS KIRISHIMA ...

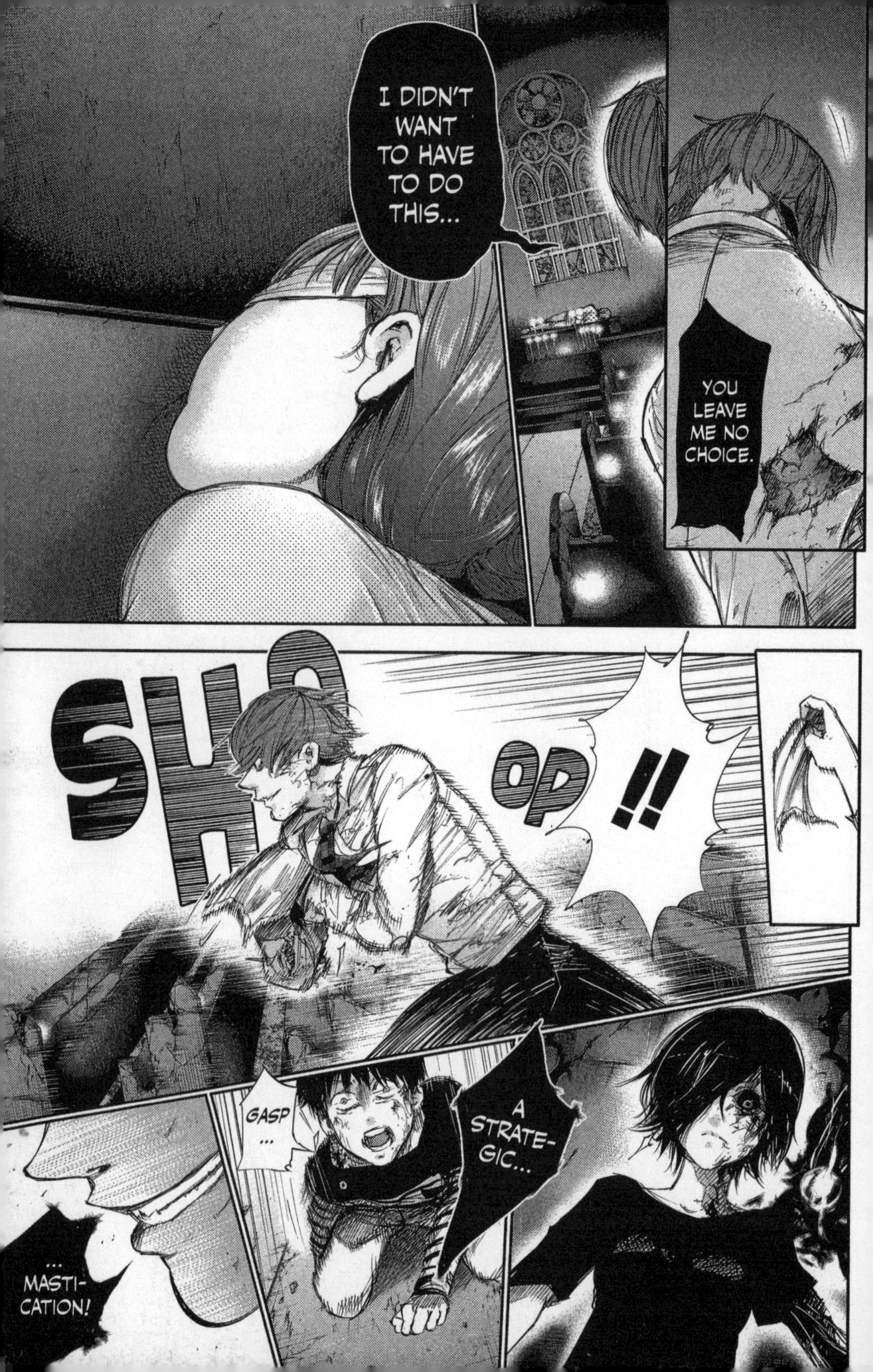
YOU LEAVE ME NO CHOICE.
I DIDN'T WANT TO HAVE TO DO THIS...
SHOOP!!
A STRATE-GIC...
GASP...
...MASTI-CATION!

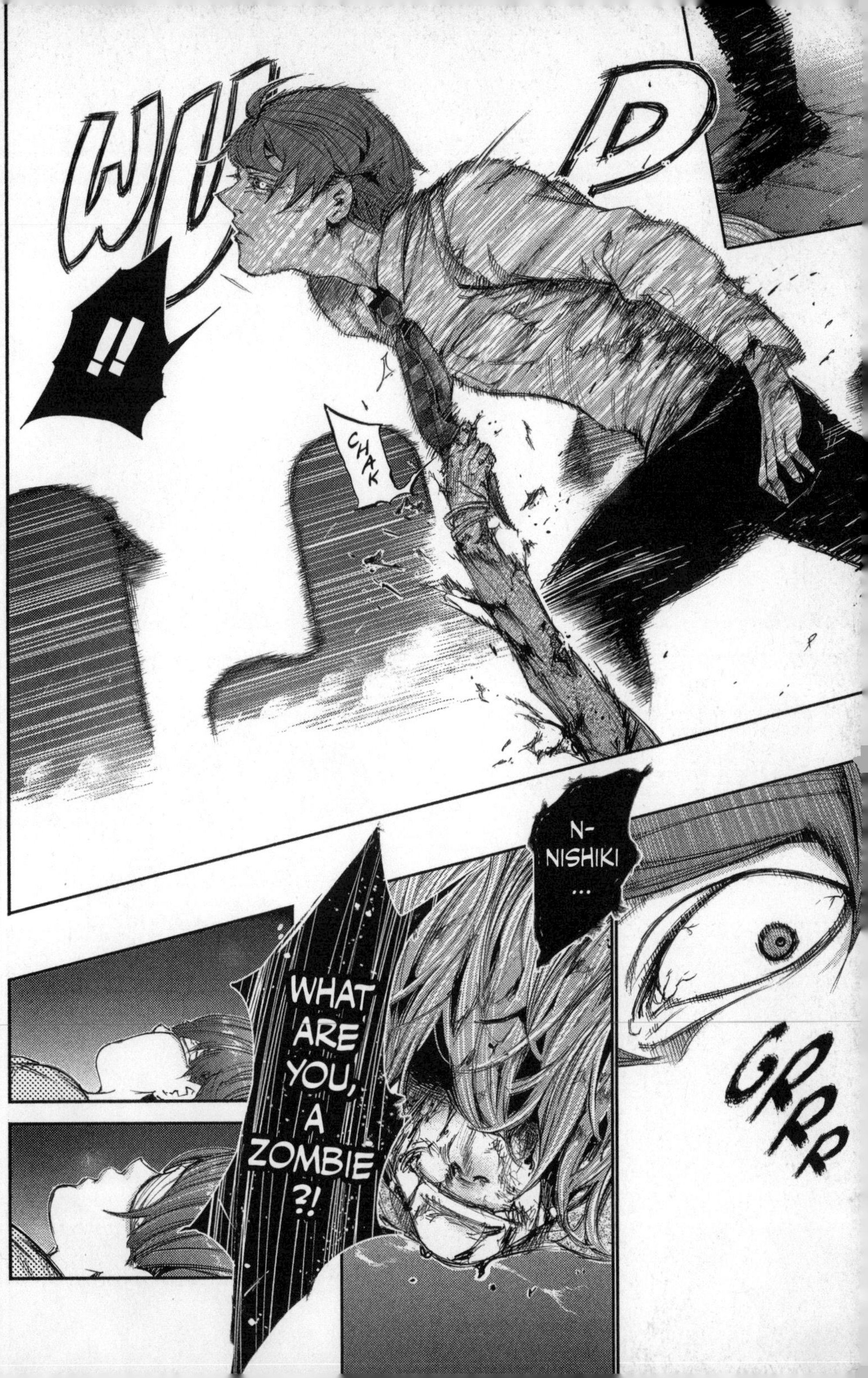
!!
CHAK
N-NISHIKI ...
GRRR
WHAT ARE YOU, A ZOMBIE ?!

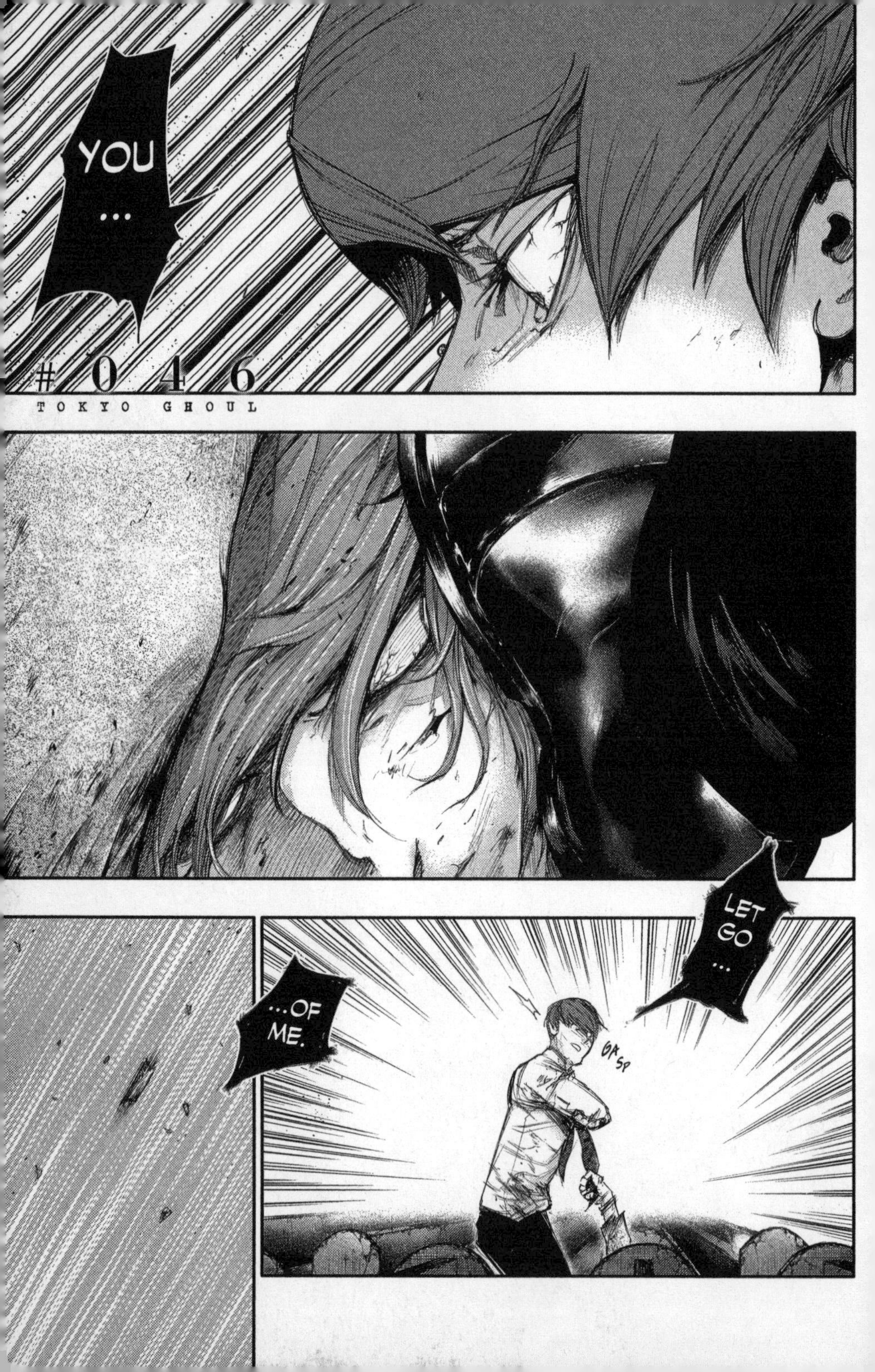
YOU ...
#046
TOKYO GHOUL
LET GO ...
...OF ME.
GASP

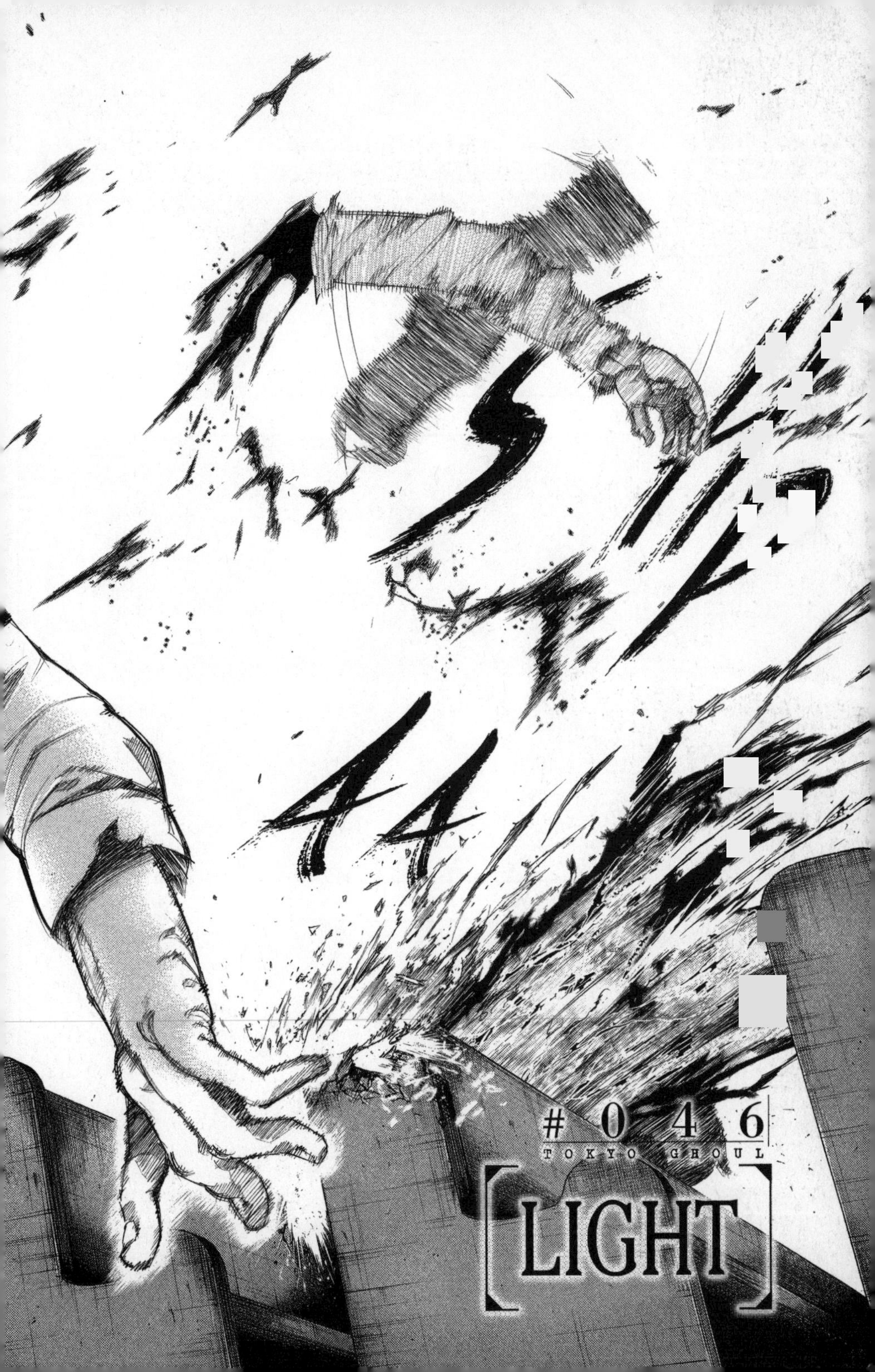

#046
TOKYO GHOUL
[LIGHT]

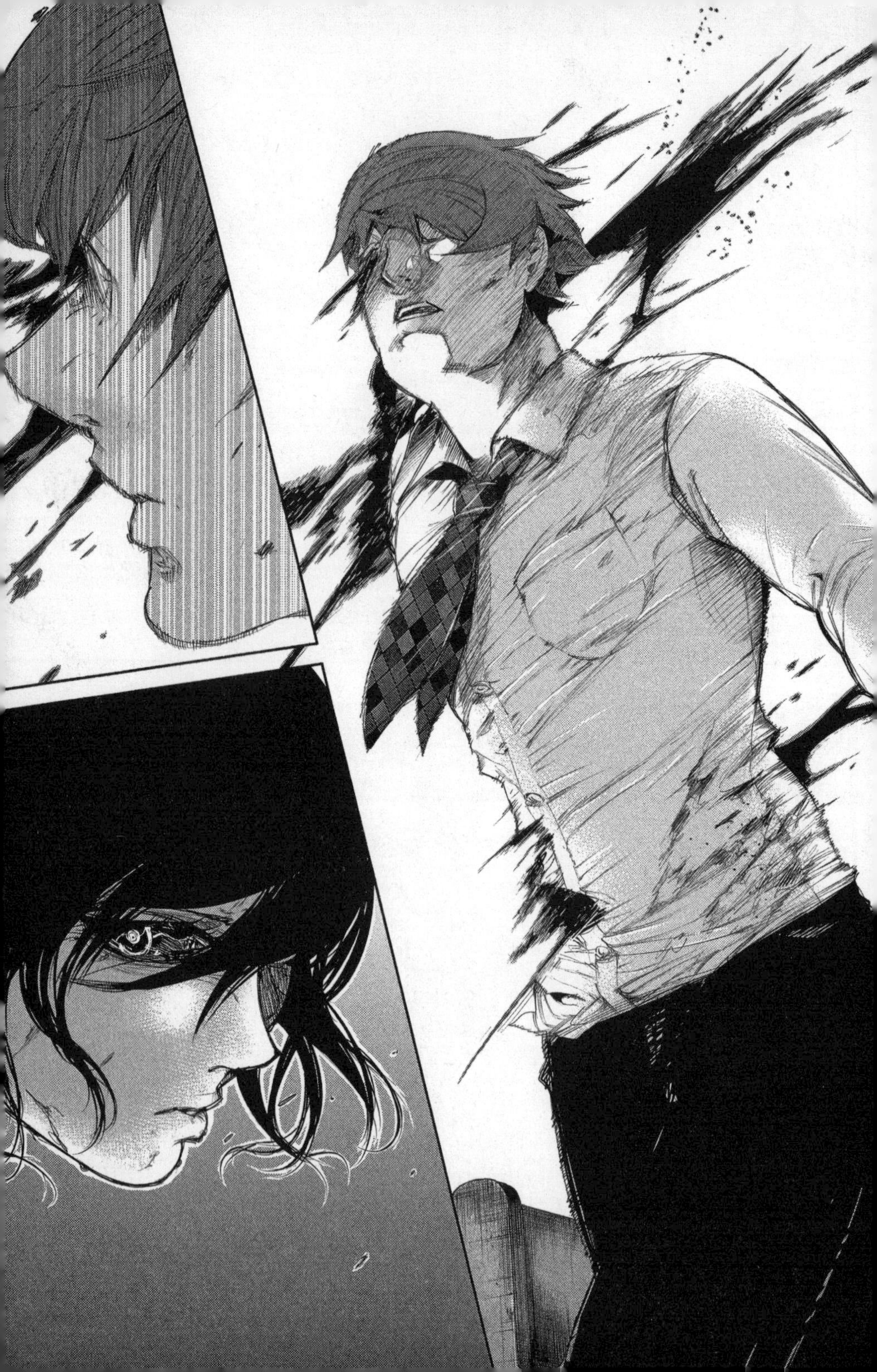

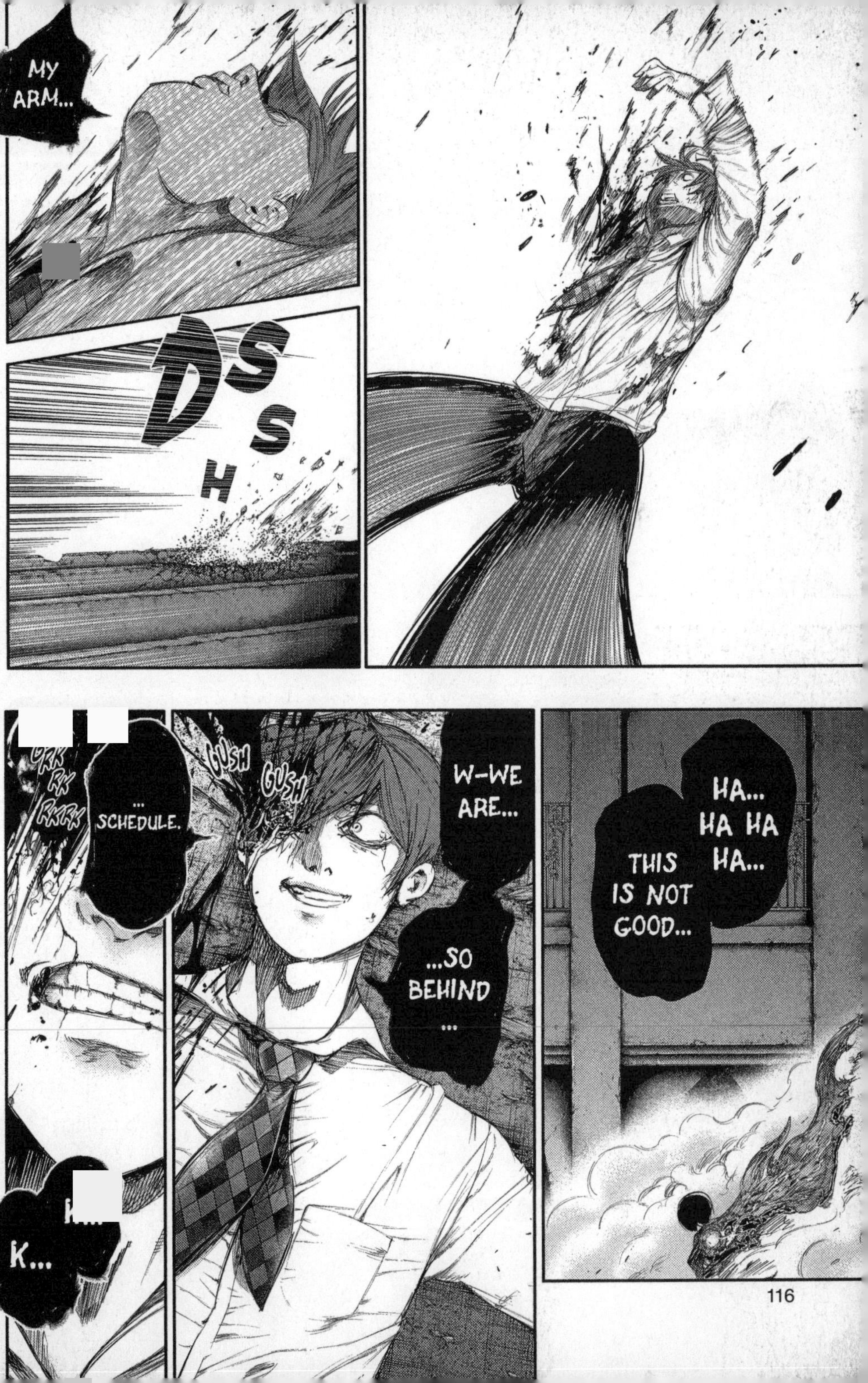
MY ARM...
DSSH
HA... HA HA HA...
THIS IS NOT GOOD...
W-WE ARE...
GUSH GUSH
...SO BEHIND ...
... SCHEDULE.
RK RKRK
K...

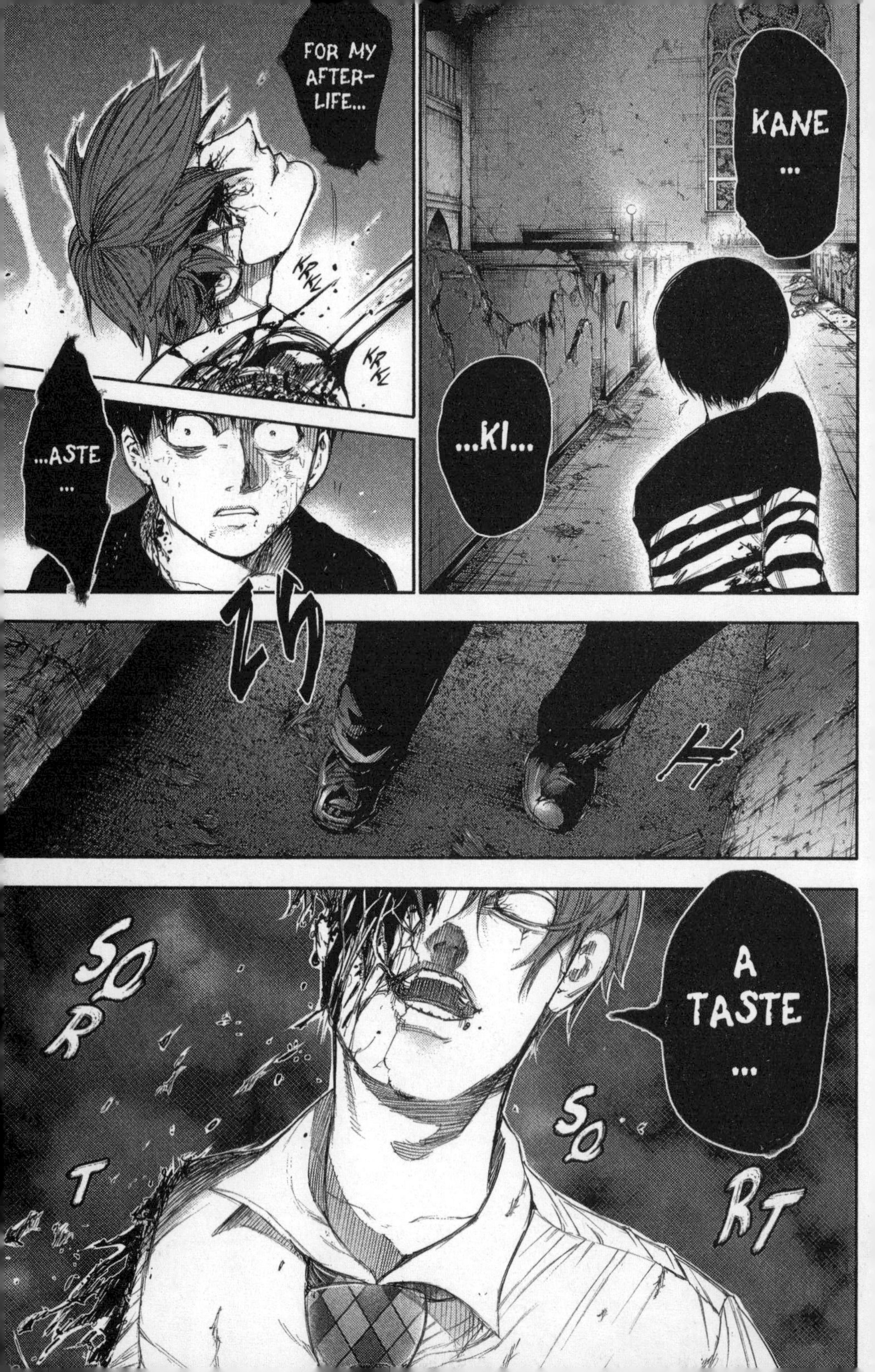
KANE ...
...KI...
FOR MY AFTER-LIFE...
...ASTE ...
A TASTE ...
SORT
SORT

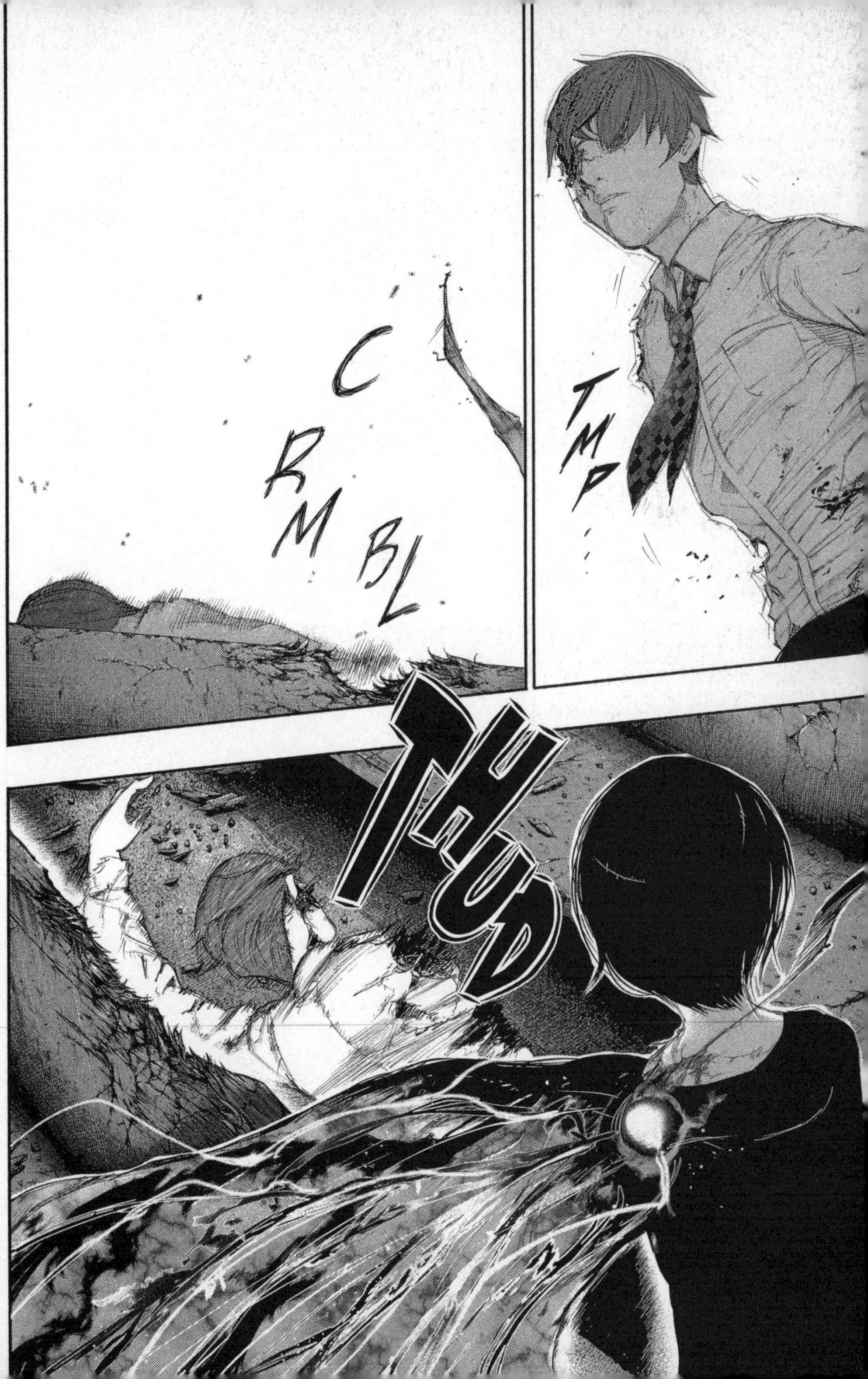
TMP
CRMBL
THUD

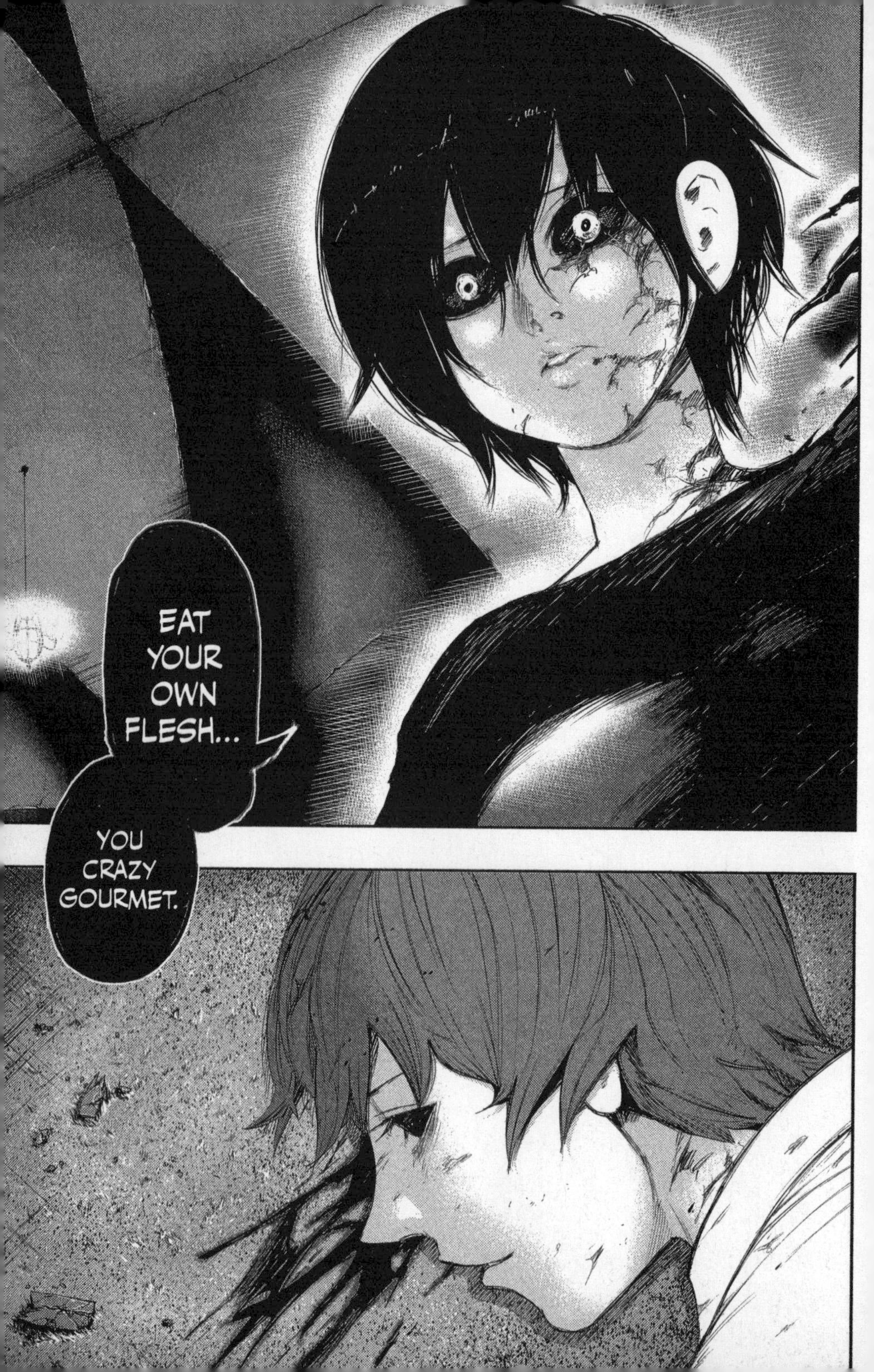
EAT YOUR OWN FLESH...
YOU CRAZY GOURMET.

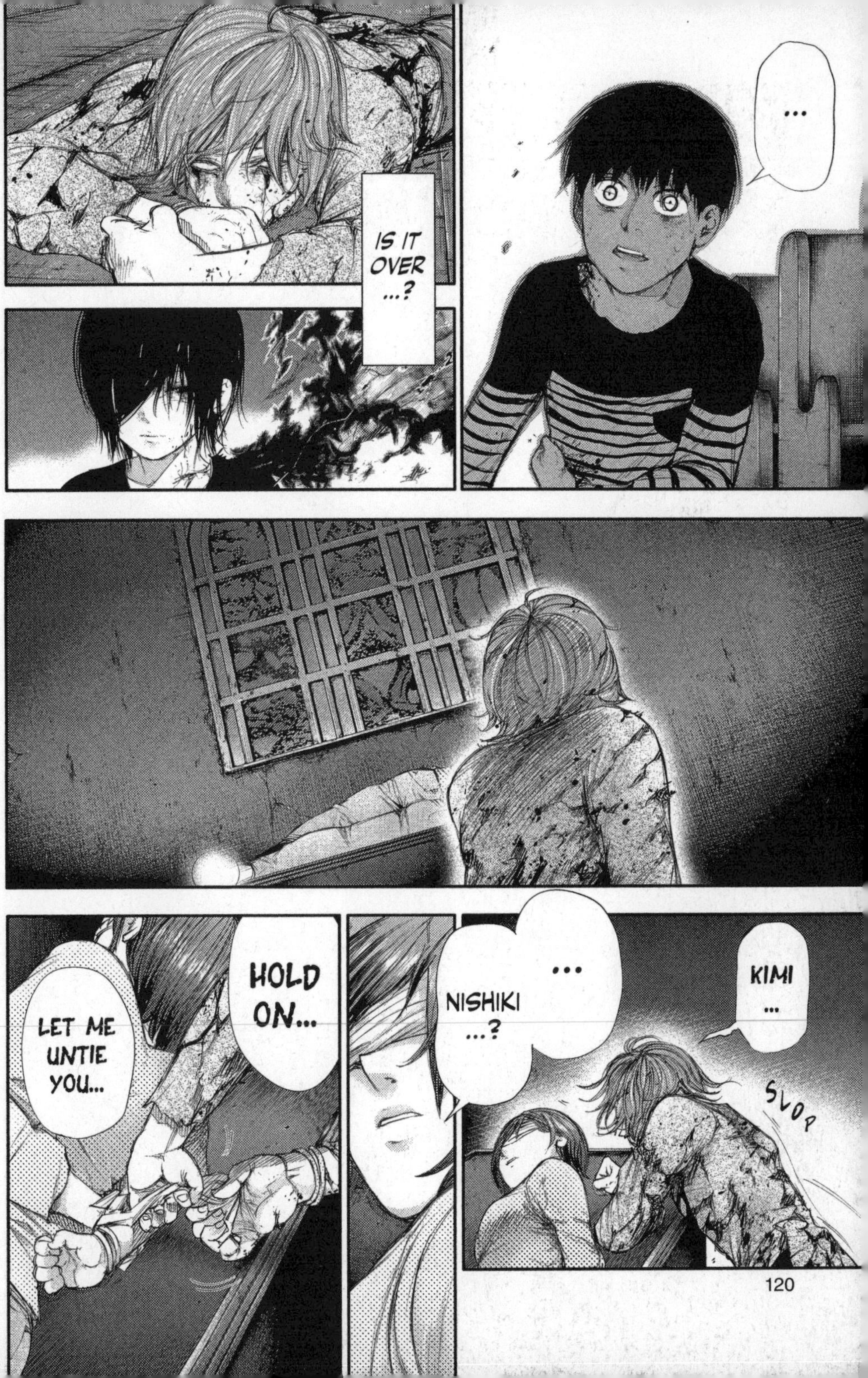
...
IS IT OVER ...?
KIMI ...
SLOP
...
NISHIKI ...?
HOLD ON...
LET ME UNTIE YOU...

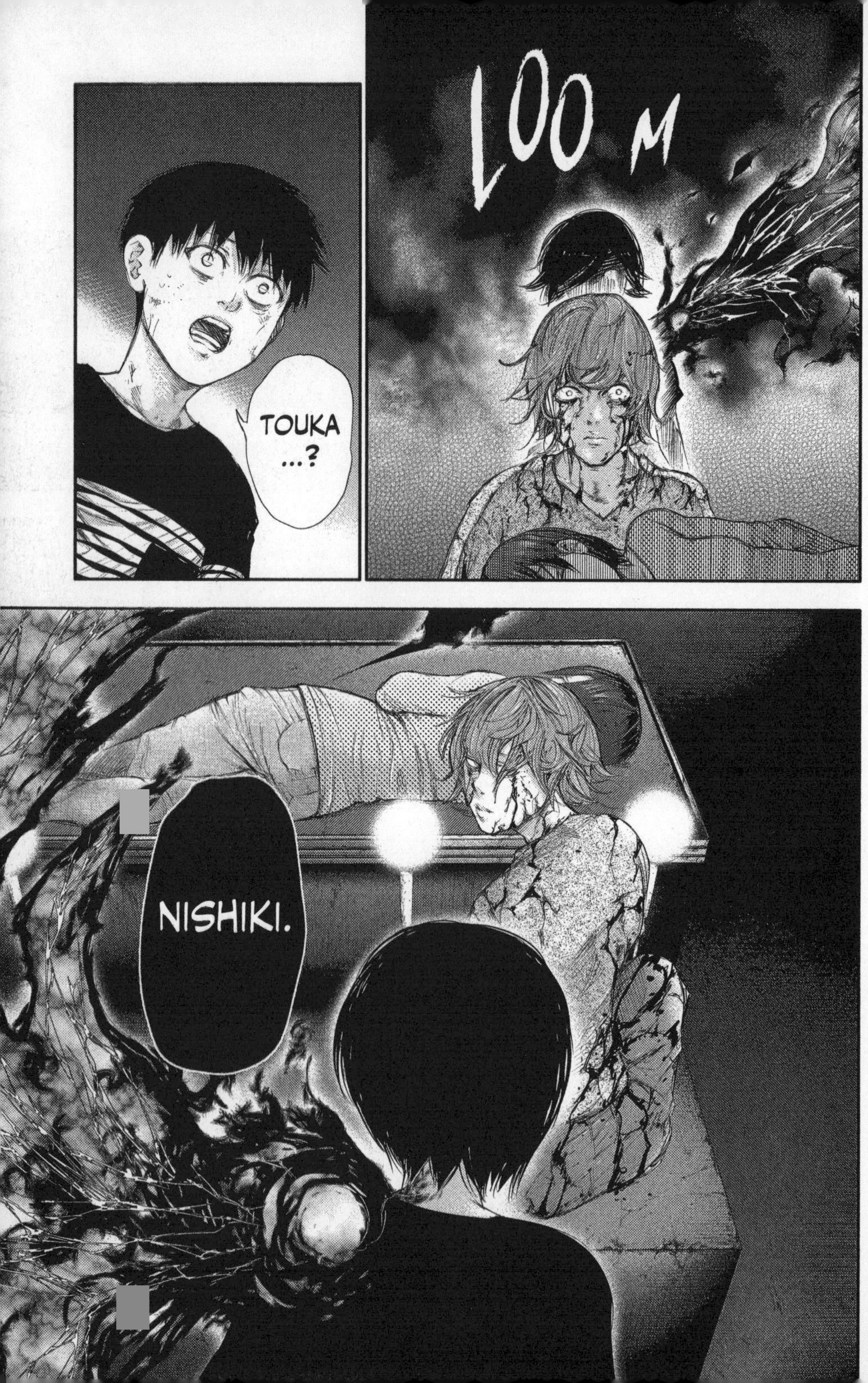
LOOM
TOUKA ...?
NISHIKI.

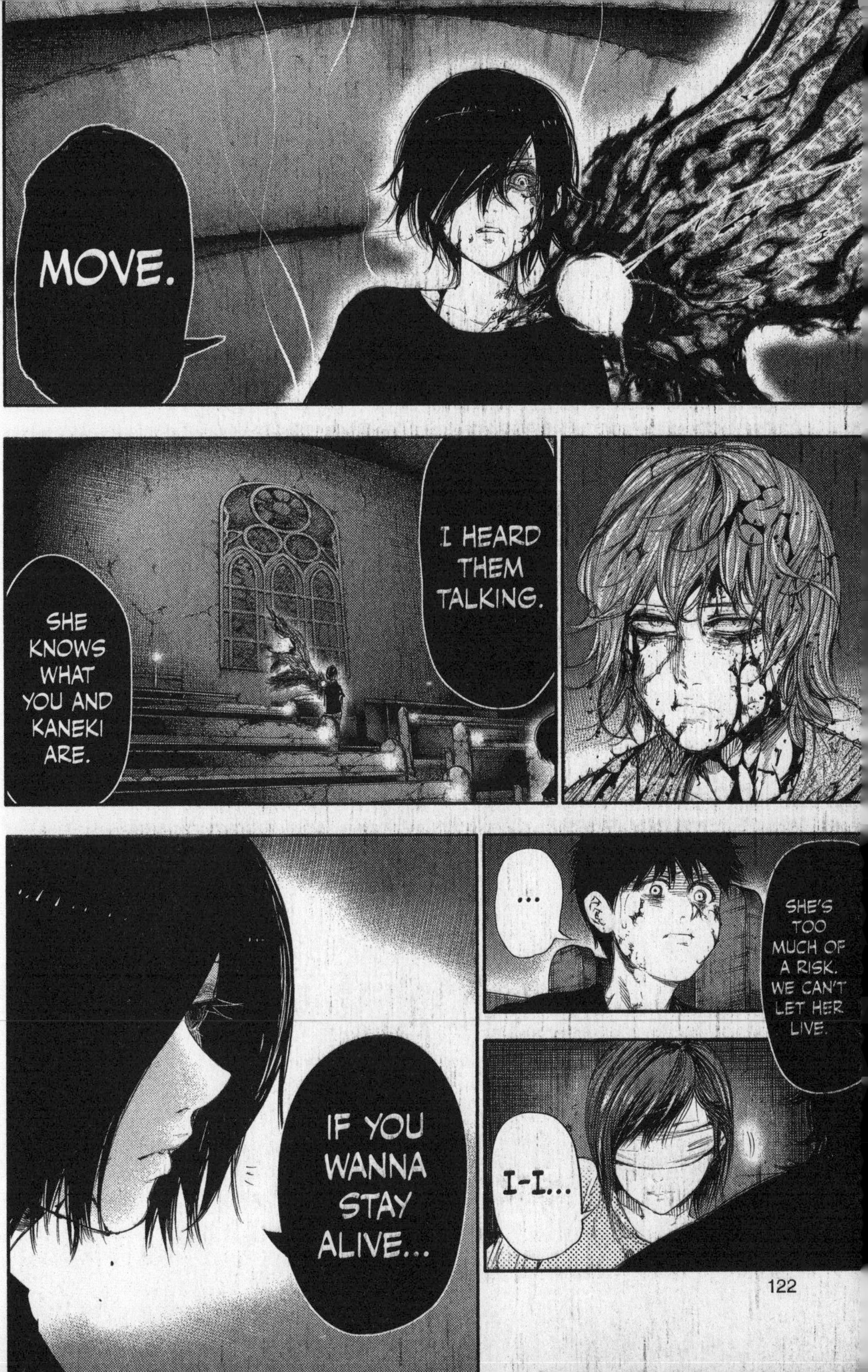
MOVE.
I HEARD THEM TALKING.
SHE KNOWS WHAT YOU AND KANEKI ARE.
SHE'S TOO MUCH OF A RISK. WE CAN'T LET HER LIVE.
...
I-I...
IF YOU WANNA STAY ALIVE...

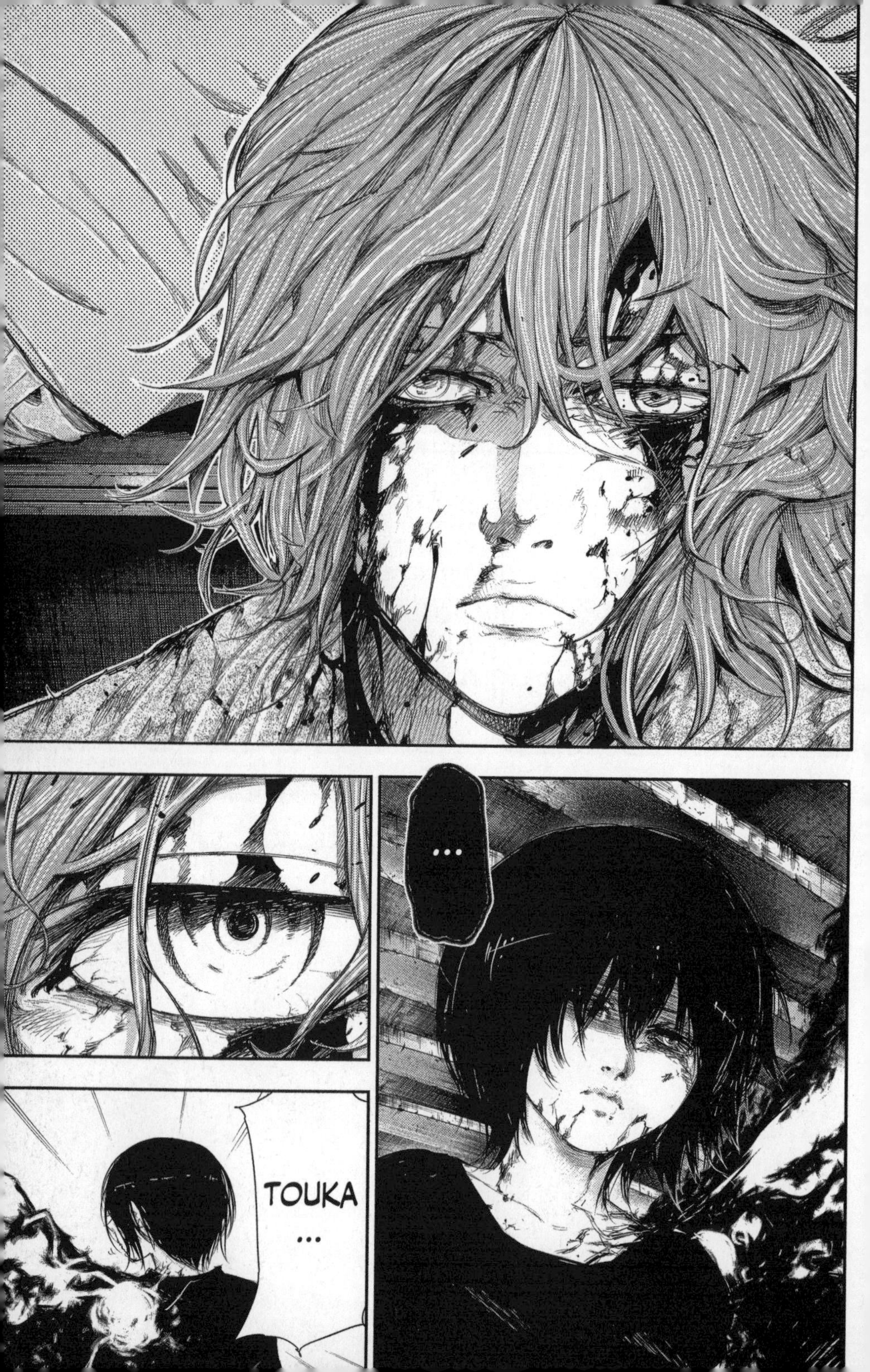
...
TOUKA
...

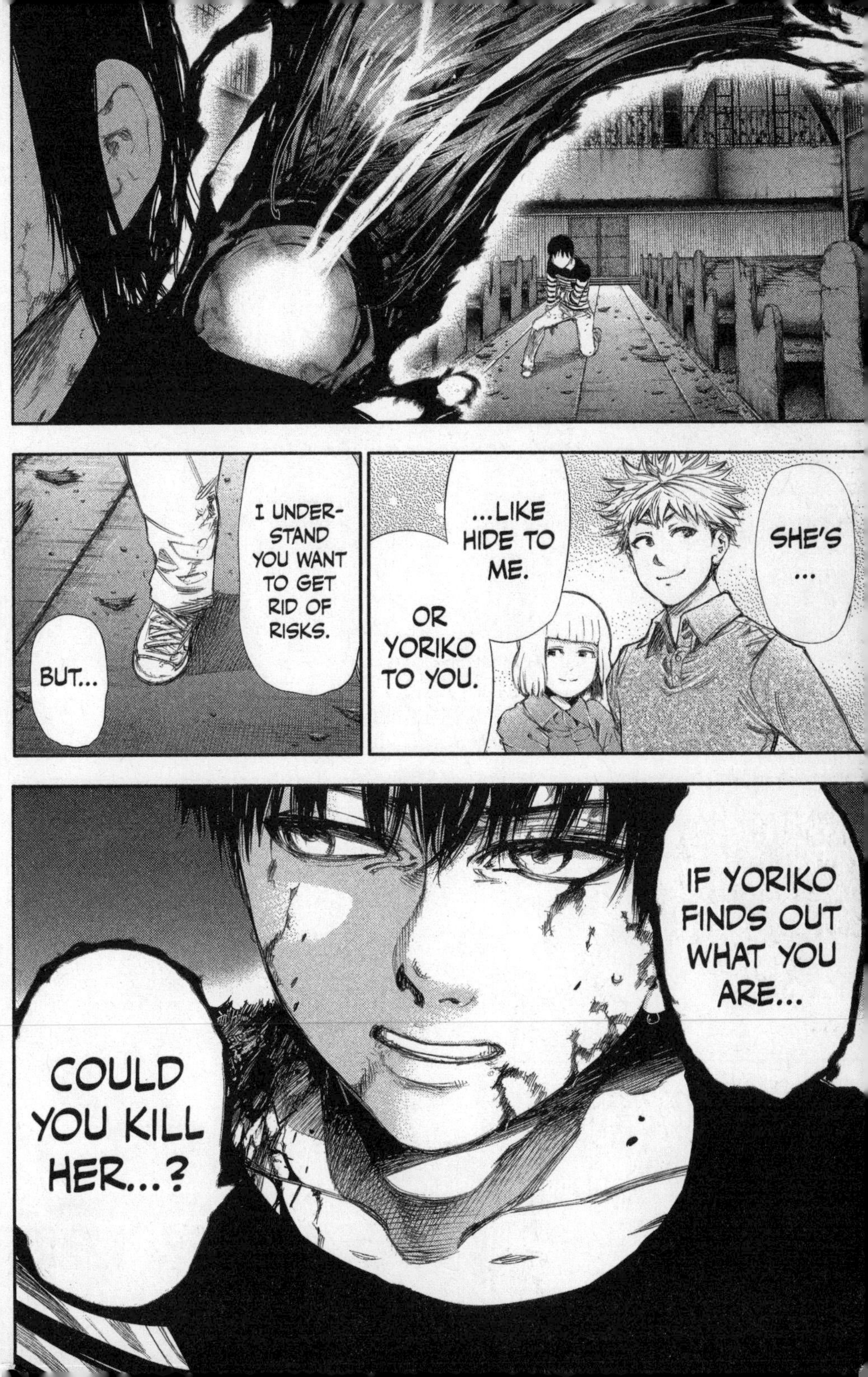
SHE'S ...
...LIKE HIDE TO ME.
OR YORIKO TO YOU.
I UNDER-STAND YOU WANT TO GET RID OF RISKS.
BUT...
IF YORIKO FINDS OUT WHAT YOU ARE...
COULD YOU KILL HER...?

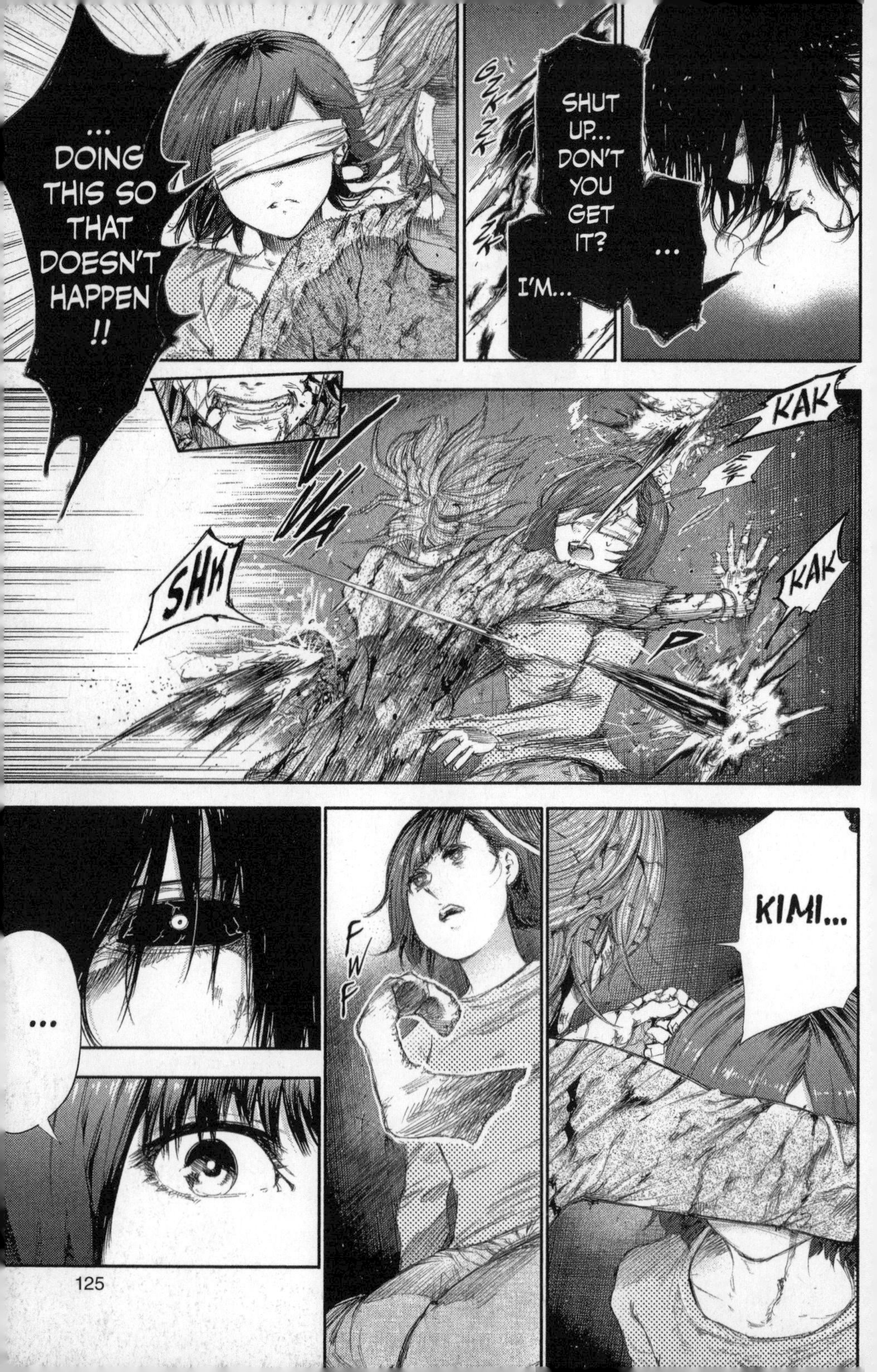
...
SHUT UP... DON'T YOU GET IT?
I'M...
... DOING THIS SO THAT DOESN'T HAPPEN !!
KAK
KAK
SHK
KIMI...
FWF
...

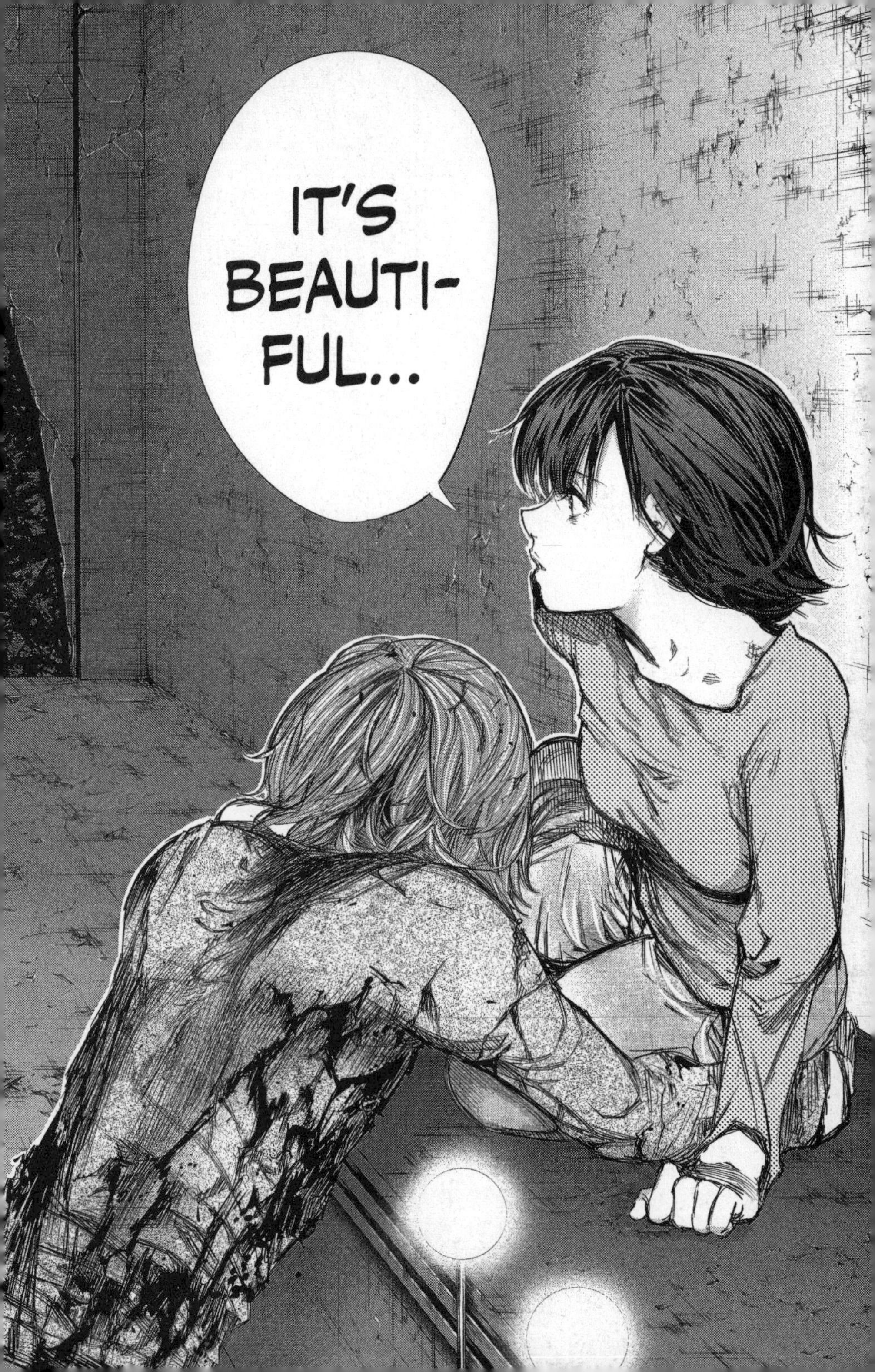
IT'S BEAUTI-FUL...

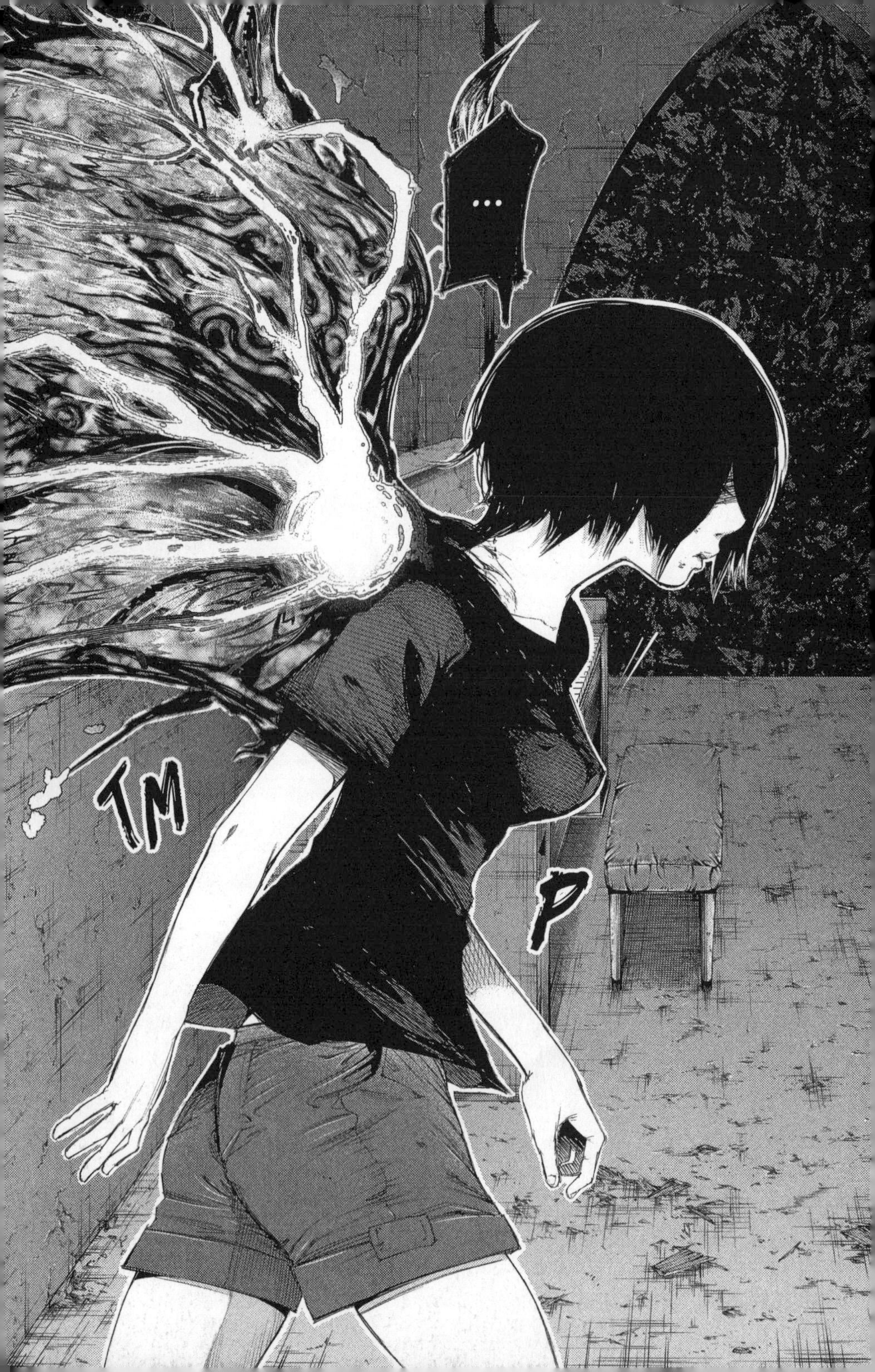
...
TMP

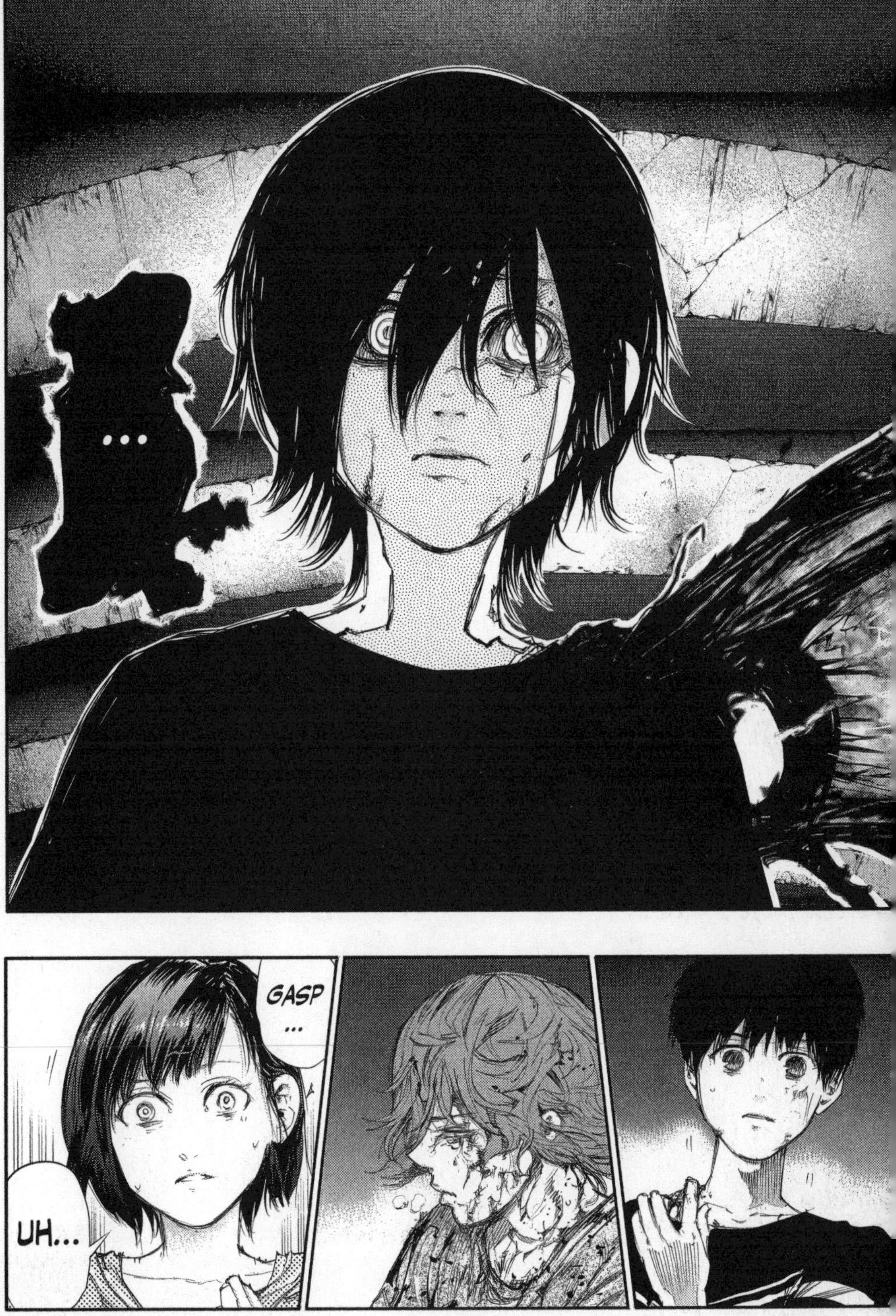
...
GASP ...
UH...

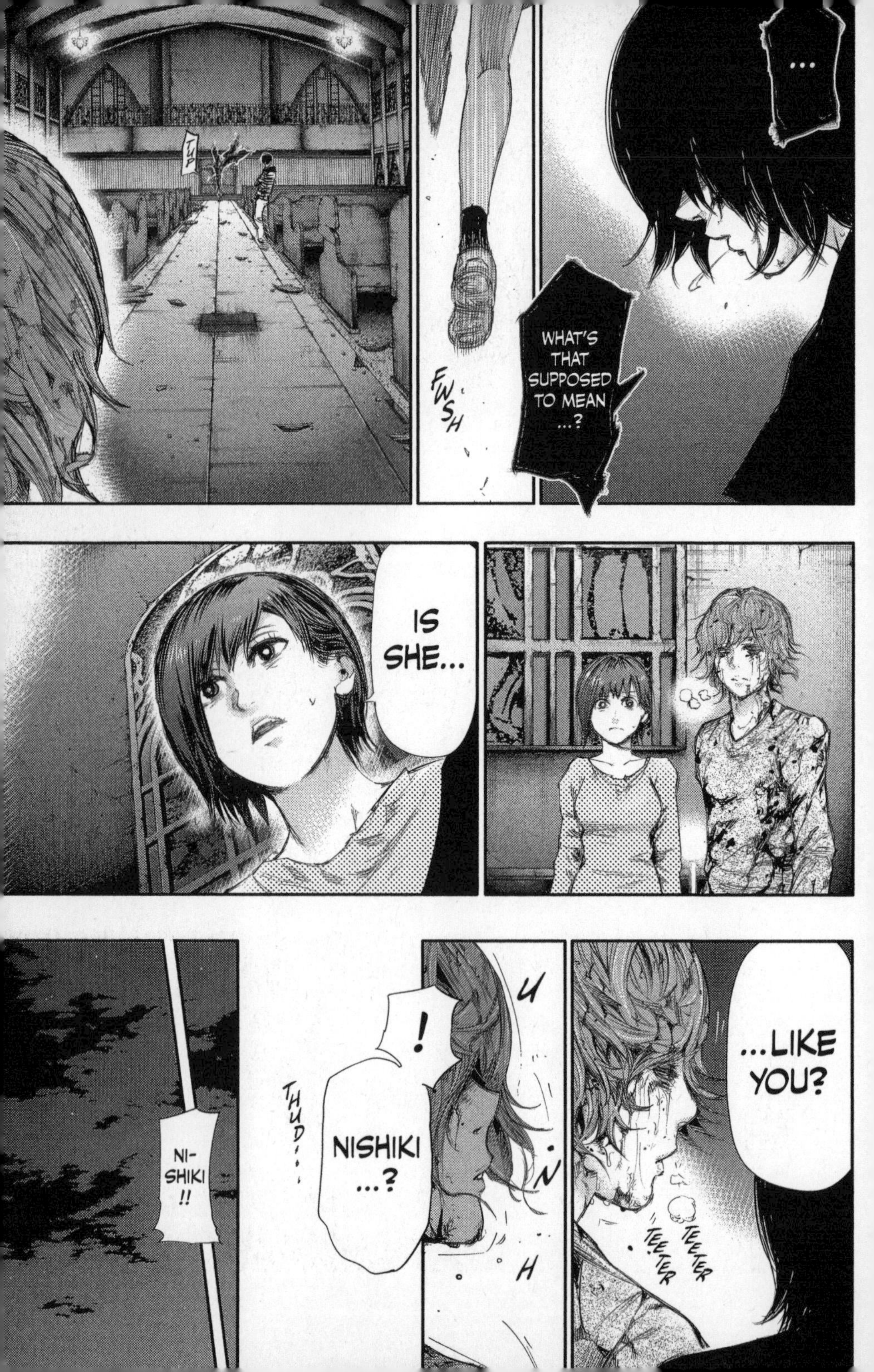
...
WHAT'S THAT SUPPOSED TO MEAN ...?
FWSH
TUP
IS SHE...
...LIKE YOU?
TEETER TEETER
UNNH
!
NISHIKI ...?
THUD
NI-SHIKI !!

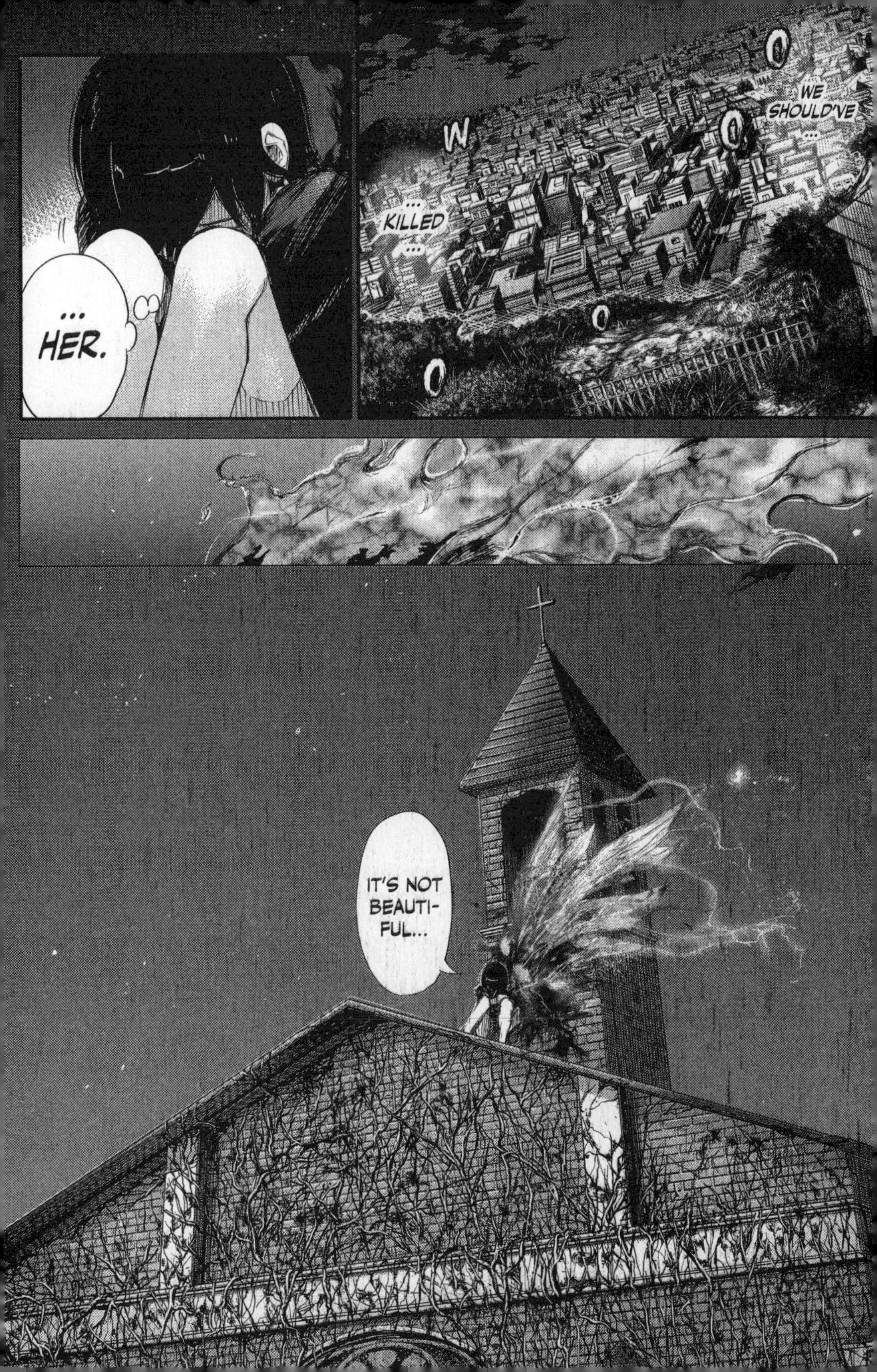
WE SHOULD'VE ...
WOOOO
... KILLED ...
... HER.
IT'S NOT BEAUTI- FUL...

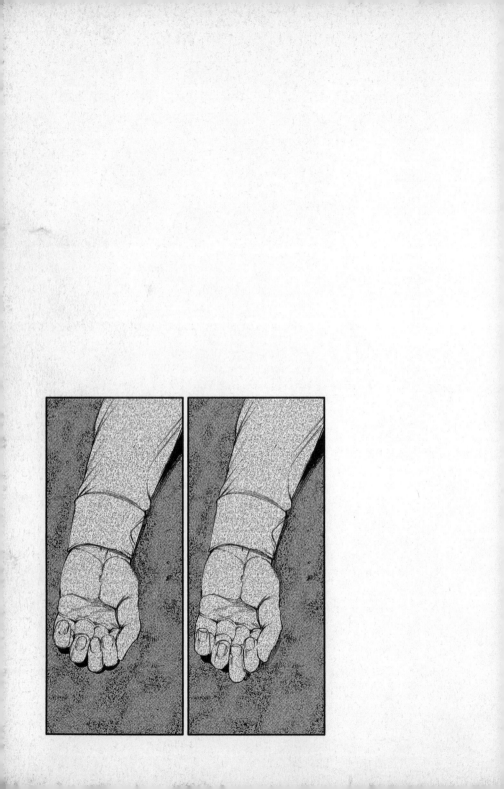

"I am Rize. I appear human. My staple
food is also...human."

Rize the Binge Eater arrives in the 20th Ward.

Where was she and what was she doing
before meeting Kaneki in #001?

Why did she choose the 20th Ward?

Rize Kamishiro was bored.

A short prologue tracing back six
months from that fateful day.

Taking place in...the 11th Ward.

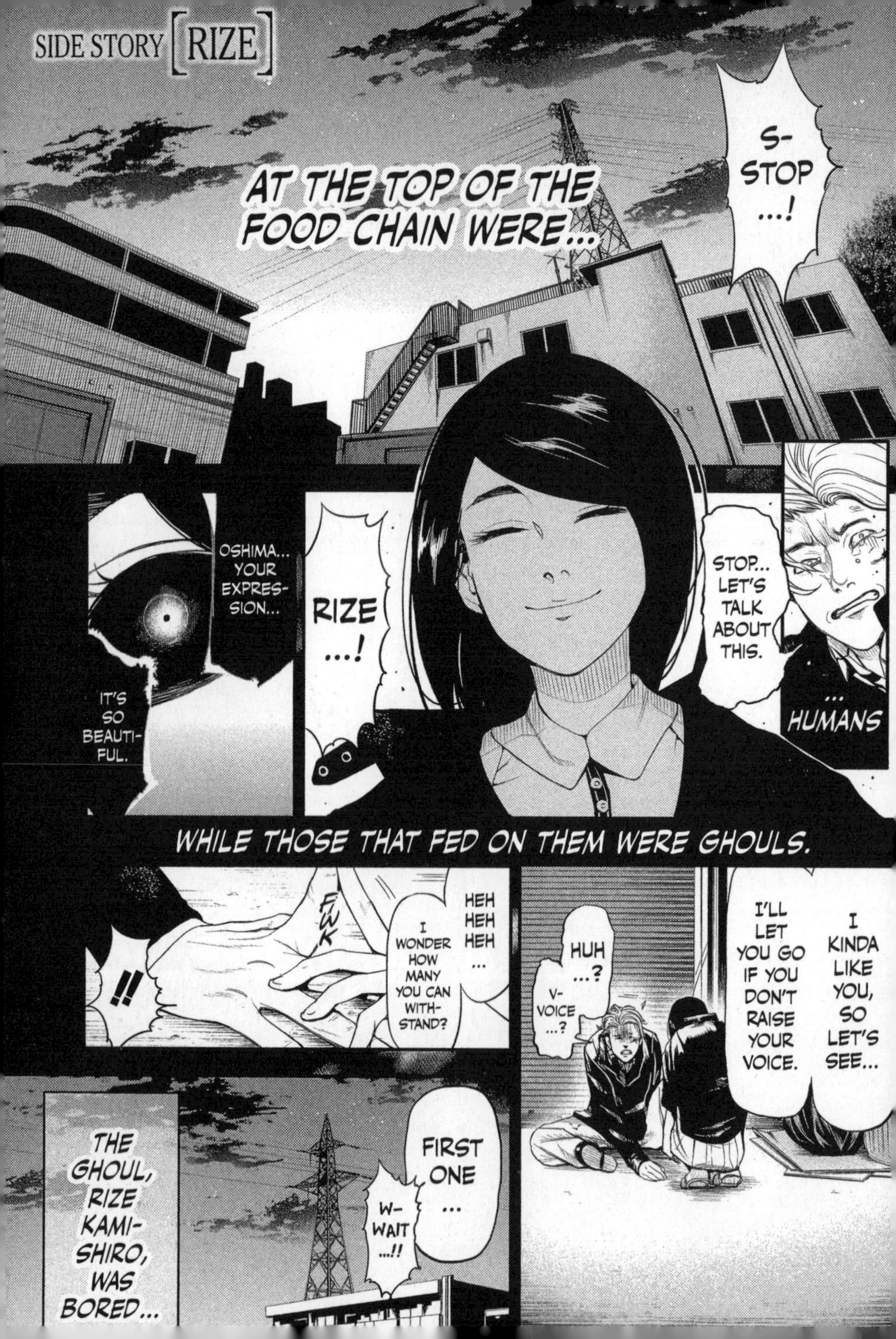
SIDE STORY [RIZE]
S-STOP...!
AT THE TOP OF THE FOOD CHAIN WERE...
STOP... LET'S TALK ABOUT THIS.
...HUMANS
RIZE...!
OSHIMA... YOUR EXPRESSION...
IT'S SO BEAUTIFUL.
WHILE THOSE THAT FED ON THEM WERE GHOULS.
I KINDA LIKE YOU, SO LET'S SEE...
I'LL LET YOU GO IF YOU DON'T RAISE YOUR VOICE.
HUH...?
V-VOICE...?
HEH HEH HEH...
I WONDER HOW MANY YOU CAN WITHSTAND?
FWK
!!
FIRST ONE...
W-WAIT...!!
THE GHOUL, RIZE KAMISHIRO, WAS BORED...

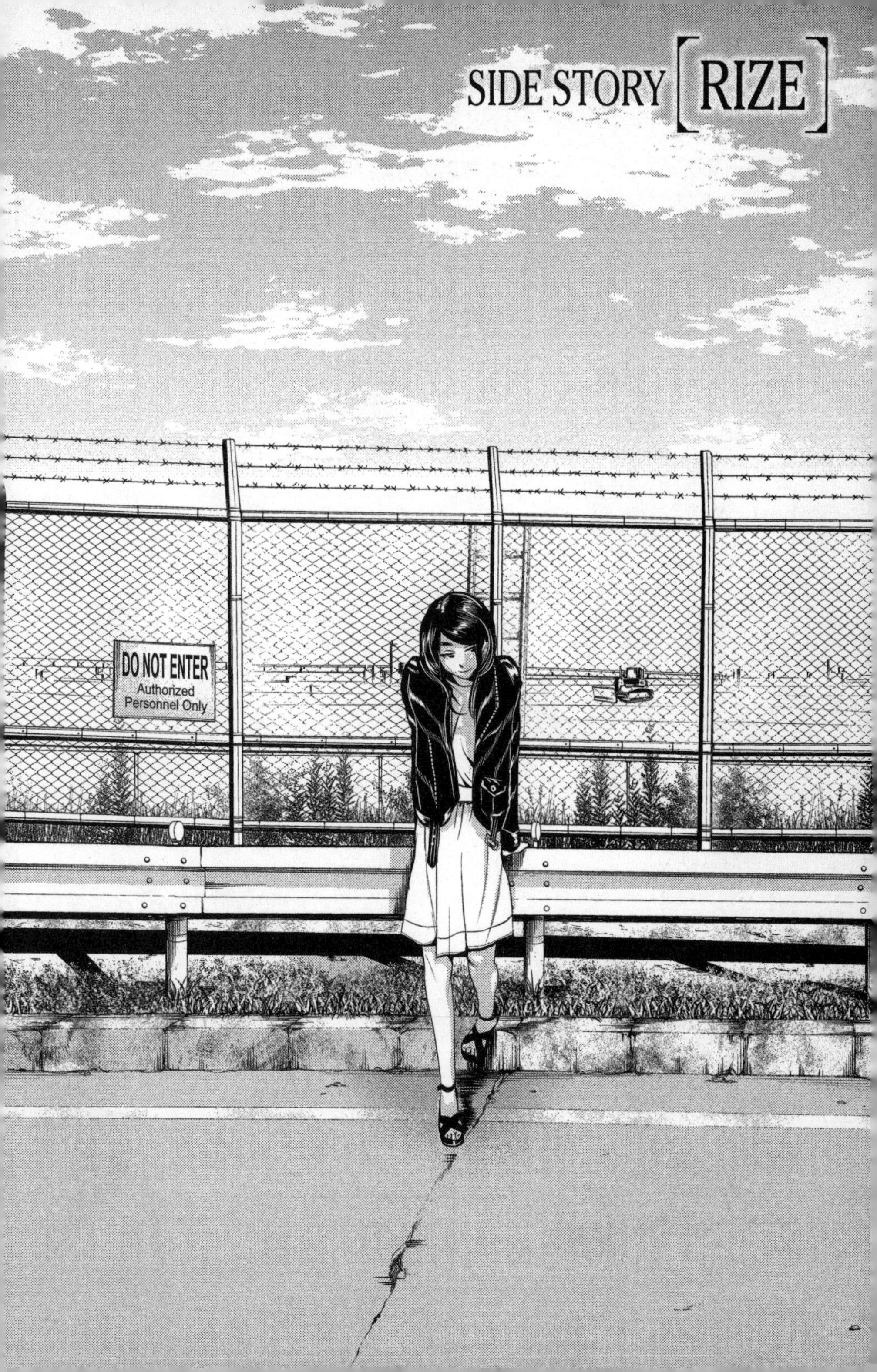
SIDE STORY [RIZE]
DO NOT ENTER
Authorized
Personnel Only

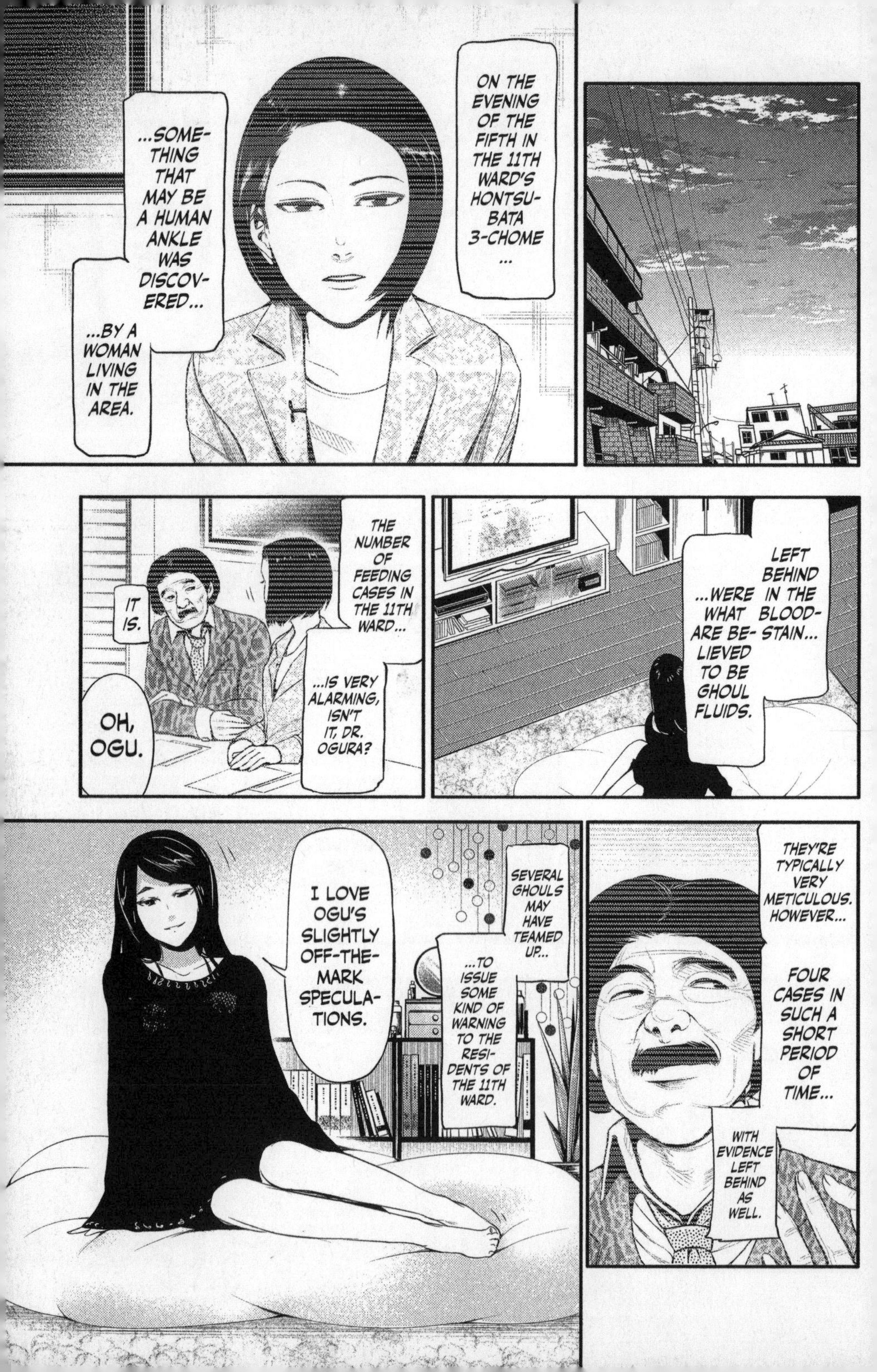
ON THE EVENING OF THE FIFTH IN THE 11TH WARD'S HONTSUBATA 3-CHOME...
...SOMETHING THAT MAY BE A HUMAN ANKLE WAS DISCOVERED...
...BY A WOMAN LIVING IN THE AREA.
LEFT BEHIND IN THE BLOODSTAIN...
...WERE WHAT ARE BELIEVED TO BE GHOUL FLUIDS.
THE NUMBER OF FEEDING CASES IN THE 11TH WARD...
...IS VERY ALARMING, ISN'T IT, DR. OGURA?
IT IS.
OH, OGU.
THEY'RE TYPICALLY VERY METICULOUS. HOWEVER...
FOUR CASES IN SUCH A SHORT PERIOD OF TIME...
WITH EVIDENCE LEFT BEHIND AS WELL.
SEVERAL GHOULS MAY HAVE TEAMED UP...
...TO ISSUE SOME KIND OF WARNING TO THE RESIDENTS OF THE 11TH WARD.
I LOVE OGU'S SLIGHTLY OFF-THE-MARK SPECULATIONS.

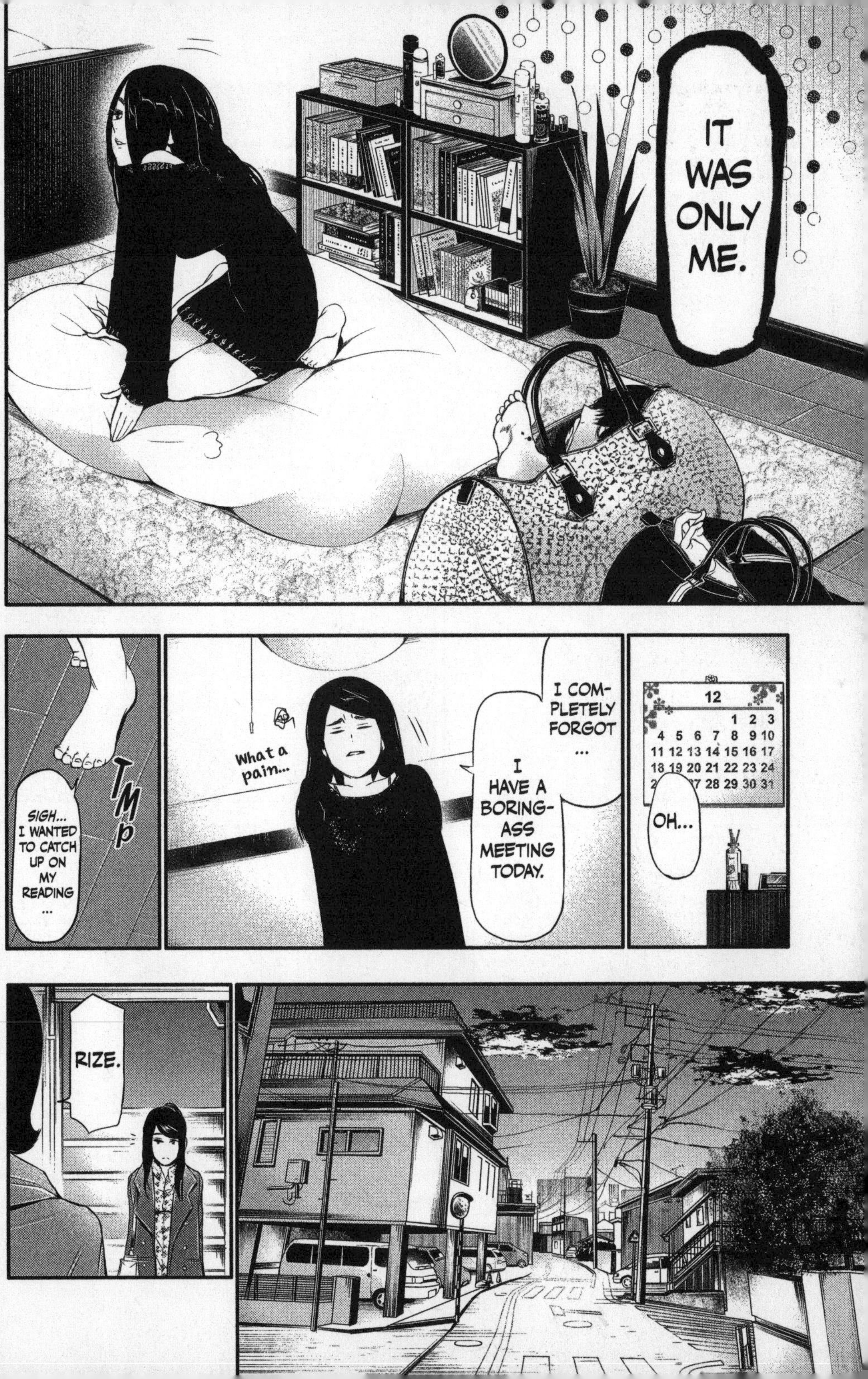
IT WAS ONLY ME.
12
OH...
I COMPLETELY FORGOT...
I HAVE A BORING-ASS MEETING TODAY.
What a pain...
TMP
SIGH... I WANTED TO CATCH UP ON MY READING...
RIZE.

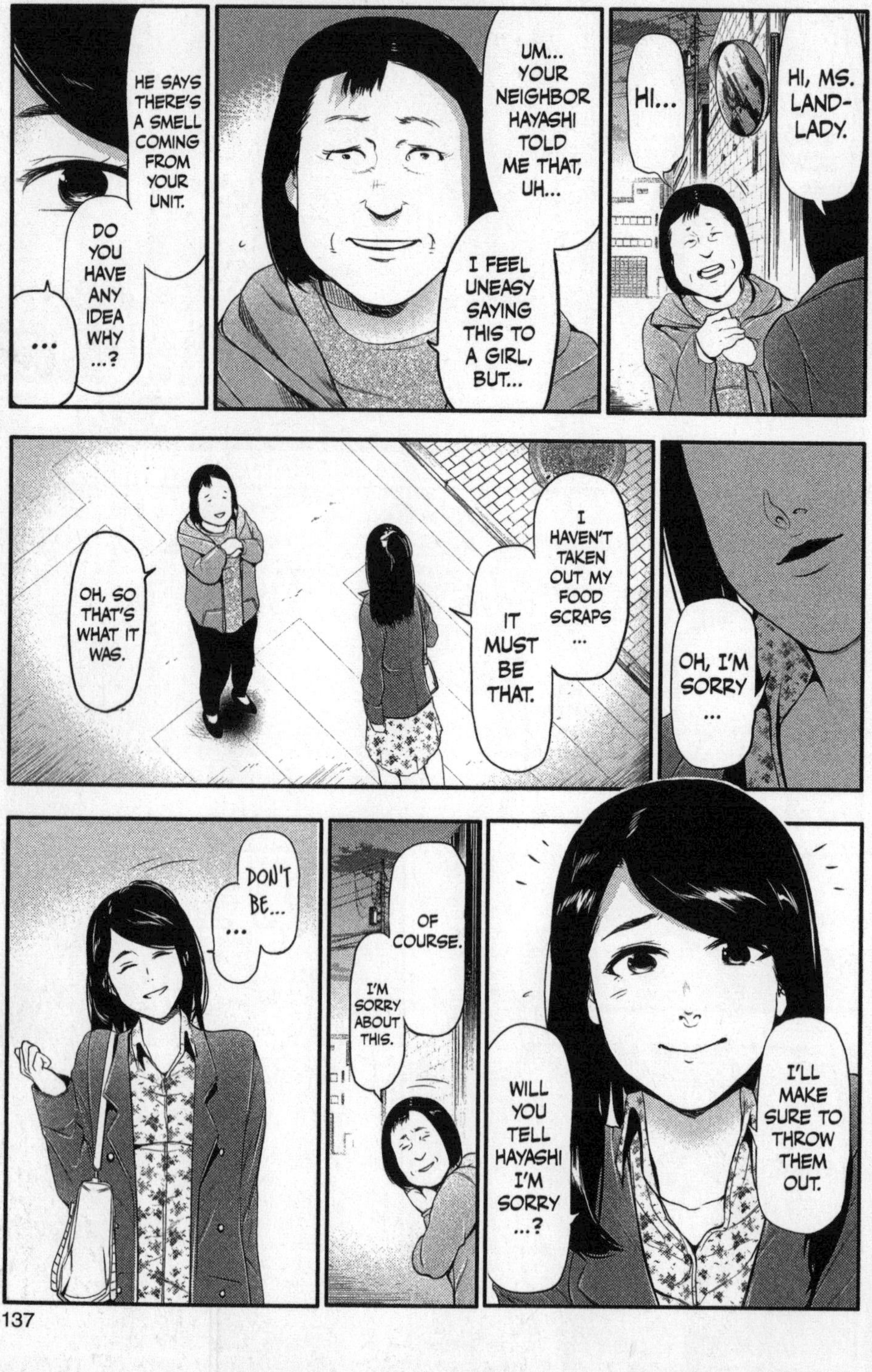
HI, MS. LANDLADY.
HI...
UM... YOUR NEIGHBOR HAYASHI TOLD ME THAT, UH...
I FEEL UNEASY SAYING THIS TO A GIRL, BUT...
HE SAYS THERE'S A SMELL COMING FROM YOUR UNIT.
DO YOU HAVE ANY IDEA WHY ...?
...
OH, I'M SORRY ...
I HAVEN'T TAKEN OUT MY FOOD SCRAPS ...
IT MUST BE THAT.
OH, SO THAT'S WHAT IT WAS.
I'LL MAKE SURE TO THROW THEM OUT.
WILL YOU TELL HAYASHI I'M SORRY ...?
OF COURSE.
I'M SORRY ABOUT THIS.
DON'T BE... ...

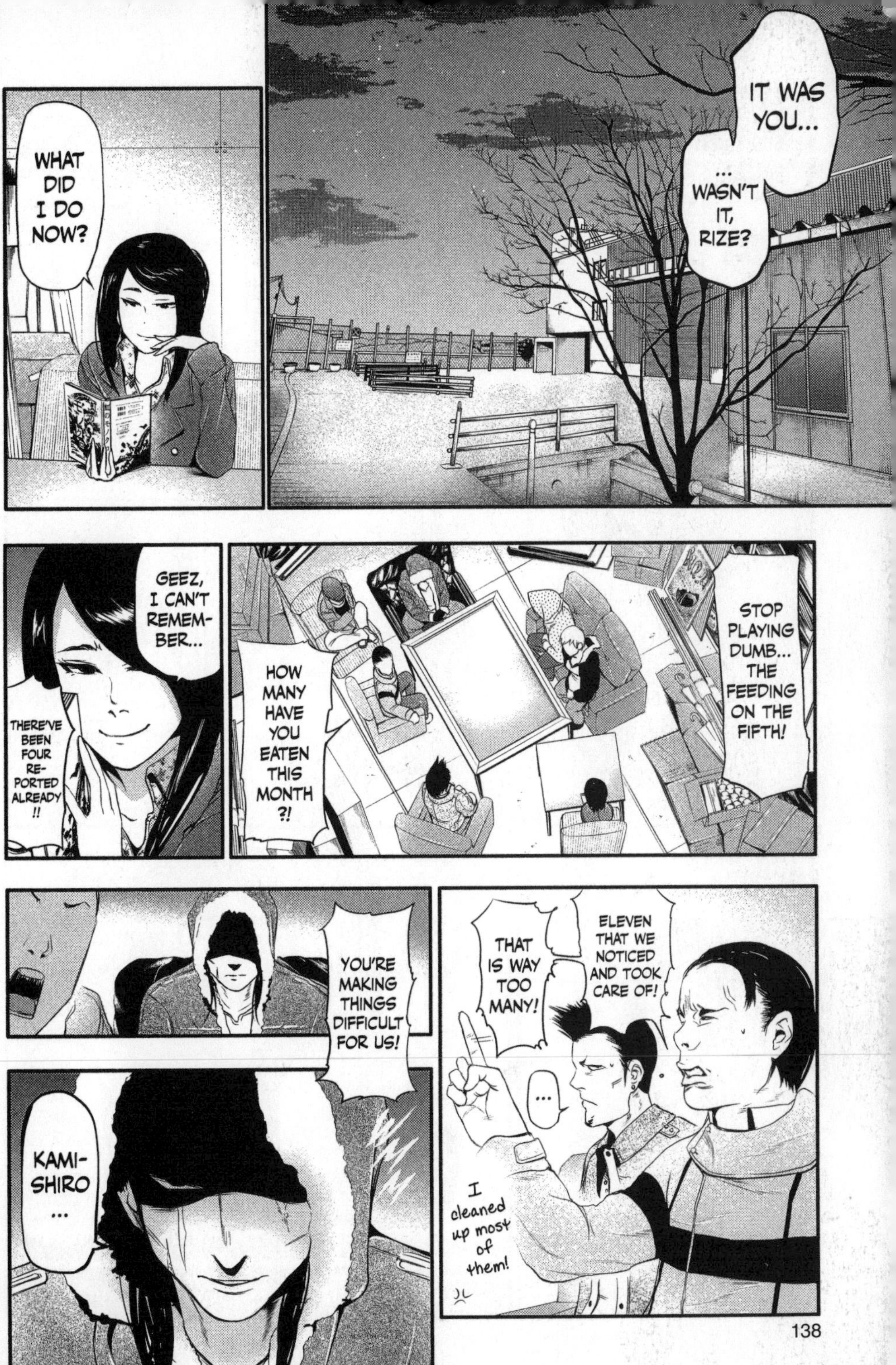
IT WAS YOU...
... WASN'T IT, RIZE?
WHAT DID I DO NOW?
STOP PLAYING DUMB... THE FEEDING ON THE FIFTH!
HOW MANY HAVE YOU EATEN THIS MONTH?!
GEEZ, I CAN'T REMEMBER...
THERE'VE BEEN FOUR REPORTED ALREADY!!
ELEVEN THAT WE NOTICED AND TOOK CARE OF!
THAT IS WAY TOO MANY!
...
I cleaned up most of them!
YOU'RE MAKING THINGS DIFFICULT FOR US!
KAMISHIRO...

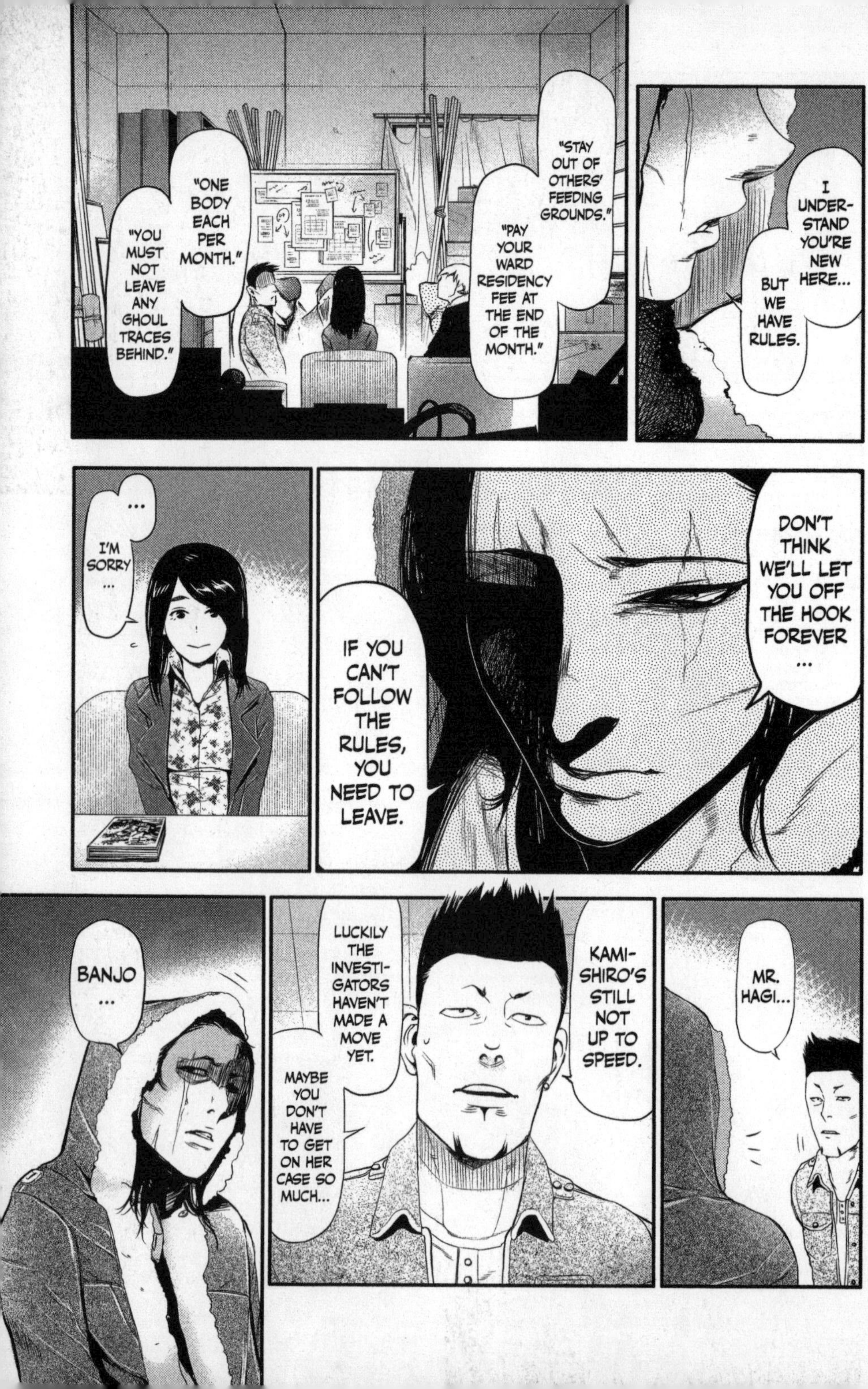
I UNDERSTAND YOU'RE NEW HERE...
BUT WE HAVE RULES.
"STAY OUT OF OTHERS' FEEDING GROUNDS."
"PAY YOUR WARD RESIDENCY FEE AT THE END OF THE MONTH."
"ONE BODY EACH PER MONTH."
"YOU MUST NOT LEAVE ANY GHOUL TRACES BEHIND."
DON'T THINK WE'LL LET YOU OFF THE HOOK FOREVER...
IF YOU CAN'T FOLLOW THE RULES, YOU NEED TO LEAVE.
...
I'M SORRY...
MR. HAGI...
KAMISHIRO'S STILL NOT UP TO SPEED.
LUCKILY THE INVESTIGATORS HAVEN'T MADE A MOVE YET.
MAYBE YOU DON'T HAVE TO GET ON HER CASE SO MUCH...
BANJO...

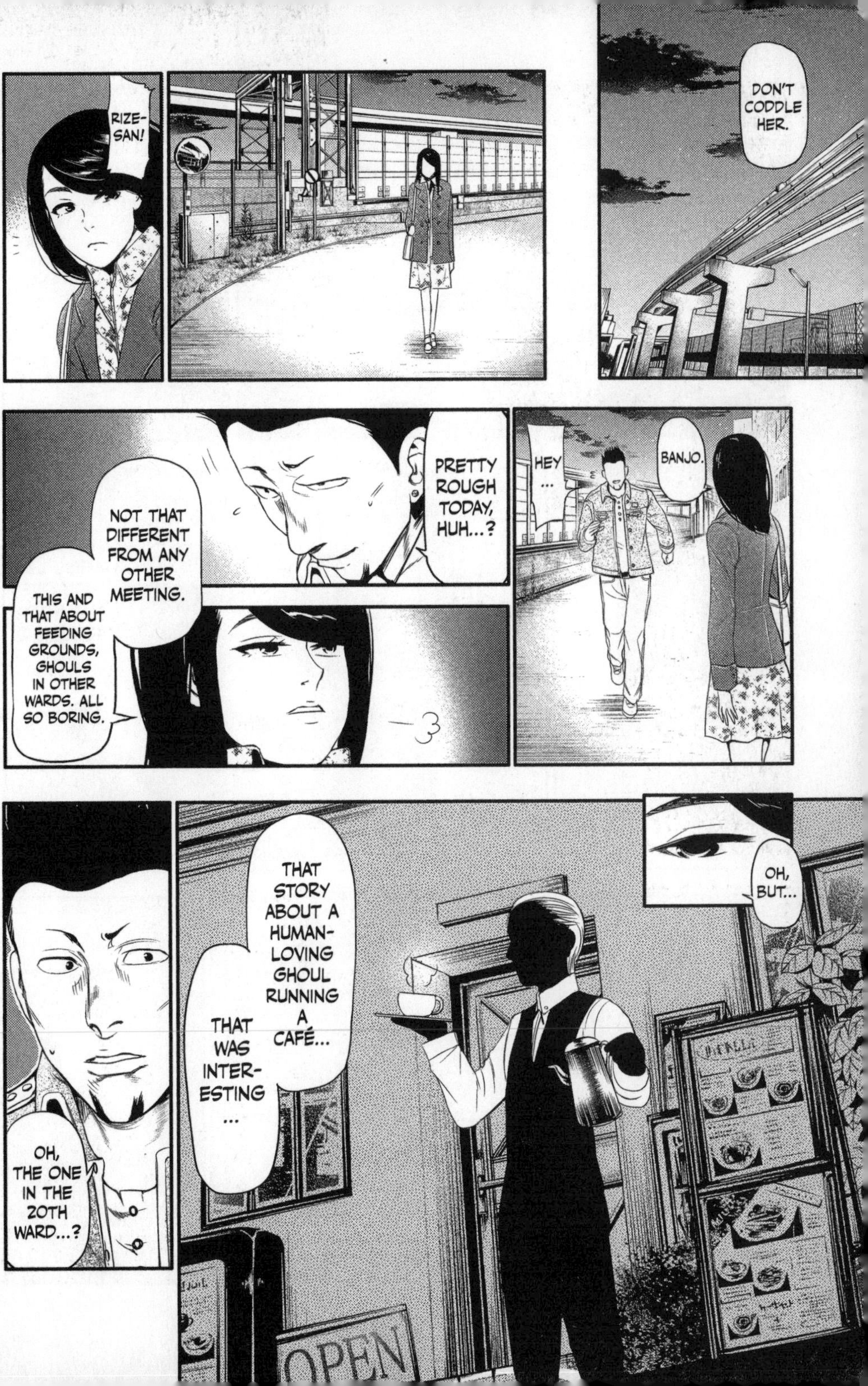
DON'T CODDLE HER.
RIZE-SAN!
BANJO.
HEY ...
PRETTY ROUGH TODAY, HUH...?
NOT THAT DIFFERENT FROM ANY OTHER MEETING.
THIS AND THAT ABOUT FEEDING GROUNDS, GHOULS IN OTHER WARDS. ALL SO BORING.
OH, BUT...
THAT STORY ABOUT A HUMAN-LOVING GHOUL RUNNING A CAFÉ...
THAT WAS INTER-ESTING ...
OPEN
OH, THE ONE IN THE 20TH WARD...?

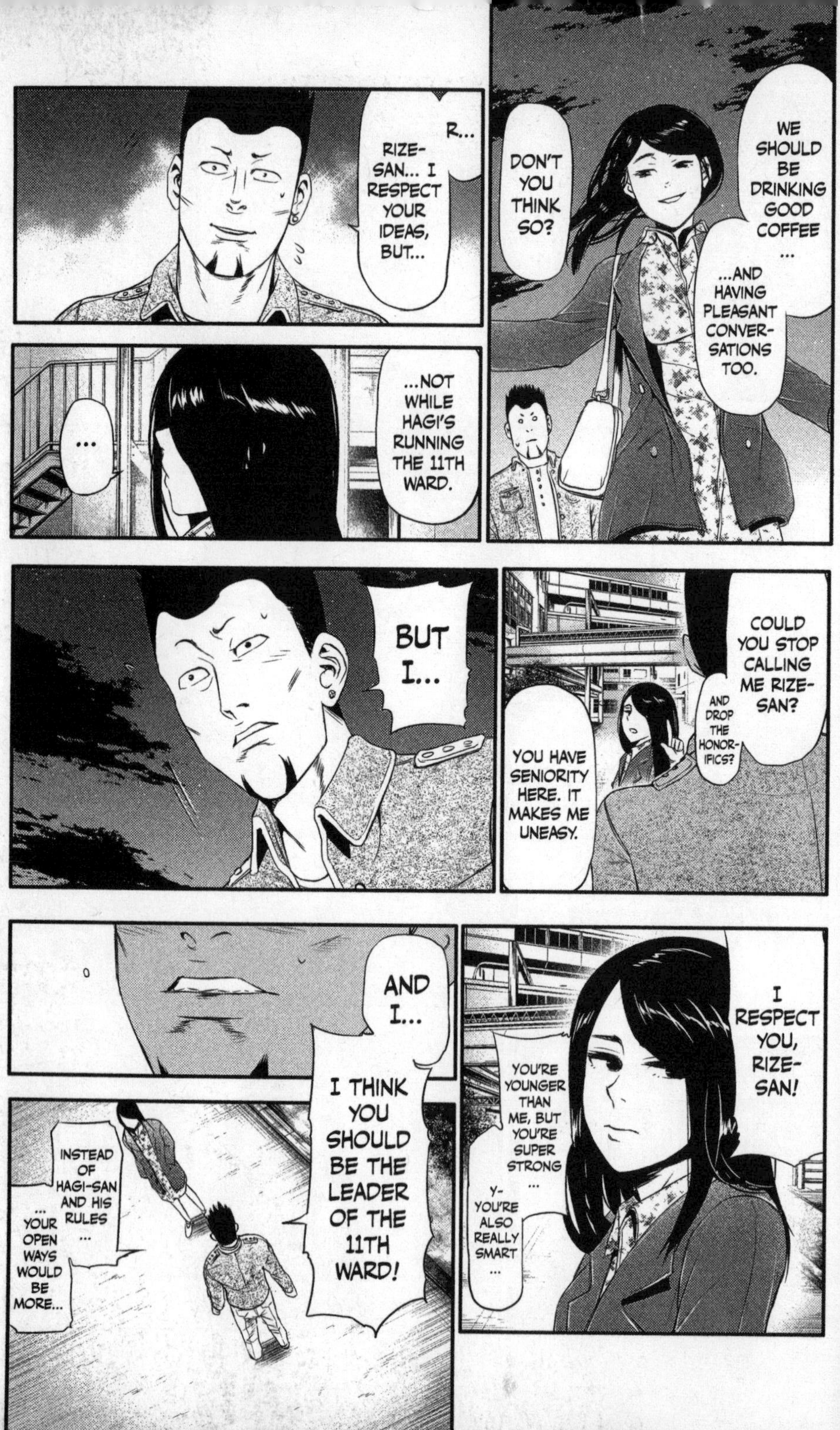
WE SHOULD BE DRINKING GOOD COFFEE...
...AND HAVING PLEASANT CONVERSATIONS TOO.
DON'T YOU THINK SO?
R...
RIZE-SAN... I RESPECT YOUR IDEAS, BUT...
...NOT WHILE HAGI'S RUNNING THE 11TH WARD.
...
COULD YOU STOP CALLING ME RIZE-SAN?
AND DROP THE HONORIFICS?
YOU HAVE SENIORITY HERE. IT MAKES ME UNEASY.
BUT I...
I RESPECT YOU, RIZE-SAN!
YOU'RE YOUNGER THAN ME, BUT YOU'RE SUPER STRONG...
Y-YOU'RE ALSO REALLY SMART...
AND I...
I THINK YOU SHOULD BE THE LEADER OF THE 11TH WARD!
INSTEAD OF HAGI-SAN AND HIS RULES...
...YOUR OPEN WAYS WOULD BE MORE...

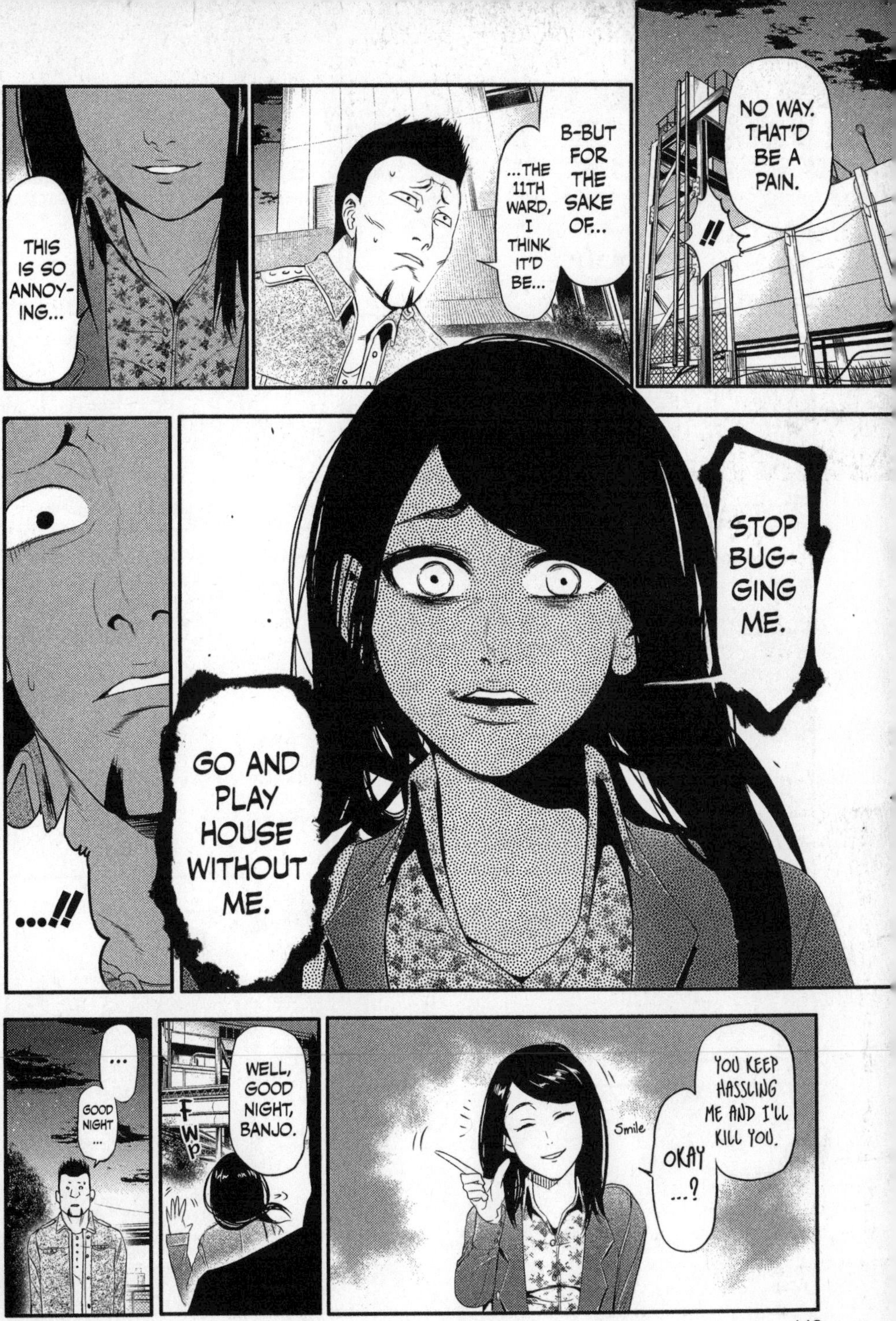
NO WAY. THAT'D BE A PAIN.
!!
B-BUT FOR THE SAKE OF...
...THE 11TH WARD, I THINK IT'D BE...
THIS IS SO ANNOY-ING...
STOP BUG-GING ME.
GO AND PLAY HOUSE WITHOUT ME.
...!!
YOU KEEP HASSLING ME AND I'LL KILL YOU.
Smile
OKAY ...?
WELL, GOOD NIGHT, BANJO.
...
GOOD NIGHT ...

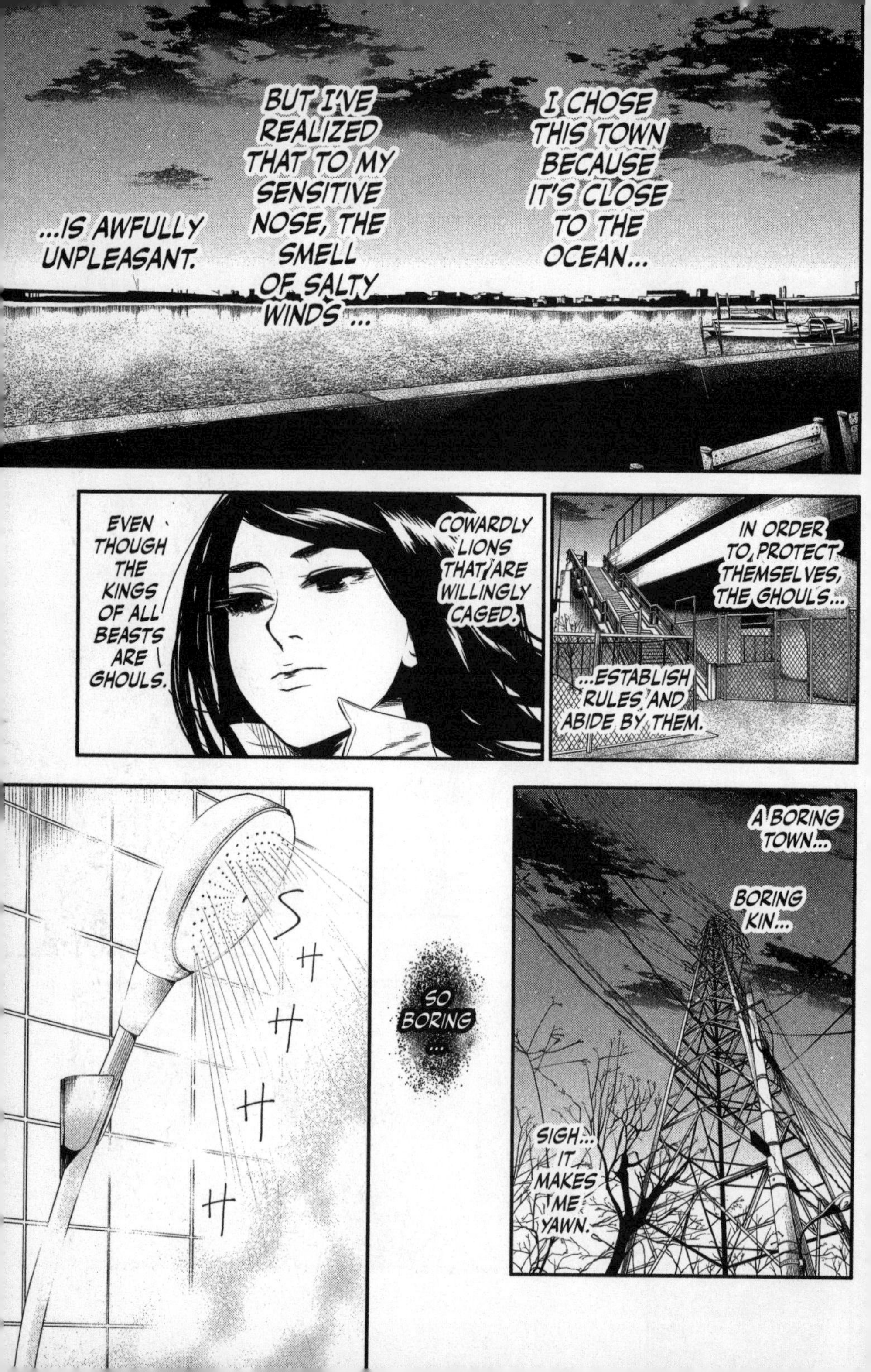
I CHOSE THIS TOWN BECAUSE IT'S CLOSE TO THE OCEAN...
BUT I'VE REALIZED THAT TO MY SENSITIVE NOSE, THE SMELL OF SALTY WINDS...
...IS AWFULLY UNPLEASANT.
IN ORDER TO PROTECT THEMSELVES, THE GHOULS...
...ESTABLISH RULES AND ABIDE BY THEM.
COWARDLY LIONS THAT ARE WILLINGLY CAGED.
EVEN THOUGH THE KINGS OF ALL BEASTS ARE GHOULS.
A BORING TOWN...
BORING KIN...
SIGH... IT MAKES ME YAWN.
SO BORING...
SHHHH

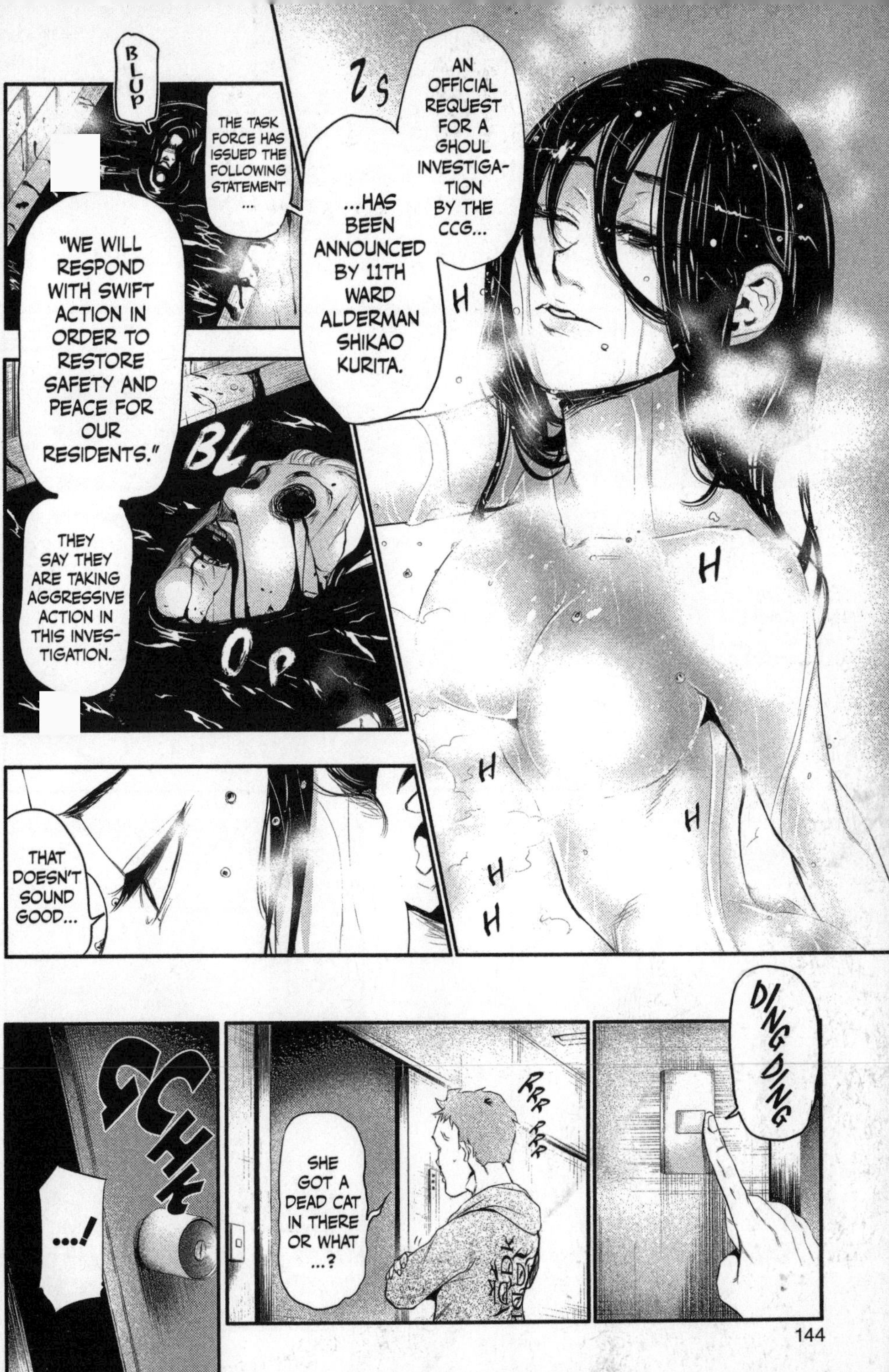
ZS
AN OFFICIAL REQUEST FOR A GHOUL INVESTIGATION BY THE CCG...
...HAS BEEN ANNOUNCED BY 11TH WARD ALDERMAN SHIKAO KURITA.
H
H
H
H
H
H
BLUP
THE TASK FORCE HAS ISSUED THE FOLLOWING STATEMENT...
"WE WILL RESPOND WITH SWIFT ACTION IN ORDER TO RESTORE SAFETY AND PEACE FOR OUR RESIDENTS."
BLOP
THEY SAY THEY ARE TAKING AGGRESSIVE ACTION IN THIS INVESTIGATION.
THAT DOESN'T SOUND GOOD...
DING DING
RRR RRR RRR
SHE GOT A DEAD CAT IN THERE OR WHAT...?
GCHK
...!

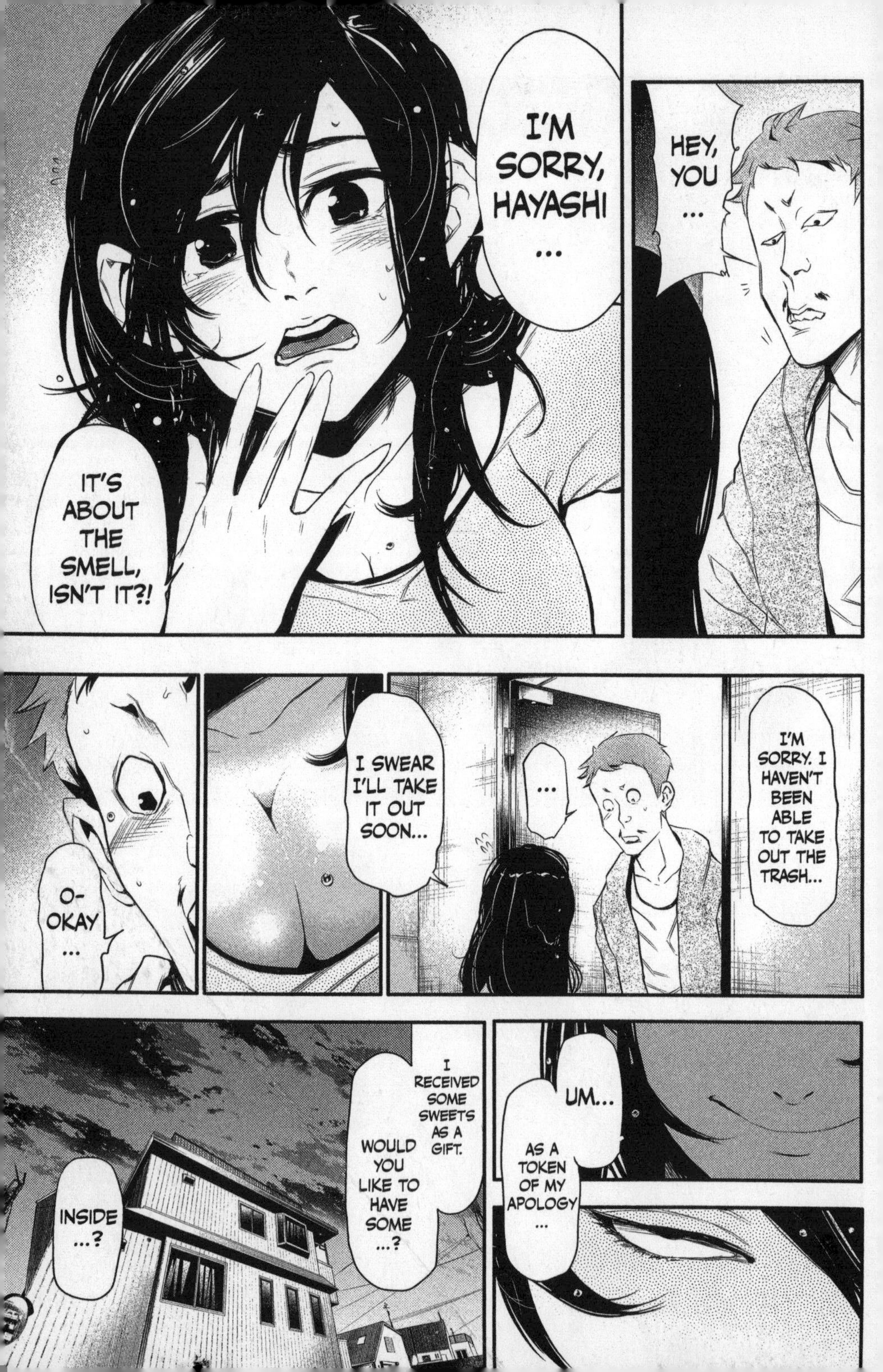
HEY, YOU ...
I'M SORRY, HAYASHI ...
IT'S ABOUT THE SMELL, ISN'T IT?!
I'M SORRY. I HAVEN'T BEEN ABLE TO TAKE OUT THE TRASH...
...
I SWEAR I'LL TAKE IT OUT SOON...
O-OKAY ...
UM...
AS A TOKEN OF MY APOLOGY ...
I RECEIVED SOME SWEETS AS A GIFT.
WOULD YOU LIKE TO HAVE SOME ...?
INSIDE ...?

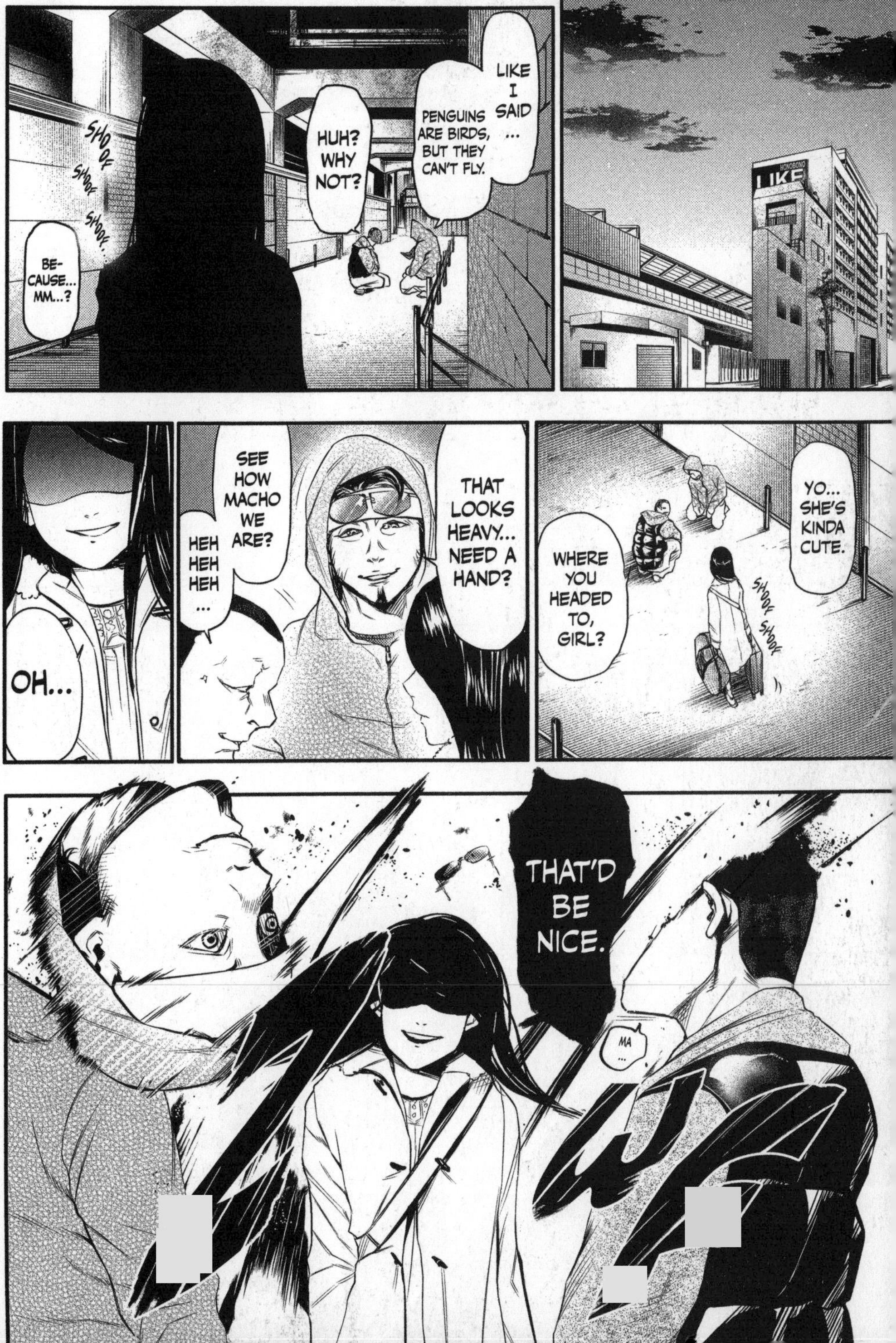
LIKE I SAID ...
PENGUINS ARE BIRDS, BUT THEY CAN'T FLY.
HUH? WHY NOT?
SHOOF
SHOOF
SHOOF
BE-CAUSE... MM...?
YO... SHE'S KINDA CUTE.
SHOOF
SHOOF
WHERE YOU HEADED TO, GIRL?
THAT LOOKS HEAVY... NEED A HAND?
SEE HOW MACHO WE ARE?
HEH HEH HEH ...
OH...
THAT'D BE NICE.
MA ...

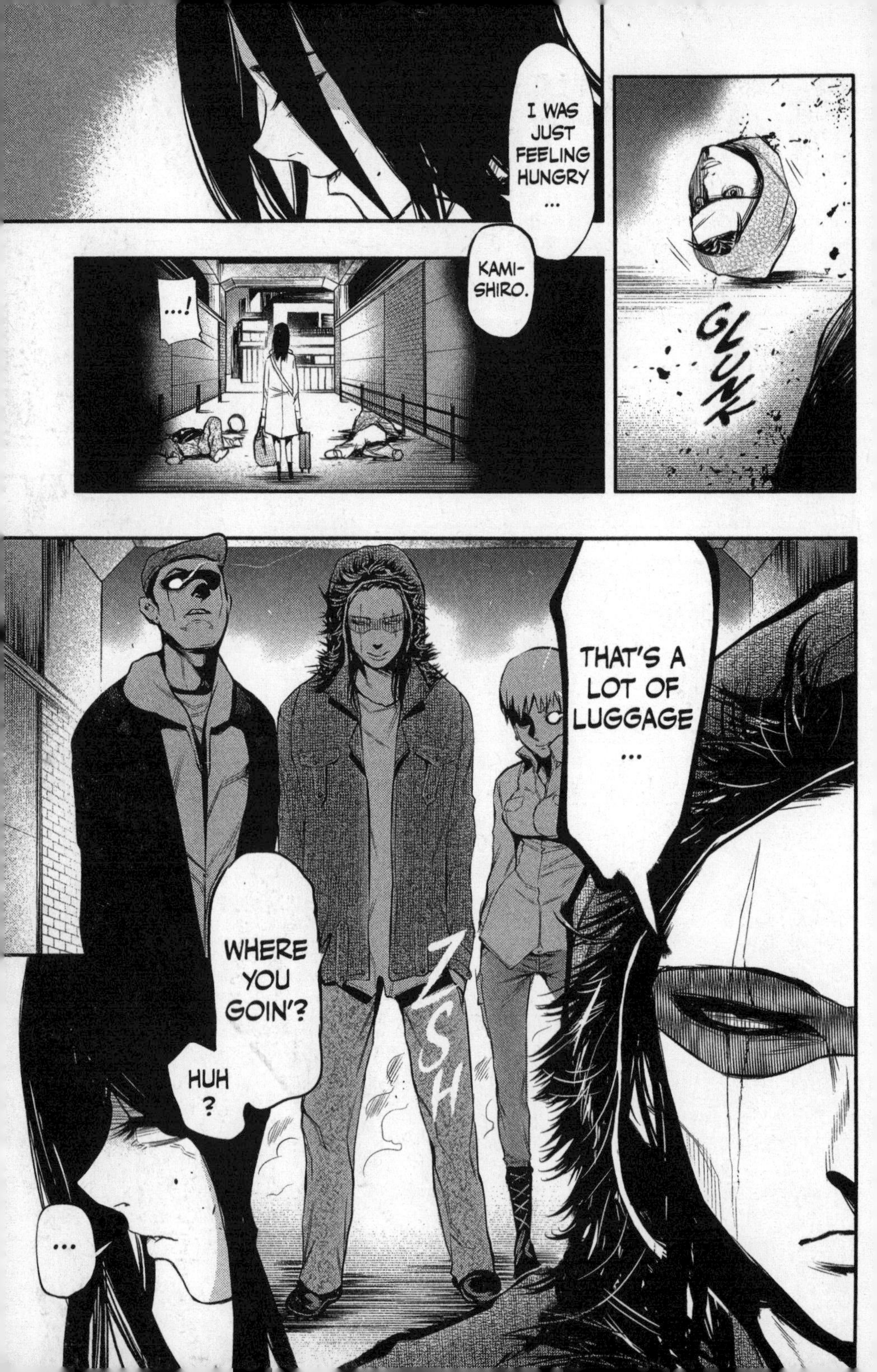
GLUNK
I WAS JUST FEELING HUNGRY ...
KAMI-SHIRO.
...!
THAT'S A LOT OF LUGGAGE ...
WHERE YOU GOIN'?
HUH?
ZSH
...

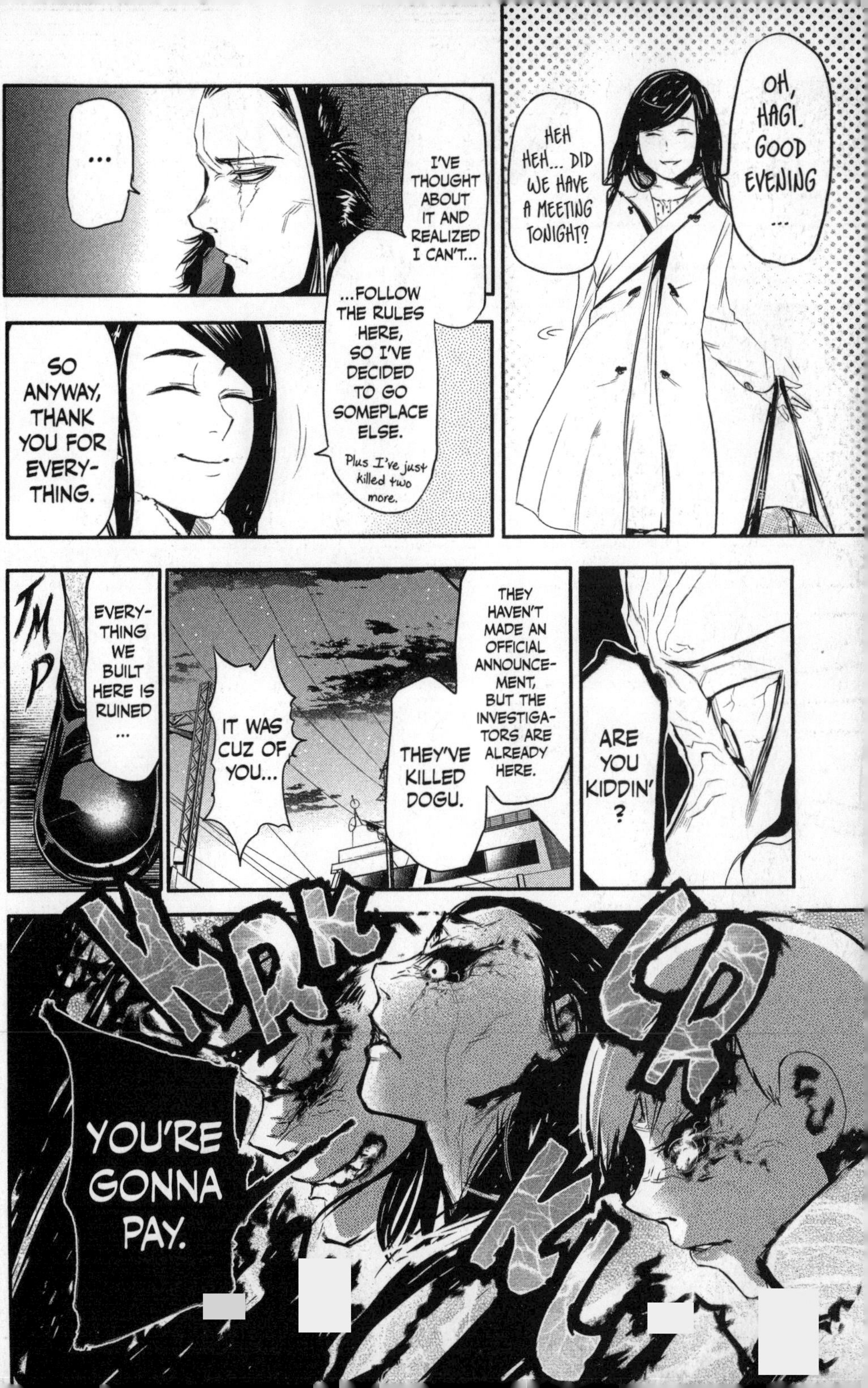
OH, HAGI. GOOD EVENING ...
HEH HEH... DID WE HAVE A MEETING TONIGHT?
I'VE THOUGHT ABOUT IT AND REALIZED I CAN'T...
...
...FOLLOW THE RULES HERE, SO I'VE DECIDED TO GO SOMEPLACE ELSE.
Plus I've just killed two more.
SO ANYWAY, THANK YOU FOR EVERY-THING.
ARE YOU KIDDIN'?
THEY HAVEN'T MADE AN OFFICIAL ANNOUNCE-MENT, BUT THE INVESTIGA-TORS ARE ALREADY HERE.
THEY'VE KILLED DOGU.
IT WAS CUZ OF YOU...
EVERY-THING WE BUILT HERE IS RUINED ...
TMP
YOU'RE GONNA PAY.

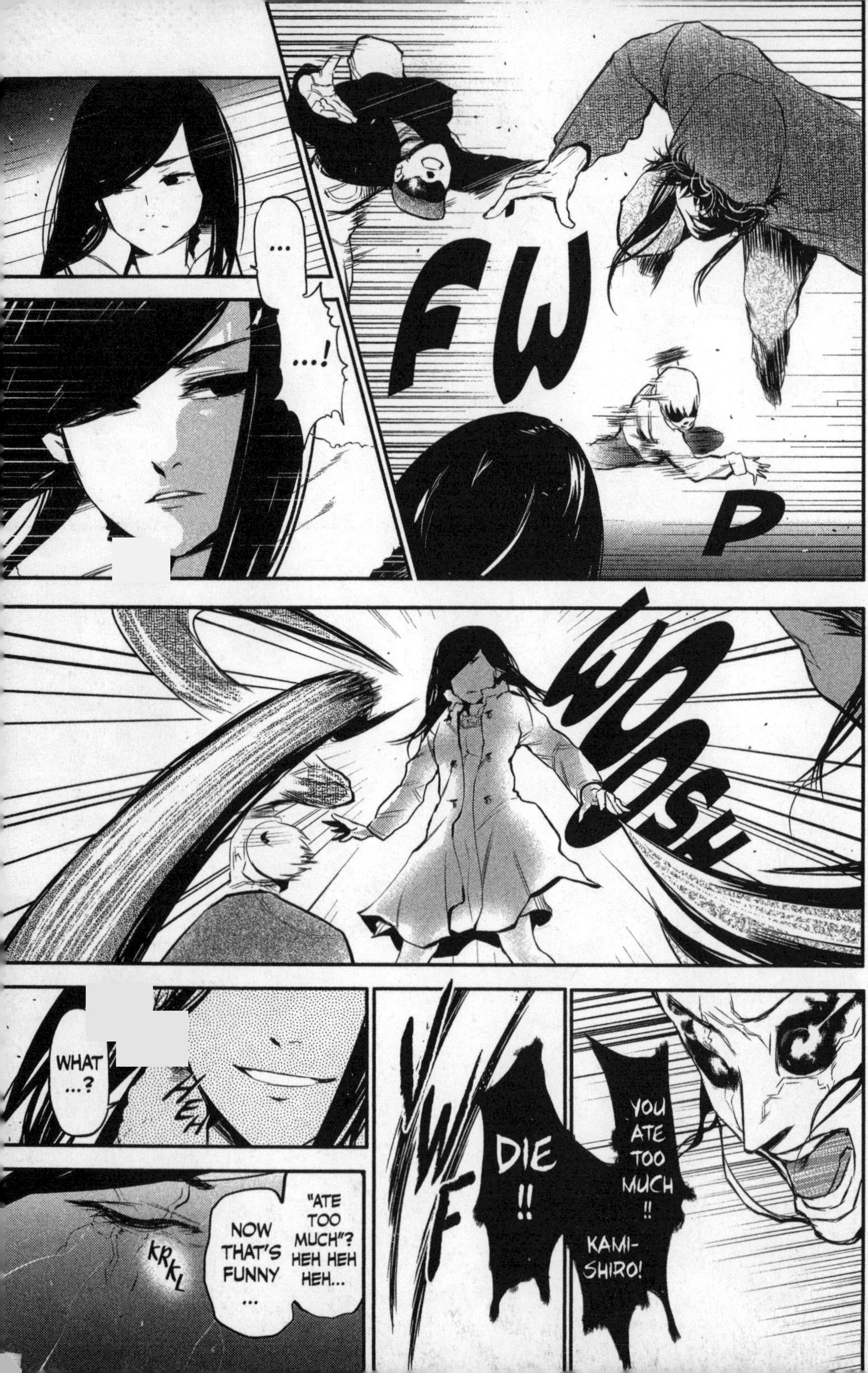
FWP
...
...!
WOOSH
YOU ATE TOO MUCH!!
KAMI-SHIRO!
VWF
DIE!!
WHAT...?
HEH
"ATE TOO MUCH"? HEH HEH HEH...
NOW THAT'S FUNNY...
KRKL

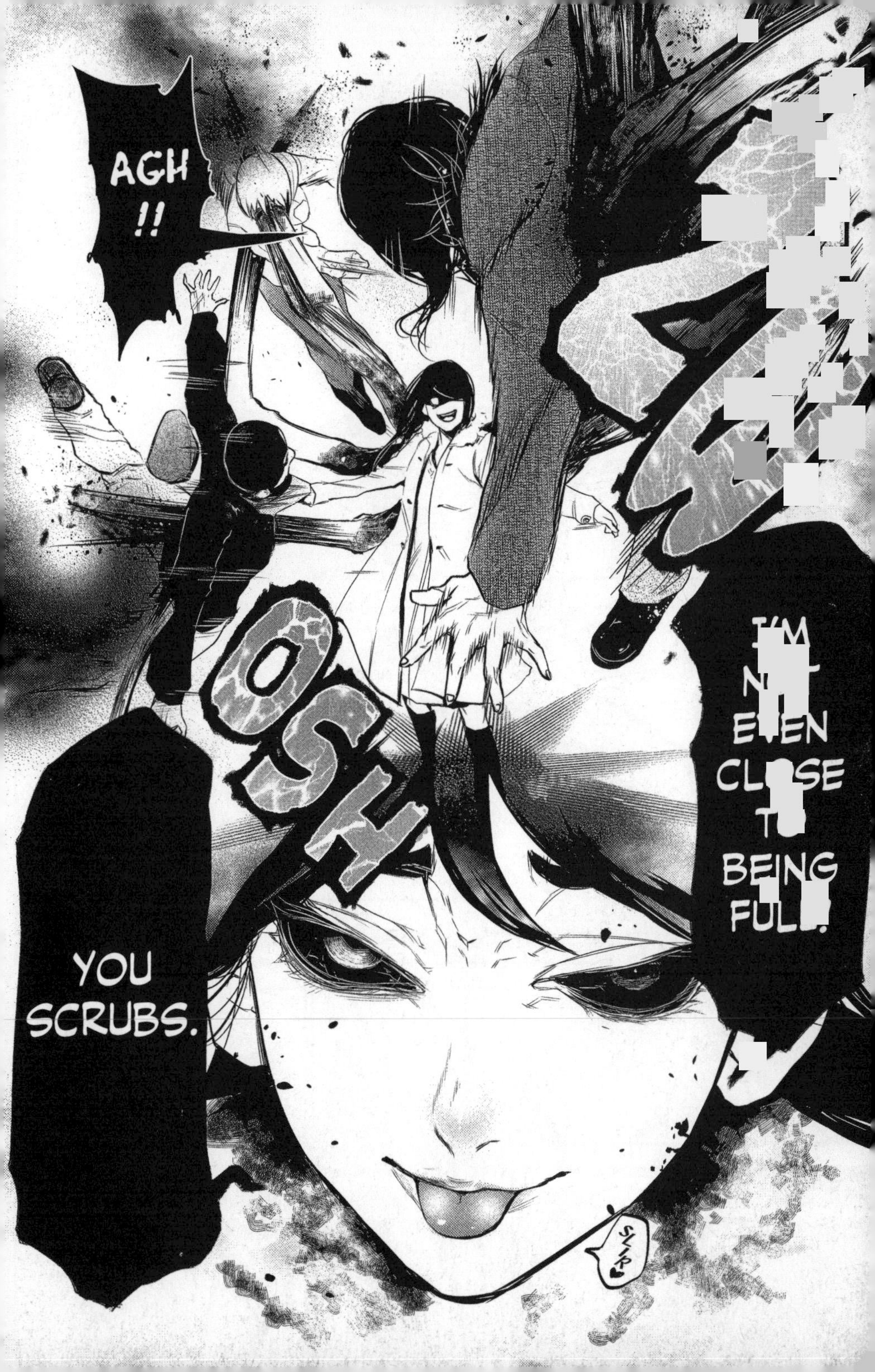
AGH !!
I'M NOT EVEN CLOSE TO BEING FULL.
OSH
YOU SCRUBS.
SLIR

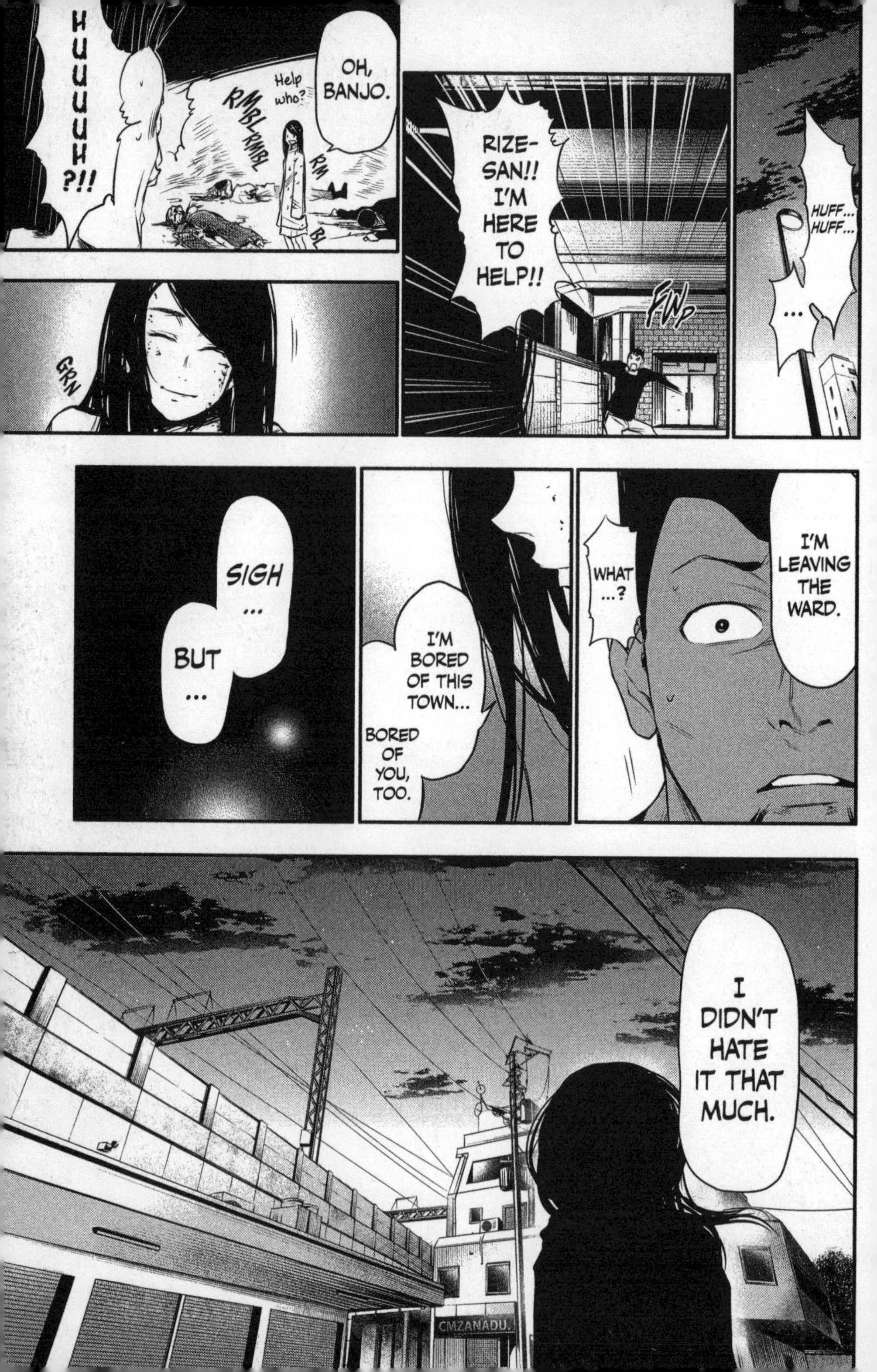
HUFF... HUFF...
...
RIZE-SAN!! I'M HERE TO HELP!!
FWP
OH, BANJO.
Help who?
RMBL RMBL
RM BL
HUUUUUH?!!
GRN
I'M LEAVING THE WARD.
WHAT...?
I'M BORED OF THIS TOWN...
BORED OF YOU, TOO.
SIGH...
BUT...
I DIDN'T HATE IT THAT MUCH.
CMZANADU.

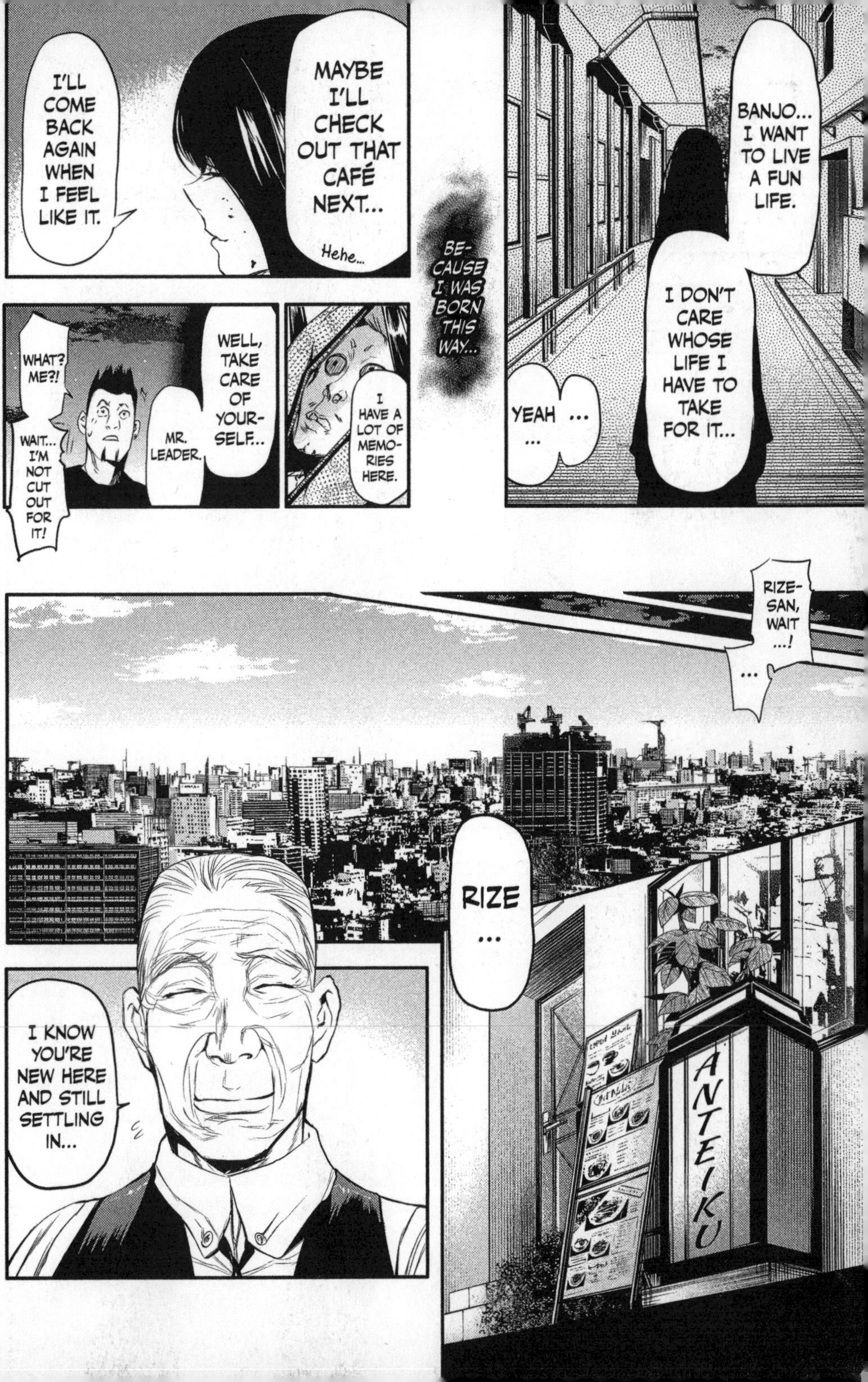
BANJO... I WANT TO LIVE A FUN LIFE.
I DON'T CARE WHOSE LIFE I HAVE TO TAKE FOR IT...
YEAH ... ...
BE-CAUSE I WAS BORN THIS WAY...
MAYBE I'LL CHECK OUT THAT CAFÉ NEXT...
Hehe...
I'LL COME BACK AGAIN WHEN I FEEL LIKE IT.
I HAVE A LOT OF MEMO-RIES HERE.
WELL, TAKE CARE OF YOUR-SELF...
MR. LEADER.
WHAT? ME?!
WAIT... I'M NOT CUT OUT FOR IT!
RIZE-SAN, WAIT ...!
...
RIZE ...
ANTEIKU
I KNOW YOU'RE NEW HERE AND STILL SETTLING IN...

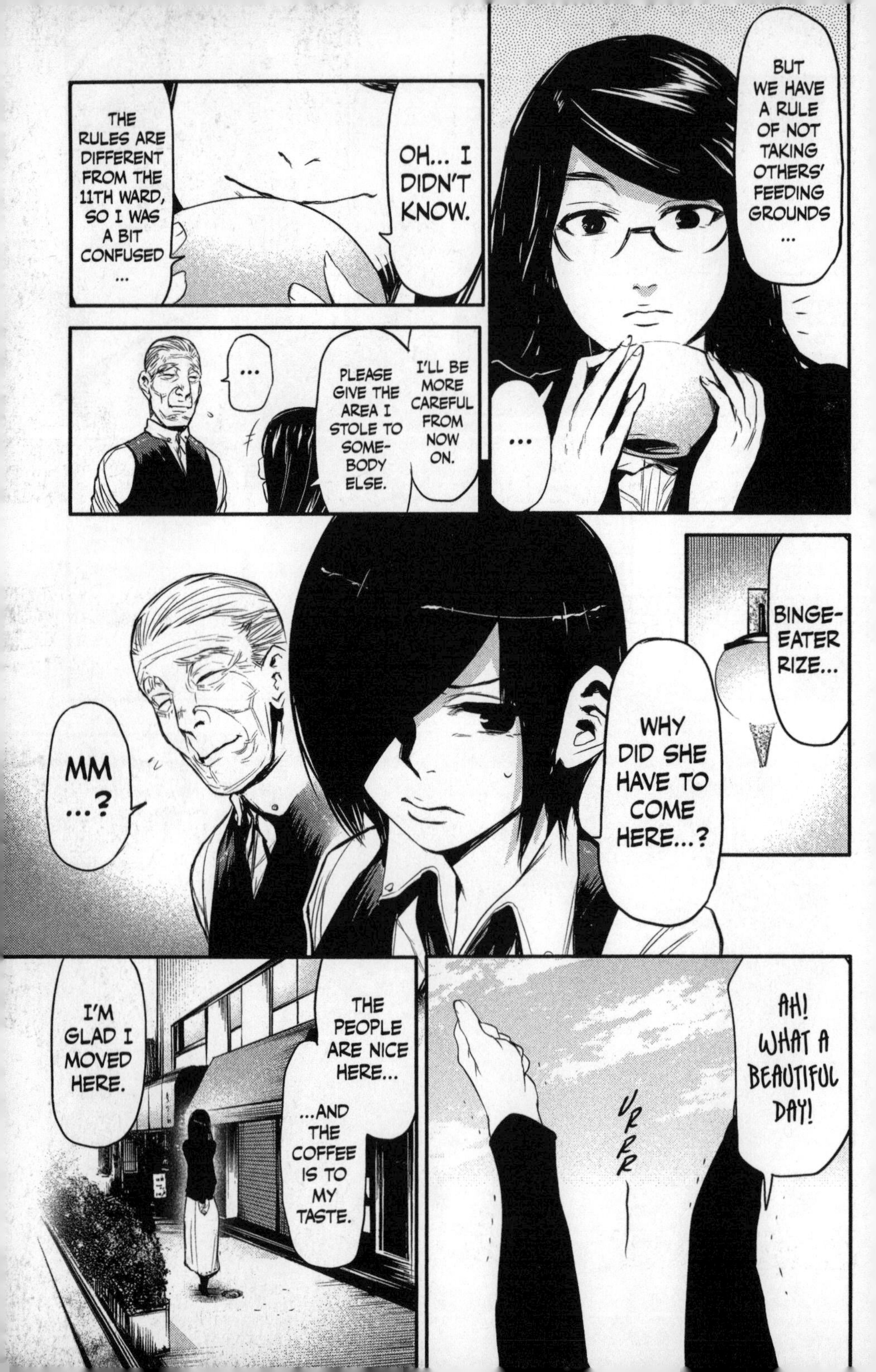
BUT WE HAVE A RULE OF NOT TAKING OTHERS' FEEDING GROUNDS ...
...
OH... I DIDN'T KNOW.
THE RULES ARE DIFFERENT FROM THE 11TH WARD, SO I WAS A BIT CONFUSED ...
I'LL BE MORE CAREFUL FROM NOW ON.
PLEASE GIVE THE AREA I STOLE TO SOMEBODY ELSE.
...
BINGE-EATER RIZE...
WHY DID SHE HAVE TO COME HERE...?
MM ...?
AH! WHAT A BEAUTIFUL DAY!
URRR
THE PEOPLE ARE NICE HERE...
...AND THE COFFEE IS TO MY TASTE.
I'M GLAD I MOVED HERE.

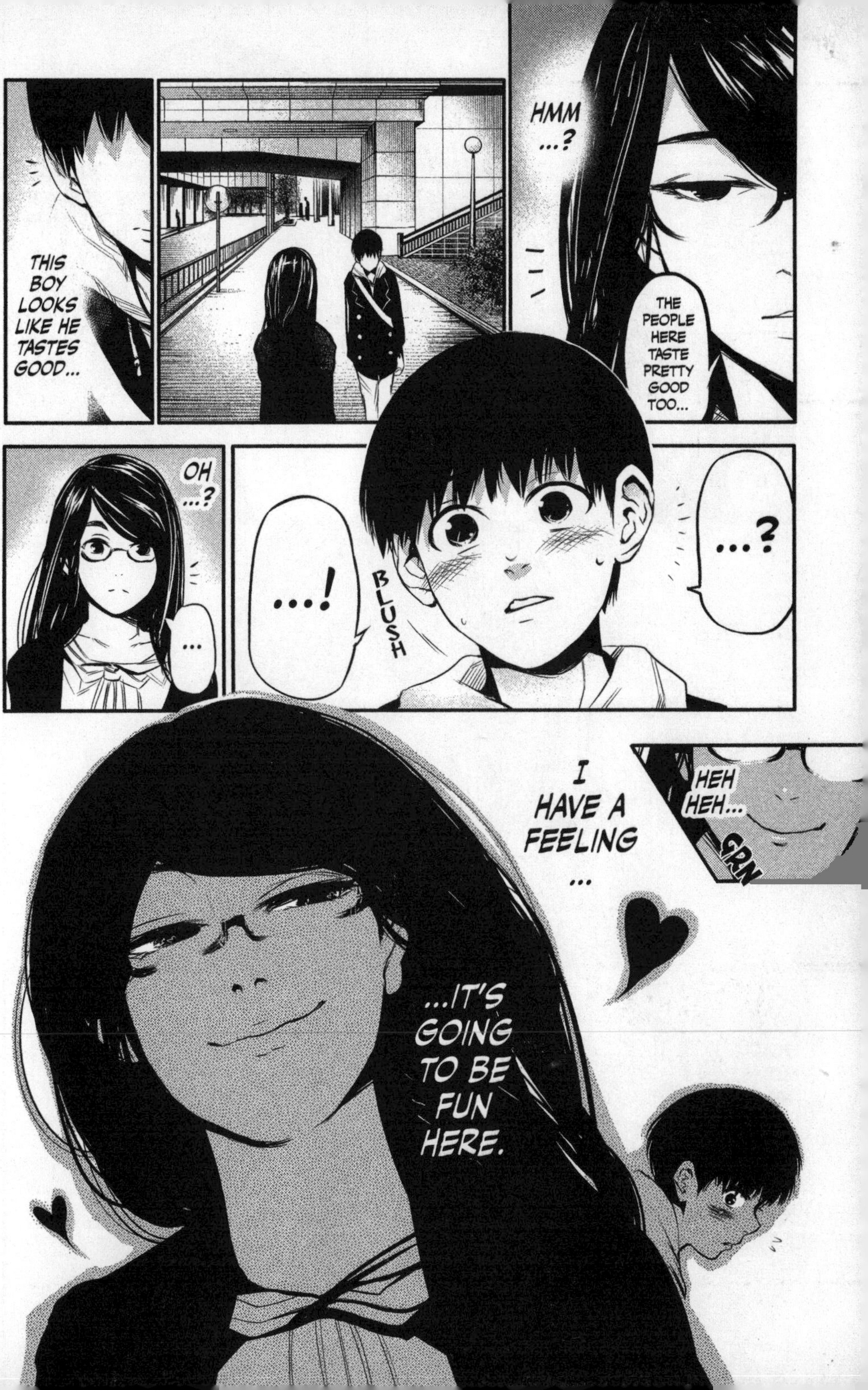
HMM ...?
THE PEOPLE HERE TASTE PRETTY GOOD TOO...
THIS BOY LOOKS LIKE HE TASTES GOOD...
...?
...!
BLUSH
OH ...?
...
HEH HEH...
GRN
I HAVE A FEELING ...
...IT'S GOING TO BE FUN HERE.

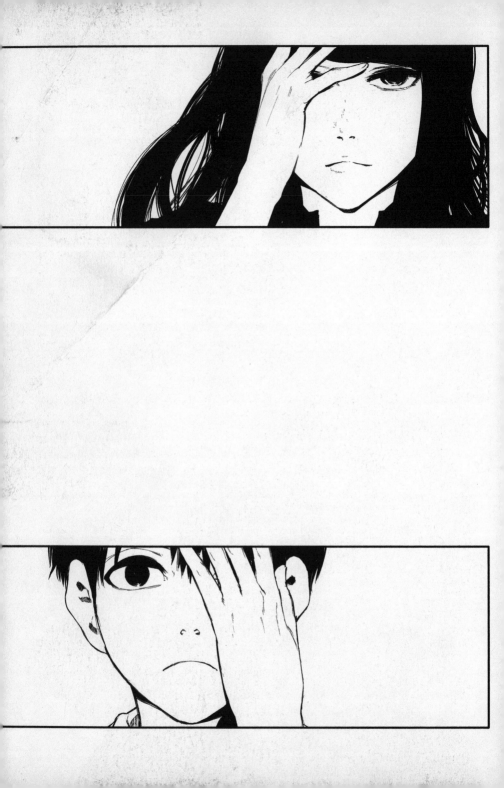

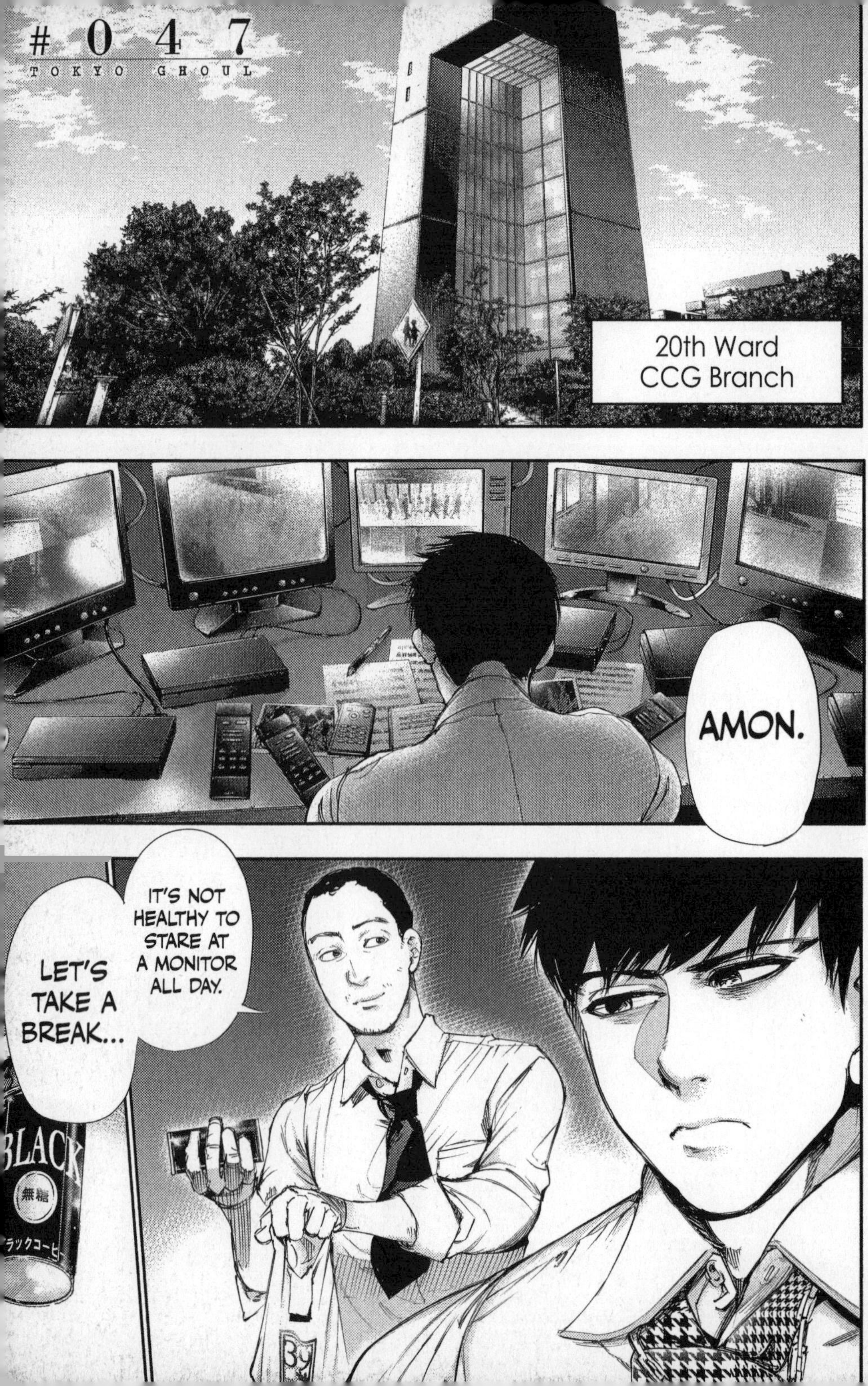
#047
TOKYO GHOUL
20th Ward CCG Branch
AMON.
IT'S NOT HEALTHY TO STARE AT A MONITOR ALL DAY.
LET'S TAKE A BREAK...
BLACK
無糖

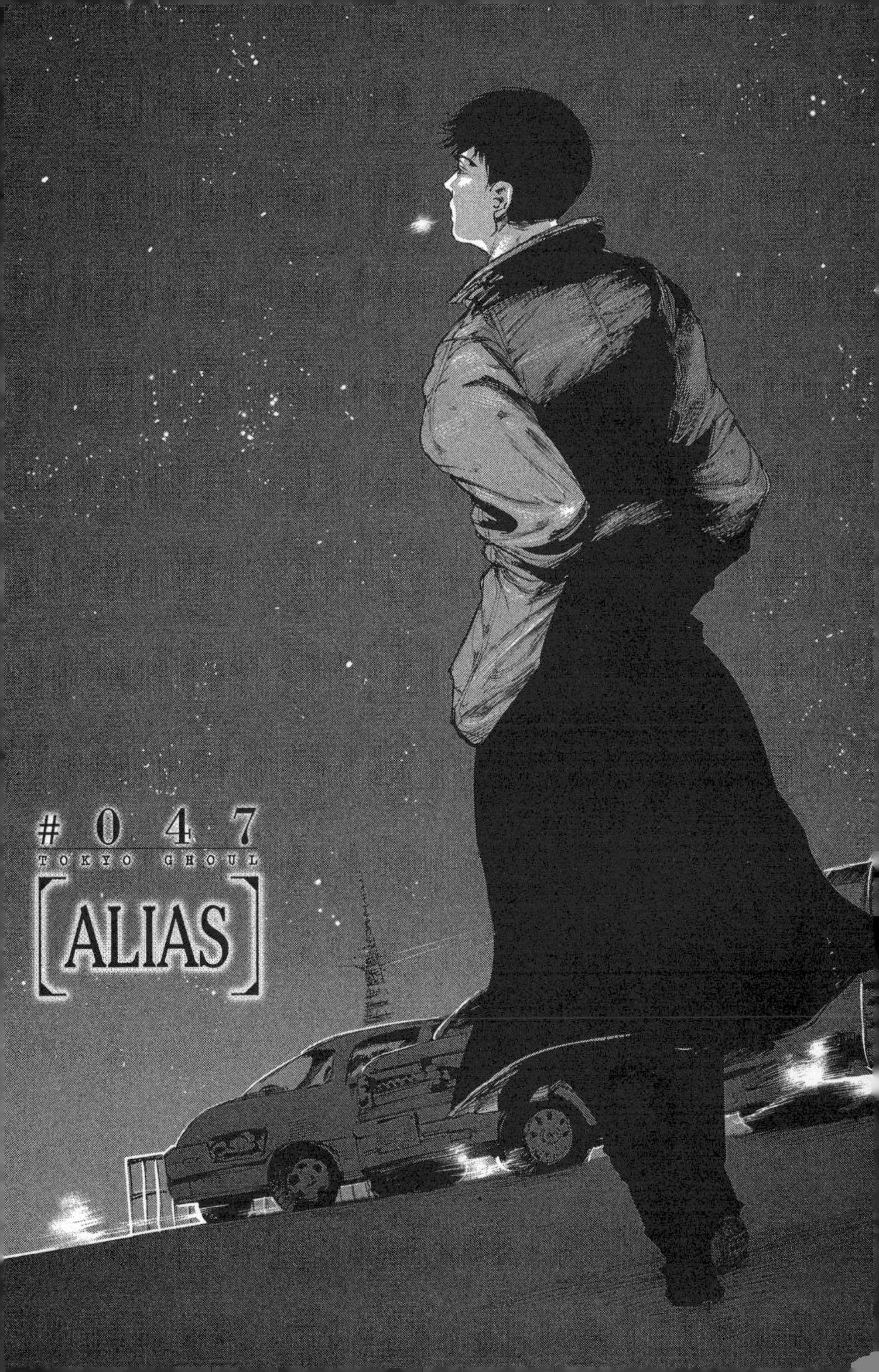
#047
TOKYO GHOUL
[ALIAS]

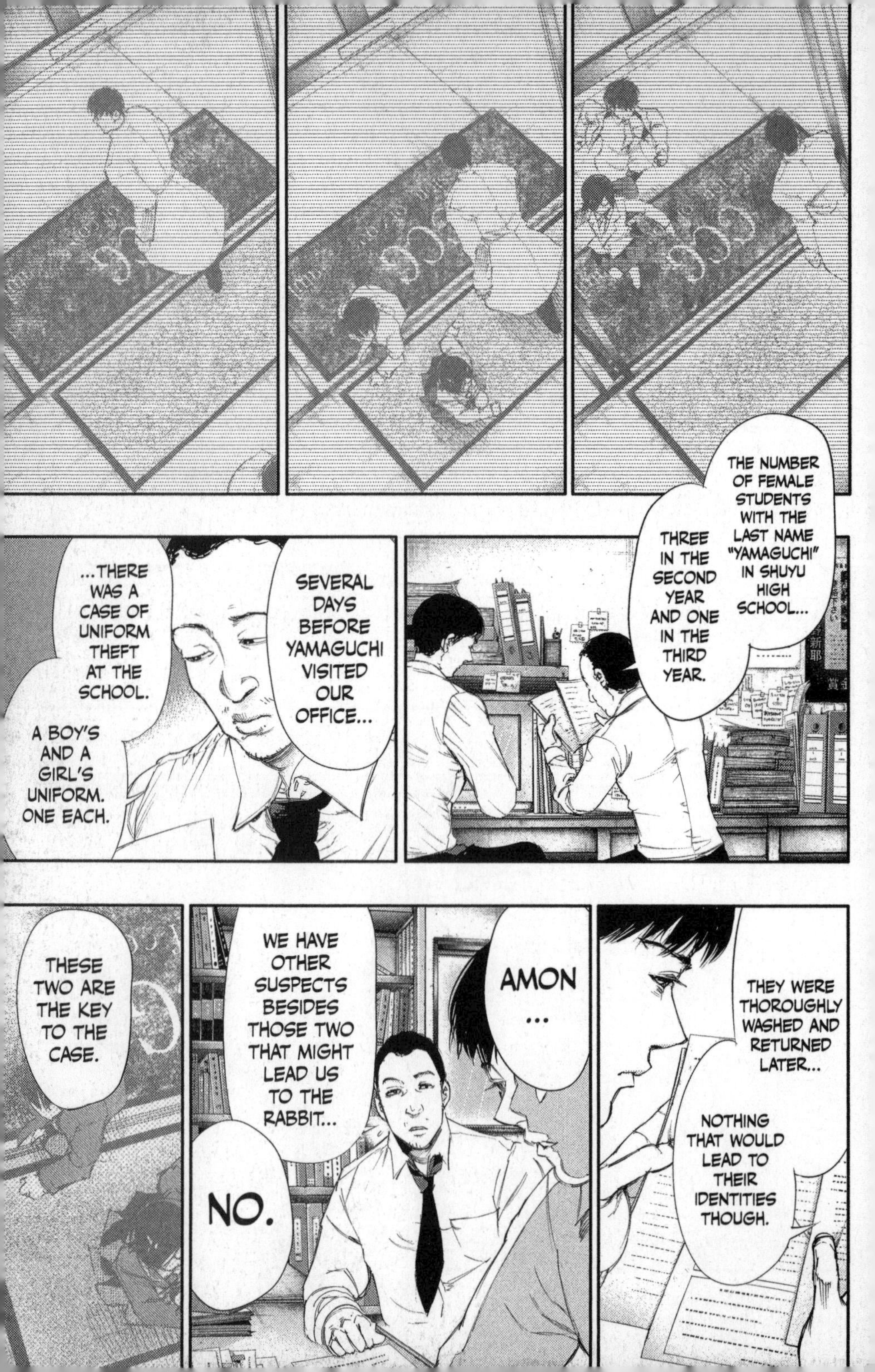
THE NUMBER OF FEMALE STUDENTS WITH THE LAST NAME "YAMAGUCHI" IN SHUYU HIGH SCHOOL...
THREE IN THE SECOND YEAR AND ONE IN THE THIRD YEAR.
SEVERAL DAYS BEFORE YAMAGUCHI VISITED OUR OFFICE...
...THERE WAS A CASE OF UNIFORM THEFT AT THE SCHOOL.
A BOY'S AND A GIRL'S UNIFORM. ONE EACH.
THEY WERE THOROUGHLY WASHED AND RETURNED LATER...
NOTHING THAT WOULD LEAD TO THEIR IDENTITIES THOUGH.
AMON ...
WE HAVE OTHER SUSPECTS BESIDES THOSE TWO THAT MIGHT LEAD US TO THE RABBIT...
NO.
THESE TWO ARE THE KEY TO THE CASE.

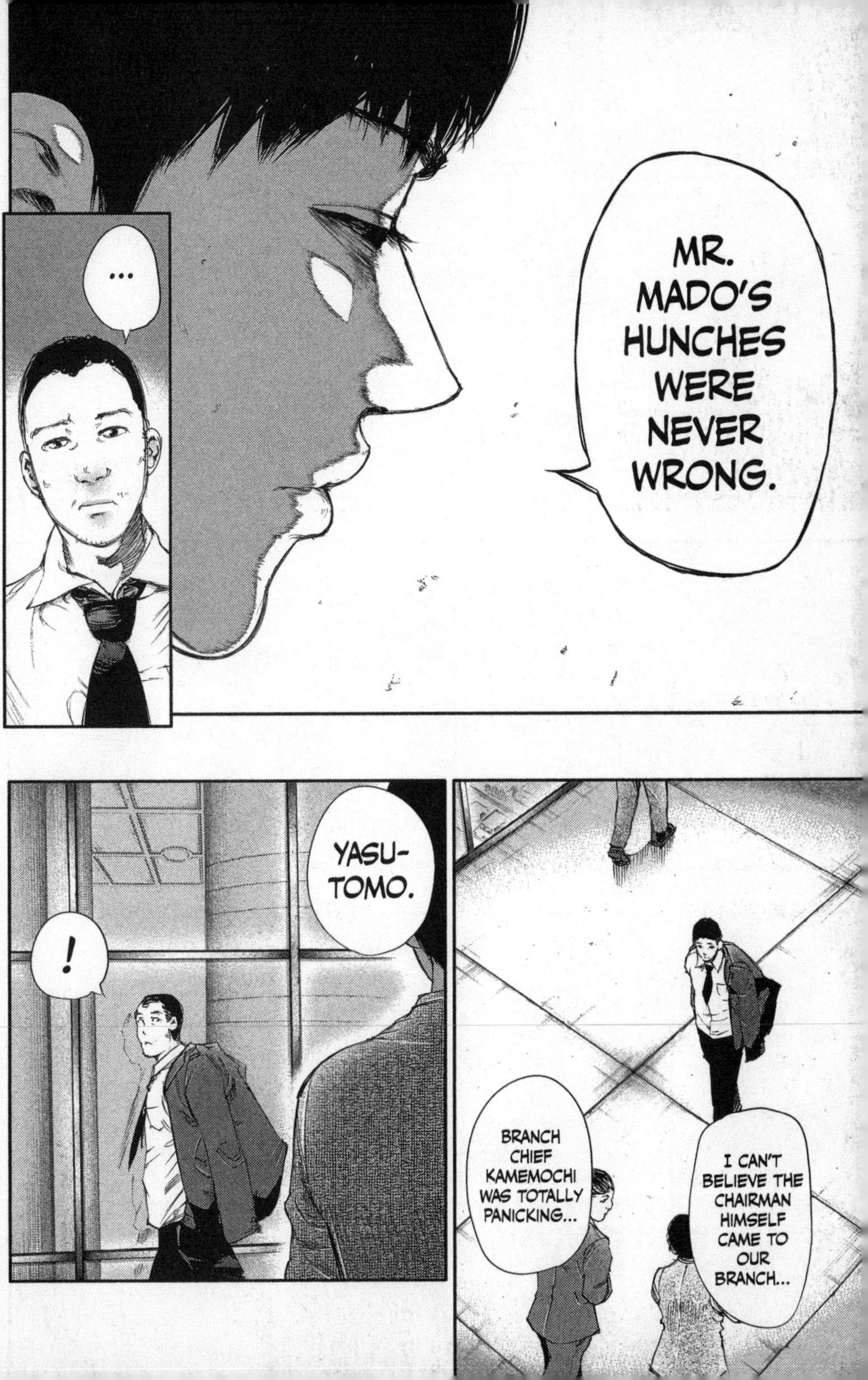
MR. MADO'S HUNCHES WERE NEVER WRONG.
...
I CAN'T BELIEVE THE CHAIRMAN HIMSELF CAME TO OUR BRANCH...
BRANCH CHIEF KAMEMOCHI WAS TOTALLY PANICKING...
YASU-TOMO.
!

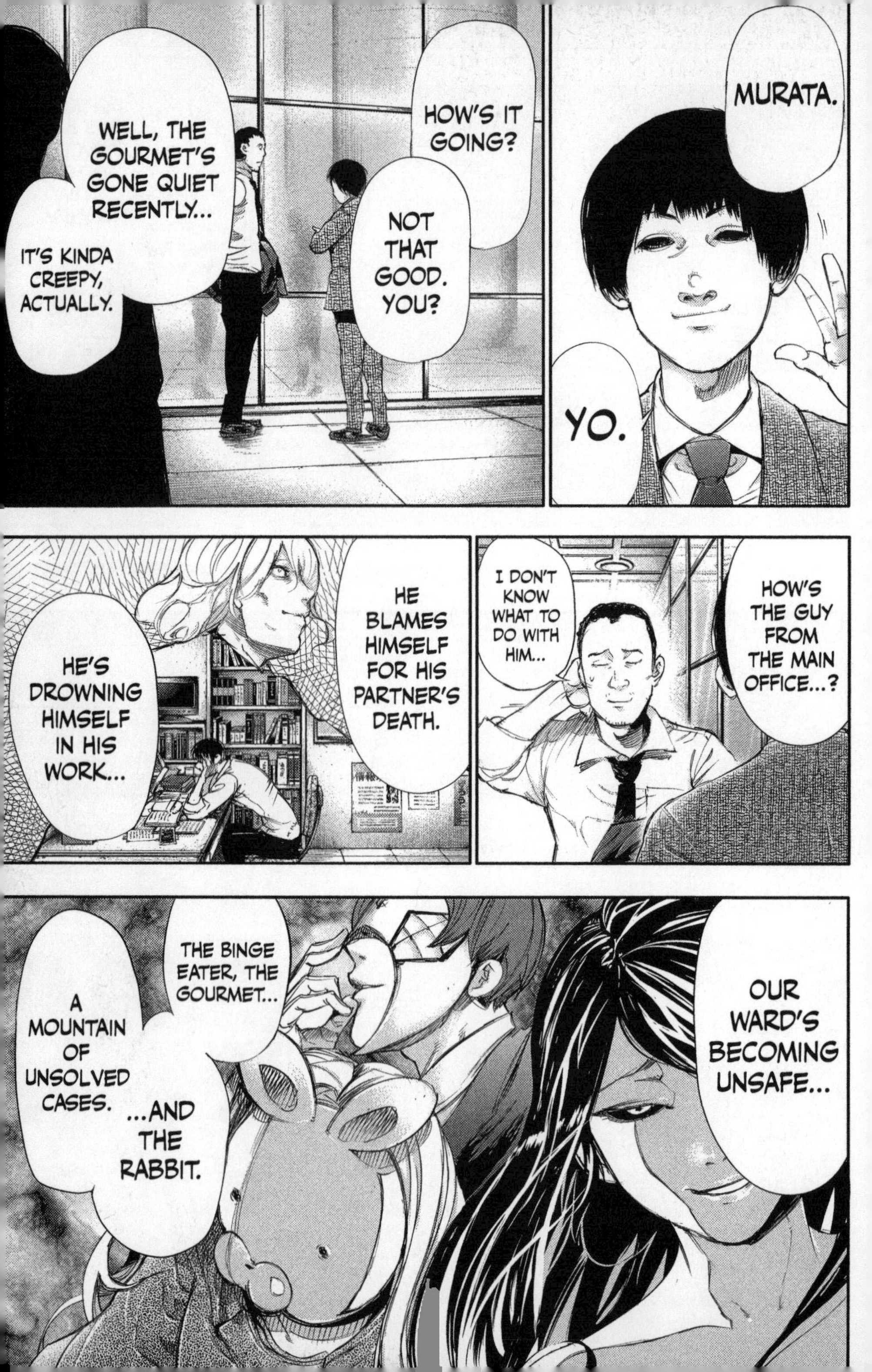
MURATA.
YO.
HOW'S IT GOING?
NOT THAT GOOD. YOU?
WELL, THE GOURMET'S GONE QUIET RECENTLY...
IT'S KINDA CREEPY, ACTUALLY.
HOW'S THE GUY FROM THE MAIN OFFICE...?
I DON'T KNOW WHAT TO DO WITH HIM...
HE BLAMES HIMSELF FOR HIS PARTNER'S DEATH.
HE'S DROWNING HIMSELF IN HIS WORK...
OUR WARD'S BECOMING UNSAFE...
THE BINGE EATER, THE GOURMET...
...AND THE RABBIT.
A MOUNTAIN OF UNSOLVED CASES.

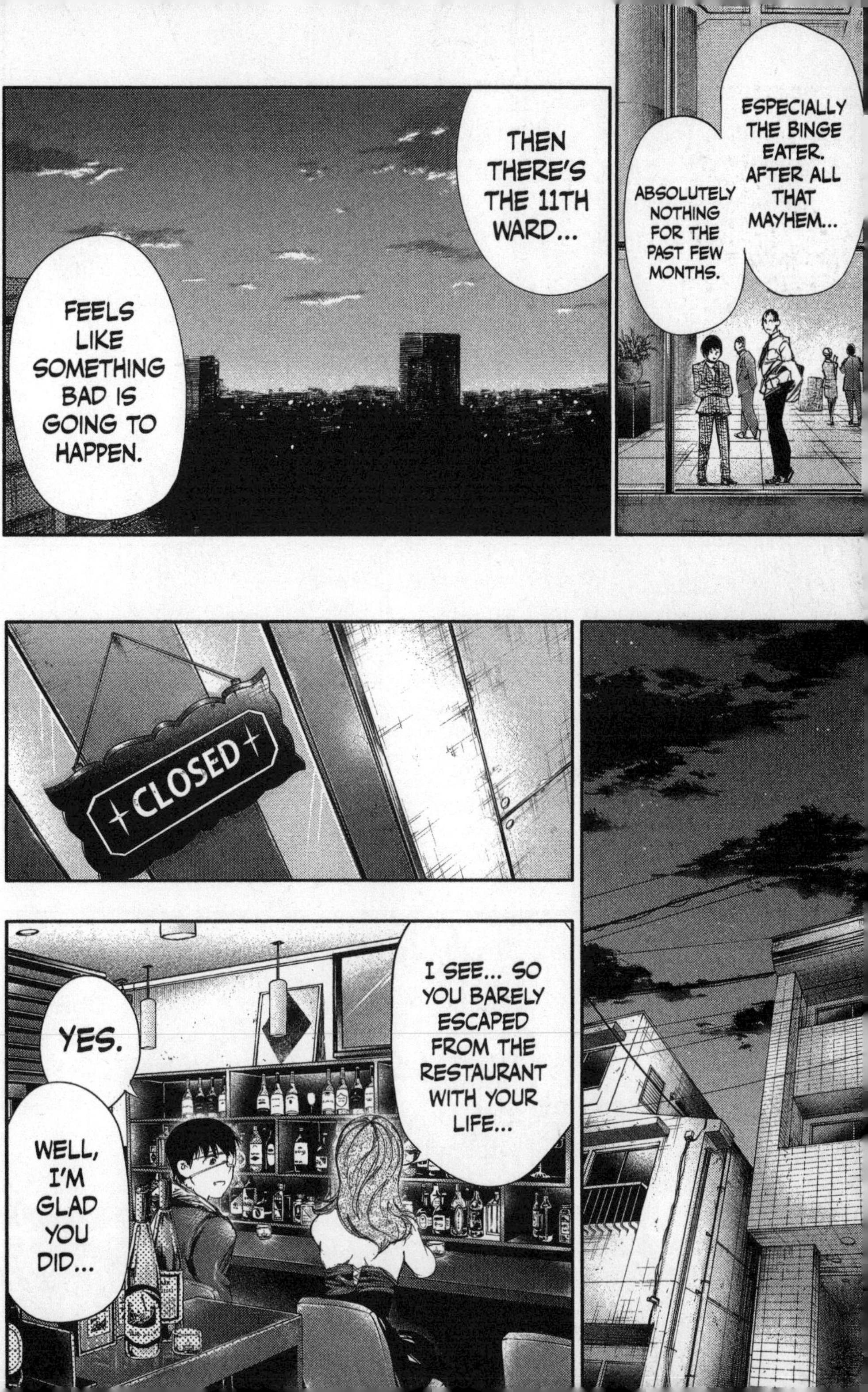
ESPECIALLY THE BINGE EATER. AFTER ALL THAT MAYHEM...
ABSOLUTELY NOTHING FOR THE PAST FEW MONTHS.
THEN THERE'S THE 11TH WARD...
FEELS LIKE SOMETHING BAD IS GOING TO HAPPEN.
CLOSED
I SEE... SO YOU BARELY ESCAPED FROM THE RESTAURANT WITH YOUR LIFE...
YES.
WELL, I'M GLAD YOU DID...

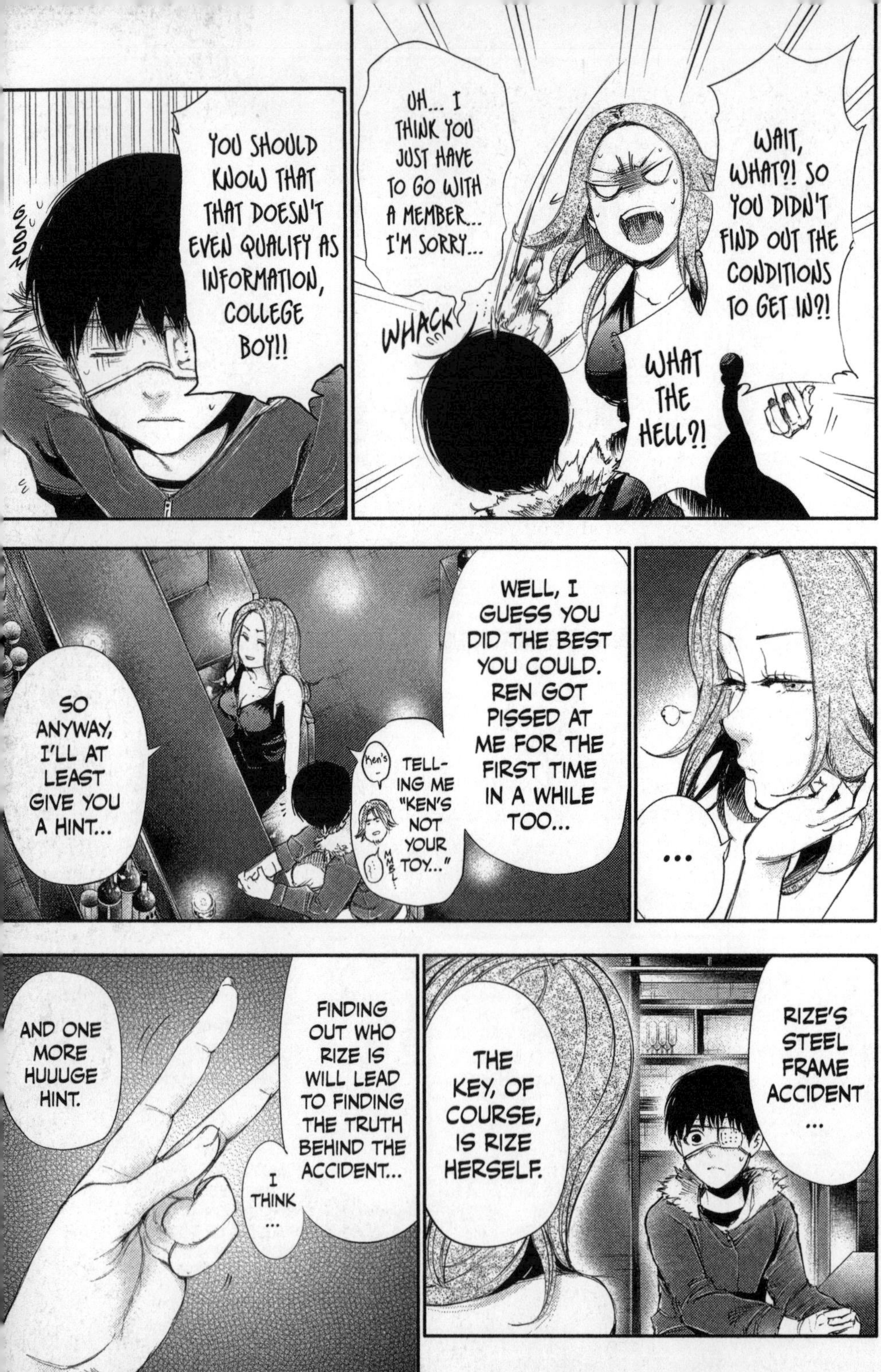
WAIT, WHAT?! SO YOU DIDN'T FIND OUT THE CONDITIONS TO GET IN?!
UH... I THINK YOU JUST HAVE TO GO WITH A MEMBER... I'M SORRY...
WHAT THE HELL?!
WHACK
YOU SHOULD KNOW THAT THAT DOESN'T EVEN QUALIFY AS INFORMATION, COLLEGE BOY!!
GLOOM
...
WELL, I GUESS YOU DID THE BEST YOU COULD. REN GOT PISSED AT ME FOR THE FIRST TIME IN A WHILE TOO...
TELLING ME "KEN'S NOT YOUR TOY..."
Ken's
MMBL
SO ANYWAY, I'LL AT LEAST GIVE YOU A HINT...
RIZE'S STEEL FRAME ACCIDENT ...
THE KEY, OF COURSE, IS RIZE HERSELF.
FINDING OUT WHO RIZE IS WILL LEAD TO FINDING THE TRUTH BEHIND THE ACCIDENT...
I THINK ...
AND ONE MORE HUUUGE HINT.

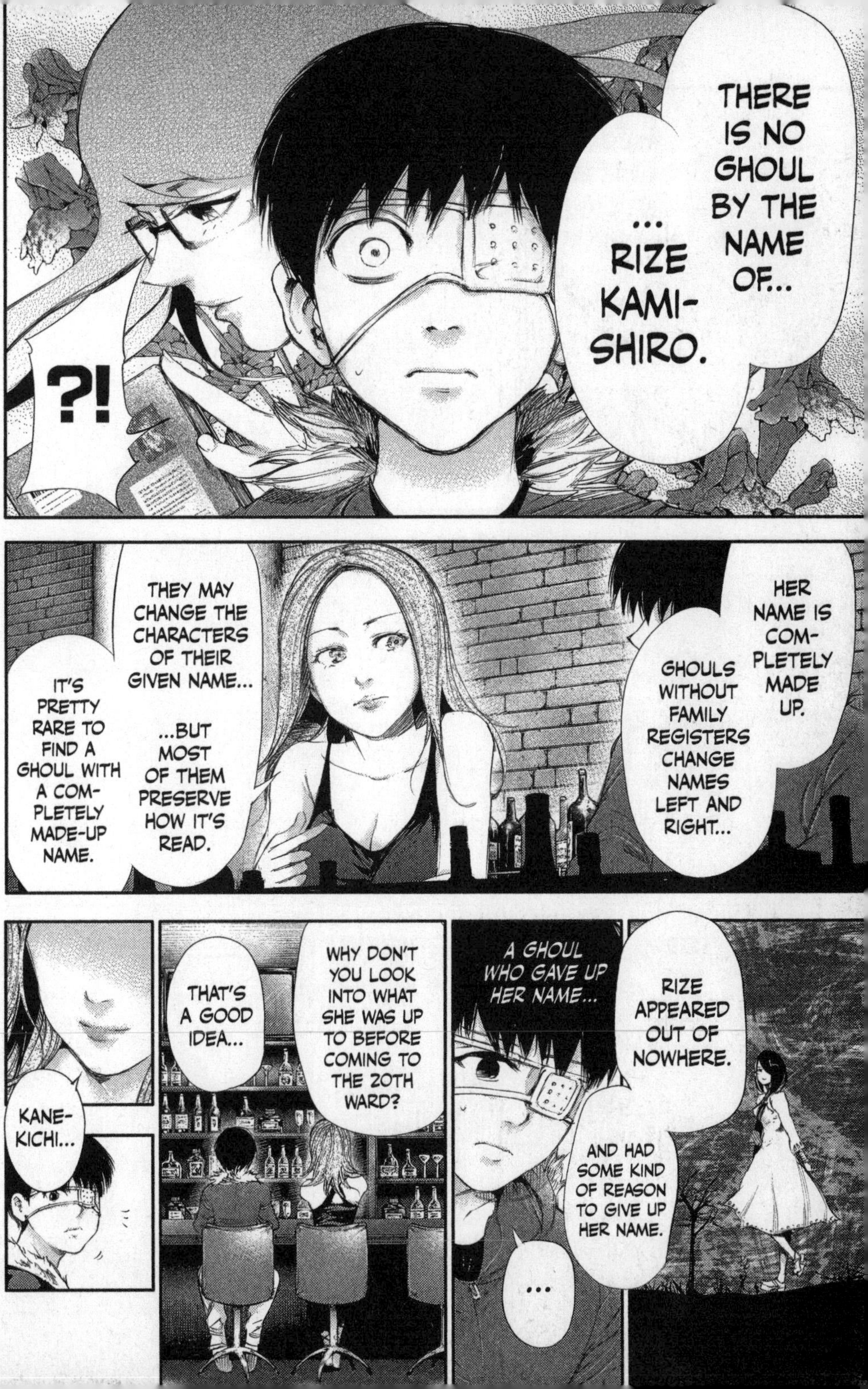
THERE IS NO GHOUL BY THE NAME OF...
... RIZE KAMI-SHIRO.
?!
HER NAME IS COM-PLETELY MADE UP.
GHOULS WITHOUT FAMILY REGISTERS CHANGE NAMES LEFT AND RIGHT...
THEY MAY CHANGE THE CHARACTERS OF THEIR GIVEN NAME...
...BUT MOST OF THEM PRESERVE HOW IT'S READ.
IT'S PRETTY RARE TO FIND A GHOUL WITH A COM-PLETELY MADE-UP NAME.
RIZE APPEARED OUT OF NOWHERE.
AND HAD SOME KIND OF REASON TO GIVE UP HER NAME.
A GHOUL WHO GAVE UP HER NAME...
...
WHY DON'T YOU LOOK INTO WHAT SHE WAS UP TO BEFORE COMING TO THE 20TH WARD?
THAT'S A GOOD IDEA...
KANE-KICHI...

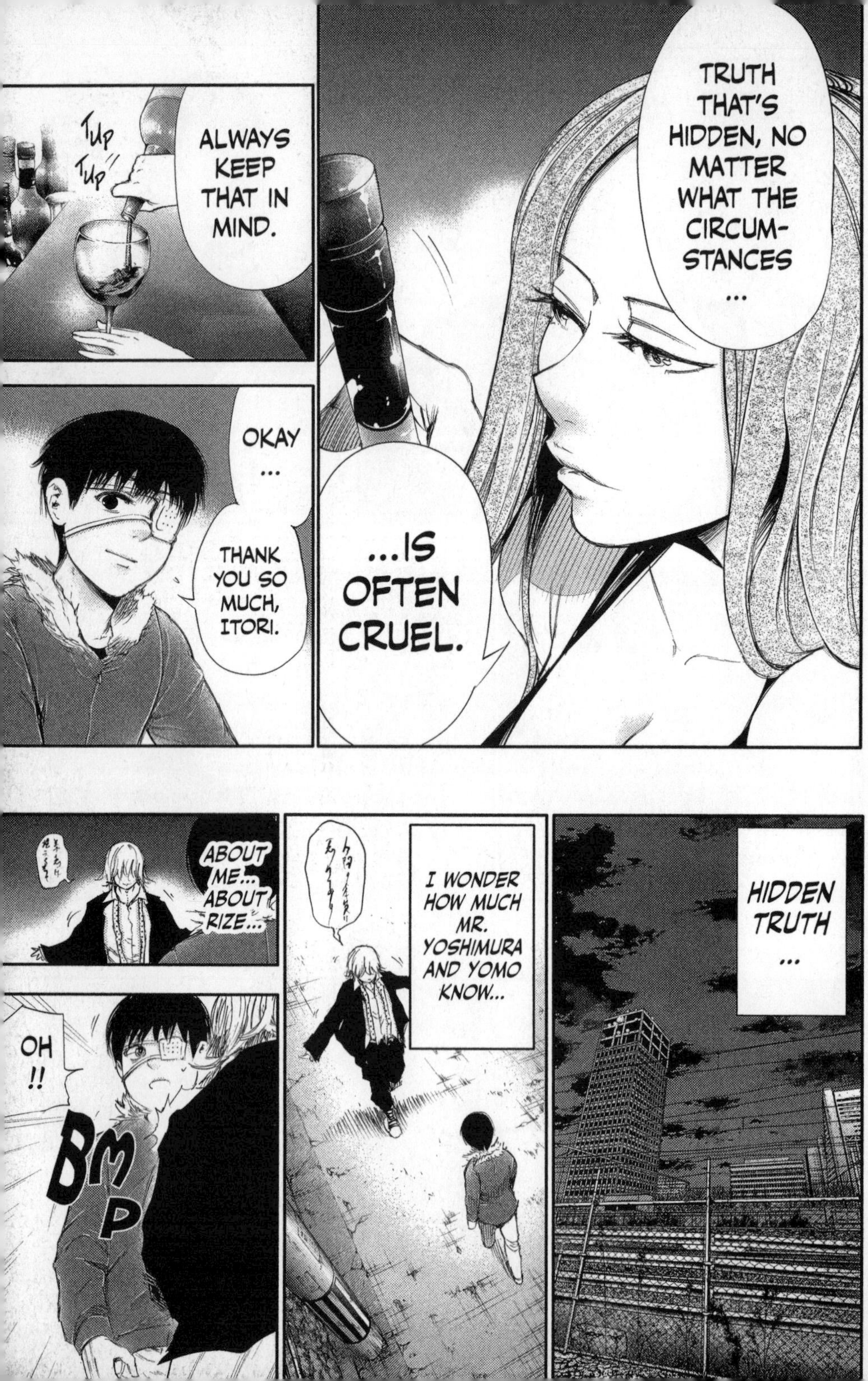
TRUTH THAT'S HIDDEN, NO MATTER WHAT THE CIRCUM-STANCES ...
...IS OFTEN CRUEL.
TUP TUP
ALWAYS KEEP THAT IN MIND.
OKAY ...
THANK YOU SO MUCH, ITORI.
HIDDEN TRUTH ...
I WONDER HOW MUCH MR. YOSHIMURA AND YOMO KNOW...
ABOUT ME... ABOUT RIZE...
OH !!
BMP

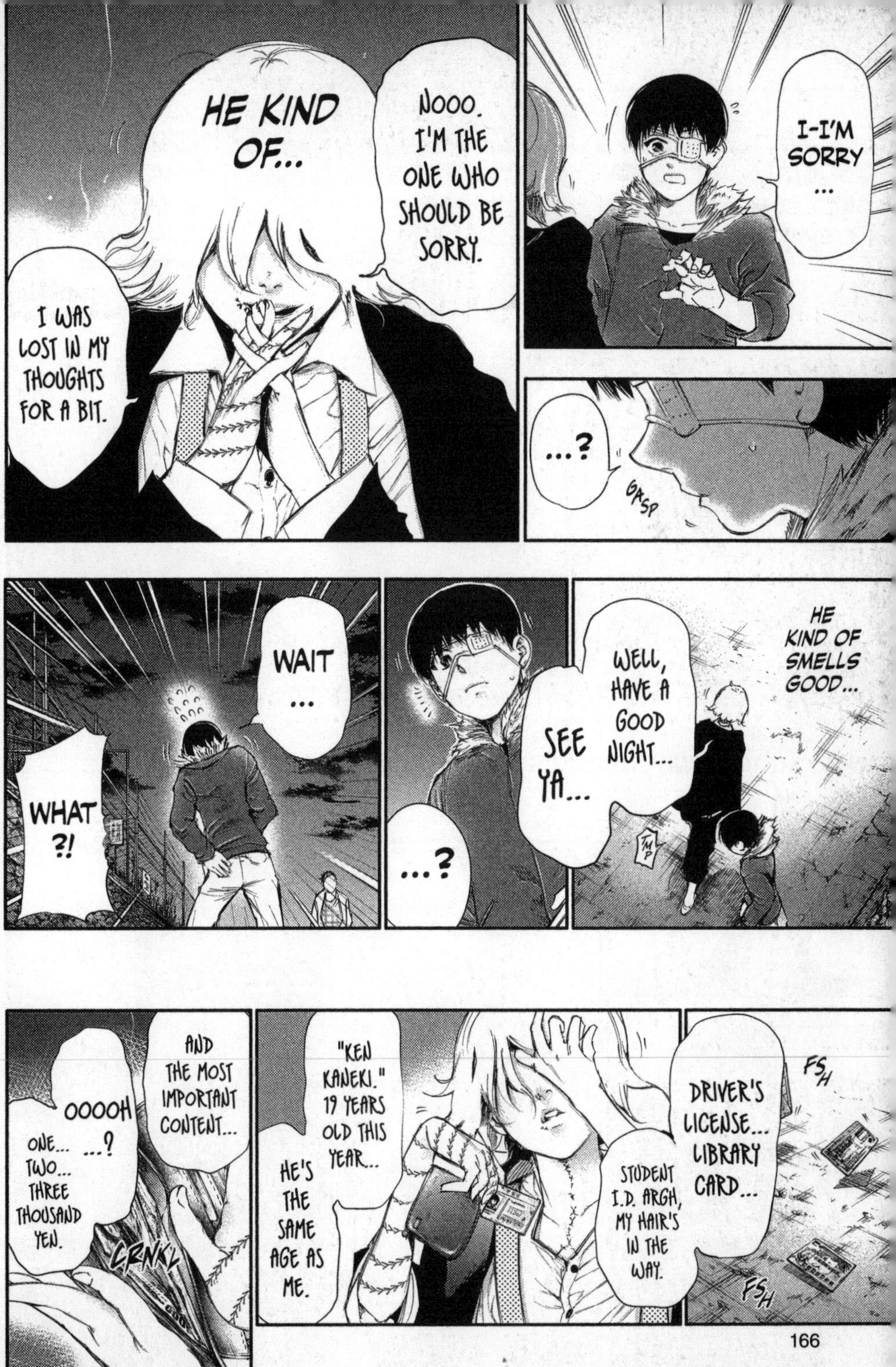
I-I'M SORRY ...
...?
GASP
NOOO. I'M THE ONE WHO SHOULD BE SORRY.
HE KIND OF...
I WAS LOST IN MY THOUGHTS FOR A BIT.
HE KIND OF SMELLS GOOD...
WELL, HAVE A GOOD NIGHT...
TMP
SEE YA...
...?
WAIT ...
WHAT ?!
FSH
DRIVER'S LICENSE... LIBRARY CARD...
STUDENT I.D. ARGH, MY HAIR'S IN THE WAY.
FSH
"KEN KANEKI." 19 YEARS OLD THIS YEAR...
HE'S THE SAME AGE AS ME.
AND THE MOST IMPORTANT CONTENT...
OOOOH ...?
ONE... TWO... THREE THOUSAND YEN.
CRNKL

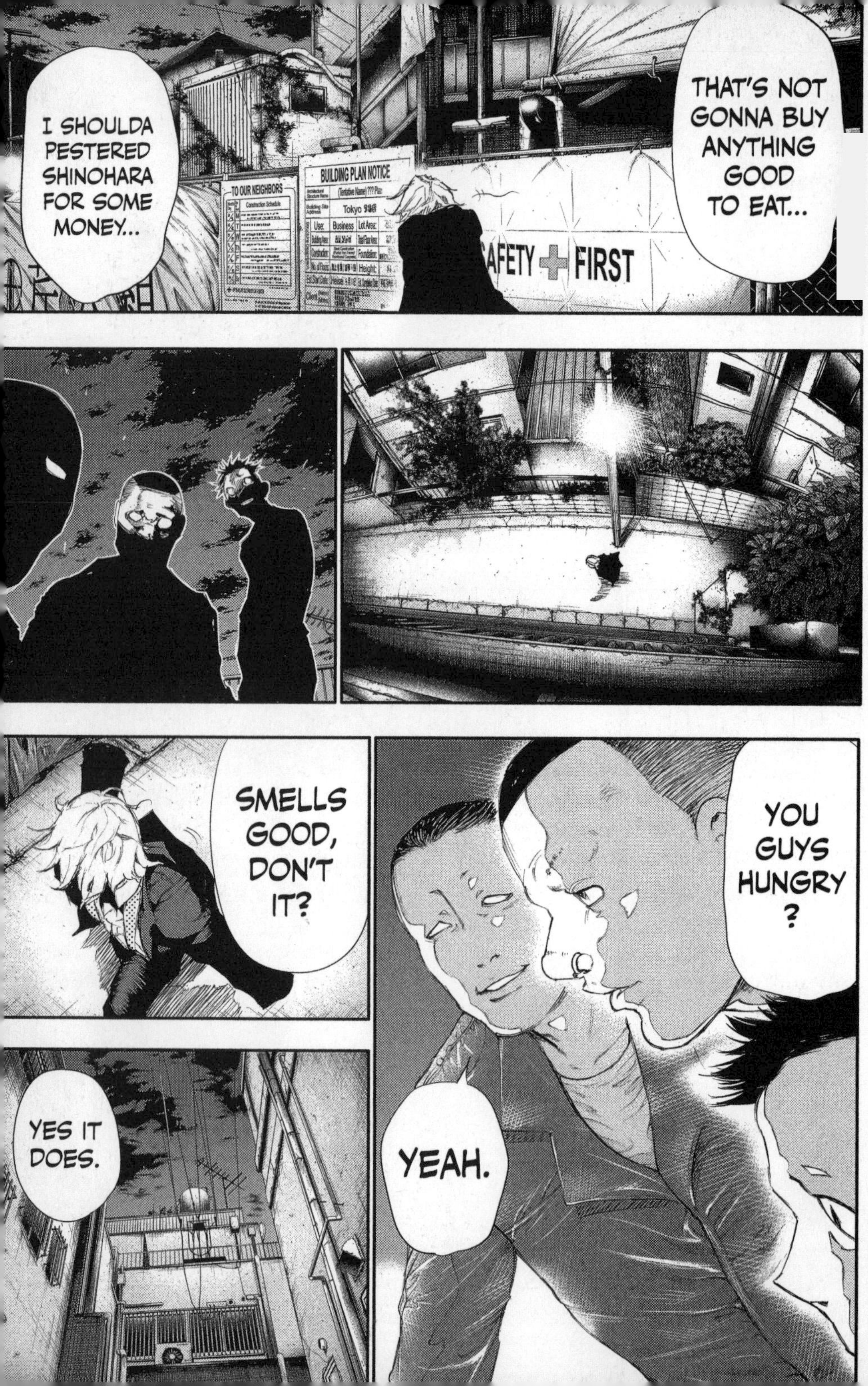
THAT'S NOT GONNA BUY ANYTHING GOOD TO EAT...
SAFETY FIRST
BUILDING PLAN NOTICE
TO OUR NEIGHBORS
I SHOULDA PESTERED SHINOHARA FOR SOME MONEY...
YOU GUYS HUNGRY?
YEAH.
SMELLS GOOD, DON'T IT?
YES IT DOES.

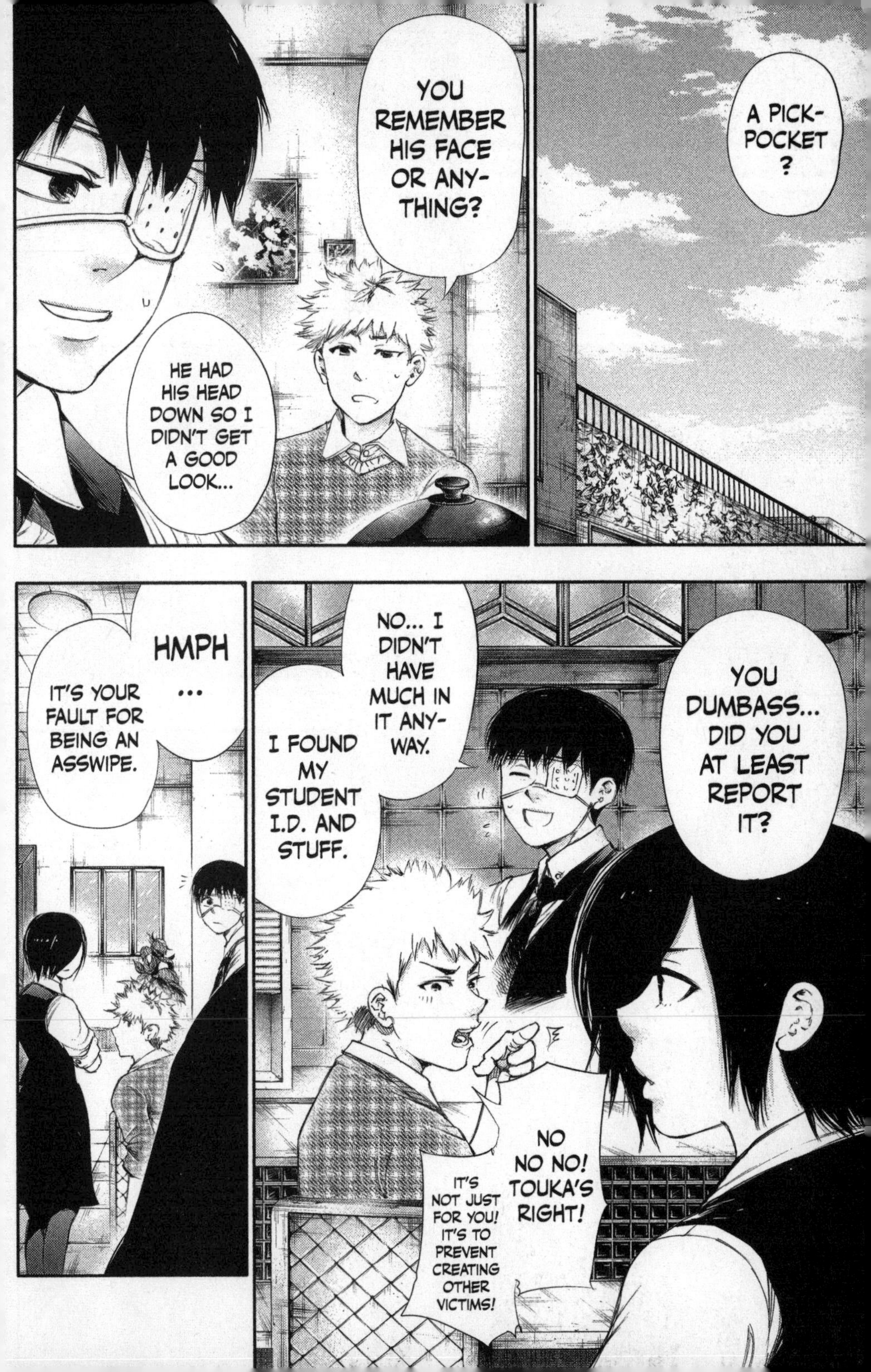
A PICK-POCKET?
YOU REMEMBER HIS FACE OR ANY-THING?
HE HAD HIS HEAD DOWN SO I DIDN'T GET A GOOD LOOK...
YOU DUMBASS... DID YOU AT LEAST REPORT IT?
NO... I DIDN'T HAVE MUCH IN IT ANY-WAY.
I FOUND MY STUDENT I.D. AND STUFF.
NO NO NO! TOUKA'S RIGHT!
IT'S NOT JUST FOR YOU! IT'S TO PREVENT CREATING OTHER VICTIMS!
HMPH...
IT'S YOUR FAULT FOR BEING AN ASSWIPE.

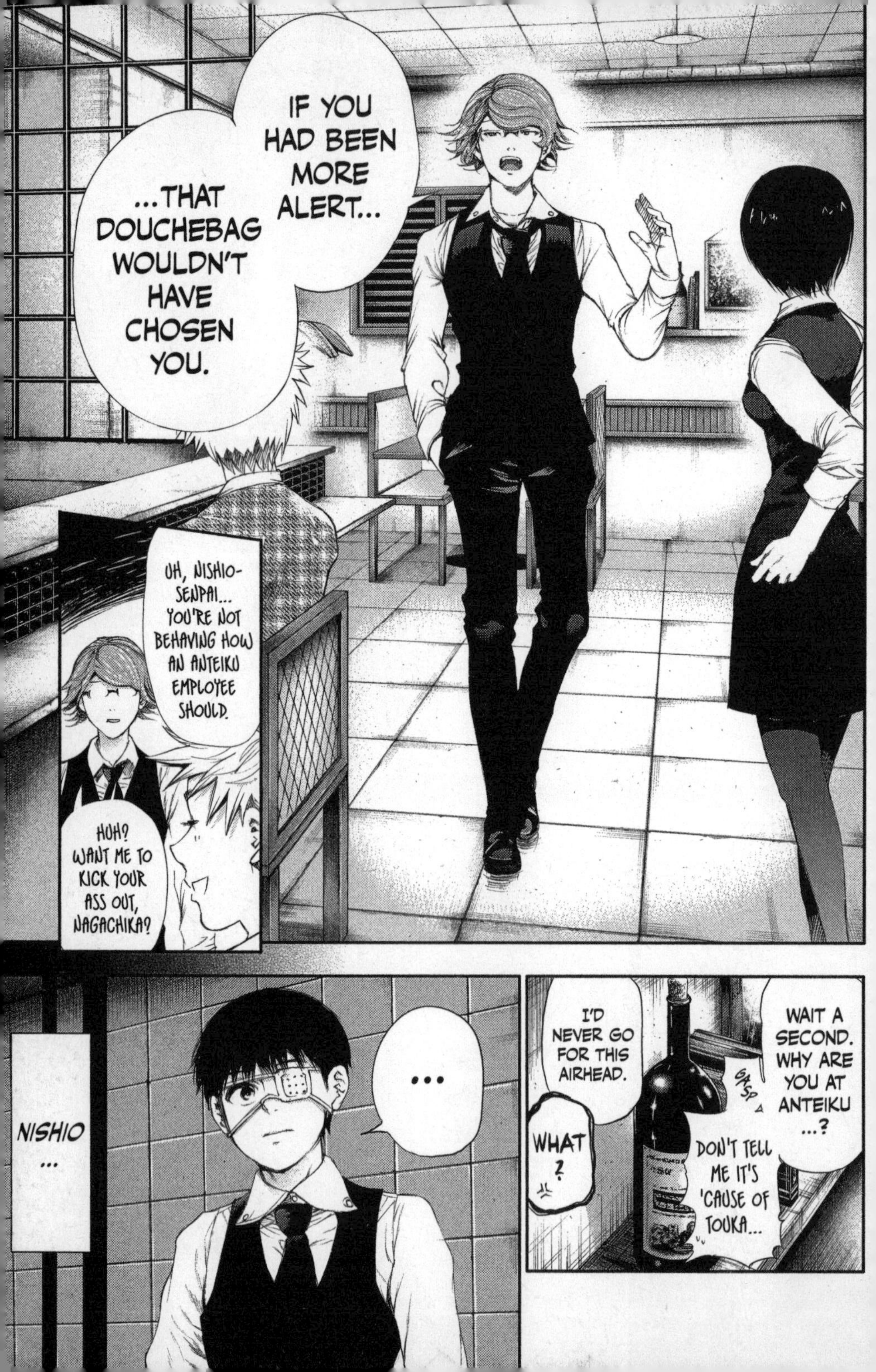
IF YOU HAD BEEN MORE ALERT...
...THAT DOUCHEBAG WOULDN'T HAVE CHOSEN YOU.
UH, NISHIO-SENPAI... YOU'RE NOT BEHAVING HOW AN ANTEIKU EMPLOYEE SHOULD.
HUH? WANT ME TO KICK YOUR ASS OUT, NAGACHIKA?
WAIT A SECOND. WHY ARE YOU AT ANTEIKU ...?
GASP
DON'T TELL ME IT'S 'CAUSE OF TOUKA...
I'D NEVER GO FOR THIS AIRHEAD.
WHAT?
...
NISHIO ...

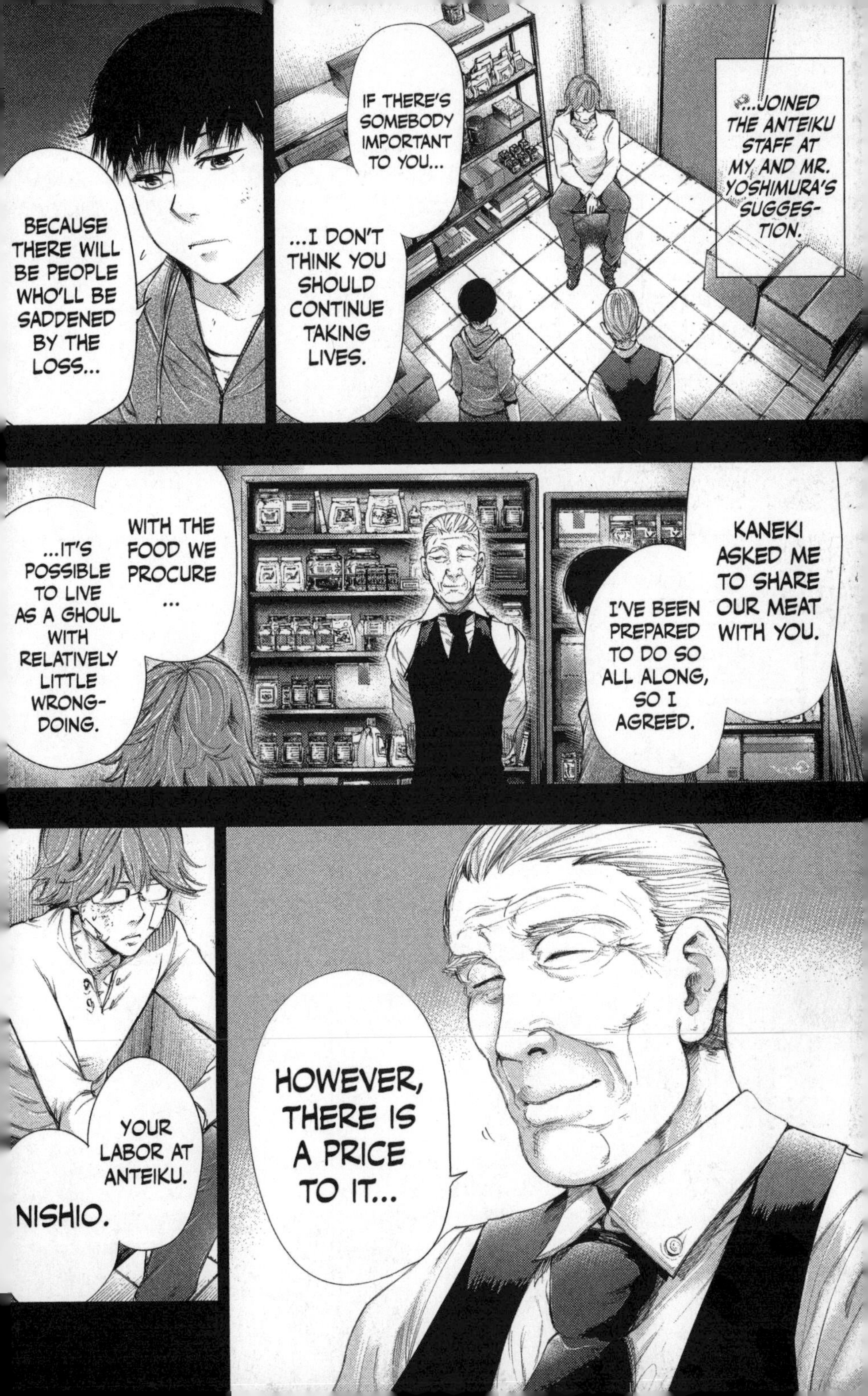
...JOINED THE ANTEIKU STAFF AT MY AND MR. YOSHIMURA'S SUGGESTION.
IF THERE'S SOMEBODY IMPORTANT TO YOU...
...I DON'T THINK YOU SHOULD CONTINUE TAKING LIVES.
BECAUSE THERE WILL BE PEOPLE WHO'LL BE SADDENED BY THE LOSS...
KANEKI ASKED ME TO SHARE OUR MEAT WITH YOU.
I'VE BEEN PREPARED TO DO SO ALL ALONG, SO I AGREED.
WITH THE FOOD WE PROCURE...
...IT'S POSSIBLE TO LIVE AS A GHOUL WITH RELATIVELY LITTLE WRONGDOING.
HOWEVER, THERE IS A PRICE TO IT...
YOUR LABOR AT ANTEIKU.
NISHIO.

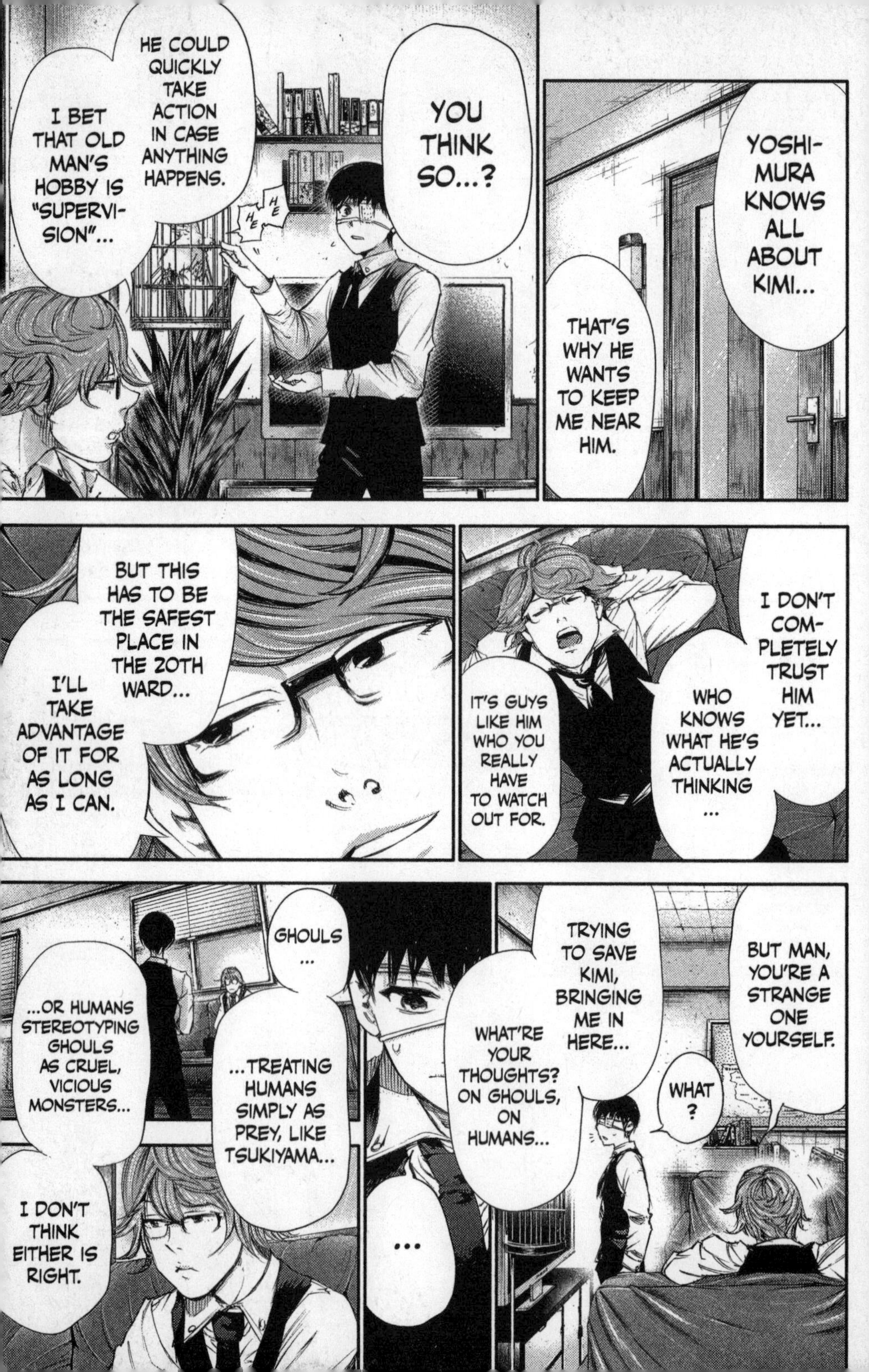
YOSHIMURA KNOWS ALL ABOUT KIMI...
THAT'S WHY HE WANTS TO KEEP ME NEAR HIM.
I BET THAT OLD MAN'S HOBBY IS "SUPERVISION"...
HE COULD QUICKLY TAKE ACTION IN CASE ANYTHING HAPPENS.
YOU THINK SO...?
HE HE
I DON'T COMPLETELY TRUST HIM YET...
WHO KNOWS WHAT HE'S ACTUALLY THINKING...
IT'S GUYS LIKE HIM WHO YOU REALLY HAVE TO WATCH OUT FOR.
BUT THIS HAS TO BE THE SAFEST PLACE IN THE 20TH WARD...
I'LL TAKE ADVANTAGE OF IT FOR AS LONG AS I CAN.
BUT MAN, YOU'RE A STRANGE ONE YOURSELF.
WHAT?
TRYING TO SAVE KIMI, BRINGING ME IN HERE...
WHAT'RE YOUR THOUGHTS? ON GHOULS, ON HUMANS...
GHOULS...
...TREATING HUMANS SIMPLY AS PREY, LIKE TSUKIYAMA...
...
...OR HUMANS STEREOTYPING GHOULS AS CRUEL, VICIOUS MONSTERS...
I DON'T THINK EITHER IS RIGHT.

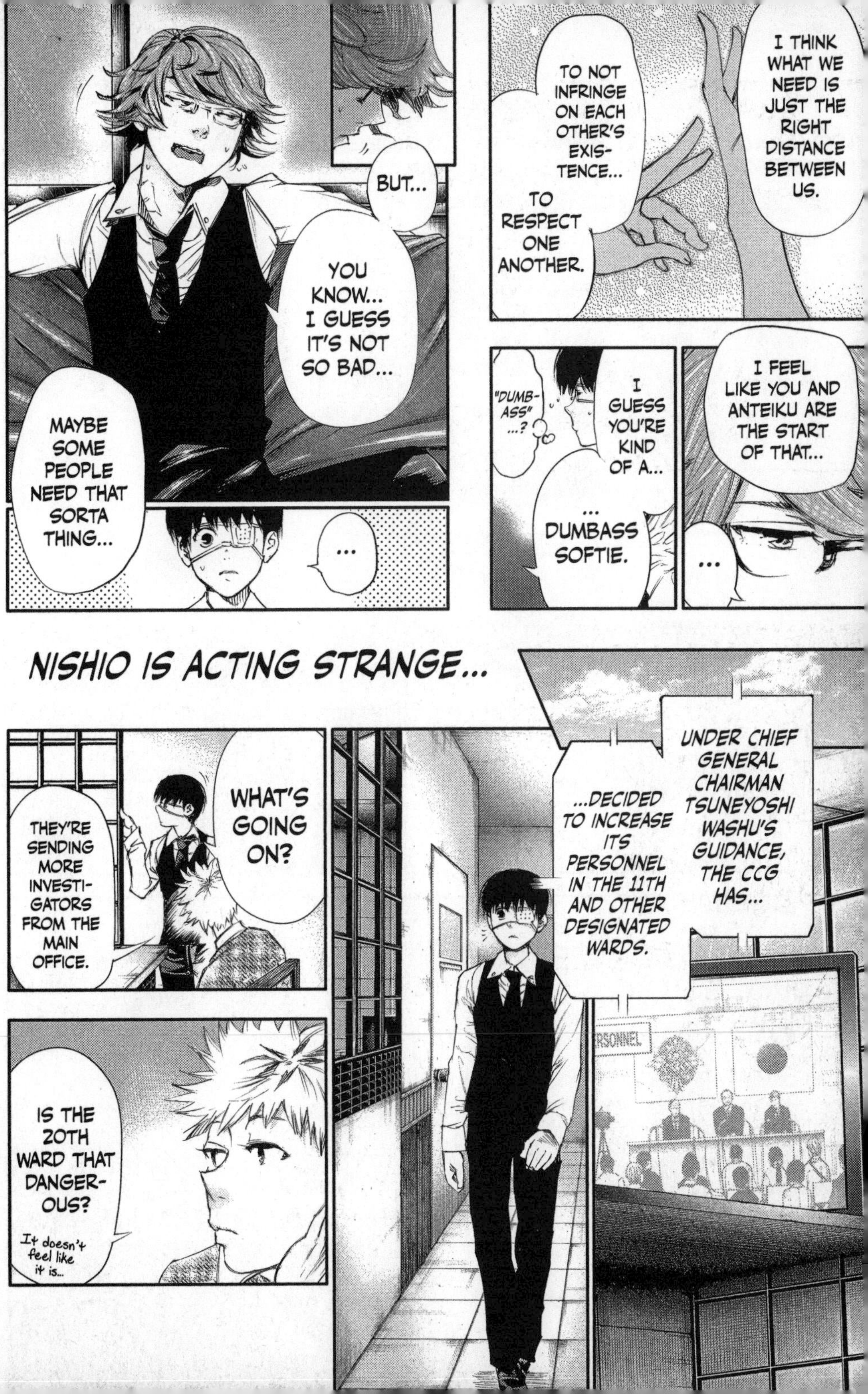
I THINK WHAT WE NEED IS JUST THE RIGHT DISTANCE BETWEEN US.
TO NOT INFRINGE ON EACH OTHER'S EXISTENCE...
TO RESPECT ONE ANOTHER.
BUT...
YOU KNOW... I GUESS IT'S NOT SO BAD...
MAYBE SOME PEOPLE NEED THAT SORTA THING...
...
I FEEL LIKE YOU AND ANTEIKU ARE THE START OF THAT...
...
I GUESS YOU'RE KIND OF A...
...DUMBASS SOFTIE.
"DUMBASS" ...?
NISHIO IS ACTING STRANGE...
UNDER CHIEF GENERAL CHAIRMAN TSUNEYOSHI WASHU'S GUIDANCE, THE CCG HAS...
...DECIDED TO INCREASE ITS PERSONNEL IN THE 11TH AND OTHER DESIGNATED WARDS.
WHAT'S GOING ON?
THEY'RE SENDING MORE INVESTIGATORS FROM THE MAIN OFFICE.
IS THE 20TH WARD THAT DANGEROUS?
It doesn't feel like it is...

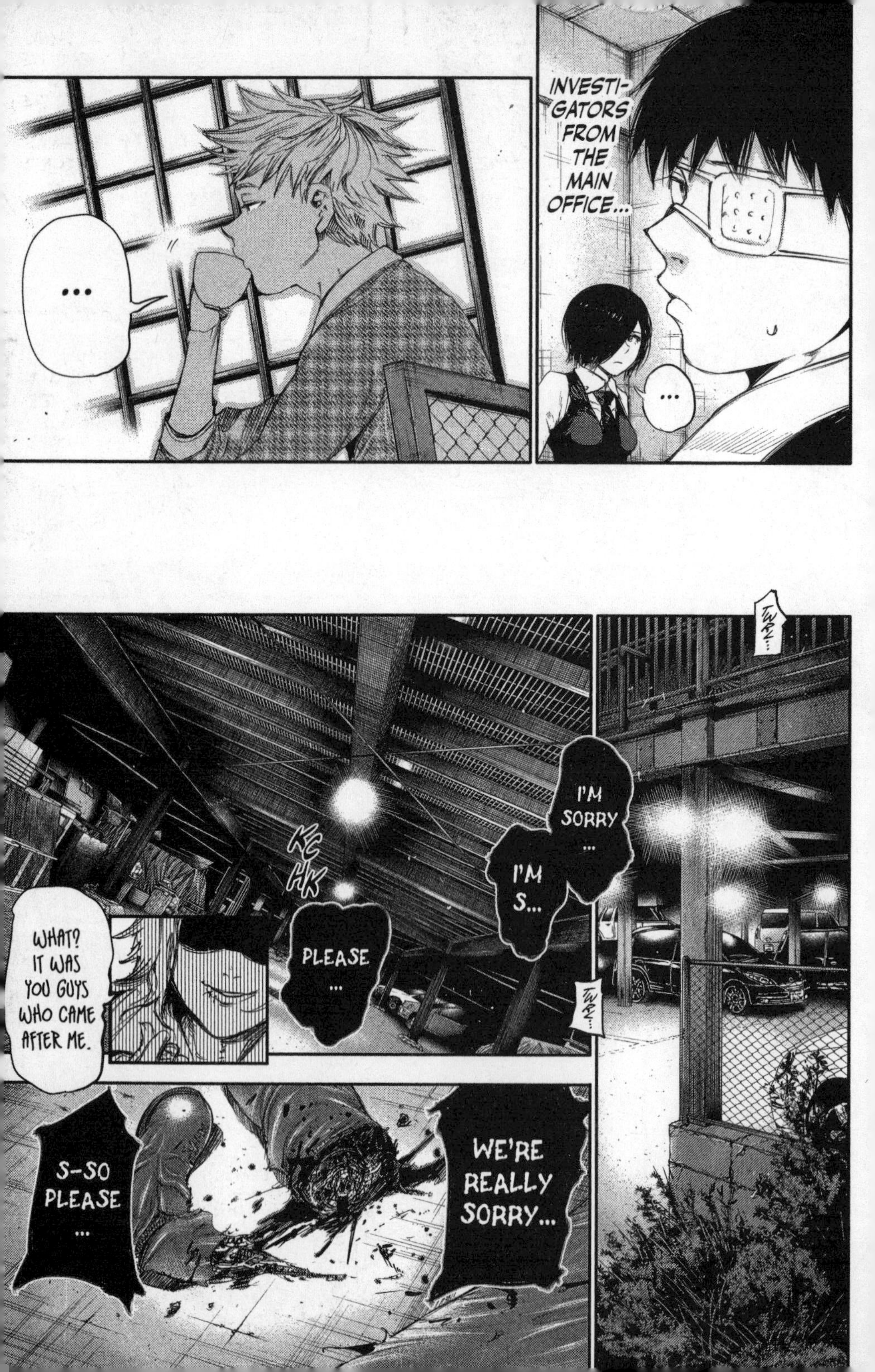
INVESTIGATORS FROM THE MAIN OFFICE...
...
...
TWRL...
TWRL...
I'M SORRY...
I'M S...
KCHK
PLEASE...
WHAT? IT WAS YOU GUYS WHO CAME AFTER ME.
WE'RE REALLY SORRY...
S-SO PLEASE...

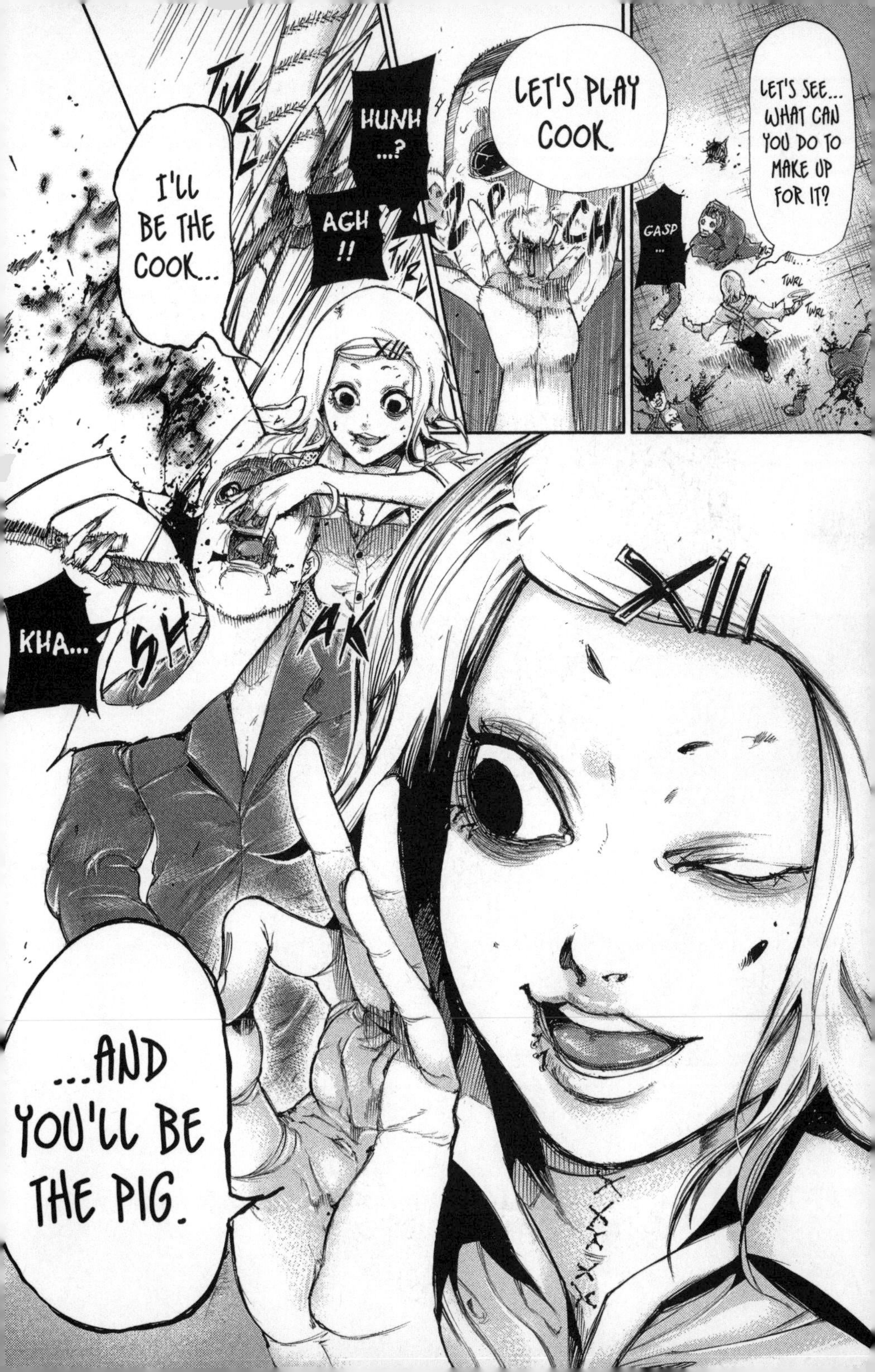
LET'S SEE... WHAT CAN YOU DO TO MAKE UP FOR IT?
GASP ...
TWRL
TWRL
LET'S PLAY COOK.
ZPCH
HUNH ...?
AGH !!
TWRL
TWRL
I'LL BE THE COOK...
KHA...
SHAK
...AND YOU'LL BE THE PIG.

#048 TOKYO GHOUL

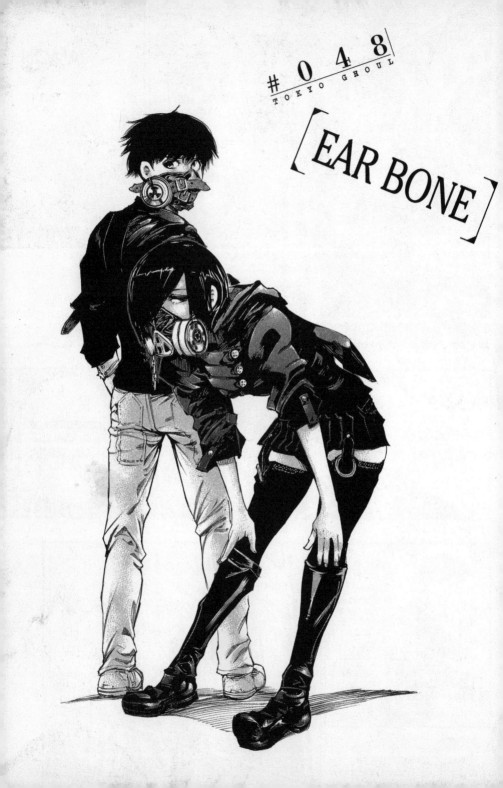

[EAR BONE]

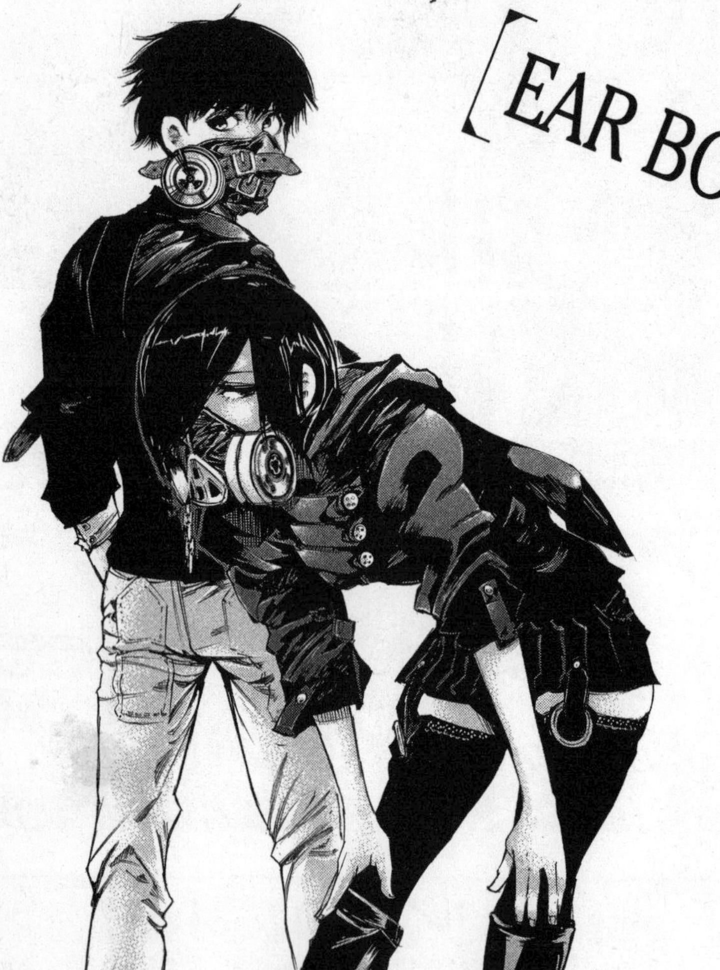

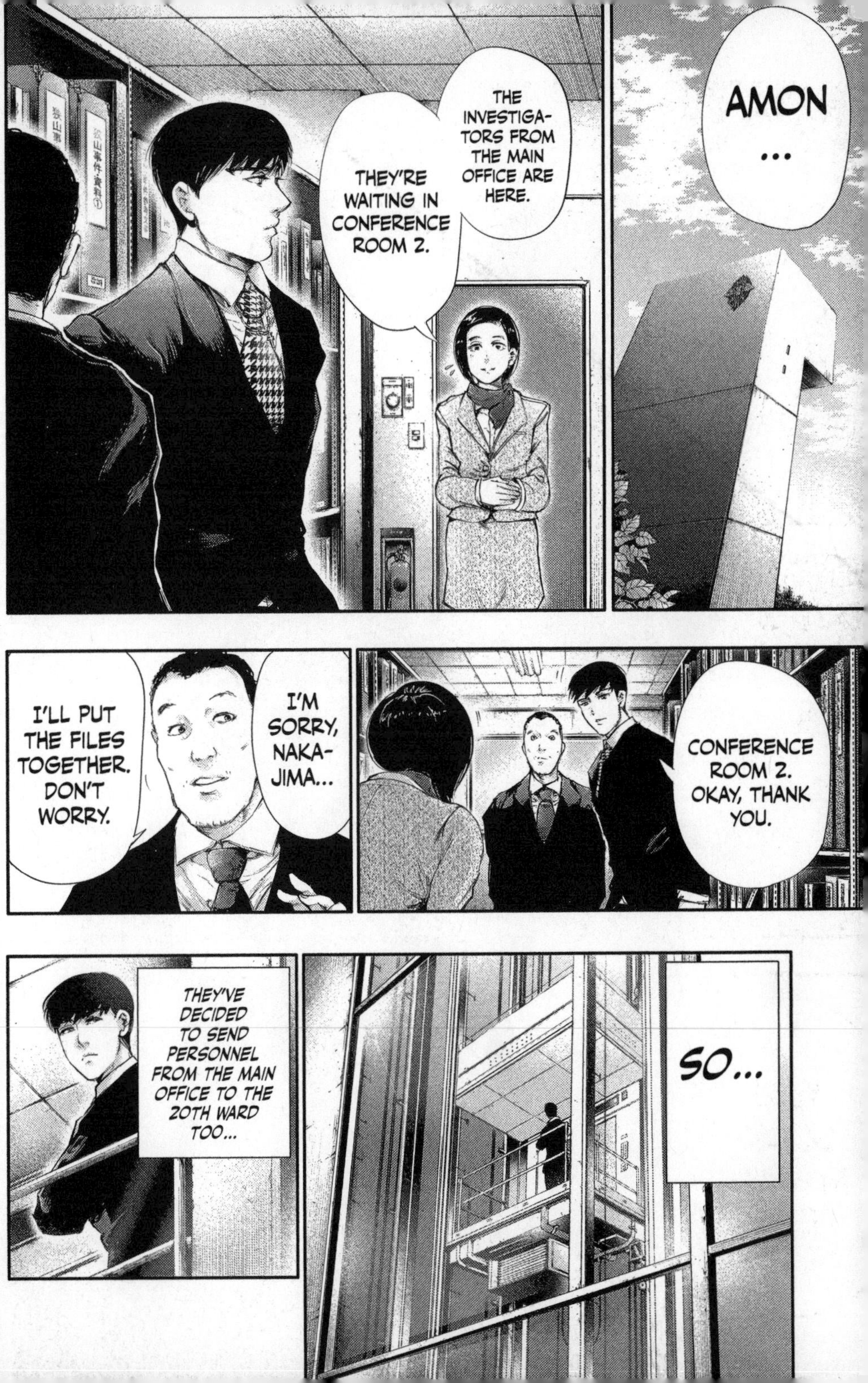
AMON ...
THE INVESTIGATORS FROM THE MAIN OFFICE ARE HERE.
THEY'RE WAITING IN CONFERENCE ROOM 2.
CONFERENCE ROOM 2. OKAY, THANK YOU.
I'M SORRY, NAKAJIMA...
I'LL PUT THE FILES TOGETHER. DON'T WORRY.
SO...
THEY'VE DECIDED TO SEND PERSONNEL FROM THE MAIN OFFICE TO THE 20TH WARD TOO...

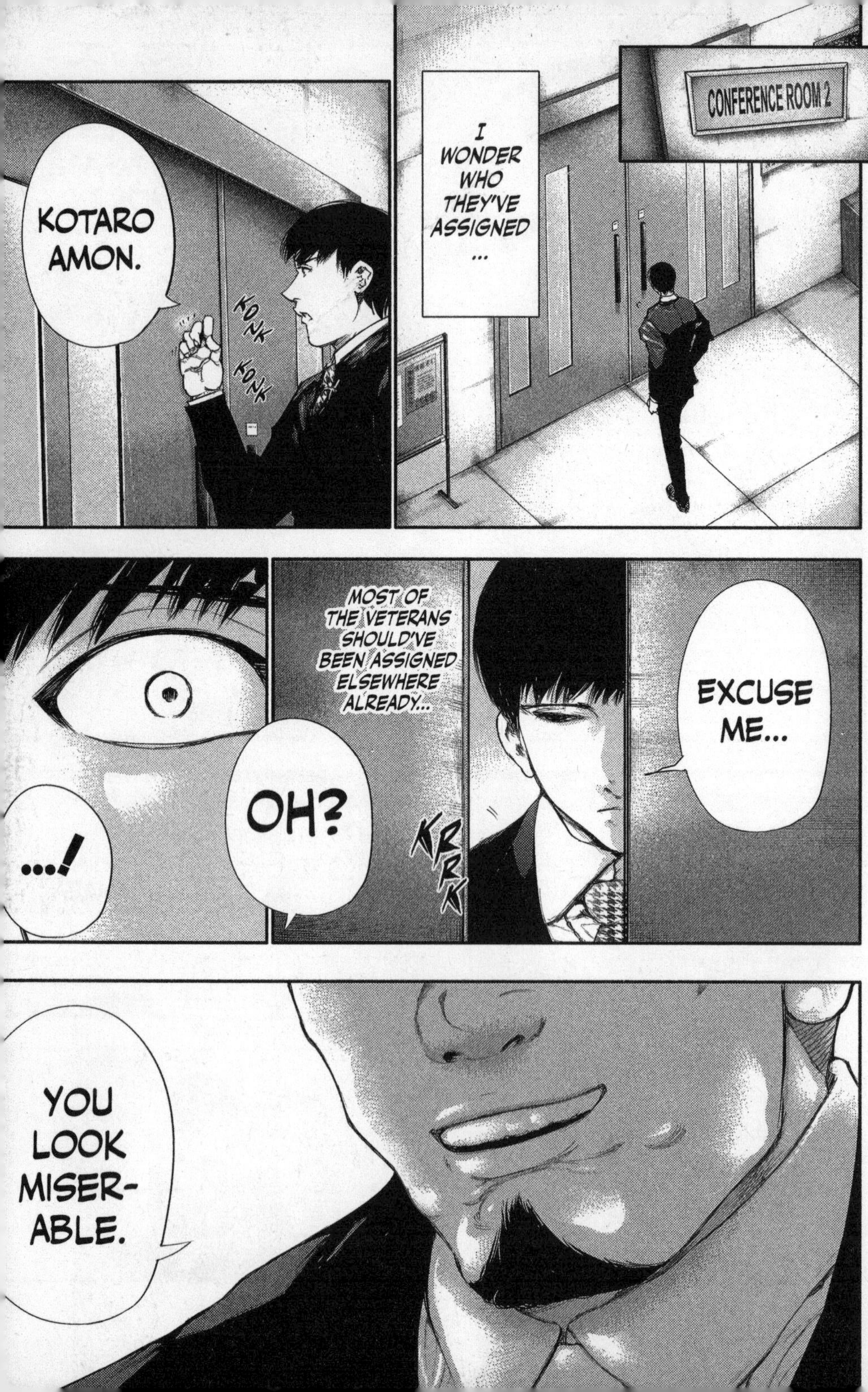
CONFERENCE ROOM 2
I WONDER WHO THEY'VE ASSIGNED ...
KONK KONK
KOTARO AMON.
EXCUSE ME...
KRRK
MOST OF THE VETERANS SHOULD'VE BEEN ASSIGNED ELSEWHERE ALREADY...
OH?
...!
YOU LOOK MISER-ABLE.

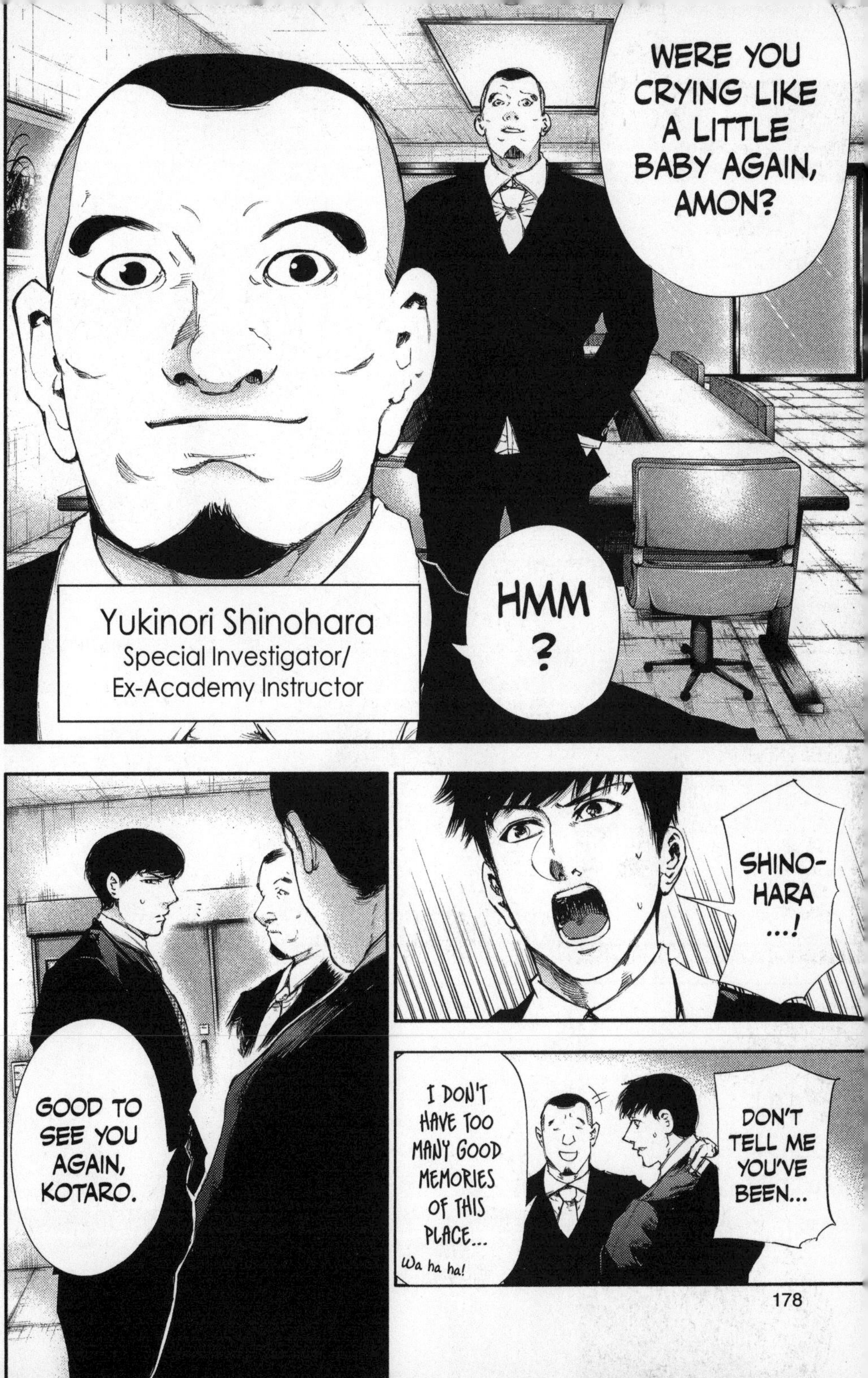
WERE YOU CRYING LIKE A LITTLE BABY AGAIN, AMON?
HMM ?
Yukinori Shinohara
Special Investigator/
Ex-Academy Instructor
SHINO-HARA ...!
DON'T TELL ME YOU'VE BEEN...
I DON'T HAVE TOO MANY GOOD MEMORIES OF THIS PLACE...
Wa ha ha!
GOOD TO SEE YOU AGAIN, KOTARO.

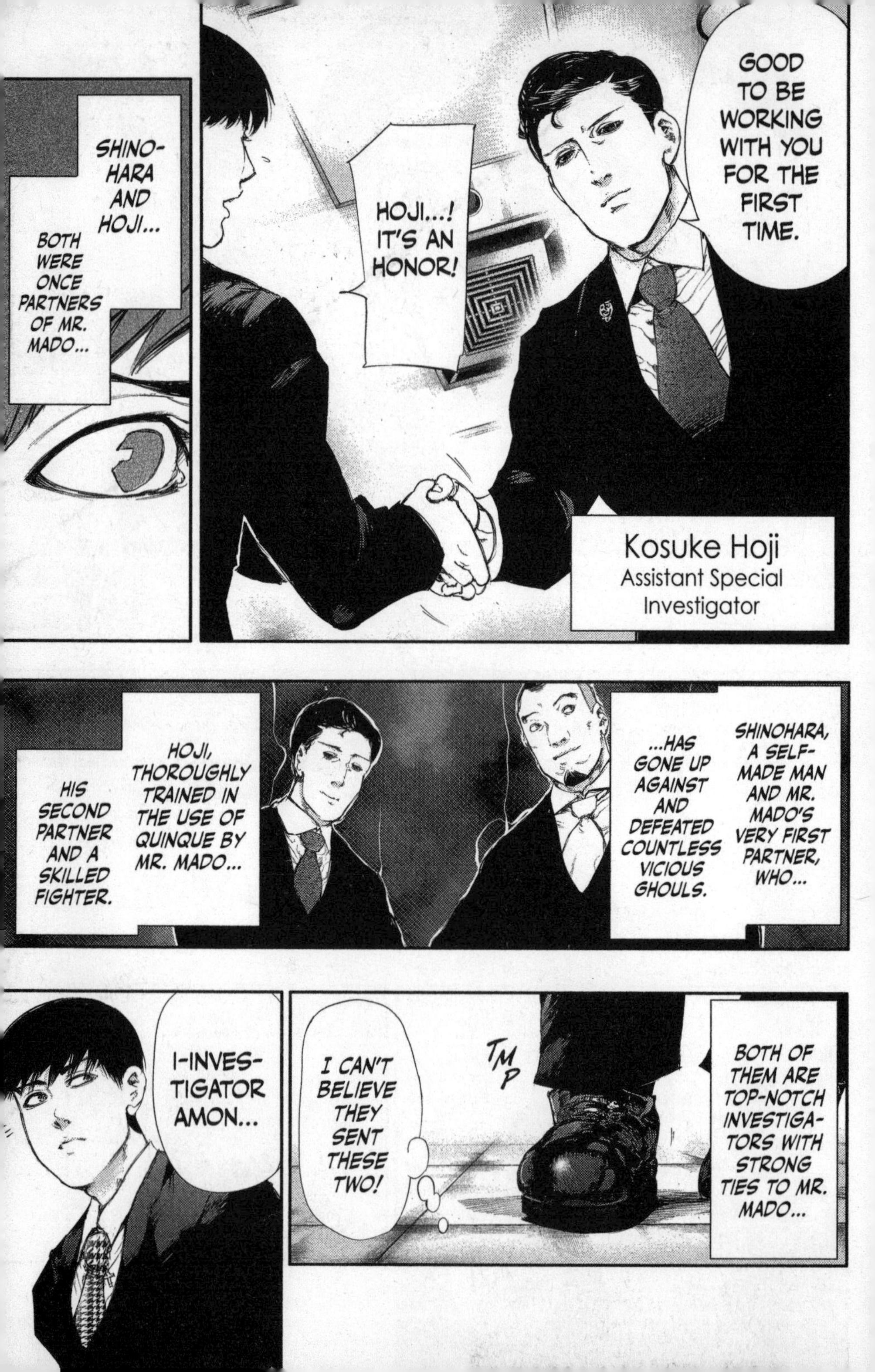
GOOD TO BE WORKING WITH YOU FOR THE FIRST TIME.
HOJI...! IT'S AN HONOR!
Kosuke Hoji
Assistant Special Investigator
SHINO-HARA AND HOJI...
BOTH WERE ONCE PARTNERS OF MR. MADO...
SHINOHARA, A SELF-MADE MAN AND MR. MADO'S VERY FIRST PARTNER, WHO...
...HAS GONE UP AGAINST AND DEFEATED COUNTLESS VICIOUS GHOULS.
HOJI, THOROUGHLY TRAINED IN THE USE OF QUINQUE BY MR. MADO...
HIS SECOND PARTNER AND A SKILLED FIGHTER.
BOTH OF THEM ARE TOP-NOTCH INVESTIGA-TORS WITH STRONG TIES TO MR. MADO...
TMP
I CAN'T BELIEVE THEY SENT THESE TWO!
I-INVES-TIGATOR AMON...

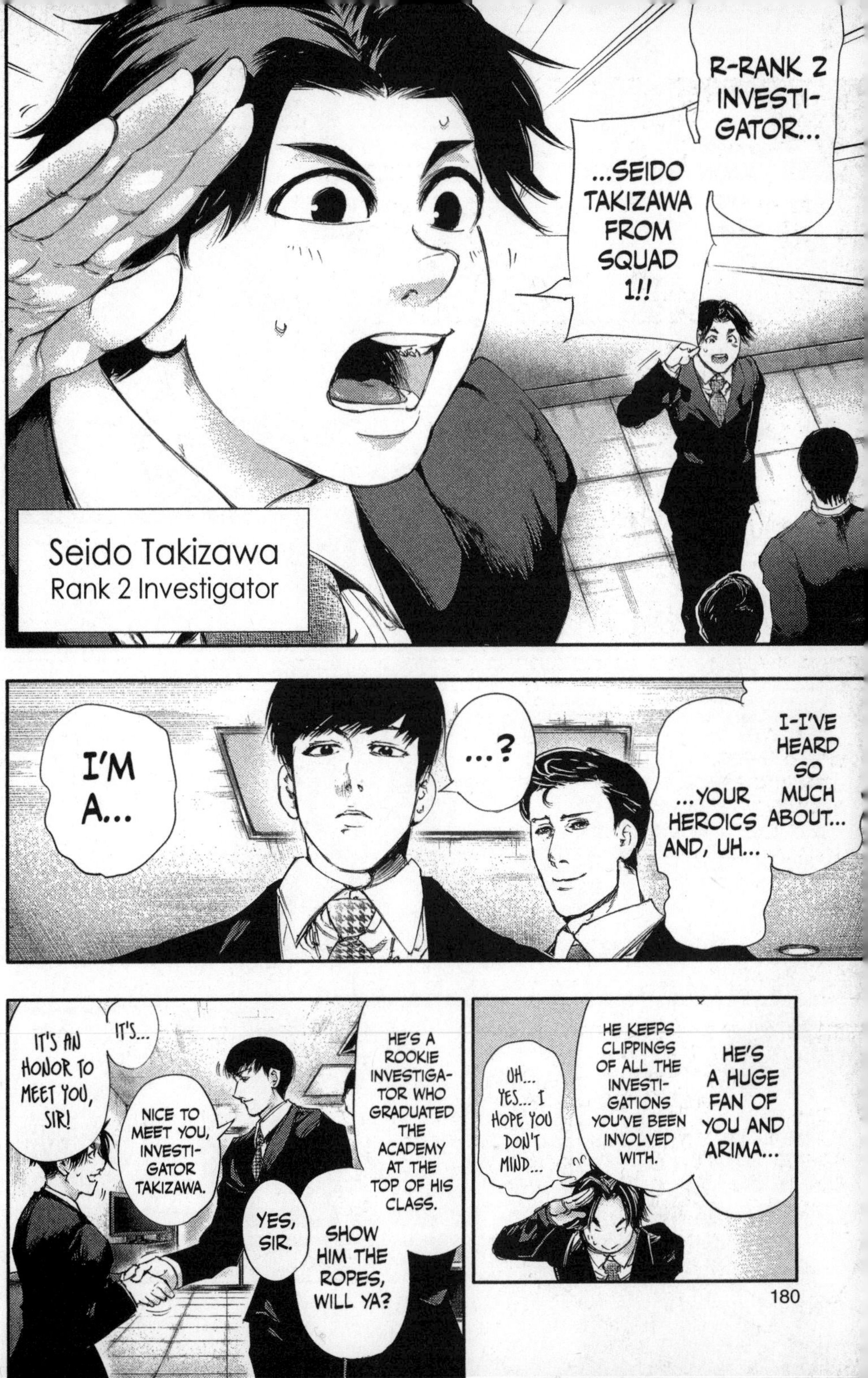
R-RANK 2 INVESTIGATOR...
...SEIDO TAKIZAWA FROM SQUAD 1!!
Seido Takizawa
Rank 2 Investigator
I-I'VE HEARD SO MUCH ABOUT...
...YOUR HEROICS AND, UH...
...?
I'M A...
HE'S A HUGE FAN OF YOU AND ARIMA...
HE KEEPS CLIPPINGS OF ALL THE INVESTIGATIONS YOU'VE BEEN INVOLVED WITH.
UH... YES... I HOPE YOU DON'T MIND...
HE'S A ROOKIE INVESTIGATOR WHO GRADUATED THE ACADEMY AT THE TOP OF HIS CLASS.
SHOW HIM THE ROPES, WILL YA?
YES, SIR.
NICE TO MEET YOU, INVESTIGATOR TAKIZAWA.
IT'S...
IT'S AN HONOR TO MEET YOU, SIR!

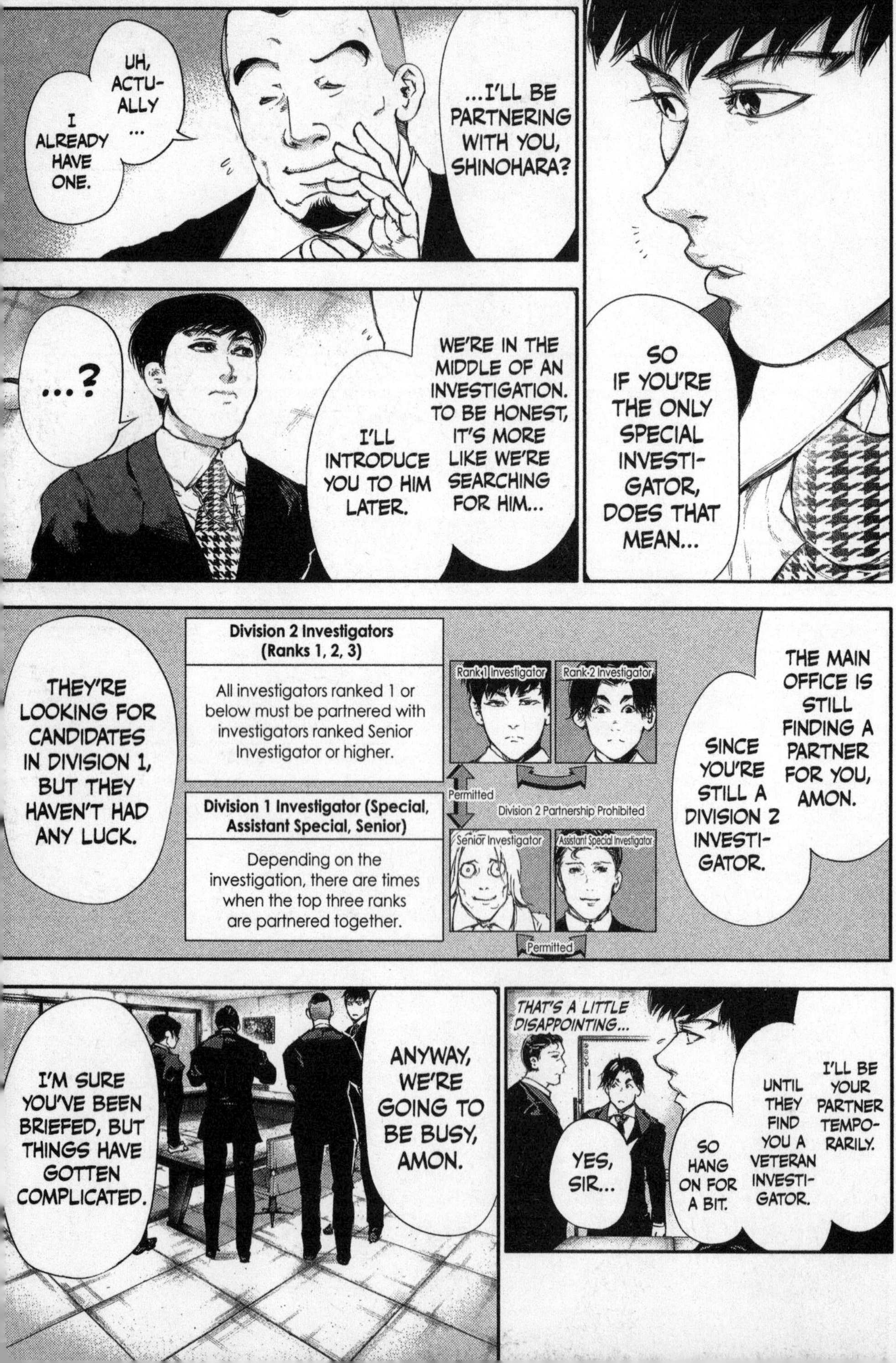
SO IF YOU'RE THE ONLY SPECIAL INVESTIGATOR, DOES THAT MEAN...
...I'LL BE PARTNERING WITH YOU, SHINOHARA?
UH, ACTUALLY...
I ALREADY HAVE ONE.
WE'RE IN THE MIDDLE OF AN INVESTIGATION. TO BE HONEST, IT'S MORE LIKE WE'RE SEARCHING FOR HIM...
I'LL INTRODUCE YOU TO HIM LATER.
...?
THE MAIN OFFICE IS STILL FINDING A PARTNER FOR YOU, AMON.
SINCE YOU'RE STILL A DIVISION 2 INVESTIGATOR.
Division 2 Investigators (Ranks 1, 2, 3)
All investigators ranked 1 or below must be partnered with investigators ranked Senior Investigator or higher.
Division 1 Investigator (Special, Assistant Special, Senior)
Depending on the investigation, there are times when the top three ranks are partnered together.
Rank 1 Investigator
Rank 2 Investigator
Division 2 Partnership Prohibited
Permitted
Senior Investigator
Assistant Special Investigator
Permitted
THEY'RE LOOKING FOR CANDIDATES IN DIVISION 1, BUT THEY HAVEN'T HAD ANY LUCK.
THAT'S A LITTLE DISAPPOINTING...
I'LL BE YOUR PARTNER TEMPORARILY.
UNTIL THEY FIND YOU A VETERAN INVESTIGATOR.
SO HANG ON FOR A BIT.
YES, SIR...
ANYWAY, WE'RE GOING TO BE BUSY, AMON.
I'M SURE YOU'VE BEEN BRIEFED, BUT THINGS HAVE GOTTEN COMPLICATED.

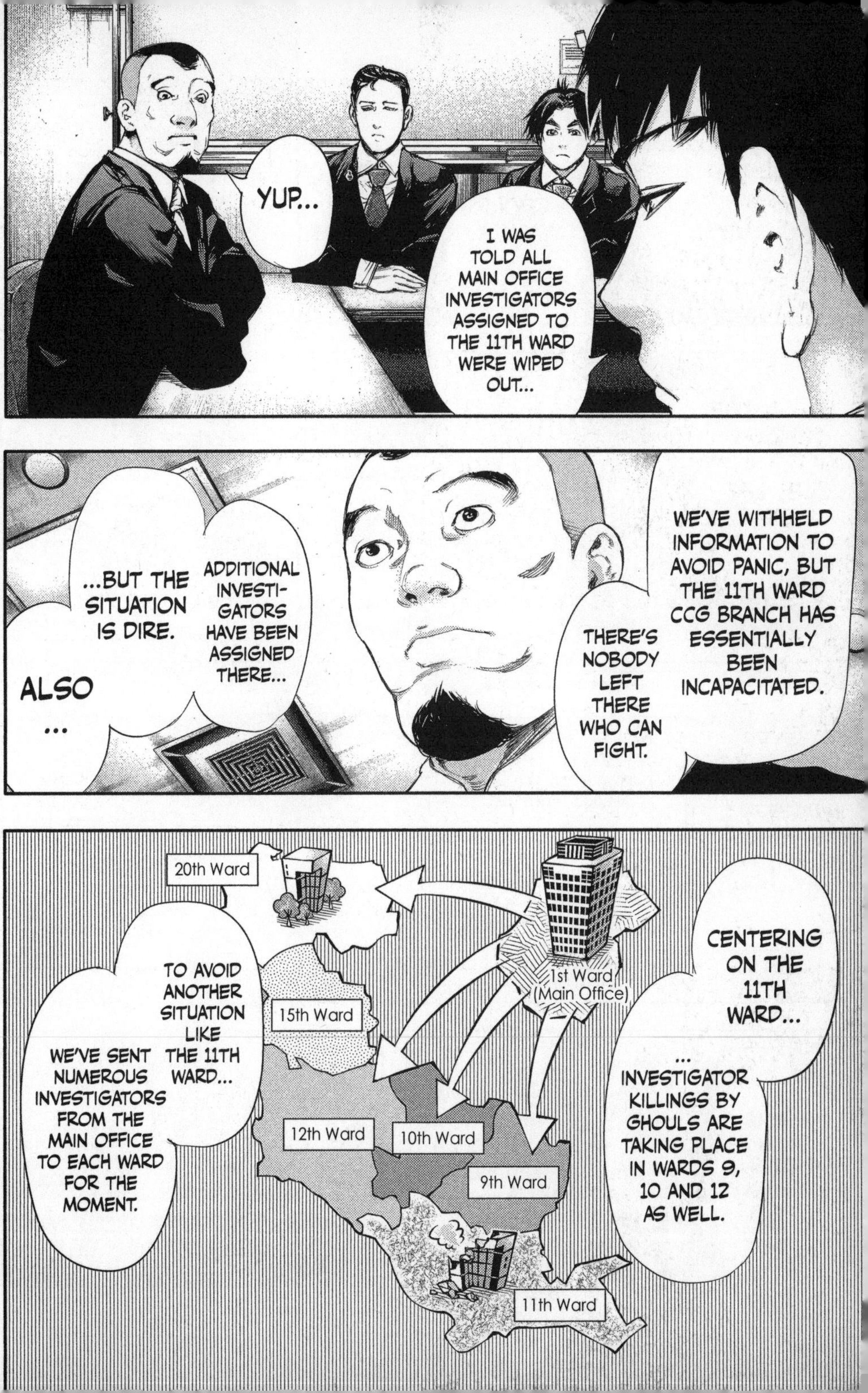
I WAS TOLD ALL MAIN OFFICE INVESTIGATORS ASSIGNED TO THE 11TH WARD WERE WIPED OUT...
YUP...
WE'VE WITHHELD INFORMATION TO AVOID PANIC, BUT THE 11TH WARD CCG BRANCH HAS ESSENTIALLY BEEN INCAPACITATED.
THERE'S NOBODY LEFT THERE WHO CAN FIGHT.
ADDITIONAL INVESTI-GATORS HAVE BEEN ASSIGNED THERE...
...BUT THE SITUATION IS DIRE.
ALSO ...
CENTERING ON THE 11TH WARD...
...INVESTIGATOR KILLINGS BY GHOULS ARE TAKING PLACE IN WARDS 9, 10 AND 12 AS WELL.
1st Ward (Main Office)
20th Ward
15th Ward
12th Ward
10th Ward
9th Ward
11th Ward
TO AVOID ANOTHER SITUATION LIKE THE 11TH WARD...
WE'VE SENT NUMEROUS INVESTIGATORS FROM THE MAIN OFFICE TO EACH WARD FOR THE MOMENT.

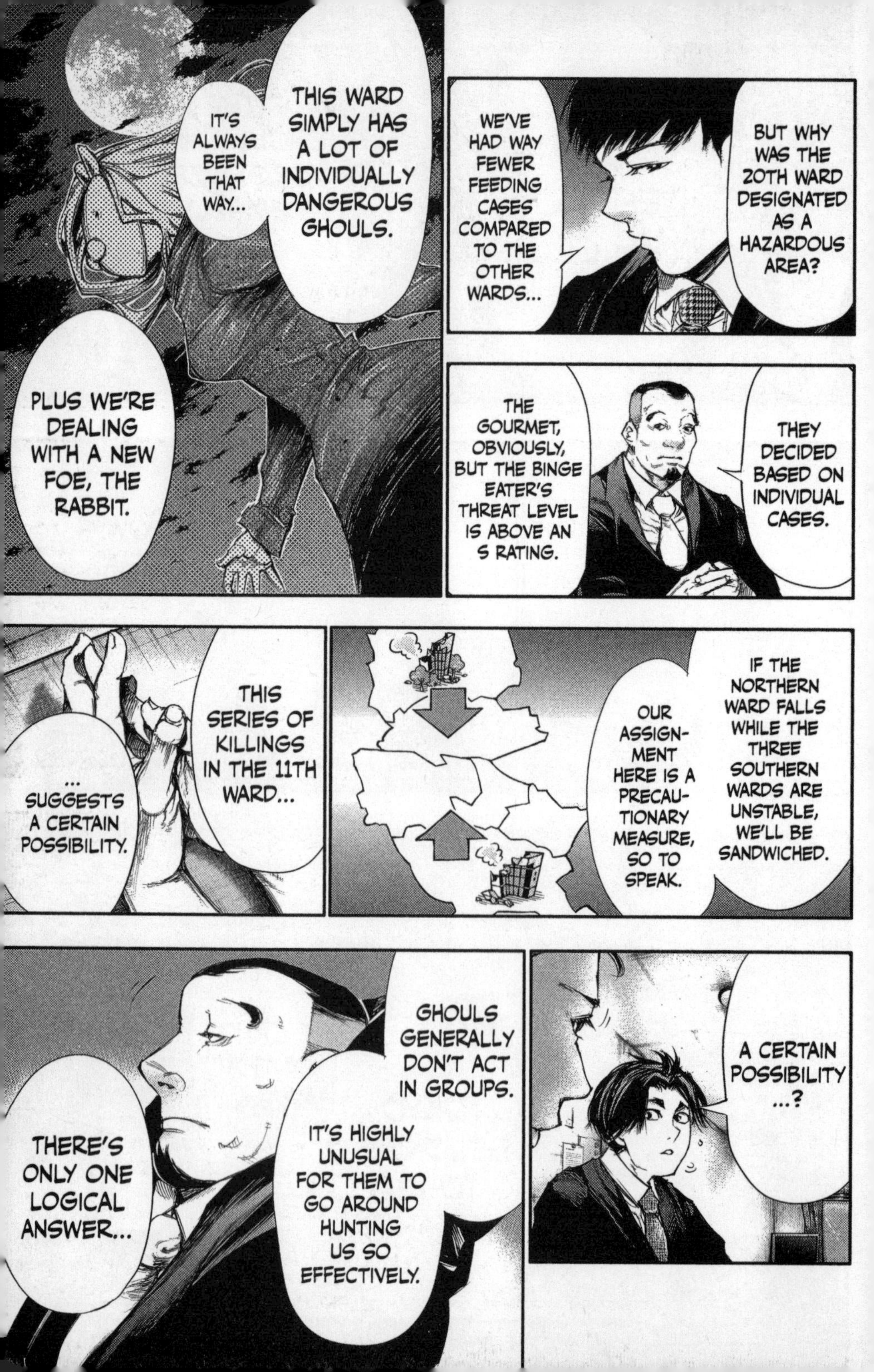
BUT WHY WAS THE 20TH WARD DESIGNATED AS A HAZARDOUS AREA?
WE'VE HAD WAY FEWER FEEDING CASES COMPARED TO THE OTHER WARDS...
THEY DECIDED BASED ON INDIVIDUAL CASES.
THE GOURMET, OBVIOUSLY, BUT THE BINGE EATER'S THREAT LEVEL IS ABOVE AN S RATING.
THIS WARD SIMPLY HAS A LOT OF INDIVIDUALLY DANGEROUS GHOULS.
IT'S ALWAYS BEEN THAT WAY...
PLUS WE'RE DEALING WITH A NEW FOE, THE RABBIT.
IF THE NORTHERN WARD FALLS WHILE THE THREE SOUTHERN WARDS ARE UNSTABLE, WE'LL BE SANDWICHED.
OUR ASSIGNMENT HERE IS A PRECAUTIONARY MEASURE, SO TO SPEAK.
THIS SERIES OF KILLINGS IN THE 11TH WARD...
...SUGGESTS A CERTAIN POSSIBILITY.
A CERTAIN POSSIBILITY...?
GHOULS GENERALLY DON'T ACT IN GROUPS.
IT'S HIGHLY UNUSUAL FOR THEM TO GO AROUND HUNTING US SO EFFECTIVELY.
THERE'S ONLY ONE LOGICAL ANSWER...

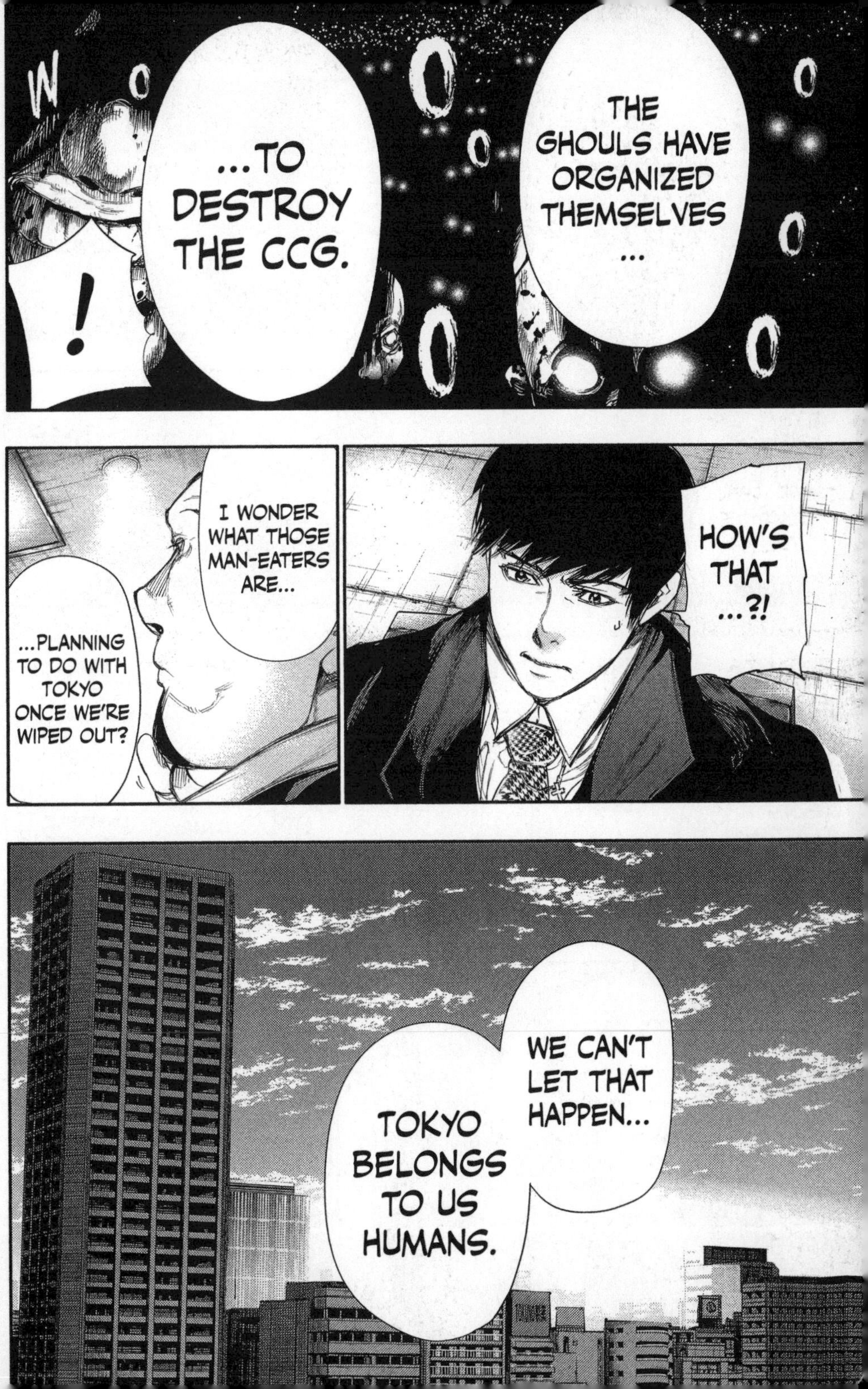
THE GHOULS HAVE ORGANIZED THEMSELVES ...
...TO DESTROY THE CCG.
HOW'S THAT ...?!
I WONDER WHAT THOSE MAN-EATERS ARE...
...PLANNING TO DO WITH TOKYO ONCE WE'RE WIPED OUT?
WE CAN'T LET THAT HAPPEN...
TOKYO BELONGS TO US HUMANS.

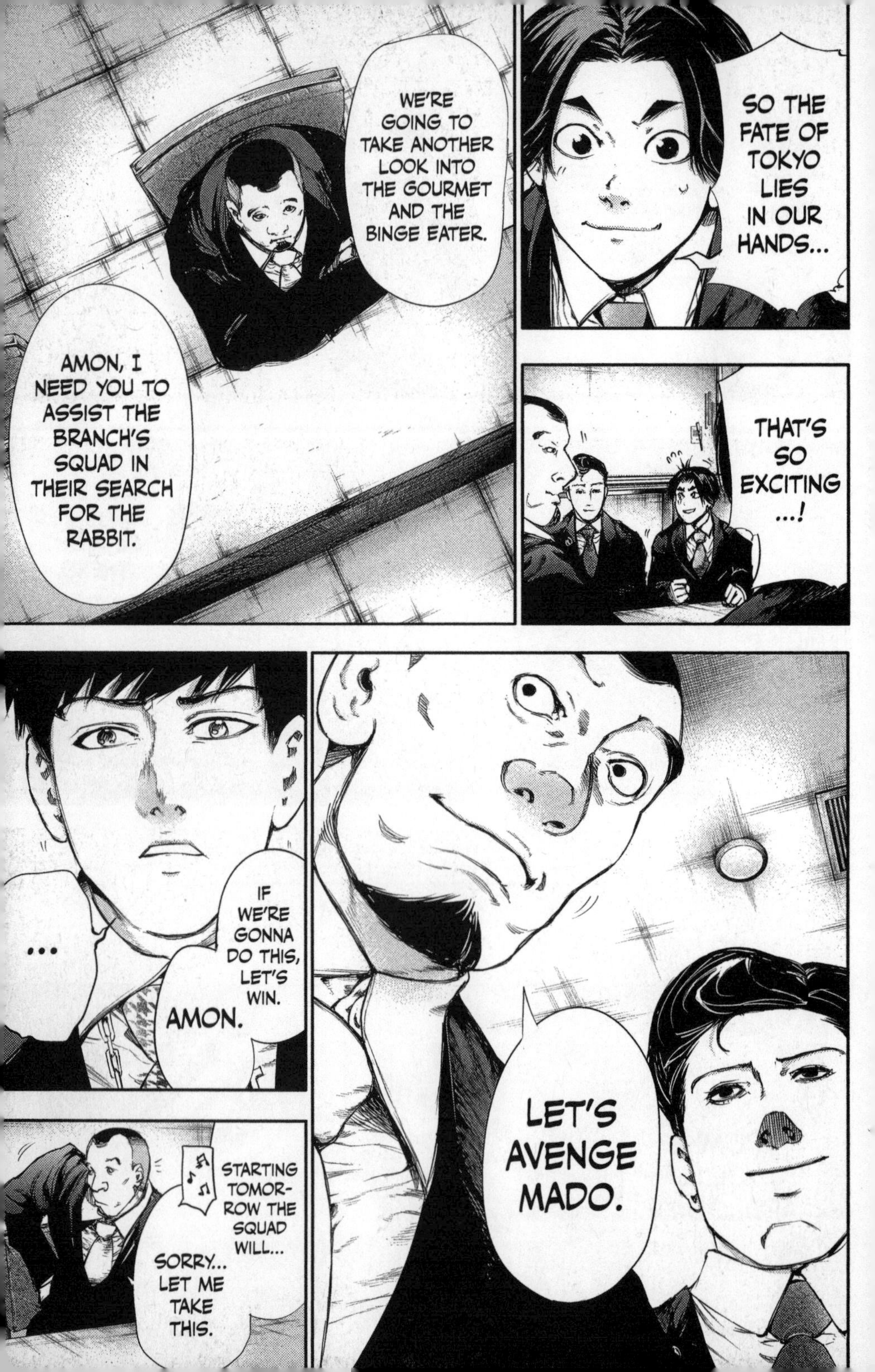
SO THE FATE OF TOKYO LIES IN OUR HANDS...
THAT'S SO EXCITING ...!
WE'RE GOING TO TAKE ANOTHER LOOK INTO THE GOURMET AND THE BINGE EATER.
AMON, I NEED YOU TO ASSIST THE BRANCH'S SQUAD IN THEIR SEARCH FOR THE RABBIT.
LET'S AVENGE MADO.
...
IF WE'RE GONNA DO THIS, LET'S WIN.
AMON.
STARTING TOMOR-ROW THE SQUAD WILL...
SORRY... LET ME TAKE THIS.

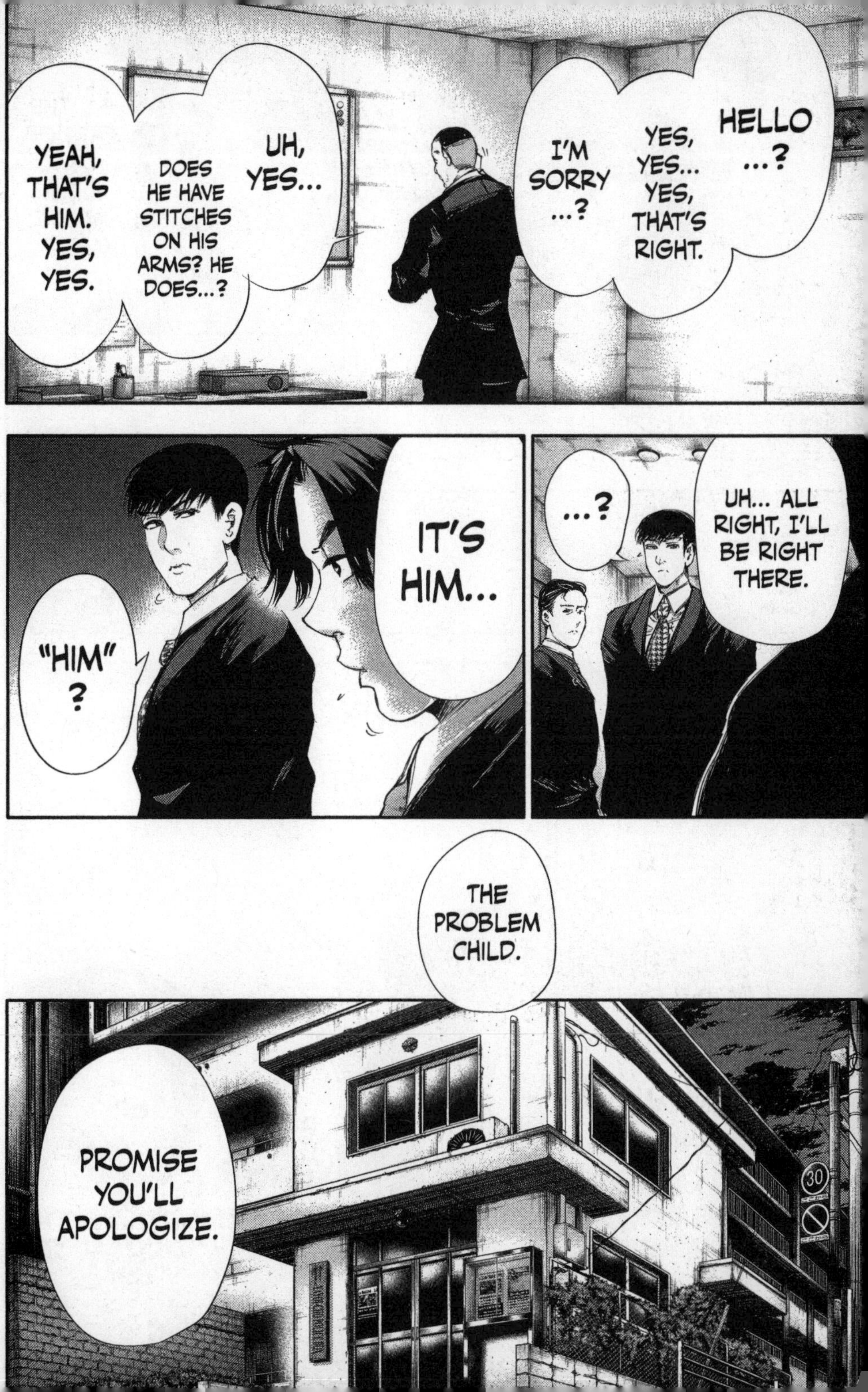
HELLO ...?
YES, YES... YES, THAT'S RIGHT.
I'M SORRY ...?
UH, YES...
DOES HE HAVE STITCHES ON HIS ARMS? HE DOES...?
YEAH, THAT'S HIM. YES, YES.
UH... ALL RIGHT, I'LL BE RIGHT THERE.
...?
IT'S HIM...
"HIM"?
THE PROBLEM CHILD.
PROMISE YOU'LL APOLOGIZE.

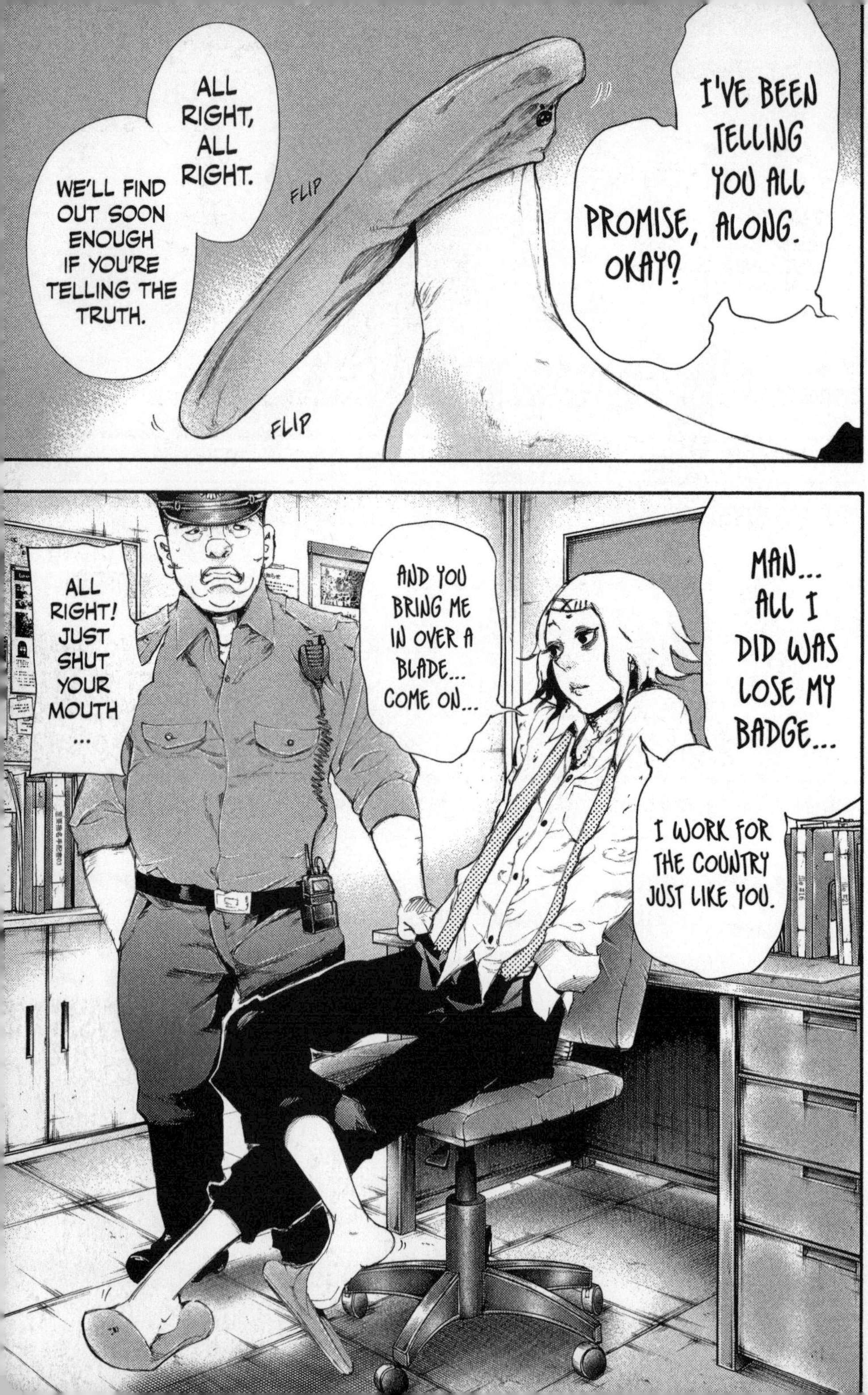
I'VE BEEN TELLING YOU ALL ALONG.
PROMISE, OKAY?
FLIP
ALL RIGHT, ALL RIGHT.
WE'LL FIND OUT SOON ENOUGH IF YOU'RE TELLING THE TRUTH.
FLIP
MAN... ALL I DID WAS LOSE MY BADGE...
I WORK FOR THE COUNTRY JUST LIKE YOU.
AND YOU BRING ME IN OVER A BLADE... COME ON...
ALL RIGHT! JUST SHUT YOUR MOUTH...

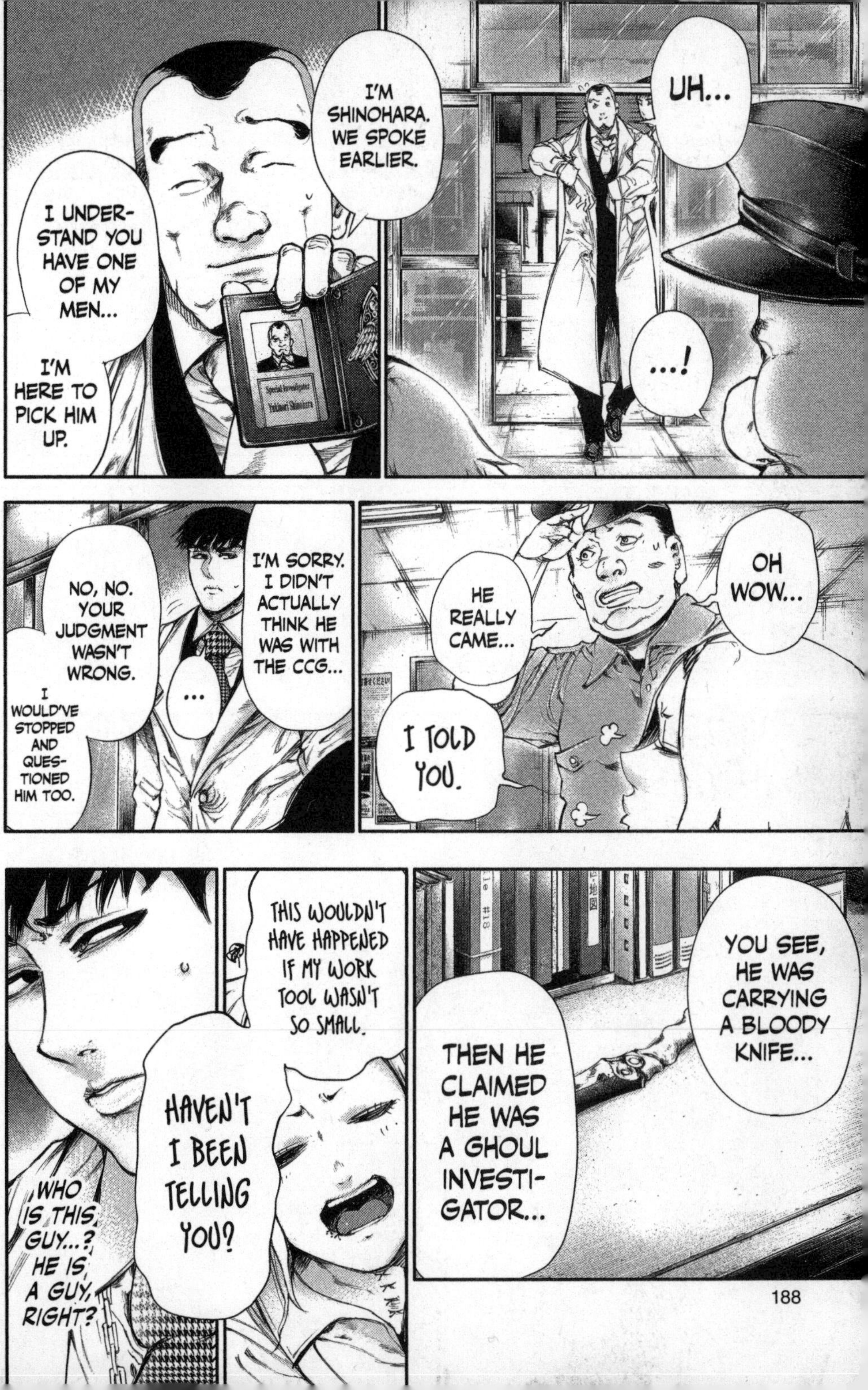
UH...
...!
I'M SHINOHARA. WE SPOKE EARLIER.
I UNDERSTAND YOU HAVE ONE OF MY MEN...
I'M HERE TO PICK HIM UP.
OH WOW...
HE REALLY CAME...
I TOLD YOU.
I'M SORRY. I DIDN'T ACTUALLY THINK HE WAS WITH THE CCG...
...
NO, NO. YOUR JUDGMENT WASN'T WRONG.
I WOULD'VE STOPPED AND QUESTIONED HIM TOO.
YOU SEE, HE WAS CARRYING A BLOODY KNIFE...
THEN HE CLAIMED HE WAS A GHOUL INVESTIGATOR...
THIS WOULDN'T HAVE HAPPENED IF MY WORK TOOL WASN'T SO SMALL.
HAVEN'T I BEEN TELLING YOU?
WHO IS THIS GUY...? HE IS A GUY, RIGHT?

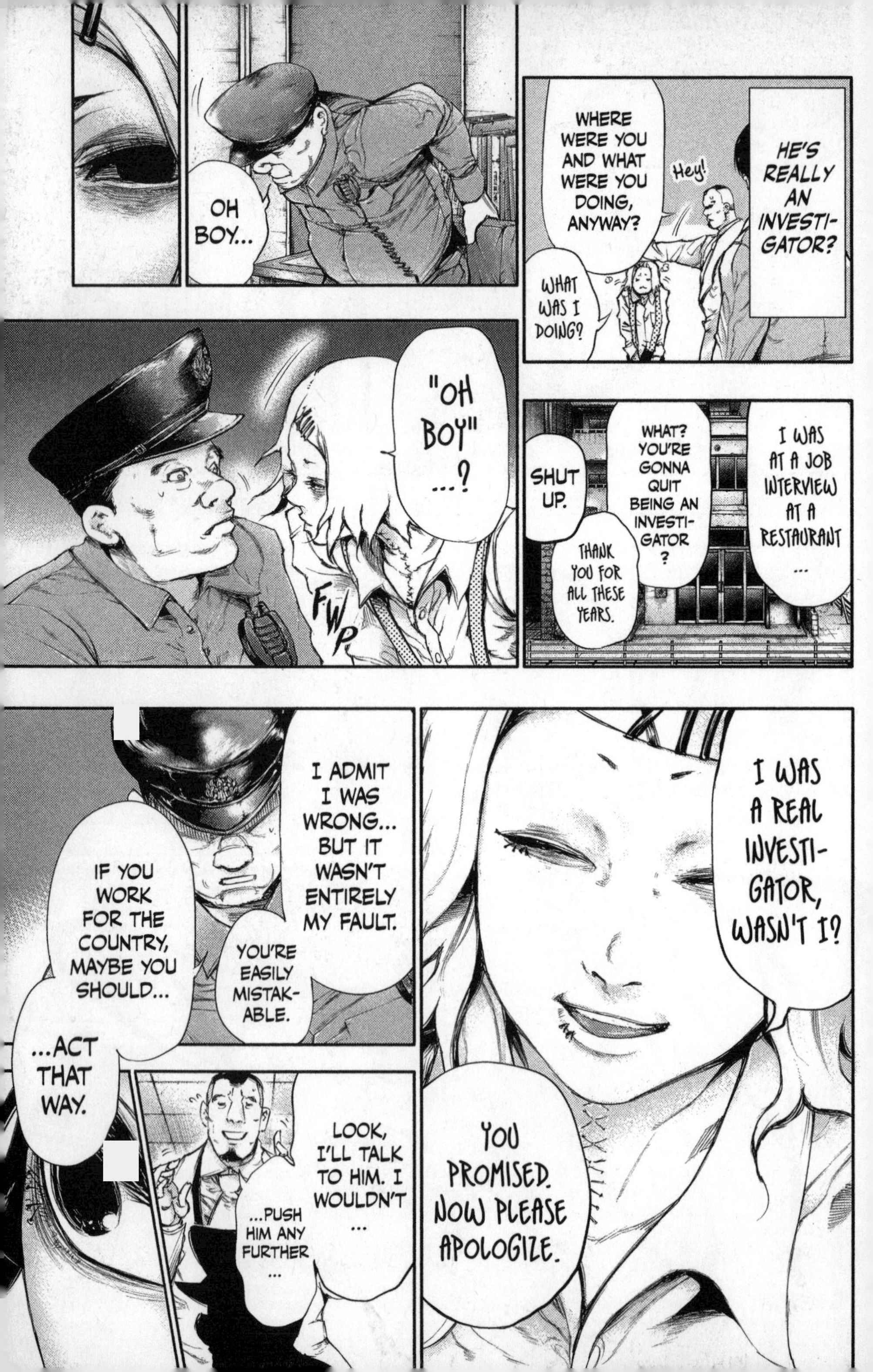
HE'S REALLY AN INVESTIGATOR?
WHERE WERE YOU AND WHAT WERE YOU DOING, ANYWAY?
Hey!
WHAT WAS I DOING?
OH BOY...
I WAS AT A JOB INTERVIEW AT A RESTAURANT ...
WHAT? YOU'RE GONNA QUIT BEING AN INVESTIGATOR ?
SHUT UP.
THANK YOU FOR ALL THESE YEARS.
"OH BOY" ...?
FWP
I WAS A REAL INVESTIGATOR, WASN'T I?
YOU PROMISED. NOW PLEASE APOLOGIZE.
I ADMIT I WAS WRONG... BUT IT WASN'T ENTIRELY MY FAULT.
YOU'RE EASILY MISTAKABLE.
IF YOU WORK FOR THE COUNTRY, MAYBE YOU SHOULD...
...ACT THAT WAY.
LOOK, I'LL TALK TO HIM. I WOULDN'T ...
...PUSH HIM ANY FURTHER ...

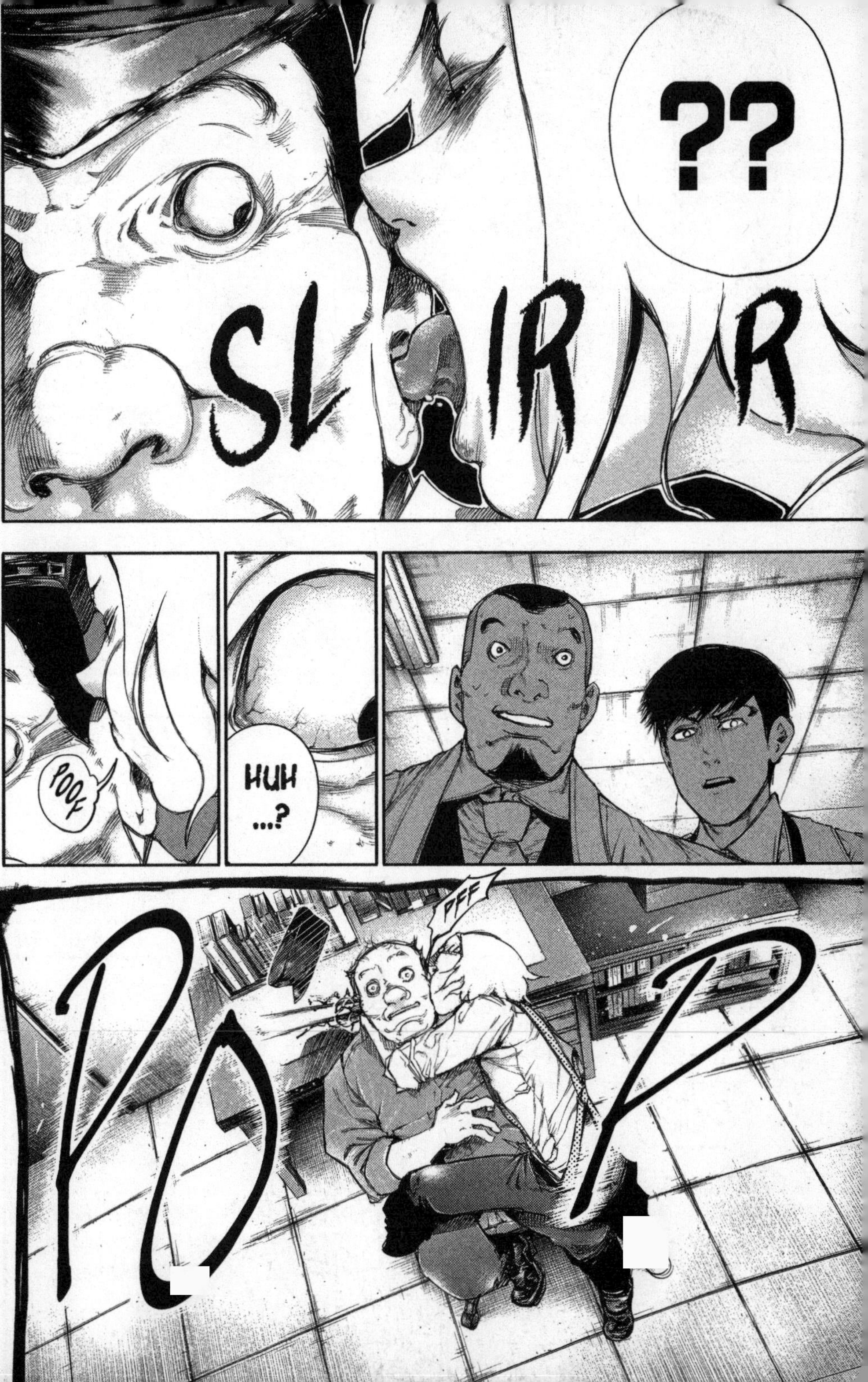
??
SLIRR
HUH ...?
POOF
PFF
POP

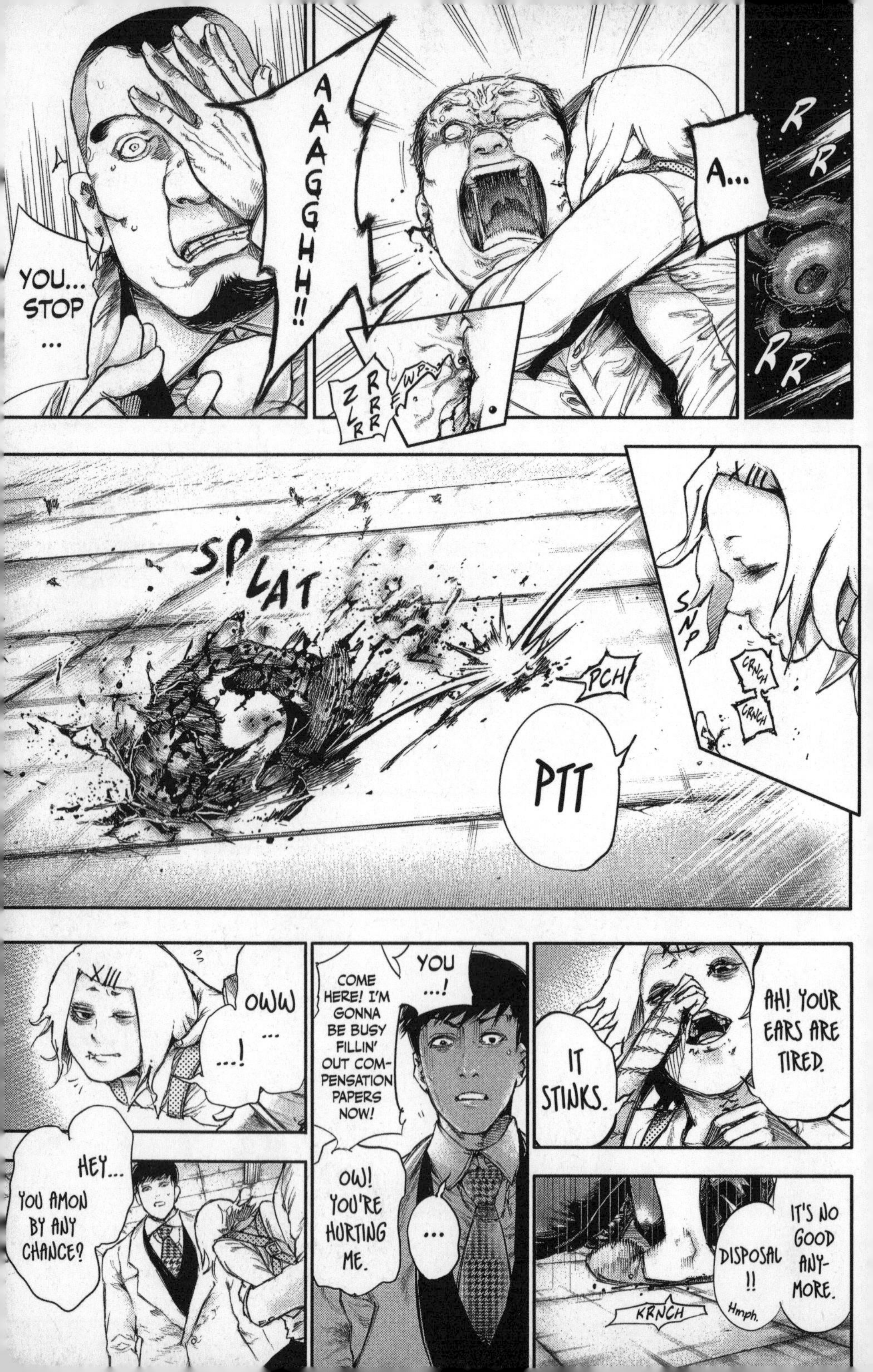
A...
RRRR
FWP...
RRRR
ZLR
AAAAGGHH!!
YOU... STOP ...
SNP
CRNCH
CRNCH
PTT
PCH
SPLAT
AH! YOUR EARS ARE TIRED.
IT STINKS.
IT'S NO GOOD ANYMORE.
DISPOSAL!!
Hmph.
KRNCH
YOU ...!
COME HERE! I'M GONNA BE BUSY FILLIN' OUT COMPENSATION PAPERS NOW!
OW! YOU'RE HURTING ME.
...
OWW ...
...!
HEY... YOU AMON BY ANY CHANCE?

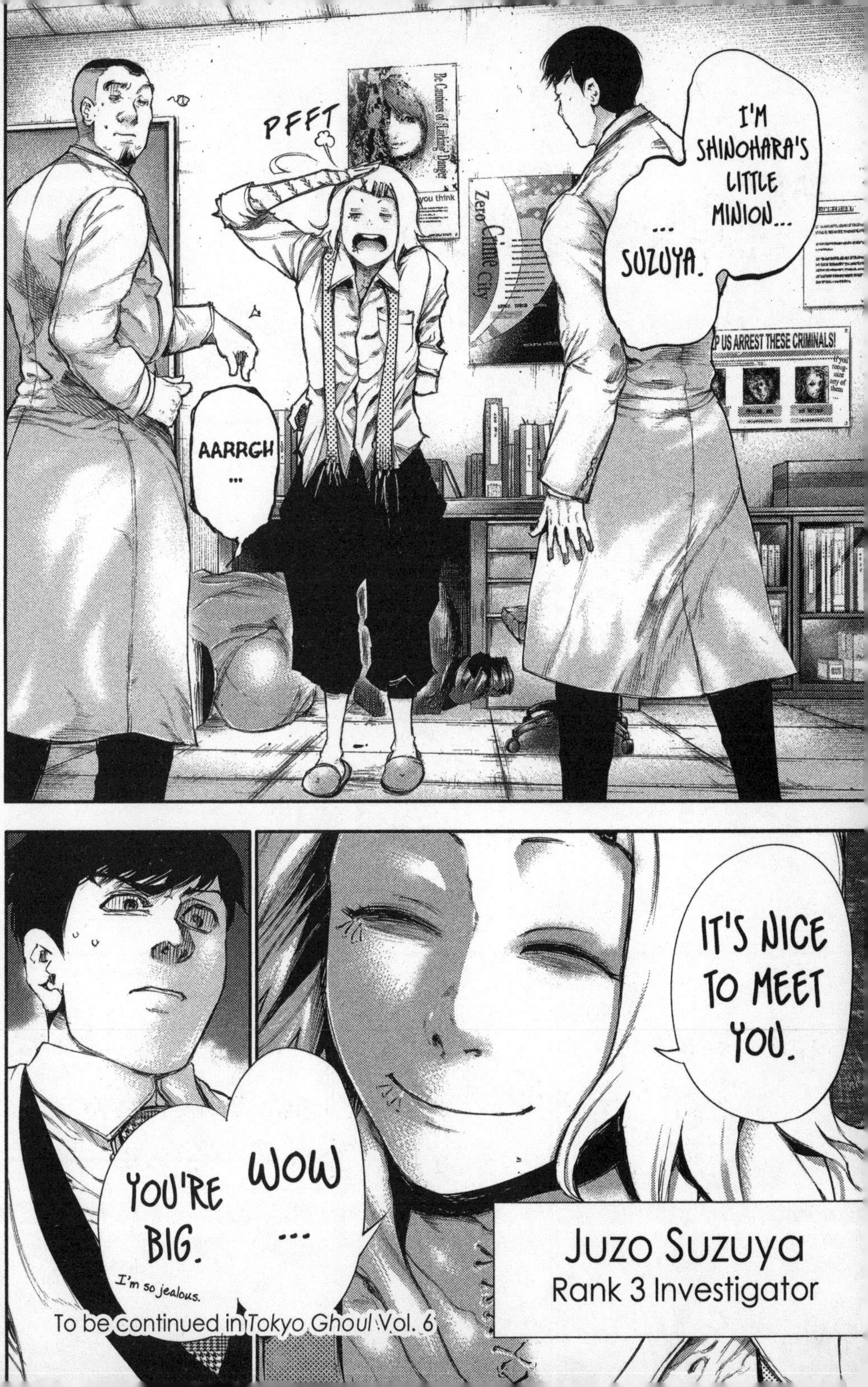
I'M SHINOHARA'S LITTLE MINION...
...SUZUYA.
PFFT
AARRGH...
IT'S NICE TO MEET YOU.
WOW...
YOU'RE BIG.
I'm so jealous.
Juzo Suzuya
Rank 3 Investigator
To be continued in Tokyo Ghoul Vol. 6

Tokyo Ghoul

Sui Ishida

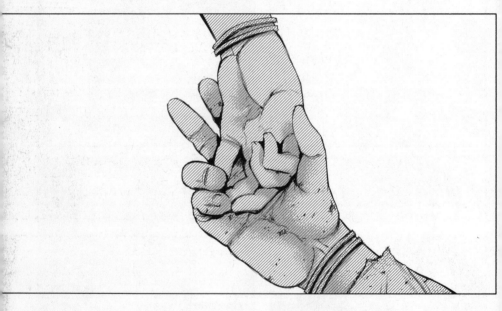

Staff Eda
    Ryuji Miyamoto
    Mizuki Ida
    Matsuzaki

Design Hideaki Shimada (L.S.D.)
Cover Miyuki Takaoka (POCKET)
Editor Jumpei Matsuo

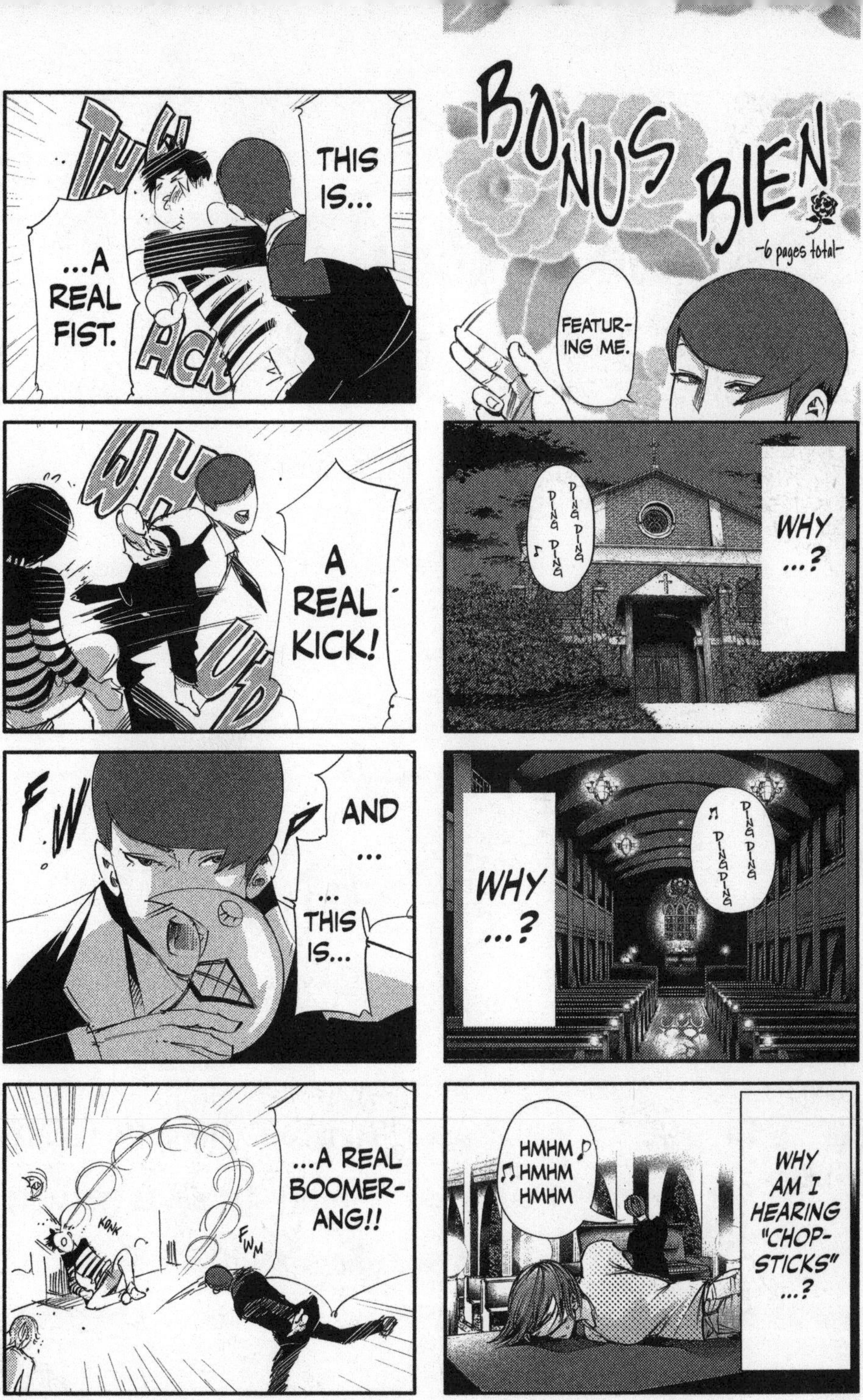
BONUS BIEN
—6 pages total—
FEATURING ME.
WHY ...?
DING DING DING DING
WHY ...?
DING DING DING DING
WHY AM I HEARING "CHOPSTICKS" ...?
HMHM HMHM HMHM
THIS IS...
...A REAL FIST.
A REAL KICK!
AND ... ... THIS IS...
...A REAL BOOMERANG!!
FWM
KONK

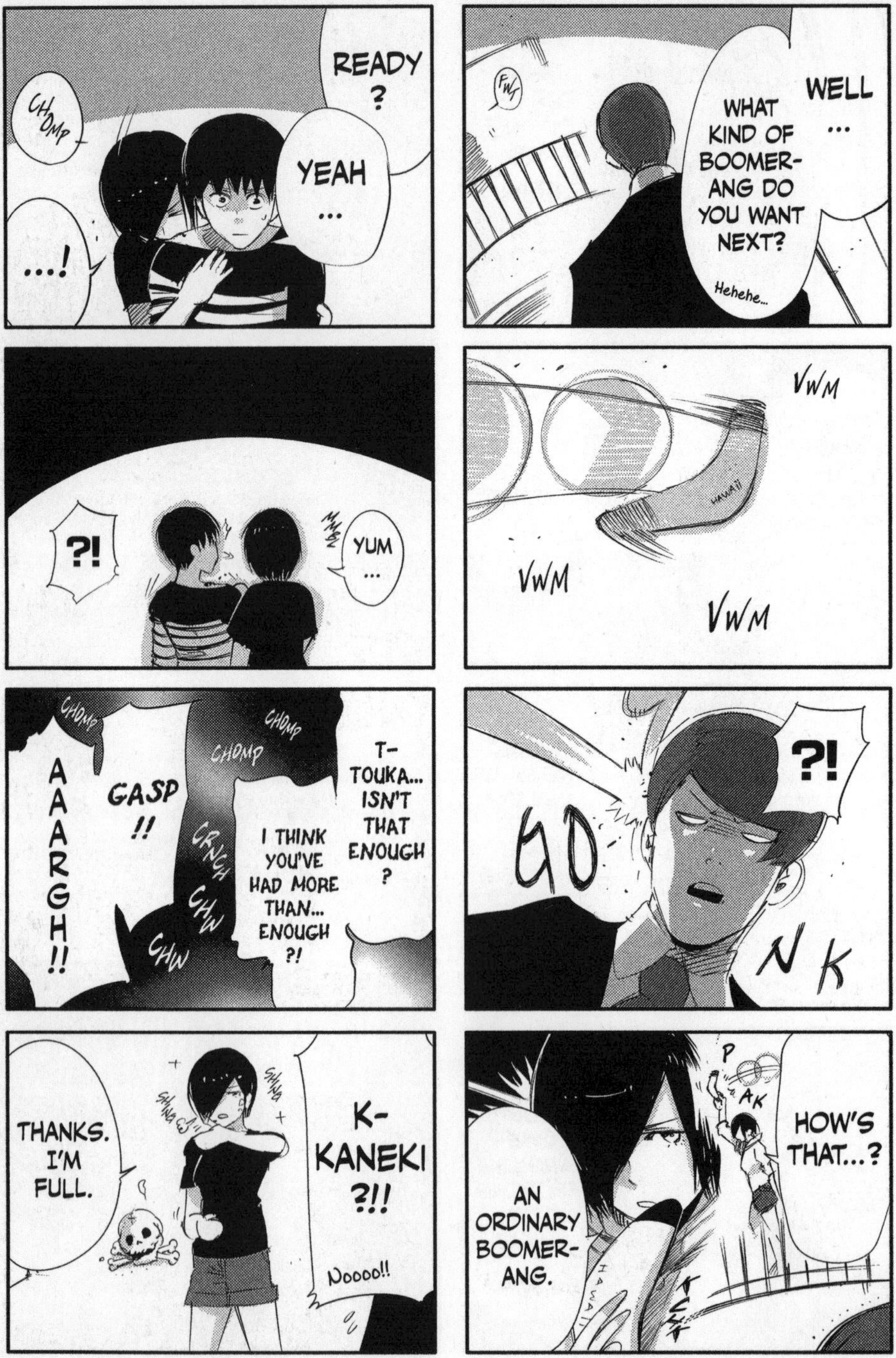
WELL...
WHAT KIND OF BOOMERANG DO YOU WANT NEXT?
Hehehe...
FWT
READY?
YEAH...
CHOMP
...!
VWM
VWM
VWM
YUM...
?!
?!
GD
NK
T-TOUKA... ISN'T THAT ENOUGH?
I THINK YOU'VE HAD MORE THAN... ENOUGH?!
CHOMP
CHOMP
CHOMP
GASP!!
AAARGH!!
CRNCH
CHW
CHW
P
AK
HOW'S THAT...?
AN ORDINARY BOOMERANG.
K-KANEKI?!!
Noooo!!
THANKS. I'M FULL.

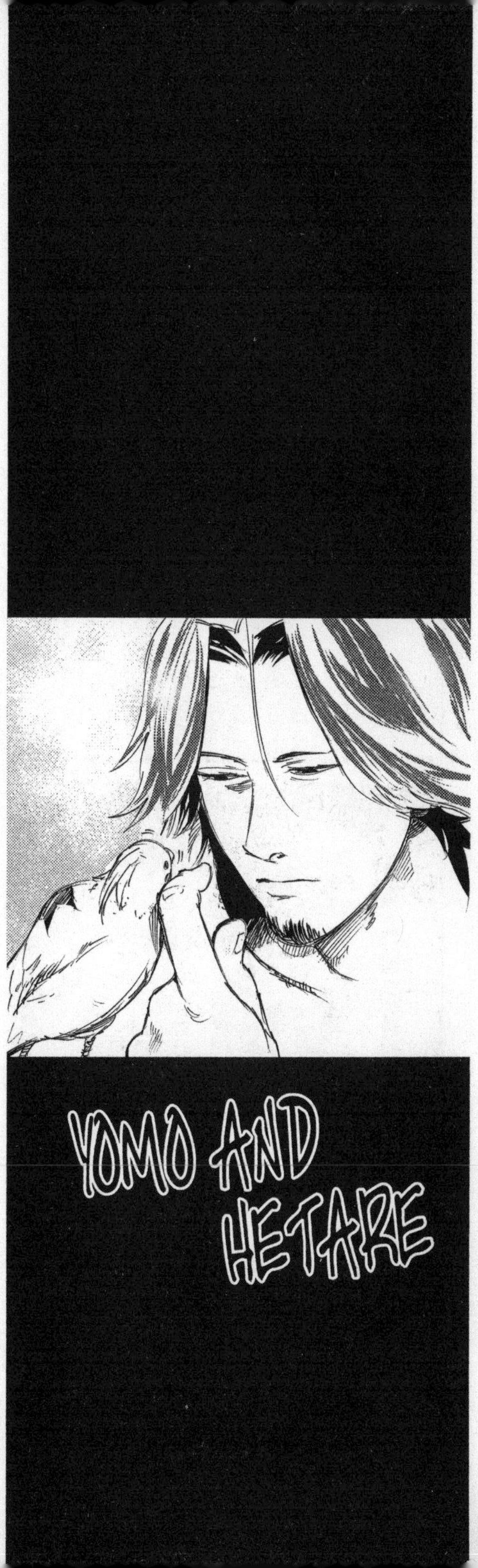
YOMO AND HETARE

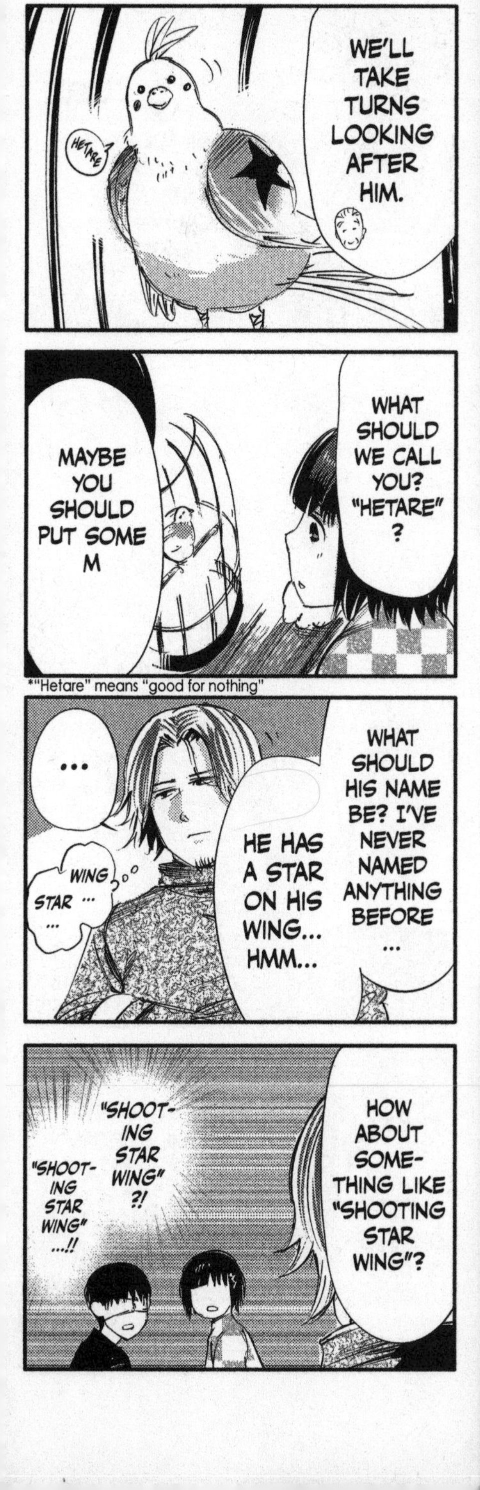
WE'LL TAKE TURNS LOOKING AFTER HIM.
HETARE
WHAT SHOULD WE CALL YOU? "HETARE" ?
MAYBE YOU SHOULD PUT SOME M
WHAT SHOULD HIS NAME BE? I'VE NEVER NAMED ANYTHING BEFORE ...
HE HAS A STAR ON HIS WING... HMM...
...
WING STAR ... ...
HOW ABOUT SOME-THING LIKE "SHOOTING STAR WING"?
"SHOOT-ING STAR WING" ?!
"SHOOT-ING STAR WING" ...!!

*"Hetare" means "good for nothing"

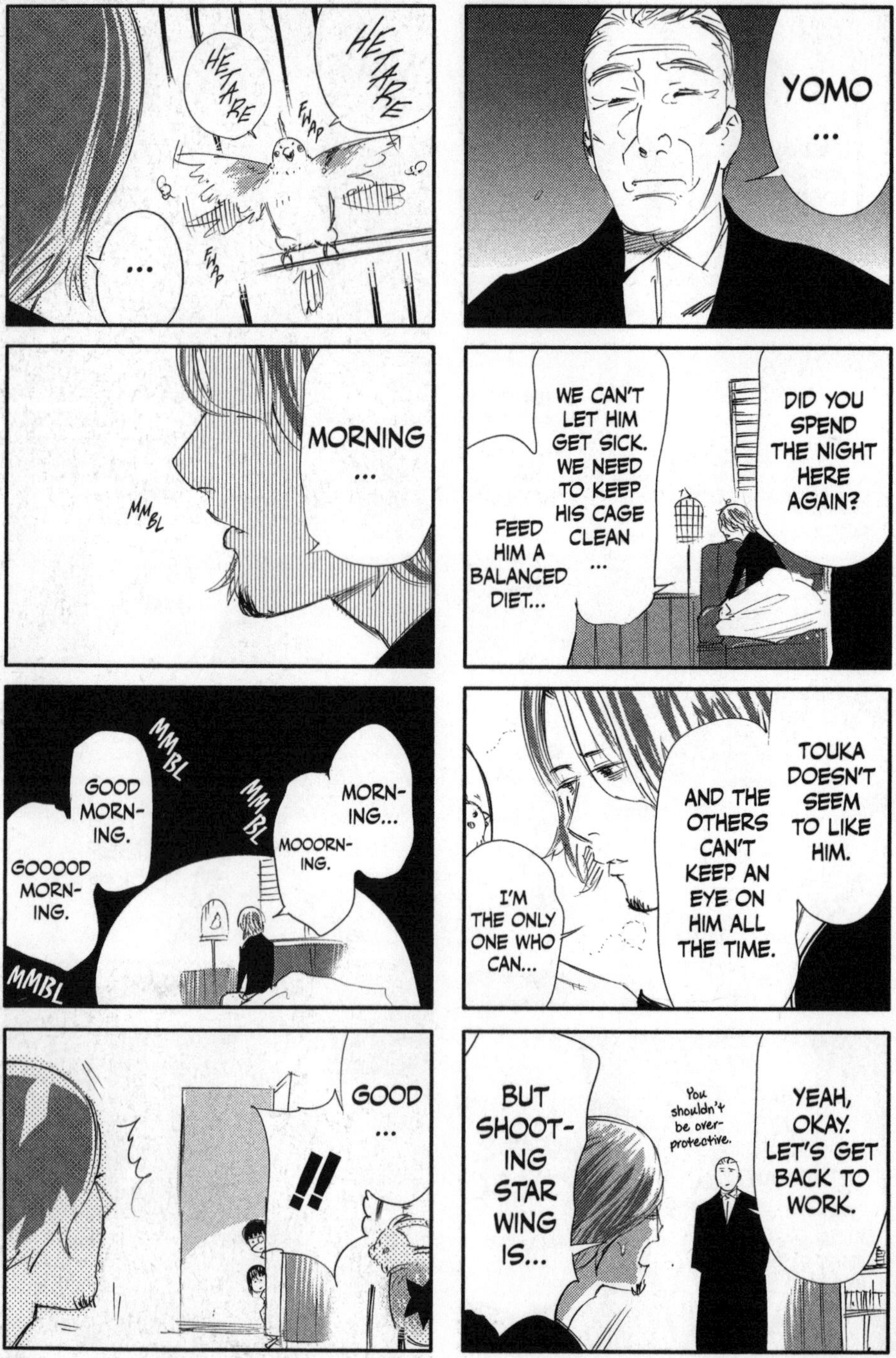
YOMO ...
HETARE
HETARE
FWAP
...
FWAP
DID YOU SPEND THE NIGHT HERE AGAIN?
WE CAN'T LET HIM GET SICK. WE NEED TO KEEP HIS CAGE CLEAN ...
FEED HIM A BALANCED DIET...
MORNING ...
MMBL
TOUKA DOESN'T SEEM TO LIKE HIM.
AND THE OTHERS CAN'T KEEP AN EYE ON HIM ALL THE TIME.
I'M THE ONLY ONE WHO CAN...
MORN-ING...
MMBL
MOOORN-ING.
MMBL
GOOD MORN-ING.
GOOOOD MORN-ING.
MMBL
YEAH, OKAY. LET'S GET BACK TO WORK.
You shouldn't be over-protective.
BUT SHOOT-ING STAR WING IS...
GOOD ...
!!

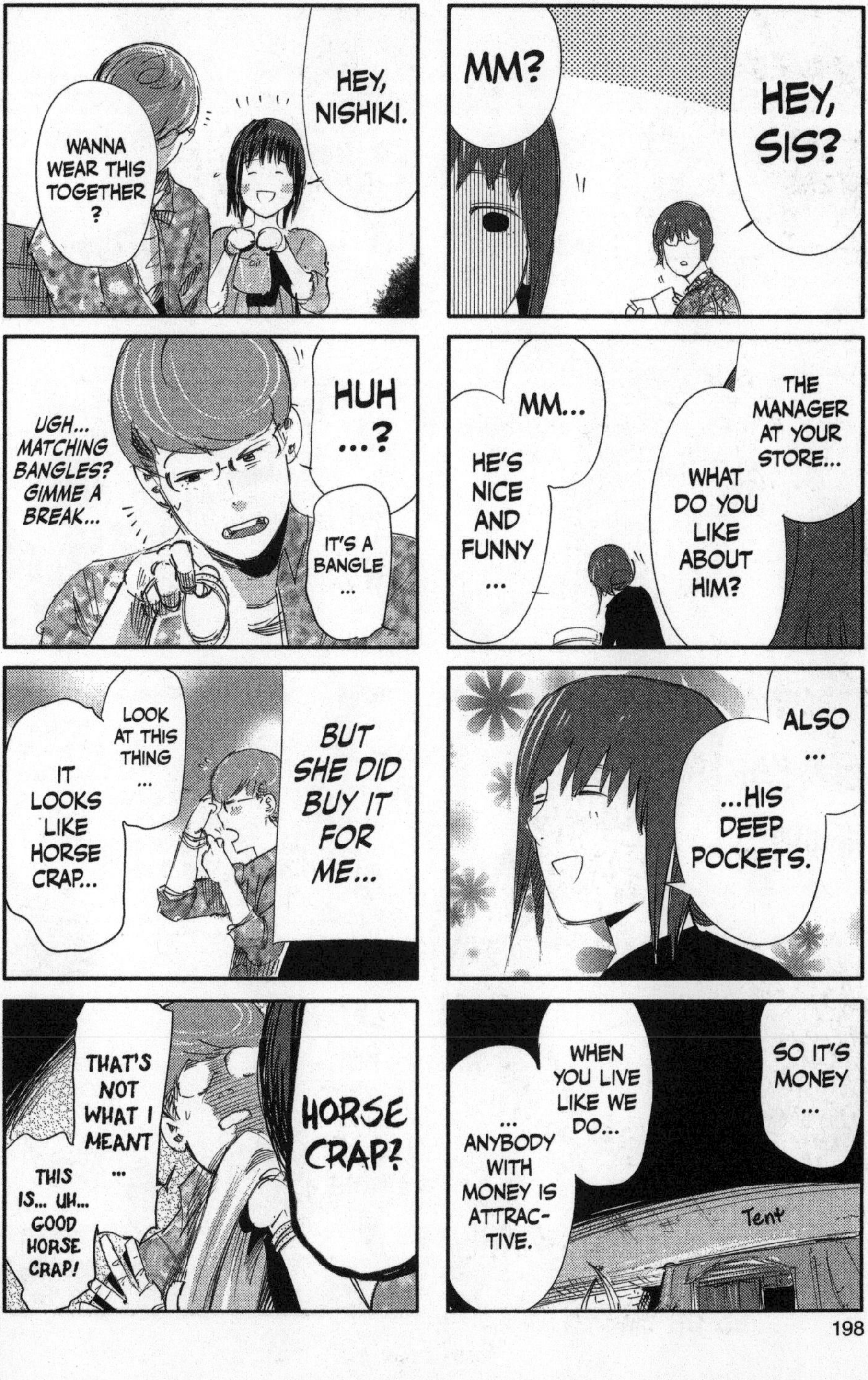
HEY, SIS?
MM?
HEY, NISHIKI.
WANNA WEAR THIS TOGETHER ?
THE MANAGER AT YOUR STORE...
WHAT DO YOU LIKE ABOUT HIM?
MM...
HE'S NICE AND FUNNY ...
HUH ...?
IT'S A BANGLE ...
UGH... MATCHING BANGLES? GIMME A BREAK...
ALSO ...
...HIS DEEP POCKETS.
BUT SHE DID BUY IT FOR ME...
LOOK AT THIS THING ...
IT LOOKS LIKE HORSE CRAP...
SO IT'S MONEY ...
WHEN YOU LIVE LIKE WE DO...
... ANYBODY WITH MONEY IS ATTRAC- TIVE.
Tent
HORSE CRAP?
THAT'S NOT WHAT I MEANT ...
THIS IS... UH... GOOD HORSE CRAP!

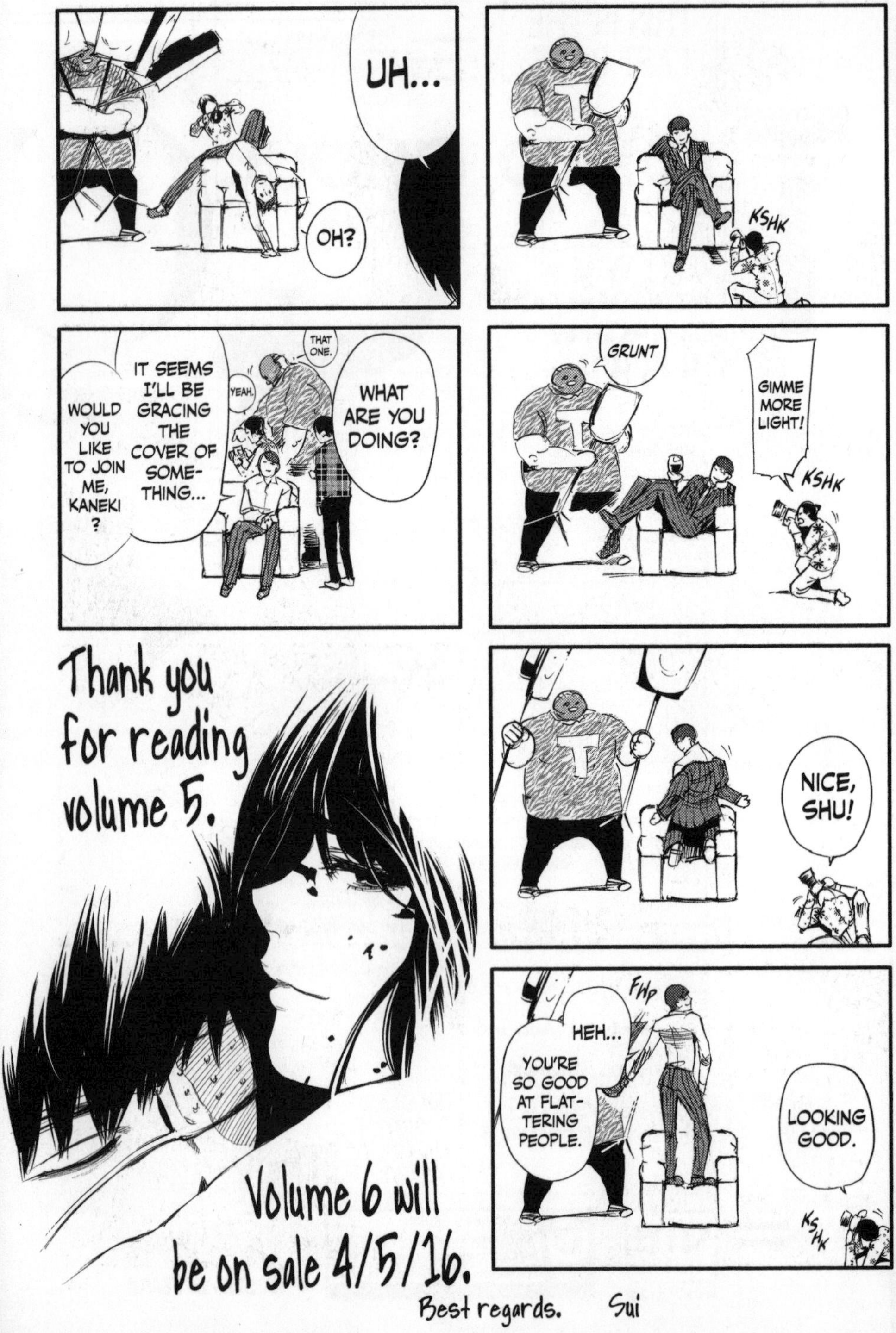
KSHK
GRUNT
GIMME MORE LIGHT!
KSHK
NICE, SHU!
FWP
HEH...
YOU'RE SO GOOD AT FLATTERING PEOPLE.
LOOKING GOOD.
KSHK
UH...
OH?
WHAT ARE YOU DOING?
THAT ONE.
YEAH.
IT SEEMS I'LL BE GRACING THE COVER OF SOMETHING...
WOULD YOU LIKE TO JOIN ME, KANEKI?
Thank you for reading volume 5.
Volume 6 will be on sale 4/5/16.
Best regards. Sui

TOKYO GHOUL

[THIS IS THE
LAST PAGE]

TOKYO GHOUL
READS
RIGHT TO LEFT

P9-CTA-050

TOKYO GHOUL

東　京　喰　種

VOLUME 5
VIZ Signature Edition

Story and art by

SUI ISHIDA

TOKYO GHOUL © 2011 by Sui Ishida
All rights reserved.
First published in Japan in 2011 by
SHUEISHA Inc., Tokyo.
English translation rights arranged by
SHUEISHA Inc.

TRANSLATION. Joe Yamazaki

TOUCH-UP ART AND LETTERING. Vanessa Satone

DESIGN. Fawn Lau

EDITOR. Joel Enos

Printed in the U.S.A.

Published by VIZ Media, LLC
P.O. Box 77010
San Francisco, CA 94107

10 9 8 7 6 5 4 3 2 1
First printing, February 2016

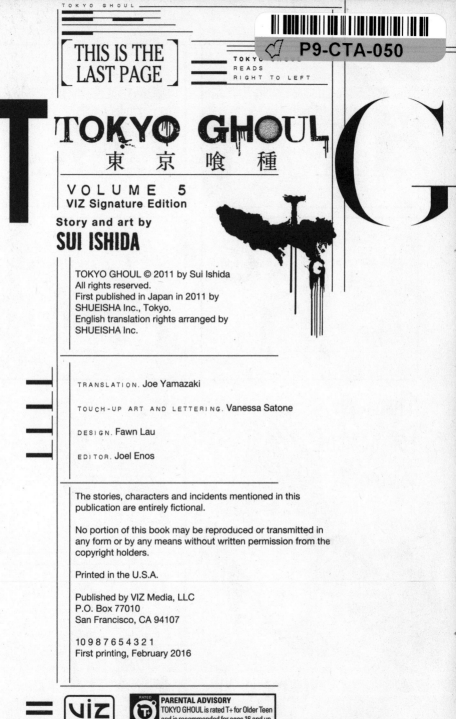

VIZ
media
www.viz.com

VIZ SIGNATURE